Essential Documents of
AMERICAN HISTORY

VOLUME
II

From Reconstruction to the
Twenty-first Century

EDITED BY BOB BLAISDELL

DOVER PUBLICATIONS, INC.
Mineola, New York

Bibliographical Note

Essential Documents of American History, Volume II: From Reconstruction to the Twenty-first Century, first published by Dover Publications, Inc., in 2016, is a new compilation of historic American documents. The source of each one has been abbreviated in brackets at the end of the respective document and can be found in the last section of this collection.

International Standard Book Number

ISBN-13: 978-0-486-80908-3
ISBN-10: 0-486-80908-0

Manufactured in the United States by RR Donnelley
80908001   2016
www.doverpublications.com

Note

It's ENLIVENING AND enlightening to read about events as they happen through these 154 documents*—dating from 1606 to 2008—that make us eyewitnesses to history. For example, during the Constitutional Convention in the summer of 1787, we can imagine some of the Founding Fathers shaking their heads ruefully during the debate over the continuance of slavery.

George Mason of Virginia lamented, "Every master of slaves is born a petty tyrant. They bring the judgment of heaven on a country. As nations cannot be rewarded or punished in the next world they must be in this." Was Mason prescient about the Civil War of 1861–1865 or simply possessed of an unusually acute moral sense?

In 1789, we learn through his first Inaugural Address that George Washington was apprehensive as he warily accepted the duties of president of the newly established nation: "Among the vicissitudes incident to life no event could have filled me with greater anxieties than that of which the notification was transmitted by your order ... On the one hand, I was summoned by my country, whose voice I can never hear but with veneration and love, from a retreat which I had chosen with the fondest predilection, and, in my flattering hopes, with an immutable decision, as the asylum of my declining years ..." Less than three years after serving his second term of office, the great man died at the longed for "asylum" of his Mount Vernon home.

Thomas Jefferson, the primary author in 1776 of the Declaration of Independence, was, as the third president, excited as he imagined the world that his chosen proxy, Captain Meriwether Lewis, would

---

*Volume I (ISBN-13: 978-0-486-79730-4) contains 83 documents, spanning 1606 to 1865. Volume II contains 71 documents, spanning 1866 to 2008.

encounter in the wilderness in and beyond the recently purchased Louisiana Territory and made his way to the Pacific Ocean. More than any other U.S. president of the eighteenth century, Jefferson demonstrated respect for the native peoples by instructing Lewis:

> In all your intercourse with the natives treat them in the most friendly & conciliatory manner which their own conduct will admit; allay all jealousies as to the object of your journey, satisfy them of it's innocence, make them acquainted with the position, extent, character, peaceable & commercial dispositions of the U. S. of our wish to be neighborly, friendly & useful to them, & of our dispositions to a commercial intercourse with them; confer with them on the points most convenient as mutual emporiums, & the articles of most desirable interchange for them & us. if a few of their influential chiefs, within practicable distance, wish to visit us, arrange such a visit with them, and furnish them with authority to call on our officers, on their entering the U. S. to have them conveyed to this place at public expense. if any of them should wish to have some of their young people brought up with us, & taught such arts as may be useful to them, we will receive, instruct & take care of them, such a mission, whether of influential chiefs, or of young people, would give some security to your own party, carry with you some matter of the kine-pox, inform those of them with whom you may be of it' efficacy as a preservative from the small-pox; and instruct & encourage them in the use of it. This may be especially done wherever you winter.[1] (We have preserved Jefferson's clipped and special spellings.)

Native American oratory is justly admired, and as recorded by witnesses, we can read the speakers' cogent arguments and discourses about this great land they love and the naive concessions they made to the multitudes of immigrants from across the Atlantic. In 1811, Tecumseh, the chief of the Shawnees, tried to unify various tribes in an alliance against the encroaching, treaty-breaking European settlers. When we learn that his persuasive, carefully reasoned arguments fell on deaf ears, we can only wonder what else he might have said to convince them.

---

[1] *Original Journals of the Lewis and Clark Expedition: 1804–1806.* Vol. 7. Edited by Reuben Gold Thwaites. New York: Dodd, Mead and Company. 1904. 250.

Too often as students of history we are like readers of tragedies, hoping that what we know is about to happen won't. Would Senator John C. Calhoun, a firebrand from South Carolina, really have stoked the flames of secession by defending and lauding the region's "peculiar institution" of slavery had he known the consequences of the Civil War, in which more than 600,000 soldiers died? Could this country of immigrants really have set out on genocidal policies against the Native peoples? As proud as we are to be Americans, our history will often shock us. Along with the glory of unprecedented achievement, there is also the shame and regret of injustice and wrongdoing.

But it's not over until it's over; improvements beckon. Lord knows we haven't achieved gender or racial equality yet, much less agreement about health care, economic and international policy, or guns and drugs. Our history shows that we've made tremendous moral progress, that in spite of each age's prejudices and limitations, we are driven toward making adjustments and corrections.

Political stand-offs can be infuriatingly frustrating, no doubt about it, and if we weren't much more than political animals, it would be hard to feel hopeful. But Americans are *social* beings, and at our best we're curious and reflective, and we can clearly see the veering of our nation's course in retrospect while wondering where we're veering now. The leaders of the American Revolution seemed to have no intention of declaring independence until they did so; the history they encountered and created surprised them, and someday the history we're making now will surprise us too. In fact, a few of the more recent documents can evoke memories of unexpected events of our own time. For instance, the 9/11 Commission Report recounting the minute-by-minute confusion and terror of the attack on the World Trade Center towers may stir haunting memories from that day for many readers.

Does our sense of history lay too much blame or credit at the feet of politicians, who, in their twists and turns, bombast and eloquence, we see speaking to the wishes and furies of the people? Probably! But these documents are not just written or spoken by the privileged; they include the bewildered and outraged viewpoints of the comparatively powerless. In his 1852 address, "What to the Slave Is the Fourth of July?" the ex-slave Frederick Douglass, one of the most extraordinary Americans in our history, forcefully expresses the contradictory feelings in the air: "I am not included within the pale of this glorious anniversary! Your high independence only reveals the immeasurable distance between us. The blessings in which you, this day, rejoice, are not enjoyed in common. The rich inheritance of justice, liberty, prosperity and independence, bequeathed by your fathers, is shared by you, not by me. The sunlight that brought light and healing to you, has brought stripes and death to me. This Fourth of July is yours, not mine. You may rejoice, I must mourn. To drag a man in fetters into the grand illuminated temple of liberty, and call upon him to join you in joyous anthems, were inhuman mockery and sacrilegious irony."

I have tried to include all the most famous documents as long as they can now be read with engagement, while avoiding blowhard self-congratulatory speeches and pronouncements, which unfortunately in political matters are always a looming part of the weather. There are documents I haven't included only because they would take a cleverer and more knowledgeable writer and reader than I to introduce them in a succinct way. For example, concerning our own time, I didn't know how to make use of the flood of documents that have been released concerning our government's squirrelly approbation of the use of torture after the 9/11 catastrophe. Given another decade or two, I might figure out which of these outrageous documents to include.

While it's impossible to sympathize with any argument for the post–Civil War's Jim Crow laws or segregation, I have chosen to let the Georgia governor George C. Wallace try to make the argument himself in 1963. His voice was loud; he spoke for himself and others. If we're ashamed by much of our history, there's plenty of shame left to think of our own personal failures and sins. The most thoughtless "truths" we once accepted as a country or individuals can now, in reflection, fill us with horror and disgust.

Just personally, on the (big open) other hand, Abraham Lincoln's words almost always make me proud to be an American. You might argue, sensibly, that not only I but nobody alive today had anything to do with anything he said or did, and so why should I feel proud for what he said or ashamed for what his opposite number, the Confederate president Jefferson Davis, said and did? Because that's the way despair of and pride in one's nation works. We agonize with not only the weaknesses of those who came before us but identify with their accomplishments. Senator Margaret Chase Smith's speech in 1950, in which she calls out a horde of her fellow senators during the Red Scare for trying to "ride to political victory on the Four

Horsemen of Calumny—Fear, Ignorance, Bigotry, and Smear," gives me hope that it's possible to be brave in the face of cynically induced hysteria; Martin Luther King, Jr.'s "I Have a Dream" speech never stops being inspiring and alluring; through the astronauts' accounts of their Apollo 11 moon landing in 1969, it seems now even more wonderful to me than when it happened in my boyhood.

Finally, the word "Documents" in our anthology title shouldn't suggest we have the facts or that we are establishing *a* truth or *the* truths about American history. We could, by substituting the word *Artifacts* for *Documents* remind ourselves that these pieces are, famous or not, maybe no more significant than *millions* of other pieces that could help us form an idea of America's history, but that, as *artifacts,* they represent only a fraction of each event yet can, nonetheless, tell us so much about the culture in which they were produced.

There are many anthologies and histories I have relied on for pointing me to some of the definitely great and famous documents of our history, and I have also relied on many previous compilers and editors for their astute introductory notes to the selections. I particularly thank Dover's senior editor, John Grafton, for his guidance over the course of this project and for several of the most informative introductory notes.

—*Bob Blaisdell*
New York City, April 2015

Contents

THE WORLD WARS

INTO THE COLD WAR

INTO THE TWENTY-FIRST CENTURY

Post-War
to World War

Congressman Thaddeus Stevens, ... the Fourteenth

*was the leader
of compromises;
pt and unsparing
urgent for confis-
His theory of recon-
ir rights, and under
ngressional action on
nstruction committee,
House had passed the
h Stevens disapproved.
y Albert Bushnell Hert*

ittee desired. It falls far short of my wishes, but it ſull... I believe it is all that can be obtained in the present state of public opinion. Not only Congress but the several States are to be consulted. Upon a careful survey of the whole ground, we did not believe that nineteen of the loyal States could be induced to ratify any proposition more stringent than this. I say nineteen, for I utterly repudiate and scorn the idea that any State not acting in the Union is to be counted on the question of ratification. It is absurd to suppose that any more than three fourths of the States that propose the amendment are required to make it valid; that States not here are to be counted as present. Relieving, then, that this is the best proposition that can be made effectual, I accept it. [. . .]

The first section prohibits the States from abridging the privileges and immunities of citizens of the United States, or unlawfully depriving them of life, liberty, or property, or of denying to any person within their jurisdiction the "equal" protection of the laws.

I can hardly believe that any person can be found who will not admit that every one of these provisions is just. They are all asserted, in some form or other, in our DECLARATION or organic law. But the Constitution limits only the action of Congress, and is not a limitation on the States. This amendment supplies that defect, and allows Congress to correct the unjust legislation of the States, so far that the law which operates upon one man shall operate *equally* upon all. Whatever law punishes a white man for a crime shall punish the black man precisely in the same way and to the same degree. Whatever law protects the white man shall afford "equal" protection to the black man. Whatever means of redress is afforded to one shall be afforded to all. Whatever law allows the white man to testify in court shall allow the man of color to do the same. These are great advantages over their present codes. Now different degrees of punishment are inflicted, not on account of the magnitude of the crime, but according to the color of the skin. Now color disqualifies a man from testifying in courts, or being tried in the same way as white men. I need not enumerate these partial and oppressive laws. Unless the Constitution should restrain them those States will all, I fear, keep up this discrimination, and crush to death the hated freedmen. Some answer, "Your civil rights bill secures the same things." That is partly true, but a law is repeatable by a majority. And I need hardly say that the first time that the South with their copperhead allies obtains the command of Congress it will be repealed. The veto of the President and their votes on the bill are conclusive evidence of that. And yet I am amazed and alarmed at the impatience of certain well-meaning Republicans at the exclusion of the rebel States until the Constitution shall be so amended as to restrain their despotic desires. This amendment once adopted cannot be annulled without two thirds of Congress. That they will hardly get. And yet certain of our distinguished friends propose to admit State after State before this becomes a part of the Constitution. What madness! Is their judgment misled by their kindness; or are they unconsciously drifting into the haven of power at the other end of the avenue? I do not suspect it, but others will.

The second section I consider the most important in the article. It fixes the basis of representation in Congress. If any State shall exclude any of her adult male citizens from the elective franchise, or abridge that right, she shall forfeit her right to representation in the same proportion. The effect of this provision will be either to compel the States to grant universal suffrage or so to shear them of their power as to keep them forever in a hopeless minority in the national Government, both legislative and executive. If they do not enfranchise the freedmen, it would give to the rebel States but thirty-seven Representatives. Thus shorn of their power, they would soon become restive. Southern pride would not long brook a hopeless minority. True it will take two, three, possibly five years before they conquer their prejudices sufficiently to allow their late slaves to become their equals at the polls. That short delay would not be injurious. In the mean time the freedmen would become more enlightened, and more fit to discharge the high duties of their new condition. In that time, too, the loyal Congress could mature their laws and so amend the Constitution as to secure the rights of every human being, and render disunion impossible. Heaven forbid that the southern States, or *any one of them,* should be represented on this floor until such monuments of freedom are built high and firm. Against our will they have been absent for four bloody years; against our will they must not come back until we are ready to receive them. Do not tell me that there are loyal representatives waiting for admission—until their States are loyal they can have no standing here. They would merely *mis*represent their constituents.

I admit that this article is not as good as the one we sent to death in the Senate. In my judgment, we shall not approach the measure of justice until we have given every adult freedman a homestead on the land where he was born and toiled and suffered. Forty acres of land and a hut would be more valuable to him than the immediate right to vote. Unless we give them this we shall receive the censure of mankind and the curse of Heaven. That article referred to provided that if *one* of the injured race was excluded the State should forfeit the right to have any of them represented. That would have hastened their full enfranchisement. This section allows the States to discriminate among the same class, and receive proportionate credit in representation. This I dislike. But it is a short step forward. The large stride which we in vain proposed is dead; the murderers must answer to the suffering race. I would not have been the perpetrator. A load of misery must sit heavy on their souls.

The third section may encounter more difference of opinion here. Among the people I believe it will be the most popular of all the provisions; it prohibits rebels from voting for members of Congress and electors of President until 1870. My only objection to it is that it is too lenient. I know that there is a morbid sensibility, sometimes called mercy, which affects a few of all classes, from the priest to the clown, which has more sympathy for the murderer on the gallows than for his victim. I hope I have a heart as capable of feeling for human woe as others. I have long since wished that capital punishment were abolished. But I never dreamed that all punishment could be dispensed with in human society. Anarchy, *treason,* and violence would reign triumphant. Here is the mildest of all punishments ever inflicted on traitors. I might not consent to the extreme severity denounced upon them by a provisional governor of Tennessee—I mean the late lamented Andrew Johnson of blessed memory—but I would have increased the severity of this section. I would be glad to see it extended to 1876, and to include all State and municipal as well as national elections. In my judgment we do not sufficiently protect the loyal men of the rebel States from the vindictive persecutions of their victorious rebel neighbors. Still I will move no amendment, nor vote for any, lest the whole fabric should tumble to pieces.

I need say nothing of the fourth section, for none dare object to it who is not himself a rebel. To the friend of justice, the friend of the Union, of the perpetuity of liberty, and the final triumph of the rights of man and their extension to every human being, let me say, sacrifice as we have done your peculiar views, and instead of vainly insisting upon the instantaneous operation of all that is right accept what is possible, and "all these things shall be added unto you."

Congressional Globe, 39 Cong., 1 sess. (F and J. Rives, Washington, 1866), 2459–2460 *passim,* May 8, 1866.

Fourteenth Amendment
Passed by Congress June 13, 1866. Ratified July 9, 1868.

Note: Article I, section 2, of the Constitution was modified by section 2 of the 14th amendment.

Section 1.
ALL PERSONS BORN or naturalized in the United States, and subject to the jurisdiction thereof, are citizens of the United States and of the State wherein they reside. No State shall make or enforce any law which shall abridge the privileges or immunities of citizens of the United States; nor shall any State deprive any person of life, liberty, or property, without due process of law; nor deny to any person within its jurisdiction the equal protection of the laws.

Section 2.

Representatives shall be apportioned among the several States according to their respective numbers, counting the whole number of persons in each State, excluding Indians not taxed. But when the right to vote at any election for the choice of electors for President and Vice-President of the United States, Representatives in Congress, the Executive and Judicial officers of a State, or the members of the Legislature thereof, is denied to any of the male inhabitants of such State, being twenty-one years of age,★ and citizens of the United States, or in any way abridged, except for participation in rebellion, or other crime, the basis of representation therein shall be reduced in the proportion which the number of such male citizens shall bear to the whole number of male citizens twenty-one years of age in such State.

Section 3.

No person shall be a Senator or Representative in Congress, or elector of President and Vice-President, or hold any office, civil or military, under the United States, or under any State, who, having previously taken an oath, as a member of Congress, or as an officer of the United States, or as a member of any State legislature, or as an executive or judicial officer of any State, to support the Constitution of the United States, shall have engaged in insurrection or rebellion against the same, or given aid or comfort to the enemies thereof. But Congress may by a vote of two-thirds of each House, remove such disability.

Section 4.

The validity of the public debt of the United States, authorized by law, including debts incurred for payment of pensions and bounties for services in suppressing insurrection or rebellion, shall not be questioned. But neither the United States nor any State shall assume or pay any debt or obligation incurred in aid of insurrection or rebellion against the United States, or any claim for the loss or emancipation of any slave; but all such debts, obligations and claims shall be held illegal and void.

Section 5.

The Congress shall have the power to enforce, by appropriate legislation, the provisions of this article.

★*Changed by section 1 of the 26th amendment.*

[AHD]

United States and Russia,
Treaty and the Alaska Purchase

March 30, 1867

The risk of encroachment by Russia had been one of the causes which induced President Monroe to give official utterance to the "Monroe Doctrine." After his statement, Russia ceased from attempts to increase her influence on the Pacific coast, and became willing to dispose of Alaska, regarding it as a possession difficult to defend and of little value. The territory was formally transferred on Oct. 18, 1867. — Note by Charles W Eliot.

CONVENTION BETWEEN THE United States of America and His Majesty the Emperor of Russia, for the Cession of the Russian Possessions in North America to the United States, Concluded at Washington March 30, 1867; Ratification Advised by Senate April 9, 1867; Ratified by President May 28, 1867; Ratifications Exchanged at Washington June 20, 1867; Proclaimed, June 20, 1867.

The United States of America and His Majesty the Emperor of all the Russia, being desirous of strengthening, if possible, the good understanding which exists between them, have, for that purpose, appointed as their Plenipotentiaries, the President of the United States, William H. Seward, Secretary of State; and His Majesty the Emperor of all the Russias, the Privy Counsellor Edward de Stoeckl, his Envoy Extraordinary and Minister Plenipotentiary to the United States;

And the said Plenipotentiaries, having exchanged their full powers, which were found to be in due form, have agreed upon and signed the following articles:

ARTICLE I

His Majesty the Emperor of all the Russias agrees to cede to the United States, by this convention, immediately upon the exchange of the ratifications thereof, all the territory and dominion now possessed by his said Majesty on the continent of America and in adjacent islands, the same being contained within the geographical limits herein set forth, to wit: The eastern limit is the line of demarcation between the Russian and the British possessions in North America, as established by the convention between Russia and Great Britain, of February 28–16, 1825, and described in Articles III and IV of said convention, in the following terms:

"Commencing from the southernmost point of the island called Prince of Wales Island, which point lies in the parallel of 54 degrees 40 minutes north latitude, and between the 131st and 133d degree of west longitude (meridian of Greenwich), the said line shall ascend to the north along the channel called Portland Channel, as far as the point of the continent where it strikes the 56th degree of north latitude; from this last-mentioned point, the line of demarcation shall follow the summit of the mountains situated parallel to the coast, as far as the point of intersection of the 141st degree of west longitude (of the same meridian); and finally, from the said point of intersection, the said meridian line of the 141st degree, in its prolongation as far as the Frozen Ocean.

"IV With reference to the line of demarcation laid down in the preceding article, it is understood—

"1st That the island called Prince of Wales Island shall belong wholly to Russia" (now, by this cession to the United States).

"2d That whenever the summit of the mountains which extend in a direction parallel to the coast from the 56th degree of north latitude to the point of intersection of the 141st degree of west longitude shall prove to be at the distance of more than ten marine leagues from the ocean, the limit between the British possessions and the line of coast which is to belong to Russia as above mentioned (that is to say, the limit to the possessions ceded by this convention), shall be formed by a line parallel to the winding of the coast, and which shall never exceed the distance of ten marine leagues therefrom."

The western limit within which the territories and dominion conveyed are contained passes through a point in Behring's Straits on the parallel of sixty-five degrees thirty minutes north latitude, at its intersection by the meridian which passes midway between the islands of Krusenstern or Ignalook, and the island of Romanoff, or Noonarbook, and proceeds due north without limitation, into the same Frozen Ocean. The same western limit, beginning at the same initial point, proceeds thence in a course nearly southwest, through Behring's Straits and Behring's Sea, so as to pass midway between the northwest point of the island of St. Lawrence and the southeast point of Cape Choukotski, to the meridian of one hundred and seventy-two west longitude; thence, from the intersection of that meridian, in a southwesterly direction, so as to pass midway between the island of Attou and the Copper Island of the Kormandorski couplet or group, in the North Pacific Ocean, to the meridian of one hundred and ninety-three degrees west longitude, so as to include in the territory conveyed the whole of the Aleutian Islands east of that meridian.

ARTICLE II

In the cession of territory and dominion made by the preceding article are included the right of property in all public lots and squares, vacant lands, and all public buildings, fortifications, barracks, and other edifices which are not private individual property. It is, however, understood and agreed, that the churches which have been built in the ceded territory by the Russian Government, shall remain the property of such members of the Greek Oriental Church resident in the territory as may choose to worship therein. Any Government archives, papers, and documents relative to the territory and dominion aforesaid, which may now be existing there, will be left in the possession of the agent of the United States; but an authenticated copy of such of them as may be required, will be, at all times, given by the United States to the Russian Government, or to such Russian officers or subjects as they may apply for.

ARTICLE III

The inhabitants of the ceded territory, according to their choice, reserving their natural allegiance, may return to Russia within three years; but if they should prefer to remain in the ceded territory, they, with the exception of uncivilized native tribes, shall be admitted to the enjoyment of all the rights, advantages, and immunities of citizens of the United States, and shall be maintained and protected in the free enjoyment of their liberty, property, and religion. The uncivilized tribes will be subject to such laws and regulations as the United States may from time to time adopt in regard to aboriginal tribes of that country.

ARTICLE IV

His Majesty, the Emperor of all the Russias shall appoint, with convenient dispatch, an agent or agents for the purpose of formally delivering to a similar agent or agents, appointed on behalf of the United States, the territory, dominion, property, dependencies, and appurtenances which are ceded as above, and for doing any other act which may be necessary in regard thereto. But the cession, with the right of immediate possession, is nevertheless to be deemed complete and absolute on the exchange of ratifications, without waiting for such formal delivery.

ARTICLE V

Immediately after the exchange of the ratifications of this convention, any fortifications or military posts which may be in the ceded territory shall be delivered to the agent of the United States, and any Russian troops which may be in the territory shall be withdrawn as soon as may be reasonably and conveniently practicable.

ARTICLE VI

In consideration of the cession aforesaid, the United States agree to pay at the Treasury in Washington, within ten months after the exchange of the ratifications of this convention, to the diplomatic representative or other agent of His Majesty the Emperor of all the Russia, duly authorized to receive the same, seven million two hundred thousand dollars in gold. The cession of territory and dominion herein made is hereby declared to be free and unencumbered by any reservations, privileges, franchises, grants, or possessions, by any associated companies, whether corporate or incorporate, Russian or any other, or by any parties, except merely private individual property-holders; and the cession hereby made conveys all the rights, franchises, and privileges now belonging to Russia in the said territory or dominion, and appurtenances thereto.

ARTICLE VII

When this convention shall have been duly ratified by the President of the United States, by and with the advice and consent of the Senate, on the one part, and, on the other, by His Majesty the Emperor of all the Russias, the ratifications shall be exchanged at Washington within three months from the date thereof or sooner if possible.

In faith, whereof the respective Plenipotentiaries have signed this convention, and thereto affixed the seals of their arms.

Done at Washington the thirtieth day of March, in the year of our Lord one thousand eight hundred and sixty-seven.

WILLIAM H. SEWARD [L. S.]
EDOUARD DE STOECKL [L. S.]

[AHD]

Red Cloud, Speech, "The Great Spirit Made Us Both"

June 16, 1870

Invited by Peter Cooper to tell "the Indian's story," the chief of the Oglala Sioux said at Cooper Union Institute in New York City: "Red Cloud arose and faced the audience, drawing his blankets around him majestically. He was greeted with an outburst of applause and waving of handkerchiefs. As soon as the tumult had subsided, he began on a somewhat high key and with a rapid utterance, his 'talk.' At the end of each sentence he paused, and stood calmly surveying the audience, while the interpreter explained his words to Dr. Crosby, and he again in stentorian tones, gave them to the immense audience. Almost every sentence was received with loud applause by the assembly," reported The New York Times.

MY BROTHERS AND my Friends who are before me today: God Almighty has made us all, and He is here to hear what I have to say to you today. The Great Spirit made us both. He gave us lands and He gave you lands. You came here and we received you as brothers. When the Almighty made you, He made you all white and clothed you. When He made us He made us with red skins and poor. When you first came we were very many and you were few. Now you are many and we are few. You do not know who appears before you to speak. He is a representative of the original American race, the first people of this continent. We are good, and not bad. The reports which you get about us are all on one side. You hear of us only as murderers and thieves. We are not so. If we had more lands to give to you we would give them, but we have no more. We are driven into a very little island, and we want you, our dear

13

friends, to help us with the Government of the United States. The
Great Spirit made us poor and ignorant. He made you rich and wise
and skillful in things which we know nothing about. The good
Father made you to eat tame game and us to eat wild game. Ask
any one who has gone through to California. They will tell you we
have treated them well. You have children. We, too, have children,
and we wish to bring them up well. We ask you to help us do it.
At the mouth of Horse Creek, in 1852, the Great Father made a
treaty with us. We agreed to let him pass through our territory
unharmed for fifty-five years. We kept our word. We committed
no murders, no depredations, until the troops came there. When
the troops were sent there trouble and disturbance arose. Since that
time there have been various goods sent from time to time to us,
but only once did they reach us, and soon the Great Father took
away the only good man he had sent us, Col. Fitzpatrick. The
Great Father said we must go to farming, and some of our men
went to farming near Fort Laramie, and were treated very badly
indeed. We came to Washington to see our Great Father that peace
might be continued. The Great Father that made us both wishes
peace to be kept; we want to keep peace. Will you help us? In 1868
men came out and brought papers. We could not read them, and
they did not tell us truly what was in them. We thought the treaty
was to remove the forts, and that we should then cease from fighting. But they wanted to send us traders on the Missouri. We did
not want to go on the Missouri, but wanted traders where we were.
When I reached Washington the Great Father explained to me
what the treaty was, and showed me that the interpreters had deceived me. All I want is right and justice. I have tried to get from
the Great Father what is right and just. I have not altogether succeeded. I want you to help me to get what is right and just. I represent the whole Sioux nation, and they will be bound by what I
say. I am no Spotted Tail, to say one thing one day and be bought
for a pin the next. Look at me. I am poor and naked, but I am the
Chief of the nation. We do not want riches, but we want to train
our children right. Riches would do us no good. We could not
take them with us to the other world. We do not want riches, we
want peace and love.

The riches that we have in this world, Secretary Cox said truly,
we cannot take with us to the next world. Then I wish to know
why Commissioners are sent out to us who do nothing but rob us

and get the riches of this world away from us! I was brought up among the traders, and those who came out there in the early times treated me well and I had a good time with them. They taught us to wear clothes and to use tobacco and ammunition. But, by and by, the Great Father sent out a different kind of men; men who cheated and drank whisky; men who were so bad that the Great Father could not keep them at home and so sent them out there. I have sent a great many words to the Great Father but they never reached him. They were drowned on the way, and I was afraid the words I spoke lately to the Great Father would not reach you, so I came to speak to you myself; and now I am going away to my home. I want to have men sent out to my people whom we know and can trust. I am glad I have come here. You belong in the East and I belong in the West, and I am glad I have come here and that we could understand one another. I am very much obliged to you for listening to me. I go home this afternoon. I hope you will think of what I have said to you. I bid you all an affectionate farewell.

[GSNA]

Chief Joseph, Speech, "I Will Fight No More Forever"

October 5, 1877

After leading his tribe of Nez Percé more than 1,600 miles, and about thirty miles from refuge in Canada, Chief Joseph (1841–1904) surrendered to General Oliver Howard at Eagle Creek, Montana. His famous words of surrender were recorded on the spot by a U.S. Army interpreter.

TELL GENERAL HOWARD I know his heart. What he told me before I have in my heart. I am tired of fighting. Our chiefs are killed. Looking Glass is dead. Too-hul-hul-sote is dead. The old men are all dead. It is the young men who say yes or no. He who led on the young men is dead. It is cold and we have no blankets. The little children are freezing to death. My people, some of them, have run away to the hills, and have no blankets, no food; no one knows where they are—perhaps freezing to death. I want to have time to look for my children and see how many of them I can find. Maybe I shall find them among the dead. Hear me, my chiefs. I am tired; my heart is sick and sad. From where the sun now stands I will fight no more forever.

[GSNA]

Susan B. Anthony, Address On Behalf of the Woman Suffrage Movement

January 23, 1880

Susan Brownell Anthony (1820–1906) was one of the most prominent and well-known civil rights leaders of the nineteenth century. Remembered mostly as an outspoken crusader for women's suffrage, Susan B. Anthony was also an important abolitionist and a pioneering figure in the temperance movement. The following address, delivered before the Committee on the Judiciary in the U.S. Senate in 1880, is a passionate appeal for the adaption of a women's suffrage amendment.

— Note by James Daley

[...] AMENDMENTS HAVE BEEN proposed to put God in the Constitution and to keep God out of the Constitution. All sorts of propositions to amend the Constitution have been made; but I ask that you allow no other amendment to be called the sixteenth but that which shall put into the hands of one-half of the entire people of the nation the right to express their opinions as to how the Constitution shall be amended henceforth. Women have the right to say whether we shall have God in the Constitution as well as men. Women have a right to say whether we shall have a national law or an amendment to the Constitution prohibiting the importation or manufacture of alcoholic liquors. We have a right to have our opinions counted on every possible question concerning the public welfare.

You ask us why we do not get this right to vote first in the school districts, and on school questions, or the questions of liquor license. It has been shown very clearly why we need something more than that. You have good enough laws to-day in every State in this Union for the suppression of what are termed the social vices; for the suppression of the grog-shops, the gambling houses, the brothels, the obscene shows. There is plenty of legislation in every State in this Union for their suppression if it could be executed. Why is the Government, why are the States and the cities, unable to execute these laws? Simply because there is a large balance of power in every city that does not want those laws executed. Consequently both parties must alike cater to that balance of political power. The party that puts a plank in its platform that the laws against the grog-shops and all the other sinks of iniquity must be executed, is the party that will not get this balance of power to vote for it, and, consequently, the party that cannot get into power.

What we ask of you is that you will make of the women of the cities a balance of political power, so that when a mayor, a member of the common council, a supervisor, a justice of the peace, a district attorney, a judge on the bench even, shall go before the people of that city as a candidate for the suffrages of the people he shall not only be compelled to look to the men who frequent the grog-shops, the brothels, and the gambling houses, who will vote for him if he is not in favor of executing the law, but that he shall have to look to the mothers, the sisters, the wives, the daughters of those deluded men to see what they will do if he does not execute the law.

We want to make of ourselves a balance of political power. What we need is the power to execute the laws. We have got laws enough. Let me give you one little fact in regard to my own city of Rochester. You all know how that wonderful whip called the temperance crusade roused the whisky ring. It caused the whisky force to concentrate itself more strongly at the ballot-box than ever before, so that when the report of the elections in the spring of 1874 went over the country the result was that the whisky ring was triumphant, and that the whisky ticket was elected more largely than ever before. Senator Thurman will remember how it was in his own State of Ohio. Everybody knows that if my friends, Mrs. ex-Governor Wallace, Mrs. Allen, and all the women of the great West could have gone to the ballot-box at those municipal elections and voted for candidates, no such result would have occurred; while you refused by the laws of the State to the women the right to have their opinions counted, every rum-seller, every drunkard, every pauper even from the poor-house, and every criminal outside of the State's prison came out on election day to express his opinion and have it counted.

The next result of that political event was that the ring demanded new legislation to protect the whisky traffic everywhere. In my city the women did not crusade the streets, but they said they would help the men to execute the law. They held meetings, sent out committees, and had testimony secured against every man who had violated the law, and when the board of excise held its meeting those women assembled, three or four hundred, in the church one morning, and marched in a solid body to the common council chamber where the board of excise was sitting. As one rum-seller after another brought in his petition for a renewal of license, who had violated the law, those women presented the testimony against him. The law of the State of New York is that no man shall have a renewal who has violated the law. But in not one case did that board refuse to grant a renewal of license because of the testimony which those women presented, and at the close of the sitting it was found that twelve hundred more licenses had been granted than ever before in the history of the State. Then the defeated women said they would have those men punished according to law.

Again they retained an attorney and appointed committees to investigate all over the city. They got the proper officer to prosecute every rum-seller. I was at their meeting. One woman reported that the officer in every city refused to prosecute the liquor dealer who had violated the law. Why? Because if he should do so he would lose the votes of all the employees of certain shops on that street, if another he would lose the votes of the railroad employees, and if another he would lose the German vote, if another Irish vote, and so on. I said to those women what I say to you, and what I know to be true to-day, that if the women of the city of Rochester had held the power of the ballot in their hands they would have been a great political balance of power.

The last report was from District Attorney Raines. The women complained of a lager-beer-garden keeper. Said the district attorney, "Ladies, you are right, this man is violating the law, everybody knows it, but if I should prosecute him I would lose the entire

German vote." Said I, "Ladies, do you not see that if the women of the city of Rochester had the right to vote District Attorney Raines would have been compelled to have stopped and counted, weighed and measured? He would have said, 'If I prosecute that lager-beer German I shall lose the, 5,000 German votes in this city, but if I fail to prosecute him and execute the laws I shall lose the votes of 20,000 women.'"

Do you not see, gentlemen, that so long as you put this power of the ballot in the hands of every possible man, rich, poor, drunk, sober, educated, ignorant, outside of the State's prison, to make or unmake, not only every law and lawmaker, but every office-holder who has to do with the executing of the law, and take the power from the hands of the women of the nation, the mothers, you put the long arm of the lever, as we call it in mechanics, in the hands of the whisky power and make it utterly impossible for regulation of sobriety to be maintained in our community? The first step to-wards social regulation and good society in towns, cities, and vil-lages is the ballot in the hands of the mothers of those places. I appeal to you especially in this matter.

I do not know what you think about the proper sphere of women. It matters little what any of us think about it. We shall each and every individual find our own proper sphere if we are left to act in freedom; but my opinion is that when the whole arena of politics and government is thrown open to women they will endeavor to do very much as they do in their homes; that the men will look after the greenback theory or the hard-money theory, that you will look after free-trade or tariff, and the women will do the home house-keeping of the government, which is to take care of the moral government and the social regulation of our home department.

It seems to me that we have the power of government outside to shape and control circumstances, but that the inside power, the government house-keeping, is powerless, and is compelled to ac-cept whatever conditions or circumstances shall be granted.

Therefore I do not ask for liquor suffrage alone, nor for school suffrage alone, because that would amount to nothing. We must be able to have a voice in the election not only of every law-maker, but of everyone who has to do either with the making or the executing of the laws.

Then you ask why we do not get suffrage by the popular-vote method, State by State? I answer, because there is no reason why I,

for instance, should desire the women of one State of this nation to
vote any more than the women of another State. I have no more
interest as regards the women of New York than I have as regards
the women of Indiana, Iowa, or any of the States represented by
the women who have come up here. The reason why I do not wish
to get this right by what you call the popular-vote method, the
State vote, is because I believe there is a United States citizenship.
I believe that this is a nation, and to be a citizen of this nation
should be a guaranty to every citizen of the right to a voice in the
Government, and should give to me my right to express my opinion. You deny to me my liberty, my freedom, if you say that I shall
have no voice whatever in making, shaping, or controlling the
conditions of society in which I live. I differ from Judge Hunt, and
I hope I am respectful when I say that I think he made a very funny
mistake when he said that fundamental rights belong to the States
and only surface rights to the National Government. I hope you
will agree with me that the fundamental right of citizenship, the
right to voice in the Government, is a national right.

The National Government may concede to the States the right to
decide by a majority as to what banks they shall have, what laws
they shall enact with regard to insurance, with regard to property,
and any other question; but I insist upon it that the National
Government should not leave it a question with the States that a
majority in any State may disfranchise the minority under any circumstances whatsoever. The franchise to you men is not secure.
You hold it to-day, to be sure, by the common consent of white
men, but if at any time, on your principle of government, the majority of any of the States should choose to amend the State constitution so as to disfranchise this or that portion of the white men by
making this or that condition, by all the decisions of the Supreme
Court and by the legislation thus far there is nothing to hinder them.

Therefore the women demand a sixteenth amendment to bring
to women the right to vote, or if you please to confer upon women
their right to vote, to protect them in it, and to secure men in their
right, because you are not secure.

I would let the States act upon almost every other question by
majorities, except the power to say whether my opinion shall be
counted. I insist upon it that no State shall decide that question. [...]

You who are here upon the floor of Congress in both Houses
are the picked men of the nation. You may say what you please

about John Morrissey, the gambler, &c.: he was head and shoulders above the rank and file of his constituency. The world may gabble ever so much about members of Congress being corrupt and being bought and sold; they are as a rule head and shoulders among the great majority who compose their State governments. There is no doubt about it. Therefore I ask of you, as representative men, as men who think, as men who study, as men who philosophize, as men who know, that you will not drive us back to the States any more, but that you will carry out this method of procedure which has been practiced from the beginning of the Government; that is, that you will put a prohibitory amendment in the Constitution and submit the proposition to the several State legislatures. The amendment which has been presented before you reads:

ARTICLE XVI

SECTION 1. The right of suffrage in the United States shall be based on citizenship, and the right of citizens of the United States to vote shall not be denied or abridged by the United States, or by any State, on account of sex, or for any reason not equally applicable to all citizens of the United States.

SECTION 2. Congress shall have power to enforce this article by appropriate legislation.

[GSAW]

Helen Hunt Jackson, Conclusion, *A Century of Dishonor: A Sketch of the United States Government's Dealings with Some of the Indian Tribes*

1881

Born in Amherst, Massachusetts, the poet and activist Helen Hunt Jackson (1830–1885) wrote A Century of Dishonor, the most important and enduring study of the country's official dealings with North America's native peoples. We present here the concluding chapter of her great work.

THERE ARE WITHIN the limits of the United States between two hundred and fifty and three hundred thousand Indians, exclusive of those in Alaska. The names of the different tribes and bands, as entered in the statistical tables of the Indian Office Reports, number nearly three hundred. One of the most careful estimates which has been made of their numbers and localities gives them as follows: "In Minnesota and States east of the Mississippi, about 32,500; in Nebraska, Kansas, and the Indian Territory, 70,650; in the Territories of Dakota, Montana, Wyoming, and Idaho, 65,000; in Nevada and the Territories of Colorado, New Mexico, Utah, and Arizona, 84,000; and on the Pacific slope, 48,000."

Of these, 130,000 are self-supporting on their own reservations, "receiving nothing from the Government except interest on their own moneys, or annuities granted them in consideration of the cession of their lands to the United States."★

★Annual Report of Indian Commissioner for 1872.

This fact alone would seem sufficient to dispose forever of the accusation, so persistently brought against the Indian, that he will not work.

Of the remainder, 84,000 are partially supported by the Government—the interest money due them and their annuities, as provided by treaty, being inadequate to their subsistence on the reservations where they are confined. In many cases, however, these Indians furnish a large part of their support—the White River Utes, for instance, who are reported by the Indian Bureau as getting sixty-six per cent. of their living by "root-digging, hunting, and fishing;" the Squaxin band, in Washington Territory, as earning seventy-five per cent., and the Chippewas of Lake Superior as earning fifty per cent., in the same way. These facts also would seem to dispose of the accusation that the Indian will not work.

There are about 55,000 who never visit an agency, over whom the Government does not pretend to have either control or care. These 55,000 "subsist by hunting, fishing, on roots, nuts, berries, etc., and by begging and stealing;" and this also seems to dispose of the accusation that the Indian will not "work for a living." There remains a small portion, about 31,000 that are entirely subsisted by the Government.

There is not among these three hundred bands of Indians one which has not suffered cruelly at the hands either of the Government or of white settlers. The poorer, the more insignificant, the more helpless the band, the more certain the cruelty and outrage to which they have been subjected. This is especially true of the bands on the Pacific slope. These Indians found themselves of a sudden surrounded by and caught up in the great influx of gold-seeking settlers, as helpless creatures on a shore are caught up in a tidal wave. There was not time for the Government to make treaties; not even time for communities to make laws. The tale of the wrongs, the oppressions, the murders of the Pacific-slope Indians in the last thirty years would be a volume by itself, and is too monstrous to be believed.

It makes little difference, however, where one opens the record of the history of the Indians; every page and every year has its dark stain. The story of one tribe is the story of all, varied only by differences of time and place; but neither time nor place makes any difference in the main facts. Colorado is as greedy and unjust in

1880 as was Georgia in 1830, and Ohio in 1795; and the United States Government breaks promises now as deftly as then, and with an added ingenuity from long practice.

One of its strongest supports in so doing is the wide-spread sentiment among the people of dislike to the Indian, of impatience with his presence as a "barrier to civilization," and distrust of it as a possible danger. The old tales of the frontier life, with its horrors of Indian warfare, have gradually, by two or three generations' telling, produced in the average mind something like an hereditary instinct of unquestioning and unreasoning aversion which it is almost impossible to dislodge or soften.

There are hundreds of pages of unimpeachable testimony on the side of the Indian; but it goes for nothing, is set down as sentimentalism or partisanship, tossed aside and forgotten.

President after president has appointed commission after commission to inquire into and report upon Indian affairs, and to make suggestions as to the best methods of managing them. The reports are filled with eloquent statements of wrongs done to the Indians, of perfidies on the part of the Government; they counsel, as earnestly as words can, a trial of the simple and unperplexing expedients of telling truth, keeping promises, making fair bargains, dealing justly in all ways and all things. These reports are bound up with the Government's Annual Reports, and that is the end of them. It would probably be no exaggeration to say that not one American citizen out of ten thousand ever sees them or knows that they exist, and yet any one of them, circulated throughout the country, read by the right-thinking, right-feeling men and women of this land, would be of itself a "campaign document" that would initiate a revolution which would not subside until the Indians' wrongs were, so far as is now left possible, righted.

In 1869 President Grant appointed a commission of nine men, representing the influence and philanthropy of six leading States, to visit the different Indian reservations, and to "examine all matters appertaining to Indian affairs."

In the report of this commission are such paragraphs as the following: "To assert that 'the Indian will not work' is as true as it would be to say that the white man will not work.

"Why should the Indian be expected to plant corn, fence lands, build houses, or do anything but get food from day to day, when experience has taught him that the product of his labor will be seized by the white man to-morrow? The most industrious white man would become a drone under similar circumstances. Nevertheless, many of the Indians" (the commissioners might more forcibly have said 130,000 of the Indians) "are already at work, and furnish ample refutation of the assertion that 'the Indian will not work.' There is no escape from the inexorable logic of facts.

"The history of the Government connections with the Indians is a shameful record of broken treaties and unfulfilled promises. The history of the border white man's connection with the Indians is a sickening record of murder, outrage, robbery, and wrongs committed by the former, as the rule, and occasional savage outbreaks and unspeakably barbarous deeds of retaliation by the latter, as the exception.

"Taught by the Government that they had rights entitled to respect, when those rights have been assailed by the rapacity of the white man, the arm which should have been raised to protect them has ever been ready to sustain the aggressor.

"The testimony of some of the highest military officers of the United States is on record to the effect that, in our Indian wars, almost without exception, the first aggressions have been made by the white man; and the assertion is supported by every civilian of reputation who has studied the subject. In addition to the class of robbers and outlaws who find impunity in their nefarious pursuits on the frontiers, there is a large class of professedly reputable men who use every means in their power to bring on Indian wars for the sake of the profit to be realized from the presence of troops and the expenditure of Government funds in their midst. They proclaim death to the Indians at all times in words and publications, making no distinction between the innocent and the guilty. They irate the lowest class of men to the perpetration of the darkest deeds against their victims, and as judges and jurymen shield them from the justice due to their crimes. Every crime committed by a white man against an Indian is concealed or palliated. Every offence committed by an Indian against a white man is borne on the wings of the post or the telegraph to the remotest corner of the land, clothed with all the horrors which the reality or imagination can throw around it. Against such influences as these the people of the United States need to be warned."

To assume that it would be easy, or by any one sudden stroke of legislative policy possible, to undo the mischief and hurt of the long past, set the Indian policy of the country right for the future, and make the Indians at once safe and happy, is the blunder of a hasty and uninformed judgment. The notion which seems to be growing more prevalent, that simply to make all Indians at once citizens of the United States would be a sovereign and instantaneous panacea for all their ills and all the Government's perplexities, is a very inconsiderate one. To administer complete citizenship of a sudden, all rounds, to all Indians, barbarous and civilized alike, would be as grotesque a blunder as to dose them all round with any one medicine, irrespective of the symptoms and needs of their diseases. It would kill more than it would cure. Nevertheless, it is true, as was well stated by one of the superintendents of Indian Affairs in 1857, that, "so long as they are not citizens of the United States, their rights of property must remain insecure against invasion. The doors of the federal tribunals being barred against them while wards and dependents, they can only partially exercise the rights of free government, or give to those who make, execute, and construe the few laws they are allowed to enact, dignity sufficient to make them respectable. While they continue individually to gather the crumbs that fall from the table of the United States, idleness, improvidence, and indebtedness will be the rule, and industry, thrift, and freedom from debt the exception. The utter absence of individual title to particular lands deprives every one among them of the chief incentive to labor and exertion—the very mainspring on which the prosperity of a people depends."

All judicious plans and measures for their safety and salvation must embody provisions for their becoming citizens as fast as they are fit, and must protect them till then in every right and particular in which our laws protect other "persons" who are not citizens.

There is a disposition in a certain class of minds to be impatient with any protestation against wrong which is unaccompanied or unprepared with a quick and exact scheme of remedy. This is illogical. "When pioneers in a new country find a tract of poisonous and swampy wilderness to be reclaimed, they do not withhold their hands from fire and axe till they see clearly which way roads should run, where good water will spring, and what crops will best grow on the redeemed land. They first clear the swamp. So, with this poisonous and baffling part of the domain of our national affairs—let us first "clear the swamp."

However great perplexity and difficulty there may be in the details of any and every plan possible for doing at this late day anything like justice to the Indian, however hard it may be for good statesmen and good men to agree upon the things that ought to be done, there certainly is, or ought to be, no perplexity whatever, no difficulty whatever, in agreeing upon certain things that ought not to be done, and which must cease to be done before the first steps can be taken toward righting the wrongs, curing the ills, and wiping out the disgrace to us of the present condition of our Indians.

Cheating, robbing, breaking promises—these three are clearly things which must cease to be done. One more thing, also, and that is the refusal of the protection of the law to the Indian's rights of property, "of life, liberty, and the pursuit of happiness."

When these four things have ceased to be done, time, statesmanship, philanthropy, and Christianity can slowly and surely do the rest. Till these four things have ceased to be done, statesmanship and philanthropy alike must work in vain, and even Christianity can reap but small harvest.

[CD]

Chinese Exclusion Act

May 6, 1882

In 1868, Chinese were encouraged to immigrate to the United States to help build the railroads. Because of growing prejudice against the immigrants on the West Coast, lawmakers put forward bills to prohibit further immigration; this was the first time Congress targeted a specific national group for exclusion. This Act of 1882 was intended to last for ten years, but was instead continually renewed. Chinese immigration remained severely restricted until the Immigration Act of 1965.

— Note by Bob Blaisdell

WHEREAS, IN THE opinion of the Government of the United States the coming of Chinese laborers to this country endangers the good order of certain localities within the territory thereof:

Therefore,

Be it enacted by the Senate and House of Representatives of the United States of America in Congress assembled, that from and after the expiration of ninety days next after the passage of this act, and until the expiration of ten years next after the passage of this act, the coming of Chinese laborers to the United States be, and the same is hereby, suspended; and during such suspension it shall not be lawful for any Chinese laborer to come, or having so come after the expiration of said ninety days, to remain within the United States.

SEC. 2. That the master of any vessel who shall knowingly bring within the United States on such vessel, and land or permit to be landed, any Chinese laborer, from any foreign port or place, shall be deemed guilty of a misdemeanor, and on conviction thereof shall be punished by a fine of not more than $500 for each and every such Chinese laborer so brought, and may be also imprisoned for a term not exceeding one year.

SEC. 3. That the two foregoing sections shall not apply to Chinese laborers who were in the United States on the 17th day of November, 1880, or who shall have come into the same before the expiration of ninety days next after the passage of this act...

SEC. 4. That for the purpose of properly identifying Chinese laborers who were in the United States on the 17th day of November, 1880, or who shall have come into the same before the expiration of ninety days next after the passage of this act, and in order to furnish them with the proper evidence of their right to go from and come to the United States of their free will and accord, as provided by the treaty between the United States and China dated November 17, 1880, the collector of customs of the district from which any such Chinese laborer shall depart from the United States shall, in person or by deputy, go on board each vessel having on board any such Chinese laborer and cleared or about to sail from his district for a foreign port, and on such vessel make a list of all such Chinese laborers, which shall be entered in registry-books to be kept for that purpose, in which shall be stated the name, age, occupation, last place of residence, physical marks or peculiarities, and all facts necessary for the identification of each of such Chinese laborers, which books shall be safely kept in the custom-house; and every such Chinese laborer so departing from the United States shall be entitled to, and shall receive, free of any charge or cost upon application therefore, from the collector or his deputy, at the time such list is taken a certificate, signed by the collector or his deputy and attested by his seal of office, in such form as the Secretary of the Treasury shall prescribe, which certificate shall contain a statement of the name, age, occupation, last place of residence, personal description, and facts of identification of the Chinese laborer to whom the certificate is issued, corresponding with the said list and registry in all particulars...

SEC. 5. That any Chinese laborer mentioned in section four of this act being in the United States, and desiring to depart from the United States by land, shall have the right to demand and receive, free of charge or cost, a certificate of identification similar to that provided for in section four of this act to be issued to such Chinese laborers as may desire to leave the United States by water; and it is hereby made the duty of the collector of customs of the district next adjoining the foreign country to which said Chinese laborer desires to go to issue such certificate, free of charge or cost, upon application by such Chinese laborer, and to enter the same upon registry-books to be kept by him for the purpose, as provided for in section four of this act. [...]

SEC. 13. That this act shall not apply to diplomatic and other officers of the Chinese Government traveling upon the business of that government, whose credentials shall be taken as equivalent to the certificate in this act mentioned, and shall exempt them and their body and household servants from the provisions of this act as to other Chinese persons.

SEC. 14. That hereafter no State court or court of the United States shall admit Chinese to citizenship; and all laws in conflict with this act are hereby repealed.

SEC. 15. That the words "Chinese laborers," wherever used in this act, shall be construed to mean both skilled and unskilled laborers and Chinese employed in mining.

Approved, May 6, 1882.

[AVA]

Sitting Bull, Tatanka Yotanka, Testimony Before A Senate Select Committee

August 21, 1883

At the Standing Rock Agency of the Hunkpapa Sioux in Dakota Territory, Sitting Bull (c. 1830–1890) bristled at the disrespectful manner of the U.S. Senators' select committee chairman: "You say you know I am Sitting Bull, but do you know what position I hold?" "I do not know any difference between you and the other Indians at this agency," replied the chairman. Sitting Bull answered: "I am here by the will of the Great Spirit, and by his will I am a chief. My heart is red and sweet, and I know it is sweet, because whatever passes near me puts out its tongue to me; and yet you men have come here to talk with us, and you say you do not know who I am. I want to tell you that if the Great Spirit has chosen any one to be the chief of this country it is myself." Finally, Sitting Bull told the senators, "You have conducted yourselves like men who have been drinking whiskey, and I came here to give you advice." And with that, Sitting Bull waved his hand, and he and the other Indians left the room. He later returned to apologize and make the following speech.

I CAME IN with a glad heart to shake hands with you, my friends, for I feel that I have displeased you; and I am here to apologize to you for my bad conduct and to take back what I said. I will take it back because I consider I have made your hearts bad. I heard that you were coming here from the Great Father's house some time before you came, and I have been sitting here like a prisoner waiting for someone to release me. I was looking for you everywhere, and I considered that when we talked with you it was the same as if we were talking with the Great Father; and I believe that what I pour out from my heart the Great Father will hear. What I take back is what I said to cause the people to leave the council, and want to apologize for leaving myself. The people acted like children, and I am sorry for it. I was very sorry when I found out that your intentions were good and entirely different from what I supposed they were. Now I will tell you my mind and I will tell everything straight. I know the Great Spirit is looking down upon me from above and will hear what I say, therefore I will do my best to talk straight; and I am in hopes that someone will listen to my wishes and help me to carry them out.

I have always been a chief, and have been made chief of all the land. Thirty-two years ago I was present at councils with the white man, and at rhythm of the Fort Rice council I was on the prairie listening to it, and since then a great many questions have been asked me about it, and I always said wait; and when the Black Hills council was held, and they asked me to give up that land, I said they must wait. I remember well all the promises that were made about that land because I have thought a great deal about them since that time. Of course I know that the Great Spirit provided me with animals for my food, but I did not stay out on the prairie because I did not wish to accept the offers of the Great Father, for I sent in a great many of my people and I told them that the Great Father was providing for them and keeping his agreements with them, and I was sending the Indians word all the time I was out that they must remember their agreements and fulfill them, and carry them out straight. When the English authorities were looking for me I heard that the Great Father's people were looking for me too. I was not lost. I knew where I was going all the time.

Previous to that time, when a Catholic priest called "White Hair" [meaning Bishop Marty] came to see me, I told him all these things plainly. He told me the wishes of the Great Father, and I made promises which I meant to fulfill, and did fulfill; and when I went over into the British possessions he followed me, and I told him everything that was in my heart, and sent him back to tell the Great Father what I told him; and General Terry sent me word afterwards to come in, because he had big promises to make me, and I sent him word that I would not throw my country away; that I considered it all mine still, and I wanted him to wait just four years for me; that I had gone over there to attend to some business of my own, and my people were doing just as any other people would do. If a man loses anything and goes back and looks carefully for it he will find it, and that is what the Indians are doing now when they ask you to give them the things that were promised them in the past; and I do not consider that they should be treated like beasts, and that is the reason I have grown up with the feelings I have. Whatever you wanted of me I have obeyed, and I have come when you called me. The Great Father sent me word that whatever he had against me in the past had been forgiven and thrown aside, and he would have nothing against me in the future, and I accepted his promises and came in; and he told me not to step aside from the white man's path, and I told him I would not, and I am doing my best to travel in that path.

I feel that my country has gotten a bad name, and I want it to have a good name; it used to have a good name; and I sit sometimes and wonder who it is that has given it a bad name. You are the only people now who can give it a good name, and I want you to take good care of my country and respect it. When we sold the Black Hills we got a very small price for it, and not what we ought to have received. I used to think that the size of the payments would remain the same all the time, but they are growing smaller all the time. I want you to tell the Great Father everything I have said, and that we want some benefit from the promises he has made to us; and I don't think I should be tormented with anything about giving up any part of my land until those promises are fulfilled—I would rather wait until that time, when I will be ready to transact any business he may desire.

I consider that my country takes in the Black Hills, and runs from the Powder River to the Missouri; and that all of this land belongs to me. Our reservation is not as large as we want it to be, and I suppose the Great Father owes us money now for land he has taken from us in the past. You white men advise us to follow your ways, and therefore I talk as I do. When you have a piece of land, and anything trespasses on it, you catch it and keep it until you get damages, and I am doing the same thing now; and I want you to tell all this to the Great Father for me. I am looking into the future for the benefit of my children, and that is what I mean, when I say I want my country taken care of for me. My children will grow up here, and I am looking ahead for their benefit, and for the benefit of my children's children, too; and even beyond that again.

I sit here and look around me now, and I see my people starving, and I want the Great Father to make an increase in the amount of food that is allowed us now, so that they may be able to live. We want cattle to butcher—I want to kill three hundred head of cattle at a time. That is the way you live, and we want to live the same way. This is what I want you to tell the Great Father when you go back home. If we get the things we want our children will be raised like the white children. When the Great Father told me to live like his people I told him to send me six teams of mules, because that is the way white people make a living, and I wanted my children to have these things to help them to make a living. I also told him to send me two spans of horses with wagons, and everything else my children would need. I also asked for a horse and buggy for my children; I was advised to follow the ways of the white man, and that is why I asked for those things. I never ask for anything that is not needed. I also asked for a cow and a bull for each family, so that they can raise cattle of their own. I asked for four yokes of oxen and wagons with them. Also a yoke of oxen and a wagon for each of my children to haul wood with. It is your own doing that I am here; you sent me here, and advised me to live as you do, and it is not right for me to live in poverty. I asked the Great Father for hogs, male and female, and for male and female sheep for my children to raise from. I did not leave out anything in the way of animals that the white men have; I asked for every one of them. I want you to tell the Great Father to send me some agricultural implements, so that I will not be obliged to work bare-handed. Whatever he sends to this agency our agent will take care of for us, and we will be satisfied because we know he will keep everything right. Whatever is sent here for us he will be pleased to take care of us. I want to tell you that our rations have been reduced to almost nothing, and many of the people have starved to death.

Now I beg of you to have the amount of rations increased so that our children will not starve, but will live better than they do now. I want clothing too, and I will ask for that too. We want all kinds of clothing for our people. Look at the men around here and see how poorly dressed they are. We want some clothing this month, and when it gets cold we want more of it to protect us from the weather. That is all I have to say.

[AIH]

Commissioner of Indian Affairs, Annual Report, "Massacre at Wounded Knee"

December 29, 1890

The Ghost Dance was a religion founded on the vision of a Nevada Paiute named Wovoka: he believed that if the participants danced hard enough and long enough, all the buffalo would come back, all the Indians' ancestors would come to life, and all the white people would be buried underground. With every tribe in America devastated by war, disease, hunger or removal, the Ghost Dance was an immediately popular activity with Native peoples. The new religion made U. S. Government officials nervous and in an attempt to suppress it, outlawed it; the army sent soldiers to arrest the chief of the Hunkpapa Sioux, Sitting Bull, who instead was killed on December 14. Two weeks later, some of Sitting Bull's followers were tracked to the Wounded Knee Creek on the Pine Ridge Reservation, and, in the confusion of a weapons search, were killed by army troops. The massacre was devastating and not forgotten; eighty-three years later, members of the American Indian Movement (AIM) made a new stand at Wounded Knee. The following pages are extracts from the report of the council that took place on February 11, 1891, with Sioux delegations and the Commissioner of Indian Affairs in Washington, D.C. and published in the U.S. Commissioner of Indian Affairs' Annual Report of 1891.

TURNING HAWK, PINE Ridge (Mr Cook, interpreter). Mr Commissioner, my purpose to-day is to tell you what I know of the condition of affairs at the agency where I live. A certain falsehood came to our agency from the west which had the effect of a fire upon the

Indians, and when this certain fire came upon our people those who had farsightedness and could see into the matter made up their minds to stand up against it and fight it. The reason we took this hostile attitude to this fire was because we believed that you yourself would not be in favor of this particular mischief-making thing; but just as we expected, the people in authority did not like this thing and we were quietly told that we must give up or have nothing to do with this certain movement. Though this is the advice from our good friends in the east, there were, of course, many silly young men who were longing to become identified with the movement, although they knew that there was nothing absolutely bad, nor did they know there was anything absolutely good, in connection with the movement.

In the course of time we heard that the soldiers were moving toward the scene of trouble. After awhile some of the soldiers finally reached our place and we heard that a number of them also reached our friends at Rosebud. Of course, when a large body of soldiers is moving toward a certain direction they inspire a more or less amount of awe, and it is natural that the women and children who see this large moving mass are made afraid of it and be put in a condition to make them run away. At first we thought that Pine Ridge and Rosebud were the only two agencies where soldiers were sent, but finally we heard that the other agencies fared likewise. We heard and saw that about half our friends at Rosebud agency, from fear at seeing the soldiers, began the move of running away from their agency toward ours (Pine Ridge), and when they had gotten inside of our reservation they there learned that right ahead of them at our agency was another large crowd of soldiers and while the soldiers were there, there was constantly a great deal of false rumor flying back and forth. The special rumor I have in mind is the threat that the soldiers had come there to disarm the Indians entirely and to take away all their horses from them. That was the oft-repeated story.

So constantly repeated was this story that our friends from Rosebud, instead of going to Pine Ridge, the place of their destination, veered off and went to some other direction toward the "Bad Lands." We did not know definitely how many, but understood there were 300 lodges of them, about 1,700 people. Eagle Pipe, Turning Bear, High Hawk, Short Bull, Lance, No Flesh, Pine Bird, Crow Dog, Two Strike, and White Horse were the leaders.

Well, the people after veering off in this way, many of them who believe in peace and order at our agency, were very anxious that some influence should be brought upon these people. In addition to our love of peace we remembered that many of these people were related to us by blood. So we sent out peace commissioners to the people who were thus running away from their agency.

I understood at the time that they were simply going away from fear because of so many soldiers. So constant was the word of these good men from Pine Ridge agency that finally they succeeded in getting away half of the party from Rosebud, from the place where they took refuge, and finally were brought to the agency at Pine Ridge. Young-Man-Afraid-of-his-Horses, Little Wound, Fast Thunder, Louis Shangreau, John Grass, Jack Red Cloud, and I were some of these peacemakers.

The remnant of the party from Rosebud not taken to the agency finally reached the wilds of the Bad Lands. Seeing that we had succeeded so well, once more we sent to the same party in the Bad Lands and succeeded in bringing these very Indians out of the depths of the Bad Lands and were being brought toward the agency. When we were about a day's journey from our agency we heard that a certain party of Indians (Big Foot's band) from the Cheyenne River agency was coming toward Pine Ridge in flight.

CAPTAIN SWORD. Those who actually went off of the Cheyenne River agency probably number 303, and there were a few from the Standing Rock reserve with them, but as to their number I do not know. There were a number of Ogallalas, old men and several school boys, coming back with that very same party, and one of the very seriously wounded boys was a member of the Ogallala boarding school at Pine Ridge agency. He was not on the warpath, but was simply returning home to his agency and to his school after a summer visit to relatives on the Cheyenne River.

TURNING HAWK. When we heard that these people were coming toward our agency we also heard this. These people were coming toward Pine Ridge agency, and when they were almost on the agency they were met by the soldiers and surrounded and finally taken to the Wounded Knee creek, and there at a given time their guns were demanded. When they had delivered them up, the men were separated from their families, from their tipis, and taken to a certain spot. When the guns were thus taken and the men thus separated, there was a crazy man, a young man of very bad influence and in fact a nobody, among that bunch of Indians fired his gun, and of course the firing of a gun must have been the breaking of a military rule of some sort, because immediately the soldiers returned fire and indiscriminate killing followed.

SPOTTED HORSE. This man shot an officer in the army; the first shot killed this officer. I was a voluntary scout at that encounter and I saw exactly what was done, and that was what I noticed; that the first shot killed an officer. As soon as this shot was fired the Indians immediately began drawing their knives, and they were exhorted from all sides to desist, but this was not obeyed. Consequently the firing began immediately on the part of the soldiers.

TURNING HAWK. All the men who were in a bunch were killed right there, and those who escaped that first fire got into the ravine, and as they went along up the ravine for a long distance they were pursued on both sides by the soldiers and shot down, as the dead bodies showed afterwards. The women were standing off at a different place from where the men were stationed, and when that firing began, those of the men who escaped the first onslaught went in one direction up the ravine, and then the women, who were bunched together at another place, went entirely in a different direction through an open field, and the women fared the same fate as the men who went up the deep ravine.

AMERICAN HORSE. The men were separated, as has already been said, from the women, and they were surrounded by the soldiers. Then came next the village of the Indians and that was entirely surrounded by the soldiers also. When the firing began, of course the people who were standing immediately around the young man who fired the first shot were killed right together, and then they turned their guns, Hotchkiss guns, etc., upon the women who were in the lodges standing there under a flag of truce, and of course as soon as they were fired upon they fled, the men fleeing in one direction and the women running in two different directions. So that there were three general directions in which they took flight.

There was a woman with an infant in her arms who was killed as she almost touched the flag of truce, and the women and children of course were strewn all along the circular village until they were dispatched. Right near the flag of truce a mother was shot down with her infant; the child not knowing that its mother was dead was still nursing, and that especially was a very sad sight. The women as they were fleeing with their babies were killed together, shot right through, and the women who were very heavy with child were also killed. All the Indians fled in these three directions, and after most all of them had been killed a cry was made that all those who were not killed or wounded should come forth and they would be safe. Little boys who were not wounded came out of their places of refuge, and as soon as they came in sight a number of soldiers surrounded them and butchered them there.

Of course we all feel very sad about this affair. I stood very loyal to the government all through those troublesome days, and believing so much in the government and being so loyal to it, my disappointment was very strong, and I have come to Washington with a very great blame on my heart. Of course it would have been all right if only the men were killed; we would feel almost grateful for it. But the fact of the killing of the women, and more especially the killing of the young boys and girls who are to go to make up the future strength of the Indian people, is the saddest part of the whole affair and we feel it very sorely.

I was not there at the time before the burial of the bodies, but I did go there with some of the police and the Indian doctor and a great many of the people, men from the agency, and we went through the battlefield and saw where the bodies were from the track of the blood.

TURNING HAWK. I had just reached the point where I said that the women were killed. We heard, besides the killing of the men, of the onslaught also made upon the women and children, and they were treated as roughly and indiscriminately as the men and boys were. Of course this affair brought a great deal of distress upon all the people, but especially upon the minds of those who stood loyal to the government and who did all that they were able to do in the matter of bringing about peace. They especially have suffered much distress and are very much hurt at heart. These peacemakers continued on in their good work, but there were a great many fickle young men who were ready to be moved by the change in the events there, and consequently, in spite of the great fire that was brought upon all, they were ready to assume any hostile attitude. These young men got themselves in readiness and went in the direction of the scene of battle so they might be of service there. They got there and finally exchanged shots with the soldiers. This party of young men was made up from Rosebud, Ogallala (Pine

Ridge), and members of any other agencies that happened to be there at the time. While this was going on in the neighborhood of Wounded Knee—the Indians and soldiers exchanging shots—the agency, our home, was also fired into by the Indians. Matters went on in this strain until the evening came on and then the Indians went off down by White Clay creek. When the agency was fired upon by the Indians from the hillside, of course to shots were returned by the Indian police who were guarding the agency buildings.

Although fighting seemed to have been in the air, yet those who believed in peace were still constant at their work. Young-Man-Afraid-of-his-Horses, who had been on a visit to some agency in the north or northwest, returned, and immediately went out to the people living about White Clay creek, on the border of the Bad Lands, and brought his people out. He succeeded in obtaining the consent of the people to come out of their place of refuge and return to the agency. Thus the remaining portion of the Indians who started from Rosebud was brought back into the agency. Mr. Commissioner, during the days of the great whirlwind out there, those good men tried to hold up a counteracting power and that was "Peace." We have now come to realize that peace has prevailed and won the day. While we were engaged in bringing about peace our property was left behind, of course, and most of us have lost everything, even down to the matter of guns with which to kill ducks, rabbits, etc, shotguns, and guns of that order. When Young-Man-Afraid brought the people in and their guns were asked for, both men who were called hostile and men who stood loyal in the government delivered up their guns.

[AIH]

The Populist Party Platform

July 4, 1892

The Populist movement formally organized itself in 1892 at a convention in Omaha. Some of the specific reforms that it called for (listed in the document below) only bore fruit in the new century.

ASSEMBLED UPON THE 116th anniversary of the Declaration of Independence, the People's Party of America, in their first national convention, invoking upon their action the blessing of Almighty God, put forth in the name and on behalf of the people of this country, the following preamble and declaration of principles:

PREAMBLE

The conditions which surround us best justify our co-operation; we meet in the midst of a nation brought to the verge of moral, political, and material ruin. Corruption dominates the ballot-box, the Legislatures, the Congress, and touches even the ermine of the bench. The people are demoralized; most of the States have been compelled to isolate the voters at the polling places to prevent universal intimidation and bribery. The newspapers are largely subsidized or muzzled, public opinion silenced, business prostrated, homes covered with mortgages, labor impoverished, and the land concentrating in the hands of capitalists. The urban workmen are denied the right to organize for self-protection, imported pauperized labor beats down their wages, a hireling standing army, unrecognized by our laws, is established to shoot them down, and they are rapidly degenerating into European conditions. The fruits of the toil of millions are boldly stolen to build up colossal fortunes for a few, unprecedented in the history of mankind; and the possessors of those, in turn, despise the republic and endanger liberty. From the same prolific womb of governmental injustice we breed the two great classes—tramps and millionaires.

The national power to create money is appropriated to enrich bondholders; a vast public debt payable in legal tender currency has been funded into gold-bearing bonds, thereby adding millions to the burdens of the people.

Silver, which has been accepted as coin since the dawn of history, has been demonetized to add to the purchasing power of gold by decreasing the value of all forms of property as well as human labor, and the supply of currency is purposely abridged to fatten usurers, bankrupt enterprise, and enslave industry. A vast conspiracy against mankind has been organized on two continents, and it is rapidly taking possession of the world. If not met and overthrown at once it forebodes terrible social convulsions, the destruction of civilization, or the establishment of an absolute despotism.

We have witnessed for more than a quarter of a century the struggles of the two great political parties for power and plunder, while grievous wrongs have been inflicted upon the suffering people. We charge that the controlling influences dominating both these parties have permitted the existing dreadful conditions to develop without serious effort to prevent or restrain them. Neither do they now promise us any substantial reform. They have agreed together to ignore, in the coming campaign, every issue but one. They propose to drown the outcries of a plundered people with the uproar of a sham battle over the tariff, so that capitalists, corporations, national banks, rings, trusts, watered stock, the demonetization of silver and the oppressions of the usurers may all be lost sight of. They propose to sacrifice our homes, lives, and children on the altar of mammon; to destroy the multitude in order to secure corruption funds from the millionaires.

Assembled on the anniversary of the birthday of the nation, and filled with the spirit of the grand general and chief who established our independence, we seek to restore the government of the Republic to the hands of "the plain people," with which class it originated. We assert our purposes to be identical with the purposes of the National Constitution; to form a more perfect union and establish justice, insure domestic tranquility, provide for the common defense, promote the general welfare, and secure the blessings of liberty for ourselves and our posterity.

We declare that this Republic can only endure as a free government while built upon the love of the whole people for each other and for the nation; that it cannot be pinned together by bayonets; that the civil war is over, and that every passion and resentment which grew out of it must die with it, and that we must be in fact, as we are in name, one united brotherhood of free men.

Our country finds itself confronted by conditions for which there is no precedent in the history of the world; our annual agricultural productions amount to billions of dollars in value, which must, within a few weeks or months, be exchanged for billions of dollars' worth of commodities consumed in their production; the existing currency supply is wholly inadequate to make this exchange; the results are falling prices, the formation of combines and rings, the impoverishment of the producing class. We pledge ourselves that if given power we will labor to correct these evils by wise and reasonable legislation, in accordance with the terms of our platform.

We believe that the power of government—in other words, of the people—should be expanded (as in the case of the postal service) as rapidly and as far as the good sense of an intelligent people and the teachings of experience shall justify, to the end that oppression, injustice, and poverty shall eventually cease in the land.

While our sympathies as a party of reform are naturally upon the side of every proposition which will tend to make men intelligent, virtuous, and temperate, we nevertheless regard these questions, important as they are, as secondary to the great issues now pressing for solution, and upon which not only our individual prosperity but the very existence of free institutions depend; and we ask all men to first help us to determine whether we are to have a republic to administer before we differ as to the conditions upon which it is to be administered, believing that the forces of reform this day organized will never cease to move forward until every wrong is remedied and equal rights and equal privileges securely established for all the men and women of this country.

PLATFORM

We declare, therefore—

First.—That the union of the labor forces of the United States this day consummated shall be permanent and perpetual; may its spirit enter into all hearts for the salvation of the Republic and the uplifting of mankind.

Second.—Wealth belongs to him who creates it, and every dollar taken from industry without an equivalent is robbery. "If any will not work, neither shall he eat." The interests of rural and civic labor are the same; their enemies are identical.

Third.—We believe that the time has come when the railroad corporations will either own the people or the people must own the railroads, and should the government enter upon the work of owning and managing all railroads, we should favor an amendment to the Constitution by which all persons engaged in the government service shall be placed under a civil-service regulation of the most rigid character, so as to prevent the increase of the power of the national administration by the use of such additional government employees.

FINANCE.—We demand a national currency, safe, sound, and flexible, issued by the general government only, a full legal tender for all debts, public and private, and that without the use of banking corporations, a just, equitable, and efficient means of distribution direct to the people, at a tax not to exceed 2 per cent. per annum, to be provided as set forth in the sub-treasury plan of the Farmers' Alliance, or a better system; also by payments in discharge of its obligations for public improvements.

1. We demand free and unlimited coinage of silver and gold at the present legal ratio of 16 to 1.

2. We demand that the amount of circulating medium be speedily increased to not less than $50 per capita.

3. We demand a graduated income tax.

4. We believe that the money of the country should be kept as much as possible in the hands of the people, and hence we demand that all State and national revenues shall be limited to the necessary expenses of the government, economically and honestly administered.

5. We demand that postal savings banks be established by the government for the safe deposit of the earnings of the people and to facilitate exchange.

TRANSPORTATION—Transportation being a means of exchange and a public necessity, the government should own and operate the railroads in the interest of the people. The telegraph, telephone, like the post-office system, being a necessity for the transmission of news, should be owned and operated by the government in the interest of the people.

LAND.—The land, including all the natural sources of wealth, is the heritage of the people, and should not be monopolized for speculative purposes, and alien ownership of land should be prohibited. All land now held by railroads and other corporations in excess of their actual needs, and all lands now owned by aliens should be reclaimed by the government and held for actual settlers only.

[HM]

William Jennings Bryan, Speech at the Democratic National Convention, "The Cross of Gold"

July 8, 1896

Bryan (1860–1925) concluded the Chicago convention's debate on the Democratic party's platform with a speech. In it, appealing to the interests of the country's working class, he emphasized several of his recent populist ideas on America's money system. Although he lost the presidential election in November to William McKinley, Bryan later served as President Woodrow Wilson's secretary of state.

I WOULD BE presumptuous, indeed, to present myself against the distinguished gentlemen to whom you have listened if this were a mere measuring of abilities; but this is not a contest between persons. The humblest citizen in all the land when clad in the armor of a righteous cause, is stronger than all the hosts of error. I come to speak to you in defense of a cause as holy as the cause of liberty—the cause of humanity. [...]

They tell us that this platform was made to catch votes. We reply to them that changing conditions make new issues; that the principles upon which Democracy rests are as everlasting as the hills, but that they must be applied to new conditions as they arise. Conditions have arisen, and we are here to meet these conditions. They tell us that the income tax ought not to be brought in here; that it is a new idea. They criticize us for our criticism of the Supreme Court of the United States. My friends, we have not criticized; we have simply called attention to what you already know. If you want criticisms, read the dissenting opinions of the court. There you will find criticisms. They say that we passed an unconstitutional law; we deny it. The income tax law was not unconstitutional when it was passed; it was not unconstitutional when it went before the Supreme Court for the first time; it did not become unconstitutional until one of the judges changed his mind, and we cannot be expected to know when a judge will change his mind. The income tax is just. It simply intends to put the burdens of government justly upon the backs of the people. I am in favor of an income tax. When I find a man who is not willing to bear his share of the burdens of the government which protects him, I find a man who is unworthy to enjoy the blessings of a government like ours.

They say that we are opposing national bank currency; it is true. If you will read what Thomas Benton said, you will find he said that, in searching history, he could find but one parallel to Andrew Jackson; that was Cicero, who destroyed the conspiracy of Cataline and saved Rome. Benton said that Cicero only did for Rome what Jackson did for us when he destroyed the bank conspiracy and saved America. We say in our platform that we believe that the right to coin and issue money is a function of government. We believe it. We believe that it is a part of sovereignty, and can no more with safety be delegated to private individuals than we could afford to delegate to private individuals the power to make penal statutes or levy taxes. Mr. Jefferson, who was once regarded as good Democratic authority, seems to have differed in opinion from the gentleman who has addressed us on the part of the minority. Those who are opposed to this proposition tell us that the issue of paper money is a function of the bank, and that the Government ought to go out of the banking business. I stand with Jefferson rather than with them, and tell them, as he did, that the issue of money is a function of government, and that the banks ought to go out of the governing business. [...]

We go forth confident that we shall win. Why? Because upon the paramount issue of this campaign there is not a spot of ground upon which the enemy will dare to challenge battle. If they tell us that the gold standard is a good thing, we shall point to their platform and tell them that their platform pledges the party to get rid of the gold standard and substitute bimetallism. If the gold standard is a good thing, why try to get rid of it? I call your attention to the fact that some of the very people who are in this convention to-day and who tell us that we ought to declare in favor of international bimetallism—thereby declaring that the gold standard is wrong and that the principle of bimetallism is better—these very people four months ago were open and avowed advocates of the gold standard, and were then telling us that we could not legislate two metals together, even with the aid of all the world. If the gold standard is a good thing, we ought to declare in favor of its retention and not in favor of abandoning it; and if the gold standard is a bad thing why should we wait until other nations are willing to help us to let go? Here is the line of battle, and we care not upon which issue they force the fight; we are prepared to meet them on either issue or on both. If they tell us that the gold standard is the standard of civilization, we reply to them that this, the most enlightened of all the nations of the earth, has never declared for a gold standard and that both the great parties this year are declaring against it. If the gold standard is the standard of civilization, why, my friends, should we not have it? If they come to meet us on that issue we can present the history of our nation. More than that; we can tell them that they will search the pages of history in vain to find a single instance where the common people of any land have ever declared themselves in favor of the gold standard. They can find where the holders of fixed investments have declared for a gold standard, but not where the masses have.

Mr. Carlisle said in 1878 that this was a struggle between "the idle holders of idle capital" and "the struggling masses, who produce the wealth and pay the taxes of the country"; and, my friends, the question we are to decide is: Upon which side will the Democratic party fight; upon the side of "the idle holders of idle capital" or upon the side of "the struggling masses"? That is the question which the party must answer first, and then it must be answered by each individual hereafter. The sympathies of the Democratic Party, as shown by the platform, are on the side of the struggling masses who have ever been the foundation of the Democratic party. There are two ideas of government. There are those who believe that, if you will only legislate to make the well-to-do prosperous, their prosperity will leak through on those below. The Democratic idea, however, has been that if you legislate to make the masses prosperous, their prosperity will find its way up through every class which rests upon them.

You come to us and tell us that the great cities are in favor of the gold standard; we reply that the great cities rest upon our broad and fertile prairies. Burn down your cities and leave our farms, and your cities will spring up again as if by magic; but destroy our farms and the grass will grow in the streets of every city in the country.

My friends, we declare that this nation is able to legislate for its own people on every question, without waiting for the aid or consent of any other nation on earth; and upon that issue we expect to carry every State in the Union. I shall not slander the inhabitants of the fair State of Massachusetts nor the inhabitants of the State of New York by saying that, when they are confronted with the proposition, they will declare that this nation is not able to attend to its own business. It is the issue of 1776 over again. Our ancestors, when but three millions in number, had the courage to declare their political independence of every other nation; shall we, their descendants, when we have grown to seventy millions, declare that we are less independent than our forefathers? No, my friends, that will never be the verdict of our people. Therefore, we care not upon what lines the battle is fought. If they say bimetallism is good, but that we cannot have it until other nations help us, we reply that, instead of having a gold standard because England has, we will restore bimetallism, and then let England have bimetallism because the United States has it. If they dare to come out in the open field and defend the gold standard as a good thing, we will fight them to the uttermost. Having behind us the producing masses of this nation and the world, supported by the commercial interests, the laboring interests, and the toilers everywhere, we will answer their demand for a gold standard by saying to them: You shall not press down upon the brow of labor this crown of thorns, you shall not crucify mankind upon a cross of gold.

[WJB]

Supreme Court, Plessy v. Ferguson

1896

After the end of Reconstruction in 1877, many southern states began passing what were commonly called "Jim Crow" laws, designed to create complete segregation between blacks and whites. This segregation extended to all areas of public life, including bathrooms, restaurants, buses, trains, etc. On June 7, 1892, Homer Plessy, a man of 1/8 black ancestry, boarded a "whites only" car on a train headed from New Orleans to Covington, Louisiana. Though he had purchased a first-class ticket, Plessy was promptly arrested and imprisoned for violating Louisiana's "Jim Crow" law. During his trial at the criminal district court of Orleans Parish, Plessy petitioned the Louisiana Supreme Court for a writ of prohibition against Judge John H. Ferguson, which would have ordered the lower court not to exercise jurisdiction in the case. When the Louisiana Supreme Court denied his petition, Plessy petitioned the U.S. Supreme Court, which accepted the jurisdiction.

Despite counsel Albion Tourgee's famous argument that separate but equal was equal only in theory—thus violating the Fourteenth Amendment—the court ruled 8 to 1 against Plessy, upholding Louisiana's segregationist policies. This led to an increase in "Jim Crow" laws throughout the South, until this case was finally overruled by Brown v. Board of Education in 1954.

— Note by James Daley.

U.S. SUPREME COURT

PLESSY V. FERGUSON, 163 U.S. 537 (1896)
163 U.S. 537
PLESSY V. FERGUSON.
No. 210.

MAY 18, 1896. [163 U.S. 537, 538] This was a petition for writs of prohibition and certiorari originally filed in the supreme court of the state by Plessy, the plaintiff in error, against the Hon. John H. Ferguson, judge of the criminal district court for the parish of Orleans, and setting forth, in substance, the following facts:

That petitioner was a citizen of the United States and a resident of the state of Louisiana, of mixed descent, in the proportion of seven-eighths Caucasian and one-eighth African blood; that the mixture of colored blood was not discernible in him, and that he was entitled to every recognition, right, privilege, and immunity secured to the citizens of the United States of the white race by its constitution and laws; that on June 7, 1892, he engaged and paid for a first-class passage on the East Louisiana Railway, from New Orleans to Covington, in the same state, and thereupon entered a passenger train, and took possession of a vacant seat in a coach where passengers of the white race were accommodated that such railroad company was incorporated by the laws of Louisiana as a common carrier, and was not authorized to distinguish between citizens according to their race, but, notwithstanding this, petitioner was required by the conductor, under penalty of ejection from said train and imprisonment, to vacate said coach, and occupy another seat, in a coach assigned by said company for persons not of the white race, and for no other reason than that petitioner was of the colored race; that, upon petitioner's refusal to comply with such order, he was, with the aid of a police officer, forcibly ejected from said coach, and hurried off to, and imprisoned in, the parish jail of [163 U.S. 537, 539] New Orleans, and there held to answer a charge made by such officer to the effect that he was guilty of having criminally violated an act of the general assembly of the state, approved July 10, 1890, in such case made and provided.

The petitioner was subsequently brought before the recorder of the city for preliminary examination, and committed for trial to the criminal district court for the parish of Orleans, where an information was filed against him in the matter above set forth, for a violation of the above act, which act the petitioner affirmed to be null and void, because in conflict with the constitution of the United States; that petitioner interposed a plea to such information, based upon the unconstitutionality of the act of the general assembly, to which the district attorney, on behalf of the state, filed a demurrer; that, upon issue being joined upon such demurrer and plea, the court sustained the demurrer, overruled the plea, and ordered petitioner to plead over to the facts set forth in the information, and that, unless the judge of the said court be enjoined by a writ of prohibition from further proceeding in such case, the court will proceed to fine and sentence petitioner to imprisonment, and thus deprive him of his constitutional rights set forth in his said plea, notwithstanding the unconstitutionality of the act under which he was being prosecuted; that no appeal lay from such sentence, and petitioner was without relief or remedy except by writs of prohibition and certiorari. Copies of the information and other proceedings in the criminal district court were annexed to the petition as an exhibit.

Upon the filing of this petition, an order was issued upon the respondent to show cause why a writ of prohibition should not issue, and be made perpetual, and a further order that the record of the proceedings had in the criminal cause be certified and transmitted to the Supreme Court.

To this order the respondent made answer, transmitting a certified copy of the proceedings, asserting the constitutionality of the law, and averring that, instead of pleading or admitting that he belonged to the colored race, the said Plessy declined and refused, either by pleading or otherwise, to admit [163 U.S. 537, 540] that he was in any sense or in any proportion a colored man.

The case coming on for hearing before the supreme court, that court was of opinion that the law under which the prosecution was had was constitutional and denied the relief prayed for by the petitioner (Ex parte Plessy, 45 La. Ann. 80, 11 South. 948); whereupon petitioner prayed for a writ of error from this court, which was allowed by the chief justice of the supreme court of Louisiana.

Mr. Justice Harlan dissenting.

A. W. Tourgee and S. F. Phillips, for plaintiff in error.

Alex. Porter Morse, for defendant in error.

Mr. Justice BROWN, after stating the facts in the foregoing language, delivered the opinion of the court.

This case turns upon the constitutionality of an act of the general assembly of the state of Louisiana, passed in 1890, providing for separate railway carriages for the white and colored races. Acts 1890, No. 111, p. 152.

The first section of the statute enacts "that all railway companies carrying passengers in their coaches in this state, shall provide equal but separate accommodations for the white, and colored races, by providing two or more passenger coaches for each passenger train, or by dividing the passenger coaches by a partition so as to secure separate accommodations: provided, that this section shall not be construed to apply to street railroads. No person or persons shall be permitted to occupy seats in coaches, other than the ones assigned to them, on account of the race they belong to."

By the second section it was enacted "that the officers of such passenger trains shall have power and are hereby required [163 U.S. 537, 541] to assign each passenger to the coach or compartment used for the race to which such passenger belongs; any passenger insisting on going into a coach or compartment to which by race he does not belong, shall be liable to a fine of twenty-five dollars, or in lieu thereof to imprisonment for a period of not more than twenty days in the parish prison, and any officer of any railroad insisting on assigning a passenger to a coach or compartment other than the one set aside for the race to which said passenger belongs, shall be liable to a fine of twenty-five dollars, or in lieu thereof to imprisonment for a period of not more than twenty days in the parish prison; and should any passenger refuse to occupy the coach or compartment to which he or she is assigned by the officer of such railway, said officer shall have power to refuse to carry such passenger on his train, and for such refusal neither he nor the railway company which he represents shall be liable for damages in any of the courts of this state."

The third section provides penalties for the refusal or neglect of the officers, directors, conductors, and employees of railway companies to comply with the act, with a proviso that "nothing in this act shall be construed as applying to nurses attending children of the other race." The fourth section is immaterial.

The information filed in the criminal district court charged, in substance, that Plessy, being a passenger between two stations within the state of Louisiana, was assigned by officers of the company to the coach used for the race to which he belonged, but he insisted upon going into a coach used by the race to which he did not belong. Neither in the information nor plea was his particular race or color averred.

The petition for the writ of prohibition averred that petitioner was seven-eighths Caucasian and one-eighth African blood; that the mixture of colored blood was not discernible in him; and that he was entitled to every right, privilege, and immunity secured to citizens of the United States of the white race; and that, upon such theory, he took possession of a vacant seat in a coach where passengers of the white race were accommodated, and was ordered by the conductor to vacate [163 U.S. 537, 542] said coach, and take a seat in another, assigned to persons of the colored race, and, having refused to comply with such demand, he was forcibly ejected, with the aid of a police officer, and imprisoned in the parish jail to answer a charge of having violated the above act.

The constitutionality of this act is attacked upon the ground that it conflicts both with the thirteenth amendment of the constitution, abolishing slavery, and the fourteenth amendment, which prohibits certain restrictive legislation on the part of the states.

1. That it does not conflict with the thirteenth amendment, which abolished slavery and involuntary servitude, except a punishment for crime, is too clear for argument. Slavery implies involuntary servitude,—a state of bondage; the ownership of mankind as a chattel, or, at least, the control of the labor and services of one man for the benefit of another, and the absence of a legal right to the disposal of his own person, property, and services. This amendment was said in the Slaughter-House Cases, 16 Wall. 36, to have been intended primarily to abolish slavery, as it had been previously known in this country, and that it equally forbade Mexican peonage or the Chinese coolie trade, when they amounted to slavery or involuntary servitude, and that the use of the word "servitude" was intended to prohibit the use of all forms of involuntary slavery, of whatever class or name. It was intimated, however, in that case, that this amendment was regarded by the statesmen of that day as insufficient to protect the colored race from certain laws which had been enacted in the Southern states, imposing upon the colored race onerous disabilities and burdens, and curtailing their rights in the pursuit of life, liberty, and property to such an extent that their freedom was of little value; and that the fourteenth amendment was devised to meet this exigency.

So, too, in the Civil Rights Cases, 109 U.S. 3, 3 Sup. Ct. 18, it was said that the act of a mere individual, the owner of an inn, a public conveyance or place of amusement, refusing accommodations to colored people, cannot be justly regarded as imposing any badge of slavery or servitude upon the applicant, but [163 U.S. 537, 543] only as involving an ordinary civil injury, properly cognizable by the laws of the state, and presumably subject to redress by those laws until the contrary appears. "It would be running the slavery question into the ground," said Mr. Justice Bradley, "to make it apply to every act of discrimination which a person may see fit to make as to the guests he will entertain, or as to the people he will take into his coach or cab or car, or admit to his concert or theater, or deal with in other matters of intercourse or business."

A statute which implies merely a legal distinction between the white and colored races—a distinction which is founded in the color of the two races, and which must always exist so long as white men are distinguished from the other race by color—has no tendency to destroy the legal equality of the two races, or re-establish a state of involuntary servitude. Indeed, we do not understand that the thirteenth amendment is strenuously relied upon by the plaintiff in error in this connection.

2. By the fourteenth amendment, all persons born or naturalized in the United States, and subject to the jurisdiction thereof, are made citizens of the United States and of the state wherein they reside; and the states are forbidden from making or enforcing any law which shall abridge the privileges or immunities of citizens of the United States, or shall deprive any person of life, liberty, or property without due process of law, or deny to any person within their jurisdiction the equal protection of the laws.

The proper construction of this amendment was first called to the attention of this court in the Slaughter-House Cases, 16 Wall. 36, which involved, however, not a question of race, but one of exclusive privileges. The case did not call for any expression of opinion as to the exact rights it was intended to secure to the colored race, but it was said generally that its main purpose was to establish the citizenship of the negro, to give definitions of citizenship of the United States and of the states, and to protect from the hostile legislation of the states the privileges and immunities of citizens of the United States, as distinguished from those of citizens of the states. [163 U.S. 537,544] The object of the amendment was undoubtedly to enforce the absolute equality of the two races before the law, but, in the nature of things, it could not have been intended to abolish distinctions based upon color, or to enforce social, as distinguished from political, equality, or a commingling of the two races upon terms unsatisfactory to either. Laws permitting, and even requiring, their separation, in places where they are liable to be brought into contact, do not necessarily imply the inferiority of either race to the other, and have been generally, if not universally, recognized as within the competency of the state legislatures in the exercise of their police power. The most common instance of this is connected with the establishment of separate schools for white and colored children, which have been held to be a valid exercise of the legislative power even by courts of states where the political rights of the colored race have been longest and most earnestly enforced.

One of the earliest of these cases is that of Roberts v. City of Boston, 5 Cush. 198, in which the supreme judicial court of Massachusetts held that the general school committee of Boston had power to make provision for the instruction of colored children in separate schools established exclusively for them, and to prohibit their attendance upon the other schools. "The great principle," said Chief Justice Shaw, "advanced by the learned and eloquent advocate for the plaintiff [Mr. Charles Sumner], is that, by the constitution and laws of Massachusetts, all persons, without distinction of age or sex, birth or color, origin or condition, are equal before the law. . . . But, when this great principle comes to be applied to the actual and various conditions of persons in society, it will not warrant the assertion that men and women are legally clothed with the same civil and political powers, and that children and adults are legally to have the same functions and be subject to the same treatment; but only that the rights of all, as they are settled and regulated by law, are equally entitled to the paternal consideration and protection of the law for their maintenance and security." It was held that the powers of the committee extended to the establishment [163 U.S. 537, 545] of separate schools for children of different ages, sexes and colors, and that they might also establish special schools for poor and neglected children, who have become too old to attend the primary school, and yet have not acquired the rudiments of learning, to enable them to enter the ordinary schools. Similar laws have been enacted by congress under its general power of legislation over the District of Columbia (sections 281–283, 310, 319, Rev. St. D. C), as well as by the legislatures of many of the states, and have been generally, if not uniformly, sustained by the courts. State v. McCann, 21 Ohio St. 210; Lehew v. Brummell (Mo. Sup.) 15 S. W. 765; Ward v. Flood, 48 Cal. 36; Bertonneau v. Directors of City Schools, 3 Woods, 177, Fed. Cas. No. 1,361; People v. Gallagher, 93 N. Y. 438; Cory v. Carter, 48 Ind. 337; Dawson v. Lee, 83 Ky. 49.

Laws forbidding the intermarriage of the two races may be said in a technical sense to interfere with the freedom of contract, and yet have been universally recognized as within the police power of the state. State v. Gibson, 36 Ind. 389.

The distinction between laws interfering with the political equality of the negro and those requiring the separation of the two races in schools, theaters, and railway carriages has been frequently drawn by this court. Thus, in Strauder v. West Virginia, 100 U.S. 303, it was held that a law of West Virginia limiting to white male persons 21 years of age, and citizens of the state, the right to sit upon juries, was a discrimination which implied a legal inferiority in civil society, which lessened the security of the right of the colored race, and was a step towards reducing them to a condition of servility. Indeed, the right of a colored man that, in the selection of jurors to pass upon his life, liberty, and property, there shall be no exclusion of his race, and no discrimination against them because of color, has been asserted in a number of cases. Virginia v. Rivers, 100 U.S. 313; Neal v. Delaware, 103 U.S. 370; ush v. Com., 107 U.S. 110, 1 Sup. Ct. 625; Gibson v. Mississippi, 162 U.S. 565, 16 Sup. Ct. 904. So, where the laws of a particular locality or the charter of a particular railway corporation has provided that no person shall be excluded from the cars on account of [163 U.S. 537, 546] color, we have held that this meant that persons of color should travel in the same car as white ones, and that the enactment was not satisfied by the company providing cars assigned exclusively to people of color, though they were as good as those which they assigned exclusively to white persons. Railroad Co. v. Brown, 17 Wall. 445.

Upon the other hand, where a statute of Louisiana required those engaged in the transportation of passengers among the states to give to all persons traveling within that state, upon vessels employed in that business, equal rights and privileges in all parts of the vessel, without distinction on account of race or color, and subjected to an action for damages the owner of such a vessel who excluded colored passengers on account of their color from the cabin set aside by him for the use of whites, it was held to be, so far as it applied to interstate commerce, unconstitutional and void. Hall v. De Cuir, 95 U.S. 485. The court in this case, however, expressly disclaimed that it had anything whatever to do with the statute as a regulation of internal commerce, or affecting anything else than commerce among the states.

In the Civil Rights Cases, 109 U.S. 3, 3 Sup. Ct. 18, it was held that an act of congress entitling all persons within the jurisdiction of the United States to the full and equal enjoyment of the accommodations, advantages, facilities, and privileges of inns, public conveyances, on land or water, theaters, and other places of public amusement, and made applicable to citizens of every race and color, regardless of any previous condition of servitude, was unconstitutional and void, upon the ground that the fourteenth amendment was prohibitory upon the states only, and the legislation authorized to be adopted by congress for enforcing it was not direct legislation on matters respecting which the states were prohibited from making or enforcing certain laws, or doing certain acts, but was corrective legislation, such as might be necessary or proper for counteracting and redressing the effect of such laws or acts. In delivering the opinion of the court, Mr. Justice Bradley observed that the fourteenth amendment "does not invest congress with power to legislate upon subjects that are within the [163 U.S. 537, 547] domain of state legislation, but to provide modes of relief against state legislation or state action of the kind referred to. It does not authorize congress to create a code of municipal law for the regulation of private rights, but to provide modes of redress against the operation of state laws, and the action of state officers, executive or judicial, when these are subversive of the fundamental rights specified in the amendment. Positive rights and privileges are undoubtedly secured by the fourteenth amendment; but they are secured by way of prohibition against state laws and state proceedings affecting those rights and privileges, and by power given to congress to legislate for the purpose of carrying such prohibition into effect; and such legislation must necessarily be predicated upon such supposed state laws or state proceedings, and be directed to the correction of their operation and effect."

Much nearer, and, indeed, almost directly in point, is the case of the Louisville, N. O. & T. Ry. Co. v. State, 133 U.S. 587, 10 Sup. Ct. 348, wherein the railway company was indicted for a violation of a statute of Mississippi, enacting that all railroads carrying passengers should provide equal, but separate, accommodations for the white and colored races, by providing two or more passenger cars for each passenger train, or by dividing the passenger cars by a partition, so as to secure separate accommodations. The case was presented in a different aspect from the one under consideration, inasmuch as it was an indictment against the railway company for failing to provide the separate accommodations, but the question considered was the constitutionality of the law. In that case, the supreme court of Mississippi (66 Miss. 662, 6 South. 203) had held that the statute applied solely to commerce within the state, and, that being the construction of the state statute by its highest court, was accepted as conclusive. "If it be a matter," said the court (page 591, 133 U. S., and page 348, 10 Sup. Ct.), "respecting commerce wholly within a state, and not interfering with commerce between the states, then, obviously, there is no violation of the commerce clause of the federal constitution.... No question arises under this section as to the power of the state to separate in different compartments interstate passengers, [163 U.S. 537, 548] or affect, in any manner, the privileges and rights of such passengers. All that we can consider is whether the state has the power to require that railroad trains within her limits shall have separate accommodations for the two races. That affecting only commerce within the state is no invasion of the power given to congress by the commerce clause."

A like course of reasoning applies to the case under consideration, since the supreme court of Louisiana, in the case of State v. Judge, 44 La. Ann. 770, 11 South. 74, held that the statute in question did not apply to interstate passengers, but was confined in its application to passengers traveling exclusively within the borders of the state. The case was decided largely upon the authority of Louisville, N. O. & T. Ry. Co. v. State, 66 Miss. 662, 6 South, 203, and affirmed by this court in 133 U.S. 587, 10 Sup. Ct. 348. In the present case no question of interference with interstate commerce can possibly arise, since the East Louisiana Railway appears to have been purely a local line, with both its termini within the state of Louisiana. Similar statutes for the separation of the two races upon public conveyances were held to be constitutional in Railroad v. Miles, 55 Pa. St. 209; Day v. Owen, 5 Mich. 520; Railway Co. v. Williams, 55 111. 185; Railroad Co. v. Wells, 85 Tenn. 613; 4 S. W. 5; Railroad Co. v. Benson, 85 Tenn. 627, 4 S. W. 5; The Sue, 22 Fed. 843; Logwood v. Railroad Co., 23 Fed. 318; McGuinn v. Forbes, 37 Fed. 639; People v. King (N. Y. App.) 18 N. E. 245; Houck v. Railway Co., 38 Fed. 226; Heard v. Railroad Co., 3 Inter St. Commerce Com. R. 111, 1 Inter St. Commerce Com. R. 428.

While we think the enforced separation of the races, as applied to the internal commerce of the state, neither abridges the privileges or immunities of the colored man, deprives him of his property without due process of law, nor denies him the equal protection of the laws, within the meaning of the fourteenth amendment, we are not prepared to say that the conductor, in assigning passengers to the coaches according to their race, does not act at his peril, or that the provision of the second section of the act that denies to the passenger compensation [163 U.S. 537, 549] in damages for a refusal to receive him into the coach in which he properly belongs is a valid exercise of the legislative power. Indeed, we understand it to be conceded by the state's attorney that such part of the act as exempts from liability the railway company and its officers is unconstitutional. The power to assign to a particular coach obviously implies the power to determine to which race the passenger belongs, as well as the power to determine who, under the laws of the particular state, is to be deemed a white, and who a colored, person. This question, though indicated in the brief of the plaintiff in error, does not properly arise upon the record in this case, since the only issue made is as to the unconstitutionality of the act, so far as it requires the railway to provide separate accommodations, and the conductor to assign passengers according to their race.

It is claimed by the plaintiff in errors that, in a mixed community, the reputations of belonging to the dominant race, in this instance the white race, is "property," in the same sense that a right of action or of inheritance is property. Conceding this to be so, for the purposes of this case, we are unable to see how this statute deprives him of, or in any way affects his right to, such property. If he be a white man, and assigned to a colored coach, he may have his action for damages against the company for being deprived of his so-called "property." Upon the other hand, if he be a colored man, and be so assigned, he has been deprived of no property, since he is not lawfully entitled to the reputation of being a white man.

In this connection, it is also suggested by the learned counsel for the plaintiff in error that the same argument that will justify the state legislature in requiring railways to provide separate accommodations for the two races will also authorize them to require separate cars to be provided for people whose hair is of a certain color, or who are aliens, or who belong to certain nationalities, or to enact laws requiring colored people to walk upon one side of the street, and white people upon the other, or requiring white men's houses to be painted white, and colored men's black, or their vehicles or business signs to be of different colors, upon the theory that one side [163 U.S. 537, 550] of the street is as good as the other, or that a house or vehicle of one color is as good as one of another color. The reply to all this is that every exercise of the police power must be reasonable, and extend only to such laws as are enacted in good faith for the promotion of the public good, and not for the annoyance or oppression of a particular class. Thus, in Yick Wo v. Hopkins, 118 U.S. 356, 6 Sup. Ct. 1064, it was held by this court that a municipal ordinance of the city of San Francisco, to regulate the carrying on of public laundries within the limits of the municipality, violated the provisions of the constitution of the United States, if it conferred upon the municipal authorities arbitrary power, at their own will, and without regard to discretion, in the legal sense of the term, to give or withhold consent as to persons or places, without regard to the competency of the persons applying or the propriety of the places selected for the carrying on of the business. It was held to be a covert attempt on the part of the municipality to make an arbitrary and unjust discrimination against the Chinese race. While this was the case of a municipal ordinance, a like principle has been held to apply to acts of a state legislature passed in the exercise of the police power. Railroad Co. v. Husen, 95 U.S. 465; Louisville & N. R. Co. v. Kentucky, 161 U.S. 677, 16 Sup. Ct. 714, and cases cited on page 700, 161 U. S., and page 714, 16 Sup. Ct.; Daggett v. Hudson, 43 Ohio St. 548, 3 N. E. 538; Capen v. Foster, 12 Pick. 485; State v. Baker, 38 Wis. 71; Monroe v. Collins, 17 Ohio St. 665; Hulseman v. Rems, 41 Pa. St. 396; Osman v. Riley, 15 Cal. 48.

So far, then, as a conflict with the fourteenth amendment is concerned, the case reduces itself to the question whether the statute of Louisiana is a reasonable regulation, and with respect to this there must necessarily be a large discretion on the part of the legislature. In determining the question of reasonableness, it is at liberty to act with reference to the established usages, customs, and traditions of the people, and with a view to the promotion of their comfort, and the preservation of the public peace and good order. Gauged by this standard, we cannot say that a law which authorizes or even requires the separation of the two races in public conveyances [163 U.S. 537, 551] is unreasonable, or more obnoxious to the fourteenth amendment than the acts of congress requiring separate schools for colored children in the District of Columbia, the constitutionality of which does not seem to have been questioned, or the corresponding acts of state legislatures.

We consider the underlying fallacy of the plaintiff's argument to consist in the assumption that the enforced separation of the two races stamps the colored race with a badge of inferiority. If this be so, it is not by reason of anything found in the act, but solely because the colored race chooses to put that construction upon it. The argument necessarily assumes that if, as has been more than once the case, and is not unlikely to be so again, the colored race should become the dominant power in the state legislature, and should enact a law in precisely similar terms, it would thereby relegate the white race to an inferior position. We imagine that the white race, at least, would not acquiesce in this assumption. The argument also assumes that social prejudices may be overcome by legislation, and that equal rights cannot be secured to the negro except by an enforced commingling of the two races. We cannot accept this proposition. If the two races are to meet upon terms of social equality, it must be the result of natural affinities, a mutual appreciation of each other's merits, and a voluntary consent of individuals. As was said by the court of appeals of New York in People v. Gallagher, 93 N. Y. 438, 448: "This end can neither be accomplished nor promoted by laws which conflict with the general sentiment of the community upon whom they are designed to operate. When the government, therefore, has secured to each of its citizens equal rights before the law, and equal opportunities for improvement and progress, it has accomplished the end for which it was organized, and performed all of the functions respecting social advantages with which it is endowed." Legislation is powerless to eradicate racial instincts, or to abolish distinctions based upon physical differences, and the attempt to do so can only result in accentuating the difficulties of the present situation. If the civil and political rights of both races be equal, one cannot be inferior to the other civilly [163 U.S. 537, 552] or politically. If one race be inferior to the other socially, the constitution of the United States cannot put them upon the same plane.

It is true that the question of the proportion of colored blood necessary to constitute a colored person, as distinguished from a white person, is one upon which there is a difference of opinion in the different states; some holding that any visible admixture of black blood stamps the person as belonging to the colored race (State v. Chavers, 5 Jones [N. C.] 1); others, that it depends upon the preponderance of blood (Gray v. State, 4 Ohio, 354; Monroe v. Collins, 17 Ohio St. 665); and still others, that the predominance of white blood must only be in the proportion of three-fourths (People v. Dean, 14 Mich. 406; Jones v. Com., 80 Va. 544). But these are questions to be determined under the laws of each state, and are not properly put in issue in this case. Under the allegations of his petition, it may undoubtedly become a question of importance whether, under the laws of Louisiana, the petitioner belongs to the white or colored race.

The judgment of the court below is therefore affirmed.

Mr. Justice BREWER did not hear the argument or participate in the decision of this case.

Mr. Justice HARLAN dissenting.

By the Louisiana statute the validity of which is here involved, all railway companies (other than street-railroad companies) carry passengers in that state are required to have separate but equal accommodations for white and colored persons, "by providing two or more passenger coaches for each passenger train, or by dividing the passenger coaches by a partition so as to secure separate accommodations." Under this statute, no colored person is permitted to occupy a seat in a coach assigned to white persons; nor any white person to occupy a seat in a coach assigned to colored persons. The managers of the railroad are not allowed to exercise any discretion in the premises, but are required to assign each passenger to some coach or compartment set apart for the exclusive use of his race. If a passenger insists upon going into a coach or compartment not set apart for persons of his race, [163 U.S. 537, 553] he is subject to be fined, or to be imprisoned in the parish jail. Penalties are prescribed for the refusal or neglect of the officers, directors, conductors, and employees of railroad companies to comply with the provisions of the act.

Only "nurses attending children of the other race" are excepted from the operation of the statute. No exception is made of colored attendants traveling with adults. A white man is not permitted to have his colored servant with him in the same coach, even if his condition of health requires the constant personal assistance of such servant. If a colored maid insists upon riding in the same coach with a white woman whom she has been employed to serve, and who may need her personal attention while traveling, she is subject to be fined or imprisoned for such an exhibition of zeal in the discharge of duty.

While there may be in Louisiana persons of different races who are not citizens of the United States, the words in the act "white and colored races" necessarily include all citizens of the United States of both races residing in that state. So that we have before us a state enactment that compels, under penalties, the separation of the two races in railroad passenger coaches, and makes it a crime for a citizen of either race to enter a coach that has been assigned to citizens of the other race.

Thus, the state regulates the use of a public highway by citizens of the United States solely upon the basis of race.

However apparent the injustice of such legislation may be, we have only to consider whether it is consistent with the constitution of the United States.

That a railroad is a public highway, and that the corporation which owns or operates it is in the exercise of public functions, is not, at this day, to be disputed. Mr. Justice Nelson, speaking for this court in New Jersey Steam Nav. Co. v. Merchants' Bank, 6 How. 344, 382, said that a common carrier was in the exercise "of a sort of public office, and has public duties to perform, from which he should not be permitted to exonerate himself without the assent of the parties concerned." Mr. Justice Strong, delivering the judgment of [163 U.S. 537, 554] this court in Olcott v. Supervisors, 16 Wall. 678, 694, said: "That railroads, though constructed by private corporations, and owned by them, is public highways, has been the doctrine of nearly all the courts ever since such conveniences for passage and transportation have had any existence. Very early the question arose whether a state's right of eminent domain could be exercised by a private corporation created for the purpose of constructing a railroad. Clearly, it could not, unless taking land for such a purpose by such an agency is taking land for public use. The right of eminent domain nowhere justifies taking property for a private use. Yet it is a doctrine universally accepted that a state legislature may authorize a private corporation to take land for the construction of such a road, making compensation to the owner. What else does this doctrine mean if not that building a railroad, though it be built by a private corporation, is an act done for a public use?" So, in Township of Pine Grove v. Talcott, 19 Wall. 666, 676: "Though the corporation [a railroad company] was private, its work was public, as much so as if it were to be constructed by the state." So, in Inhabitants of Worcester v. Western R. Corp., 4 Metc. (Mass.) 564: "The establishment of that great thoroughfare is regarded as a public work, established by public authority, intended for the public use and benefit, the use of which is secured to the whole community, and constitutes, therefore, like a canal, turnpike, or highway, a public easement." "It is true that the real and personal property, necessary to the establishment and management of the railroad, is vested in the corporation; but it is in trust for the public."

In respect of civil rights, common to all citizens, the constitution of the United States does not, I think, permit any public authority to know the race of those entitled to be protected in the enjoyment of such rights. Every true man has pride of race, and under appropriate circumstances, when the rights of others, his equals before the law, are not to be affected, it is his privilege to express such pride and to take such action based upon it as to him seems proper. But I deny that any legislative body or judicial tribunal may have regard to the [163 U.S. 537, 555] race of citizens when the civil rights of those citizens are involved. Indeed, such legislation as that here in question is inconsistent not only with that equality of rights which pertains to citizenship, national and state, but with the personal liberty enjoyed by everyone within the United States.

The thirteenth amendment does not permit the withholding or the deprivation of any right necessarily inhering in freedom. It not only struck down the institution of slavery as previously existing in the United States, but it prevents the imposition of any burdens or disabilities that constitute badges of slavery or servitude. It decreed universal civil freedom in this country. This court has so adjudged. But, that amendment having been found inadequate to the protection of the rights of those who had been in slavery, it was followed by the fourteenth amendment, which added greatly to the dignity and glory of American citizenship, and to the security of personal liberty, by declaring that "all persons born or naturalized in the United States, and subject to the jurisdiction thereof, are citizens of the United States and of the state wherein they reside," and that "no state shall make or enforce any law which shall abridge the privileges or immunities of citizens of the United States; nor shall any state deprive any person of life, liberty or property without due process of law, nor deny to any person within its jurisdiction the equal protection of the laws." These two amendments, if enforced according to their true intent and meaning, will protect all the civil rights that pertain to freedom and citizenship. Finally, and to the end that no citizen should be denied, on account of his race, the privilege of participating in the political control of his country, it was declared by the fifteenth amendment that "the right of citizens of the United States to vote shall not be denied or abridged by the United States or by any state on account of race, color or previous condition of servitude."

These notable additions to the fundamental law were welcomed by the friends of liberty throughout the world. They removed the race line from our governmental systems. They had, as this court has said, a common purpose, namely, to secure "to a race recently emancipated, a race that through [163 U.S. 537, 556] many generations have been held in slavery, all the civil rights that the superior race enjoy." They declared, in legal effect, this court has further said, "that the law in the states shall be the same for the black as for the white; that all persons, whether colored or white, shall stand equal before the laws of the states; and in regard to the colored race, for whose protection the amendment was primarily designed, that no discrimination shall be made against them by law because of their color." We also said: "The words of the amendment, it is true, are prohibitory, but they contain a necessary implication of a positive immunity or right, most valuable to the colored race,—the right to exemption from unfriendly legislation against them distinctively as colored; exemption from legal discriminations, implying inferiority in civil society, lessening the security of their enjoyment of the rights which others enjoy; and discriminations which are steps towards reducing them to the condition of a subject race." It was, consequently, adjudged that a state law that excluded citizens of the colored race from juries, because of their race, however well qualified in other respects to discharge the duties of jurymen, was repugnant to the fourteenth amendment. Strauder v. West Virginia, 100 U.S. 303, 306, 307 S.; Virginia v. Rives, Id. 313; Exparte Virginia, Id. 339; Neal v. Delaware, 103 U.S. 370, 386; Bush v. Com., 107 U.S. 110, 116, 1 S. Sup. Ct. 625. At the present term, referring to the previous adjudications, this court declared that "underlying all of those decisions is the principle that the constitution of the United States, in its present form, forbids, so far as civil and political rights are concerned, discrimination by the general government or the states against any citizen because of his race. All citizens are equal before the law." Gibson v. State, 162 U.S. 565, 16 Sup. Ct. 904.

The decisions referred to show the scope of the recent amendments of the constitution. They also show that it is not within the power of a state to prohibit colored citizens, because of their race, from participating as jurors in the administration of justice.

It was said in argument that the statute of Louisiana does [163 U.S. 537, 557] not discriminate against either race, but prescribes a rule applicable alike to white and colored citizens. But this argument does not meet the difficulty. Everyone knows that the statute in question had its origin in the purpose, not so much to exclude white persons from railroad cars occupied by blacks, as to exclude colored people from coaches occupied by or assigned to white persons. Railroad corporations of Louisiana did not make discrimination among whites in the matter of accommodation for travelers. The thing to accomplish was, under the guise of giving equal accommodation for whites and blacks, to compel the latter to keep to themselves while traveling in railroad passenger coaches. No one would be so wanting in candor as to assert the contrary. The fundamental objection, therefore, to the statute, is that it interferes with the personal freedom of citizens. "Personal liberty," it has been well said, "consists in the power of locomotion, of changing situation, or removing one's person to whatsoever places one's own inclination may direct, without imprisonment or restraint, unless by due course of law." 1 Bl. Comm. *134. If a white man and a black man choose to occupy the same public conveyance on a public highway, it is their right to do so; and no government, proceeding alone on grounds of race, can prevent it without infringing the personal liberty of each.

It is one thing for railroad carriers to furnish, or to be required by law to furnish, equal accommodations for all whom they are under a legal duty to carry. It is quite another thing for government to forbid citizens of the white and black races from traveling in the same public conveyance and to punish officers of railroad companies for permitting persons of the two races to occupy the same passenger coach. If a state can prescribe, as a rule of civil conduct, that whites and blacks shall not travel as passengers in the same railroad coach, why may it not so regulate the use of the streets of its cities and towns as to compel white citizens to keep on one side of a street, and black citizens to keep on the other? Why may it not, upon like grounds, punish whites and blacks who ride together in street cars or in open vehicles on a public road [163 U.S. 537, 558] or street? Why may it not require sheriffs to assign whites to one side of a court room, and blacks to the other? And why may it not also prohibit the commingling of the two races in the galleries of legislative halls or in public assemblages convened for the consideration of the political questions of the day? Further, if this statute of Louisiana is consistent with the personal liberty of citizens, why may not the state require the separation in railroad coaches of native and naturalized citizens of the United States, or of Protestants and Roman Catholics?

The answer given at the argument to these questions was that regulations of the kind they suggest would be unreasonable, and could not, therefore, stand before the law. Is it meant that the determination of questions of legislative power depends upon the inquiry whether the statute whose validity is questioned is, in the judgment of the courts, a reasonable one, taking all the circumstances into consideration? A statute may be unreasonable merely because a sound public policy forbade its enactment. But I do not understand that the courts have anything to do with the policy or expediency of legislation. A statute may be valid, and yet, upon grounds of public policy, may well be characterized as unreasonable. Mr. Sedgwick correctly states the rule when he says that, the legislative intention being clearly ascertained, "the courts have no other duty to perform than to execute the legislative will, without any regard to their views as to the wisdom or justice of the particular enactment." Sedg. St. & Const. Law, 324. There is a dangerous tendency in these latter days to enlarge the functions of the courts, by means of judicial interference with the will of the people as expressed by the legislature. Our institutions have the distinguishing characteristic that the three departments of government are co-ordinate and separate. Each must keep within the limits defined by the constitution. And the courts best discharge their duty by executing the will of the lawmaking power, constitutionally expressed, leaving the results of legislation to be dealt with by the people through their representatives. Statutes must always have a reasonable construction. Sometimes they are to be construed strictly, sometimes literally, in order to carry out the legislative [163 U.S. 537, 559] will. But, however construed, the intent of the legislature is to be respected if the particular statute in question is valid, although the courts, looking at the public interests, may conceive the statute to be both unreasonable and impolitic. If the power exists to enact a statute, that ends the matter so far as the courts are concerned. The adjudged cases in which statutes have been held to be void, because unreasonable, are those in which the means employed by the legislature were not at all germane to the end to which the legislature was competent.

The white race deems itself to be the dominant race in this country. And so it is, in prestige, in achievements, in education, in wealth, and in power. So, I doubt not, it will continue to be for all time, if it remains true to its great heritage, and holds fast to the principles of constitutional liberty. But in view of the constitution, in the eye of the law, there is in this country no superior, dominant, ruling class of citizens. There is no caste here. Our constitution is color-blind, and neither knows nor tolerates classes among citizens. In respect of civil rights, all citizens are equal before the law. The humblest is the peer of the most powerful. The law regards man as man, and takes no account of his surroundings or of his color when his civil rights as guaranteed by the supreme law of the land are involved. It is therefore to be regretted that this high tribunal, the final expositor of the fundamental law of the land, has reached the conclusion that it is competent for a state to regulate the enjoyment by citizens of their civil rights solely upon the basis of race.

In my opinion, the judgment this day rendered will, in time, prove to be quite as pernicious as the decision made by this tribunal in the Dred Scott Case.

It was adjudged in that case that the descendants of Africans who were imported into this country, and sold as slaves, were not included nor intended to be included under the word "citizens" in the constitution, and could not claim any of the rights and privileges which that instrument provided for and secured to citizens of the United States; that, at time of the adoption of the constitution, they were "considered as a subordinate and inferior class of beings, who had been subjugated by the dominant [163 U.S. 537, 560] race, and, whether emancipated or not, yet remained subject to their authority, and had no rights or privileges but such as those who held the power and the government might choose to grant them." 17 How. 393, 404. The recent amendments of the constitution, it was supposed, had eradicated these principles from our institutions. But it seems that we have yet, in some of the states, a dominant race,—a superior class of citizens,—which assumes to regulate the enjoyment of civil rights, common to all citizens, upon the basis of race. The present decision, it may well be apprehended, will not only stimulate aggressions, more or less brutal and irritating, upon the admitted rights of colored citizens, but will encourage the belief that it is possible, by means of state enactments, to defeat the beneficent purposes which the people of the United States had in view when they adopted the recent amendments of the constitution, by one of which the blacks of this country were made citizens of the United States and of the states in which they respectively reside, and whose privileges and immunities, as citizens, the states are forbidden to abridge. Sixty millions of whites are in no danger from the presence here of eight millions of blacks. The destinies of the two races, in this country, are indissolubly linked together, and the interests of both require that the common government of all shall not permit the seeds of race hate to be planted under the sanction of law. What can more certainly arouse race hate, what more certainly create and perpetuate a feeling of distrust between these races, than state enactments which, in fact, proceed on the ground that colored citizens are so inferior and degraded that they cannot be allowed to sit in public coaches occupied by white citizens? That, as all will admit, is the real meaning of such legislation as was enacted in Louisiana.

The sure guaranty of the peace and security of each race is the clear, distinct, unconditional recognition by our governments, national and state, of every right that inheres in civil freedom, and of the equality before the law of all citizens of the United States, without regard to race. State enactments regulating the enjoyment of civil rights upon the basis of race, and cunningly devised to defeat legitimate results of the [163 U.S. 537, 561] war, under the pretense of recognizing equality of rights, can have no other result than to render permanent peace impossible, and to keep alive a conflict of races, the continuance of which must do harm to all concerned. This question is not met by the suggestion that social equality cannot exist between the white and black races in this country. That argument, if it can be properly regarded as one, is scarcely worthy of consideration; for social equality no more exists between two races when traveling in a passenger coach or a public highway than when members of the same races sit by each other in a street car or in the jury box, or stand or sit with each other in a political assembly, or when they use in common the streets of a city or town, or when they are in the same room for the purpose of having their names placed on the registry of voters, or when they approach the ballot box in order to exercise the high privilege of voting.

There is a race so different from our own that we do not permit those belonging to it to become citizens of the United States. Persons belonging to it are, with few exceptions, absolutely excluded from our country. I allude to the Chinese race. But, by the statute in question, a Chinaman can ride in the same passenger coach with white citizens of the United States, while citizens of the black race in Louisiana, many of whom, perhaps, risked their lives for the preservation of the Union, who are entitled, by law, to participate in the political control of the state and nation, who are not excluded, by law or by reason of their race, from public stations of any kind, and who have all the legal rights that belong to white citizens, are yet declared to be criminals, liable to imprisonment, if they ride in a public coach occupied by citizens of the white race. It is scarcely just to say that a colored citizen should not object to occupying a public coach assigned to his own race. He does not object, nor, perhaps, would he object to separate coaches for his race if his rights under the law were recognized. But he does object, and he ought never to cease objecting, that citizens of the white and black races can be adjudged criminals because they sit, or claim the right to sit, in the same public coach on a public highway. [163 U.S. 537, 562] The arbitrary separation of citizens, on the basis of race, while they are on a public highway, is a badge of servitude wholly inconsistent with the civil freedom and the equality before the law established by the constitution. It cannot be justified upon any legal grounds.

If evils will result from the commingling of the two races upon public highways established for the benefit of all, they will be infinitely less than those that will surely come from state legislation regulating the enjoyment of civil rights upon the basis of race. We boast of the freedom enjoyed by our people above all other peoples. But it is difficult to reconcile that boast with a state of the law which, practically, puts the brand of servitude and degradation upon a large class of our fellow citizens,—our equals before the law. The thin disguise of "equal" accommodations for passengers in railroad coaches will not mislead anyone, nor atone for the wrong this day done.

The result of the whole matter is that while this court has frequently adjudged, and at the present term has recognized the doctrine, that a state cannot, consistently with the constitution of the United States, prevent white and black citizens, having the required qualifications for jury service, from sitting in the same jury box, it is now solemnly held that a state may prohibit white and black citizens from sitting in the same passenger coach on a public highway, or may require that they be separated by a "partition" when in the same passenger coach. May it not now be reasonably expected that astute men of the dominant race, who affect to be disturbed at the possibility that the integrity of the white race may be corrupted, or that its supremacy will be imperiled, by contact on public highways with black people, will endeavor to procure statutes requiring white and black jurors to be separated in the jury box by a "partition," and that, upon retiring from the court room to consult as to their verdict, such partition, if it be a movable one, shall be taken to their consultation room, and set up in such way as to prevent black jurors from coming too close to their brother jurors of the white race. If the "partition" used in the court room happens to be stationary, provision could be made for screens with openings through [163 U.S. 537, 563] which jurors of the two races could confer as to their verdict without coming into personal contact with each other. I cannot see but that, according to the principles this day announced, such state legislation, although conceived in hostility to, and enacted for the purpose of humiliating, citizens of the United States of a particular race, would be held to be consistent with the constitution.

I do not deem it necessary to review the decisions of state courts to which reference was made in argument. Some, and the most important, of them, are wholly inapplicable, because rendered prior to the adoption of the last amendments of the constitution, when colored people had very few rights which the dominant race felt obliged to respect. Others were made at a time when public opinion, in many localities, was dominated by the institution of slavery; when it would not have been safe to do justice to the black man; and when, so far as the rights of blacks were concerned, race prejudice was, practically, the supreme law of the land. Those decisions cannot be guides in the era introduced by the recent amendments of the supreme law, which established universal civil freedom, gave citizenship to all born or naturalized in the United States, and residing here, obliterated the race line from our systems of governments, national and state, and placed our free institutions upon the broad and sure foundation of the equality of all men before the law.

I am of opinion that the state of Louisiana is inconsistent with the personal liberty of citizens, white and black, in that state, and hostile to both the spirit and letter of the constitution of the United States. If laws of like character should be enacted in the several states of the Union, the effect would be in the highest degree mischievous. Slavery, as an institution tolerated by law, would, it is true, have disappeared from our country; but there would remain a power in the states, by sinister legislation, to interfere with the full enjoyment of the blessings of freedom, to regulate civil rights, common to all citizens, upon the basis of race, and to place in a condition of legal inferiority a large body of American citizens, now constituting a part of the political community, called the [163 U.S. 537, 564] "People of the United States," for whom, and by whom through representatives, our government is administered. Such a system is inconsistent with the guaranty given by the constitution to each state of a republican form of government, and may be stricken down by congressional action, or by the courts in the discharge of their solemn duty to maintain the supreme law of the land, anything in the constitution or laws of any state to the contrary notwithstanding.

For the reason stated, I am constrained to withhold my assent from the opinion and judgment of the majority.

[LD]

Women's Christian Temperance Union, Declaration of Principles

1902

The Women's Christian Temperance Union was, in the words of its president, Lillian M. N. Stevens, "an organization of Christian women banded together for the protection of the home, the abolition of the liquor traffic and the triumph of Chirst's Golden Rule in custom and law."[1] Its efforts at legalizing a nationwide prohibition of alcoholic beverages resulted in 1919 in the ratification of the Eighteenth Amendment: "the manufacture, sale, or transportation of intoxicating liquors within, the importation thereof into, or the exportation thereof from the United States and all territory subject to the jurisdiction thereof for beverage purposes is hereby prohibited. " (The Twenty-First Amendment, in 1933, repealed it.)

WE BELIEVE IN the coming of His Kingdom, whose service is perfect freedom, because His laws, written in our members as well as in nature and in grace, are perfect, converting the soul.

We believe in the gospel of the Golden Rule, and that each man's habits of life should be an example safe and beneficent for every other man to follow.

We believe that God created both man and woman in His own image, and therefore we believe in one standard of purity for both men and women, and in the equal right of all to hold opinions and to express the same with equal freedom.

---

[1] Lillian M. N. Stevens. "The Work of the National Woman's Christian Temperance Union." In *The Annals of the American Academy of Political and Social Science.* Philadelphia. November 1908. 508.

We believe in a living wage; in an eight-hour day; in courts of conciliation and arbitration; in justice as opposed to greed of gain; in "peace on earth and good-will to men."

We therefore formulate, and for ourselves adopt the following pledge, asking our sisters and brothers of a common danger and a common hope, to make common cause with us, in working its reasonable and helpful precepts into the practice of everyday life.

I hereby solemnly promise, God helping me, to abstain from all distilled, fermented and malt liquors, including wine, beer and cider, and to employ all proper means to discourage the use of and traffic in the same.

To confirm and enforce the rationale of this pledge we declare our purpose to educate the young; to form a better public sentiment; to reform, so far as possible, by religious, ethical and scientific means, the drinking classes; to seek the transforming power of divine grace for ourselves and all for whom we work, that they and we may willfully transcend no law of pure and wholesome living; and finally we pledge ourselves to labor and to pray that all these principles, founded upon the Gospel of Christ, may be worked out into the customs of society and the laws of the land.

[AAA]

W. E. B. Du Bois, Credo

1904

The great African-American Author, William Edward Burghardt Du Bois (1868–1963), not a religious man or inclined to lead political movements, seemed to surprise himself by occasionally composing in the mode of a secular preacher. This manifesto became one of the primary documents of twentieth-century American social equality. Du Bois's great biographer, David Levering Lewis, notes: "A good many black people heard the thunder of avenging racial parity. They would hang the 'Credo' on their living room walk after Du Bois included it in Darkwater sixteen years later, just as their grandchildren would mount 'I Have a Dream' on theirs."[1]

I BELIEVE IN God who made of one blood all races that dwell on earth. I believe that all men, black and brown and white, are brothers, varying, through Time and Opportunity, in form and gift and feature, but differing in no essential particular, and alike in soul and in the possibility of infinite development.

Especially do I believe in the Negro Race; in the beauty of its genius, the sweetness of its soul, and its strength in that meekness which shall yet inherit this turbulent Earth.

I believe in pride of race and lineage and self; in pride of self so deep as to scorn injustice to other selves; in pride of lineage so great as to despise no man's father; in pride of race so chivalrous as neither to offer bastardy to the weak nor beg wedlock of the strong,

---

[1] David Levering Lewis. *W. E. B. Du Bois: Biography of a Race: 1868–1919.* New York: Henry Holt. 1993. 312.

knowing that men may be brothers in Christ, even though they be not brothers-in-law.

I believe in Service—humble reverent service, from the blackening of boots to the whitening of souls; for Work is Heaven, Idleness Hell, and Wage is the "Well done!" of the Master who summoned all them that labor and are heavy laden, making no distinction between the black sweating cotton-hands of Georgia and the First Families of Virginia, since all distinction not based on deed is devilish and not divine.

I believe in the Devil and his angels, who wantonly work to narrow the opportunity of struggling human beings, especially if they be black; who spit in the faces of the fallen, strike them that cannot strike again, believe the worst and work to prove it, hating the image which their Maker stamped on a brother's soul.

I believe in the Prince of Peace. I believe that War is Murder. I believe that armies and navies are at bottom the tinsel and braggadocio of oppression and wrong; and I believe that the wicked conquest of weaker and darker nations by nations whiter and stronger but foreshadows the death of that strength.

I believe in Liberty for all men; the space to stretch their arms and their souls; the right to breathe and the right to vote, the freedom to choose their friends, enjoy the sunshine and ride on the railroads, uncursed by color; thinking, dreaming, working as they will in a kingdom of God and love.

I believe in the training of children black even as white; the leading out of little souls into the green pastures and beside the still waters, not for pelf or peace, but for Life lit by some large vision of beauty and goodness and truth; lest we forget, and the sons of the fathers, like Esau, for mere meat barter their birthright in a mighty nation.

Finally, I believe in Patience—patience with the weakness of the Weak and the strength of the Strong, the prejudice of the Ignorant and the ignorance of the Blind; patience with the tardy triumph of Joy and the mad chastening of Sorrow—patience with God.

ATLANTA UNIVERSITY, ATLANTA, GA.

[DB]

President Theodore Roosevelt, Fourth Annual Message to Congress, "The Roosevelt Corollary to the Monroe Doctrine"

December 6, 1904

President Theodore Roosevelt (1858–1919) was a popular, active and dynamic politician. In this address he was, as usual, variously charming and alarming, candid and blustery: "In asserting the Monroe Doctrine, in taking such steps as we have taken in regard to Cuba, Venezuela, and Panama, and in endeavoring to circumscribe the theatre of war in the Far East, and to secure the open door in China, we have acted in our own interest as well as in the interest of humanity at large." His doctrine seems to have led to several instances of American intervention in Latin America.

IN TREATING OF our foreign policy and of the attitude that this great Nation should assume in the world at large, it is absolutely necessary to consider the Army and the Navy, and the Congress, through which the thought of the Nation finds its expression, should keep ever vividly in mind the fundamental fact that it is impossible to treat our foreign policy, whether this policy takes shape in the effort to secure justice for others or justice for ourselves, save as conditioned upon the attitude we are willing to take toward our Army, and especially toward our Navy. It is not merely unwise, it is contemptible, for a nation, as for an individual, to use high-sounding language to proclaim its purposes, or to take positions which are ridiculous if unsupported by potential force, and then to refuse to provide this force. If there is no intention of providing and of keeping the force necessary to back up a strong attitude, then it is far better not to assume such an attitude.

The steady aim of this Nation, as of all enlightened nations, should be to strive to bring ever nearer the day when there shall prevail throughout the world the peace of justice. There are kinds of peace which are highly undesirable, which are in the long run as destructive as any war. Tyrants and oppressors have many times made a wilderness and called it peace. Many times peoples who were slothful or timid or shortsighted, who had been enervated by ease or by luxury, or misled by false teachings, have shrunk in unmanly fashion from doing duty that was stern and that needed self-sacrifice, and have sought to hide from their own minds their shortcomings, their ignoble motives, by calling them love of peace. The peace of tyrannous terror, the peace of craven weakness, the peace of injustice, all these should be shunned as we shun unrighteous war. The goal to set before us as a Nation, the goal which should be set before all mankind, is the attainment of the peace of justice, of the peace which comes when each nation is not merely safeguarded in its own rights, but scrupulously recognizes and performs its duty toward others. Generally peace tells for righteousness; but if there is conflict between the two, then our fealty is due first to the cause of righteousness. Unrighteous wars are common, and unrighteous peace is rare; but both should be shunned. The right of freedom and the responsibility for the exercise of that right cannot be divorced. One of our great poets has well and finely said that freedom is not a gift that tarries long in the hands of cowards. Neither does it tarry long in the hands of those too slothful, too dishonest, or too unintelligent to exercise it. The eternal vigilance which is the price of liberty must be exercised, sometimes to guard against outside foes; although of course far more often to guard against our own selfish or thoughtless shortcomings.

If these self-evident truths are kept before us, and only if they are so kept before us, we shall have a clear idea of what our foreign policy in its larger aspects should be. It is our duty to remember that a nation has no more right to do injustice to another nation, strong or weak, than an individual has to do injustice to another individual; that the same moral law applies in one case as in the other. But we must also remember that it is as much the duty of the Nation to guard its own rights and its own interests as it is the duty of the individual so to do. Within the Nation the individual has now delegated this right to the State, that is, to the representative of all the individuals, and it is a maxim of the law that for every wrong there is a remedy. But in international law we have not advanced by any means as far as we have advanced in municipal law. There is as yet no judicial way of enforcing a right in international law. When one nation wrongs another, or wrongs many others, there is no tribunal before which the wrongdoer can be brought. Either it is necessary supinely to acquiesce in the wrong, and thus put a premium upon brutality and aggression, or else it is necessary for the aggrieved nation valiantly to stand up for its rights. Until some method is devised by which there shall be a degree of international control over offending nations, it would be a wicked thing for the most civilized powers, for those with most sense of international obligations and with keenest and most generous appreciation of the difference between right and wrong, to disarm. If the great civilized nations of the present day should completely disarm, the result would mean an immediate recrudescence of barbarism in one form or another. Under any circumstances a sufficient armament would have to be kept up to serve the purposes of international police; and until international cohesion and the sense of international duties and rights are far more advanced than at present, a nation desirous both of securing respect for itself and of doing good to others must have a force adequate for the work which it feels is allotted to it as its part of the general world duty. Therefore it follows that a self-respecting, just, and far-seeing nation should on the one hand endeavor by every means to aid in the development of the various movements which tend to provide substitutes for war, which tend to render nations in their actions toward one another, and indeed toward their own peoples, more responsive to the general sentiment of humane and civilized mankind; and on the other hand it should keep prepared, while scrupulously avoiding wrongdoing itself, to repel any wrong, and in exceptional cases to take action, which in a more advanced stage of international relations would come under the head of the exercise of the international police. A great free people owe it to itself and to all mankind not to sink into helplessness before the powers of evil.

We are in every way endeavoring to help on, with cordial good-will, every movement which will tend to bring us into more friendly relations with the rest of mankind. In pursuance of this policy I shall shortly lay before the Senate treaties of arbitration with all powers which are willing to enter into these treaties with us. It is not possible at this period of the world's development to agree to arbitrate all matters, but there are many matters of possible difference between us and other nations which can be thus arbitrated. Furthermore, at the request of the Interparliamentary Union, an eminent body composed of practical statesmen from all countries, I have asked the Powers to join with this Government in a second Hague conference, at which it is hoped that the work already so happily begun at The Hague may be carried some steps further toward completion. This carries out the desire expressed by the first Hague conference itself.

It is not true that the United States feels any land hunger or entertains any projects as regards the other nations of the Western Hemisphere save such as are for their welfare. All that this country desires is to see the neighboring countries stable, orderly, and prosperous. Any country whose people conduct them well can count upon our hearty friendship. If a nation shows that it knows how to act with reasonable efficiency and decency in social and political matters, if it keeps order and pays it obligations, it need fear no interference from the United States. Chronic wrongdoing, or an impotence which results in a general loosening of the ties of civilized society, may in America, as elsewhere, ultimately require intervention by some civilized nation, and in the Western Hemisphere the adherence of the United States to the Monroe Doctrine may force the United States, however reluctantly, in flagrant cases of such wrongdoing or impotence, to the exercise of an international police power. If every country washed by the Caribbean Sea would show the progress in stable and just civilization which with the aid of the Platt amendment Cuba has shown since our troops left the island, and which so many of the republics in both Americas are constantly and brilliantly showing, all question of interference by this Nation with their affairs would be at an end. Our interests and those of our southern neighbors are in reality identical. They have great natural riches, and if within their borders the reign of law and justice obtains, prosperity is sure to come to them. While they thus obey the primary laws of civilized society they may rest assured that they will be treated by us in a spirit of cordial and helpful sympathy. We would interfere with them only in the last resort, and then only if it became evident that their inability or unwillingness to do justice at home and abroad had violated the rights of the United States or had invited foreign aggression to the detriment of the entire body of American nations. It is a mere truism to say that every nation, whether in America or anywhere else, which desires to maintain its freedom, its independence, must ultimately realize that the right of such independence can not be separated from the responsibility of making good use of it.

In asserting the Monroe Doctrine, in taking such steps as we have taken in regard to Cuba, Venezuela, and Panama, and in endeavoring to circumscribe the theatre of war in the Far East, and to secure the open door in China, we have acted in our own interest as well as in the interest of humanity at large. There are, however, cases in which, while our own interests are not greatly involved, strong appeal is made to our sympathies. Ordinarily it is very much wiser and more useful for us to concern ourselves with striving for our own moral and material betterment here at home than to concern ourselves with trying to better the condition of things in other nations. We have plenty of sins of our own to war against, and under ordinary circumstances we can do more for the general uplifting of humanity by striving with heart and soul to put a stop to civic corruption, to brutal lawlessness and violent race prejudices here at home than by passing resolutions about wrongdoing elsewhere. Nevertheless there are occasional crimes committed on so vast a scale and of such peculiar horror as to make us doubt whether it is not our manifest duty to endeavor at least to show our disapproval of the deed and our sympathy with those who have suffered by it. The cases must be extreme in which such a course is justifiable. There must be no effort made to remove the mote from our brother's eye if we refuse to remove the beam from our own. But in extreme cases action may be justifiable and proper. What form the action shall take must depend upon the circumstances of the case; that is, upon the degree of the atrocity and upon our power to remedy it. The cases in which we could interfere by force of arms as we interfered to put a stop to intolerable conditions in Cuba are necessarily very few. Yet it is not to be expected that a people like ours, which in spite of certain very obvious shortcomings, nevertheless as a whole shows by its consistent practice its belief in the principles of civil and religious liberty and of orderly freedom, a people among whom even the worst crime, like the crime of lynching, is never more than sporadic, so that individuals and not classes are molested in their fundamental rights—it is inevitable that such a nation should desire eagerly to give expression to its horror on an occasion like that of the massacre of the Jews in Kishineff, or when it witnesses such systematic and long-extended cruelty and oppression as the cruelty and oppression of which the Armenians have been the victims, and which have won for them the indignant pity of the civilized world. [...]

[TR]

President Theodore Roosevelt, Seventh Annual Message to Congress, "The Conservation of Our Natural Resources"

December 3, 1907

As president from 1901 to 1909, Theodore Roosevelt did more for conserving our natural resources and lands than anyone before or since. A bird-lover from boyhood, he made himself into a fearless, bullying conservationist, joyfully taking on lumber conglomerates and oil companies, bending and stretching his executive powers for the good of generations to come.

TO THE SENATE AND HOUSE OF REPRESENTATIVES:

THE CONSERVATION OF our natural resources and their proper use constitute the fundamental problem which underlies almost every other problem of our national life. . . . As a nation we not only enjoy a wonderful measure of present prosperity but if this prosperity is used aright it is an earnest of future success such as no other nation will have. The reward of foresight for this nation is great and easily foretold. But there must be the look ahead, there must be a realization of the fact that to waste, to destroy, our natural resources, to skin and exhaust the land instead of using it so as to increase its usefulness, will result in undermining in the days of our children the very prosperity which we ought by right to hand down to them amplified and developed. For the last few years, through several agencies, the government has been endeavoring to get our people to look ahead and to substitute a planned and orderly development of our resources in place of a haphazard striving for immediate profit. Our great river systems should be developed as national water highways, the Mississippi, with its tributaries, standing first in importance, and the Columbia second, although there are many others of importance on the Pacific, the Atlantic, and the Gulf slopes. The National Government should undertake this work, and I hope a beginning will be made in the present Congress; and the greatest of all our rivers, the Mississippi, should receive special attention. From the Great Lakes to the mouth of the Mississippi there should be a deep waterway, with deep waterways leading from it to the East and the West. Such a waterway would practically mean the extension of our coastline into the very heart of our country. It would be of incalculable benefit to our people. If begun at once it can be carried through in time appreciably to relieve the congestion of our great freight-carrying lines of railroads. The work should be systematically and continuously carried forward in accordance with some well-conceived plan. The main streams should be improved to the highest point of efficiency before the improvement of the branches is attempted; and the work should be kept free from every taint of recklessness or jobbery. The inland waterways which lie just back of the whole Eastern and Southern coasts should likewise be developed. Moreover, the development of our waterways involves many other important water problems, all of which should be considered as part of the same general scheme. The government dams should be used to produce hundreds of thousands of horse-power as an incident to improving navigation; for the annual value of the unused water-powered of the United States perhaps exceeds the annual value of the products of all our mines. As an incident to creating the deep waterways down the Mississippi, the government should build along its whole lower length levees which, taken together with the control of the headwaters, will at once and forever put a complete stop to all threat of floods in the immensely fertile delta region. The territory lying adjacent to the Mississippi along its lower course will thereby become one of the most prosperous and populous, as it already is one of the most fertile, farming regions in the entire world. I have appointed an inland waterways commission to study and outline a

comprehensive scheme of development along all the lines indicated. Later I shall lay its report before the Congress.

Irrigation should be far more extensively developed than at present, not only in the States of the Great Plains and the Rocky Mountains, but in many others, as, for instance, in large portions of the
South Atlantic and Gulf States, where it should go hand in hand with
the reclamation of swampland. The Federal Government should seriously devote itself to this task, realizing that utilization of waterways
and water –power, forestry, irrigation, and the reclamation of lands
threatened with overflow, are all interdependent parts of the same
problem. The work of the Reclamation Service in developing the
larger opportunities of the Western half of our country for irrigation
is more important than almost any other movement. The constant
purpose of the government in connection with the Reclamation
Service has been to use the water resources of the public lands for the
ultimate greatest good of the greatest number; in other words, to put
upon the land permanent home-makers, to use and develop it for
themselves and for their children and children's children. . . .

The effort of the government to deal with the public land has
been based upon the same principle as that of the Reclamation
Service. The land law system which was designed to meet the needs
of the fertile and well-watered regions of the Middle West has
largely broken down when applied to the drier regions of the Great
Plains, the mountains, and much of the Pacific slope, where a farm
of 160 acres is inadequate for self-support. . . .Three years ago a
public-lands commission was appointed to scrutinize the law, and
defects, and recommend a remedy. Their examination specifically
showed the existence of great fraud upon the public domain, and
their recommendations for changes in the law were made with the
design of conserving the natural resources of every part of the public lands by putting it to its best use. Especial attention was called
to the prevention of settlement by the passage of great areas of
public land into the hands of a few men, and to the enormous waste
caused by unrestricted grazing upon the open range. The recommendations of the Public-Lands Commission are sound, for they
are especially in the interest of the actual home-maker; and where
the small home-maker cannot at present utilize the land they provide that the government shall keep control of it so that it may not
be monopolized by a few men. The Congress has not yet acted
upon these recommendations, but they are so just and proper, so

essential to our national welfare, that I feel confident, if the Congress will take time to consider them, that they will ultimately be adopted.

Some such legislation as that proposed is essential in order to preserve the great stretches of public grazing-land which are unfit for cultivation under present methods and are valuable only for the forage which they supply. These stretches amount in all to some 300,000,000 acres, and are open to the free grazing of cattle, sheep, horses, and goats, without restriction. Such a system, or lack of system, means that the range is not so much used as wasted by abuse. As the West settles, the range becomes more and more overgrazed. Much of it cannot be used to advantage unless it is fenced, for fencing is the only way by which to keep in check the owners of nomad flocks which roam hither and thither, utterly destroying the pastures and leaving a waste behind so that their presence is incompatible with the presence of home-makers. The existing fences are all illegal. ... All these fences, those that are hurtful and those that are beneficial, are alike illegal and must come down. But it is an outrage that the law should necessitate such action on the part of the Administration. The unlawful fencing of public lands for private grazing must be stopped, but the necessity which occasioned it must be provided for. The Federal Government should have control of the range, whether by permit or lease, as local necessities may determine. Such control could secure the great benefit of legitimate fencing, while at the same time securing and promoting the settlement of the country. . . . The government should part with its title only to the actual home-maker, not to the profit-maker who does not care to make a home. Our prime object is to secure the rights and guard the interests of the small ranchman, the man who ploughs and pitches hay for himself. It is this small ranchman, this actual settler and home-maker, who in the long run is most hurt by permitting thefts of the public land in whatever form.

Optimism is a good characteristic, but if carried to an excess it becomes foolishness. We are prone to speak of the resources of this country as inexhaustible; this is not so. The mineral wealth of the country, the coal, iron, oil, gas, and the like, does not reproduce itself, and therefore is certain to be exhausted ultimately; and wastefulness in dealing with it today means that our descendants will feel the exhaustion a generation or two before they otherwise would. But there are certain other forms of waste which could be entirely stopped—the waste of soil by washing, for instance, which is among the most dangerous of all wastes now in progress in the United States, is easily preventable, and so that this present enormous loss of fertility is entirely unnecessary. The preservation or replacement of the forests is one of the most important means of preventing this loss. We have made a beginning in forest preservation, but ... so rapid has been the rate of exhaustion of timber in the United States in the past, and so rapidly is the remainder being exhausted, that the country is unquestionably on the verge of a timber famine which will be felt in every household in the land. . . . The present annual consumption of lumber is certainly three times as great as the annual growth; and if the consumption and growth continue unchanged, practically all our lumber will be exhausted in another generation, while long before the limit to complete exhaustion is reached the growing scarcity will make itself felt in many blighting ways upon our national welfare. About twenty per cent of our forested territory is now reserved in national forests, but these do not include the most valuable timberlands, and in any event the proportion is too small to expect that the reserves can accomplish more than a mitigation of the trouble which is ahead for the nation. . . . We should acquire in the Appalachian and White Mountain regions all the forest-lands that it is possible to acquire for the use of the nation. These lands, because they form a national asset, are as emphatically national as the rivers which they feed, and which flow through so many States before they reach the ocean.

[DH]

Ida B. Wells-Barnett, Speech, "This Awful Slaughter"

May 8, 1909

Born to slaves, Ida B. Wells-Barnett (1862–1931) was educated at Rust University in Mississippi and Fisk University in Tennessee, before going on to a much lauded career as a journalist. Over the course of her career, Wells-Barnett wrote for the Memphis Free Speech *(of which she was part owner), the* Chicago Conservator *and the* New York Age, *making a name for herself through her one-woman journalistic crusade against lynching. The following speech was delivered at the NAACP's first annual conference in Atlanta, Georgia.*

— Note by James Daley

THE LYNCHING RECORD for a quarter of a century merits the thoughtful study of the American people. It presents three salient facts:

First, lynching is color-line murder. Second, crimes against women are the excuse, not the cause. Third, it is a national crime and requires a national remedy.

Proof that lynching follows the color line is to be found in the statistics which have been kept for the past twenty-five years. During the few years preceding this period and while frontier law existed, the executions showed a majority of white victims. Later, however, as law courts and authorized judiciary extended into the far West, lynch law rapidly abated, and its white victims became few and far between.

Just as the lynch-law regime came to a close in the West, a new mob movement started in the South. This was wholly political, its purpose being to suppress the colored vote by intimidation and murder. Thousands of assassins banded together under the name of Ku Klux Klans, "Midnight Raiders," "Knights of the Golden Circle," et cetera, et cetera, spread a reign of terror, by beating, shooting and killing colored people by the thousands. In a few years, the purpose was accomplished, and the black vote was suppressed. But mob murder continued.

From 1882, in which year fifty-two were lynched, down to the present, lynching has been along the color line. Mob murder increased yearly until in 1892 more than two hundred victims were lynched and statistics show that 3,284 men, women and children have been put to death in this quarter of a century. During the last ten years from 1899 to 1908 inclusive the number lynched was 959. Of this number 102 were white, while the colored victims numbered 857. No other nation, civilized or savage, burns its criminals; only under that Stars and Stripes is the human holocaust possible. Twenty-eight human beings burned at the stake, one of them a woman and two of them children, is the awful indictment against American civilization—the gruesome tribute which the nation pays to the color line.

Why is mob murder permitted by a Christian nation? What is the cause of this awful slaughter? This question is answered almost daily—always the same shameless falsehood that "Negroes are lynched to protect womanhood." Standing before a Chautauqua assemblage, John Temple Graves, at once champion of lynching and apologist for lynchers, said: "The mob stands today as the most potential bulwark between the women of the South and such a carnival of crime as would infuriate the world and precipitate the annihilation of the Negro race." This is the never-varying answer of lynched and their apologists. All know that it is untrue. The cowardly lyncher revels in murder, then seeks to shield him from public execration by claiming devotion to woman. But truth is mighty and the lynching record discloses the hypocrisy of the lynched as well as his crime.

The Springfield, Illinois, mob rioted for two days, the militia of the entire state was called out, two men were lynched, hundreds of people driven from their homes, all because a white woman said a Negro assaulted her. A mad mob went to the jail, tried to lynch the victim of her charge and, not being able to find him, proceeded to pillage and burn the town and to lynch two innocent men. Later, after the police had found that the woman's charge was false, she published a retraction, the indictment was dismissed and the intended victim discharged. But the lynched victims were dead. Hundreds were homeless and Illinois was disgraced.

As a final and complete refutation of the charge that lynching is occasioned by crimes against women, a partial record of lynchings is cited; 285 persons were lynched for causes as follows:

Unknown cause, 92; no cause, 10; race prejudice, 49; miscegenation, 7; informing, 12; making threats, 11; keeping saloon, 3; practicing fraud, 5; practicing voodooism, 2; bad reputation, 8; unpopularity, 3; mistaken identity, 5; using improper language, 3; violation of contract, 1; writing insulting letter, 2; eloping, 2; poisoning horse, 1; poisoning well, 2; by white caps, 9; vigilantes, 14; Indians, 1; moonshining, 1; refusing evidence, 2; political causes, 5; disputing, 1; disobeying quarantine regulations, 2; slapping a child, 1; turning state's evidence, 3; protecting a Negro, 1; to prevent giving evidence, 1; knowledge of larceny, 1; writing letter to white woman, 1; asking white woman to marry, 1; jilting girl, 1; having smallpox, 1; concealing criminal, 2; threatening political exposure, 1; self-defense, 6; cruelty, 1; insulting language to woman, 5; quarreling with white man, 2; colonizing Negroes, 1; throwing stones, 1; quarreling, 1; gambling, 1.

Is there a remedy, or will the nation confess that it cannot protect its protectors at home as well as abroad? Various remedies have been suggested to abolish the lynching infamy, but year after year, the butchery of men, women and children continues in spite of plea and protest. Education is suggested as a preventive, but it is as grave a crime to murder an ignorant man as it is a scholar. True, few educated men have been lynched, but the hue and cry once started stops at no bounds, as was clearly shown by the lynchings in Atlanta, and in Springfield, Illinois.

Agitation, though helpful, will not alone stop the crime. Year after year statistics are published, meetings are held, resolutions are adopted and yet lynchings go on. Public sentiment does measurably decrease the sway of mob law, but the irresponsible bloodthirsty criminals who swept through the streets of Springfield, beating an inoffensive law-abiding citizen to death in one part of the town, and in another torturing and shooting to death a man who for threescore years had made a reputation for honesty, integrity and sobriety, had raised a family and had accumulated property, were not deterred from their heinous crimes by either education or agitation.

The only certain remedy is an appeal to law. Lawbreakers must be made to know that human life is sacred and that every citizen of this country is first a citizen of the United States and secondly a citizen of the state in which he belongs. This nation must assert itself and protect its federal citizenship at home as well as abroad. The strong arm of the government must reach across state lines whenever unbridled lawlessness defies state laws and must give to the individual under the Stars and Stripes the same measure of protection it gives to him when he travels in foreign lands.

Federal protection of American citizenship is the remedy for lynching. Foreigners are rarely lynched in America. If, by mistake, one is lynched, the national government quickly pays the damages. The recent agitation in California against the Japanese compelled this nation to recognize that federal power must yet assert itself to protect the nation from the treason of sovereign states. Thousands of American citizens have been put to death and no President has yet raised his hand in effective protest, but a simple insult to a native of Japan was quite sufficient to stir the government at Washington to prevent the threatened wrong. If the government has power to protect a foreigner from insult, certainly it has power to save a citizen's life.

The practical remedy has been more than once suggested in Congress. Senator Gallinger, of New Hampshire, in a resolution introduced in Congress called for an investigation "with the view of ascertaining whether there is a remedy for lynching which Congress may apply." The Senate Committee has under consideration a bill drawn by A. E. Pillsbury, formerly Attorney General of Massachusetts, providing for federal prosecution of lynchers in cases where the state fails to protect citizens or foreigners. Both of these resolutions indicate that the attention of the nation has been called to this phase of the lynching question.

As a final word, it would be a beginning in the right direction if this conference can see its way clear to establish a bureau for the investigation and publication of the details of every lynching, so that the public could know that an influential body of citizens has made it a duty to give the widest publicity to the facts in each case; that it will make an effort to secure expressions of opinion all over the country against lynching for the sake of the country's fair name; and lastly, but by no means least, to try to influence the daily papers of the country to refuse to become accessory to mobs either before or after the fact.

Several of the greatest riots and most brutal burnt offerings of the mobs have been suggested and incited by the daily papers of the offending community. If the newspaper which suggests lynching in its accounts of an alleged crime, could be held legally as well as morally responsible for reporting that "threats of lynching were heard"; or, "it is feared that if the guilty one is caught, he will be lynched"; or, "there were cries of 'lynch him,' and the only reason the threat was not carried out was because no leader appeared," a long step toward a remedy will have been taken.

In a multitude of counsel there is wisdom. Upon the grave question presented by the slaughter of innocent men, women and children there should be an honest, courageous conference of patriotic, law-abiding citizens anxious to punish crime promptly, impartially and by due process of law, also to make life, liberty and property secure against mob rule.

Time was when lynching appeared to be sectional, but now it is national—a blight upon our nation, mocking our laws and disgracing our Christianity. "With malice toward none but with charity for all" let us undertake the work of making the "law of the land" effective and supreme upon every foot of American soil—a shield to the innocent; and to the guilty, punishment swift and sure.

[GSAA]

Emma Goldman, Speech, "The Tragedy of Women's Emancipation"

1910

"ONE OF THE most accomplished, magnetic speakers in American history, she crisscrossed the country lecturing on anarchism, the new drama, the new school, the new woman, birth control, crime and punishment. Subject to stubborn and sometimes brutal police and vigilante attempts to silence her, she joyfully waged countless free-speech fights along lines later followed by the Wobblies (Industrial Workers of the World). Her activities moved radicals and even some liberals to action against threats to freedom of expression."[1]

Emma Goldman (1869–1940), born in Russia, came to the United States in 1890. She first delivered this essay as a lecture in Philadelphia in 1904. She collected, revised, and published some of her lectures in December 1910 in *Anarchism and Other Essays*. "History tells us that every oppressed class gained true liberation from its masters through its own efforts," she writes. "It is necessary that woman learn that lesson that she realize that her freedom will reach as far as her power to achieve her freedom reaches."

THE TRAGEDY OF
WOMEN'S EMANCIPATION

I begin with an admission: Regardless of all political and economic theories, treating of the fundamental differences between

---

[1] Richard Drinnon, "Introduction." In Emma Goldman, *Anarchism and Other Essays* (New York: Dover Publications, Inc., 1969), vii.

various groups within the human race, regardless of class and race distinctions, regardless of all artificial boundary lines between woman's rights and man's rights, I hold that there is a point where these differentiations may meet and grow into one perfect whole.

With this I do not mean to propose a peace treaty. The general social antagonism which has taken hold of our entire public life today, brought about through the force of opposing and contradictory interests, will crumble to pieces when the reorganization of our social life, based upon the principles of economic justice, shall have become a reality.

Peace or harmony between the sexes and individuals does not necessarily depend on a superficial equalization of human beings; nor does it call for the elimination of individual traits and peculiarities. The problem that confronts us today, and which the nearest future is to solve, is how to be one's self and yet in oneness with others, to feel deeply with all human beings and still retain one's own characteristic qualities. This seems to me to be the basis upon which the mass and the individual, the true democrat and the true individuality, man and woman, can meet without antagonism and opposition. The motto should not be: Forgive one another; rather, Understand one another. The oft-quoted sentence of Madame de Staël: "To understand everything means to forgive everything," has never particularly appealed to me; it has the odor of the confessional; to forgive one's fellow-being conveys the idea of pharisaical superiority. To understand one's fellow-being suffices. The admission partly represents the fundamental aspect of my views on the emancipation of woman and its effect upon the entire sex.

Emancipation should make it possible for woman to be human in the truest sense. Everything within her that craves assertion and activity should reach its fullest expression; all artificial barriers should be broken, and the road towards greater freedom cleared of every trace of centuries of submission and slavery.

This was the original aim of the movement for woman's emancipation. But the results so far achieved have isolated woman and have robbed her of the fountain springs of that happiness which is so essential to her. Merely external emancipation has made of the modern woman an artificial being, who reminds one of the products of French arboriculture with its arabesque trees and shrubs, pyramids, wheels, and wreaths; anything, except the forms which would be reached by the expression of her own inner qualities.

Such artificially grown plants of the female sex are to be found in large numbers, especially in the so-called intellectual sphere of our life.

Liberty and equality for woman! What hopes and aspirations these words awakened when they were first uttered by some of the noblest and bravest souls of those days. The sun in all his light and glory was to rise upon a new world; in this world woman was to be free to direct her own destiny—an aim certainly worthy of the great enthusiasm, courage, perseverance, and ceaseless effort of the tremendous host of pioneer men and women, who staked everything against a world of prejudice and ignorance.

My hopes also move towards that goal, but I hold that the emancipation of woman, as interpreted and practically applied today, has failed to reach that great end. Now, woman is confronted with the necessity of emancipating herself from emancipation, if she really desires to be free. This may sound paradoxical, but is, nevertheless, only too true.

What has she achieved through her emancipation? Equal suffrage in a few States. Has that purified our political life, as many well-meaning advocates predicted? Certainly not. Incidentally, it is really time that persons with plain, sound judgment should cease to talk about corruption in politics in a boarding-school tone. Corruption of politics has nothing to do with the morals, or the laxity of morals, of various political personalities. Its cause is altogether a material one. Politics is the reflex of the business and industrial world, the mottos of which are: "To take is more blessed than to give"; "buy cheap and sell dear"; "one soiled hand washes the other." There is no hope even that woman, with her right to vote, will ever purify politics.

Emancipation has brought woman economic equality with man; that is, she can choose her own profession and trade; but as her past and present physical training has not equipped her with the necessary strength to compete with man, she is often compelled to exhaust all her energy, use up her vitality, and strain every nerve in order to reach the market value. Very few ever succeed, for it is a fact that women teachers, doctors, lawyers, architects, and engineers are neither met with the same confidence as their male colleagues, nor receive equal remuneration. And those that do reach that enticing equality generally do so at the expense of their physical and psychical well-being. As to the great mass of working girls and women, how much independence is gained if the narrowness and lack of freedom of the home is exchanged for the narrowness and lack of freedom of the factory, sweat-shop, department store, or office? In addition is the burden which is laid on many women of looking after a "home, sweet home"—cold, dreary, disorderly, uninviting—after a day's hard work. Glorious independence! No wonder that hundreds of girls are so willing to accept the first offer of marriage, sick and tired of their "independence" behind the counter, at the sewing or typewriting machine. They are just as ready to marry as girls of the middle class, who long to throw off the yoke of parental supremacy. A so-called independence which leads only to earning the merest subsistence is not so enticing, not so ideal, that one could expect woman to sacrifice everything for it. Our highly praised independence is, after all, but a slow process of dulling and stifling woman's nature, her love instinct, and her mother instinct.

Nevertheless, the position of the working girl is far more natural and human than that of her seemingly more fortunate sister in the more cultured professional walks of life—teachers, physicians, lawyers, engineers, etc., who have to make a dignified, proper appearance, while the inner life is growing empty and dead.

The narrowness of the existing conception of woman's independence and emancipation; the dread of love for a man who is not her social equal; the fear that love will rob her of her freedom and independence; the horror that love or the joy of motherhood will only hinder her in the full exercise of her profession—all these together make of the emancipated modern woman a compulsory vestal, before whom life, with its great clarifying sorrows and its deep, entrancing joys, rolls on without touching or gripping her soul.

Emancipation, as understood by the majority of its adherents and exponents, is of too narrow a scope to permit the boundless love and ecstasy contained in the deep emotion of the true woman, sweetheart, mother, in freedom.

The tragedy of the self-supporting or economically free woman does not lie in too many, but in too few experiences. True, she surpasses her sister of past generations in knowledge of the world and human nature; it is just because of this that she feels deeply the lack of life's essence, which alone can enrich the human soul, and without which the majority of women have become mere professional automatons.

That such a state of affairs was bound to come was foreseen by those who realized that, in the domain of ethics, there still remained many decaying ruins of the time of the undisputed superiority of man; ruins that are still considered useful. And, what is more important, a goodly number of the emancipated are unable to get along without them. Every movement that aims at the destruction of existing institutions and the replacement thereof with something more advanced, more perfect, has followers who in theory stand for the most radical ideas, but who, nevertheless, in their every–day practice, are like the average Philistine, feigning respectability and clamoring for the good opinion of their opponents. There are, for example, Socialists, and even Anarchists, who stand for the idea that property is robbery, yet who will grow indignant if anyone owe them the value of a half-dozen pins. […]

A rich intellect and a fine soul are usually considered necessary attributes of a deep and beautiful personality. In the case of the modern woman, these attributes serve as a hindrance to the complete assertion of her being. For over a hundred years the old form of marriage, based on the Bible, "till death doth part," has been denounced as an institution that stands for the sovereignty of the man over the woman, of her complete submission to his whims and commands, and absolute dependence on his name and support. Time and again it has been conclusively proved that the old matrimonial relation restricted woman to the function of man's servant and the bearer of his children. And yet we find many emancipated women who prefer marriage, with all its deficiencies, to the narrowness of an unmarried life; narrow and unendurable because of the chains of moral and social prejudice that cramp and bind her nature.

The explanation of such inconsistency on the part of many advanced women is to be found in the fact that they never truly understood the meaning of emancipation. They thought that all that was needed was independence from external tyrannies; the internal tyrants, far more harmful to life, and growth—ethical and social conventions—were left to take care of themselves; and they have taken care of themselves. They seem to get along as beautifully in the heads and hearts of the most active exponents of woman's emancipation, as in the heads and hearts of our grandmothers.

These internal tyrants, whether they be in the form of public opinion or what will mother say, or brother, father, aunt, or relative of any sort; what will Mrs. Grundy, Mr. Comstock, the employer, the Board of Education say? All these busybodies, moral detectives, jailers of the human spirit, what will they say? Until woman has learned to defy them all, to stand firmly on her own ground and to insist upon her own unrestricted freedom, to listen to the voice of her nature, whether it call for life's greatest treasure, love for a man, or her most glorious privilege, the right to give birth to a child, she cannot call herself emancipated. How many emancipated women are brave enough to acknowledge that the voice of love is calling, wildly beating against their breasts, demanding to be heard, to be satisfied. [...]

The greatest shortcoming of the emancipation of the present day lies in its artificial stiffness and its narrow respectabilities, which produce an emptiness in woman's soul that will not let her drink from the fountain of life. I once remarked that there seemed to be a deeper relationship between the old-fashioned mother and hostess, ever on the alert for the happiness of her little ones and the comfort of those she loved, and the truly new woman, than between the latter and her average emancipated sister. The disciples of emancipation pure and simple declared me a heathen, fit only for the stake. Their blind zeal did not let them see that my comparison between the old and the new was merely to prove that a goodly number of our grandmothers had more blood in their veins, far more humor and wit, and certainly a greater amount of naturalness, kind-heartedness, and simplicity, than the majority of our emancipated professional women who fill the colleges, halls of learning, and various offices. This does not mean a wish to return to the past, nor does it condemn woman to her old sphere, the kitchen and the nursery.

Salvation lies in an energetic march onward towards a brighter and clearer future. We are in need of unhampered growth out of old traditions and habits. The movement for woman's emancipation has so far made but the first step in that direction. It is to be hoped that it will gather strength to make another. The right to vote, or equal civil rights, may be good demands, but true emancipation begins neither at the polls nor in courts. It begins in woman's soul. History tells us that every oppressed class gained true liberation from its masters through its own efforts. It is necessary that woman learn that lesson that she realize that her freedom will reach as far as her power to achieve her freedom reaches. It is, therefore, far more important for her to begin with her inner regeneration, to cut loose from the weight of prejudices, traditions, and customs. The demand for equal rights in every vocation of life is just and fair; but, after all, the most vital right is the right to love and be loved. Indeed, if partial emancipation is to become a complete and true emancipation of woman, it will have to do away with the ridiculous notion that to be loved, to be sweetheart and mother, is synonymous with being slave or subordinate. It will have to do away with the absurd notion of the dualism of the sexes, or that man and woman represent two antagonistic worlds.

Pettiness separates; breadth unites. Let us be broad and big. Let us not overlook vital things because of the bulk of trifles confronting us. A true conception of the relation of the sexes will not admit of conqueror and conquered; it knows of but one great thing: to give of one's self boundlessly, in order to find one's self richer, deeper, better. That alone can fill the emptiness, and transform the tragedy of woman's emancipation into joy, limitless joy.

[CW]

John Muir, *The Yosemite,*
"Hetch Hetchy Valley"

1912

The conservationist John Muir (1838–1914) helped educate Americans about the need for preserving our beautiful wilderness from commercial exploitation. Here he advocates for the preservation of the Hetch Hetchy Valley, which was being coveted by the City and County of San Francisco as a site for a reservoir. In 1913 President Woodrow Wilson signed a law allowing for the valley's flooding by the building of a dam on the Tuolumne River.

YOSEMITE IS SO wonderful that we are apt to regard it as an exceptional creation, the only valley of its kind in the world; but Nature is not so poor as to have only one of anything. Several other yosemites have been discovered in the Sierra that occupy the same relative positions on the Range and were formed by the same forces in the same kind of granite. One of these, the Hetch Hetchy Valley, is in the Yosemite National Park about twenty miles from Yosemite and is easily accessible to all sorts of travelers by a road and trail that leaves the Big Oak Flat road at Bronson Meadows a few miles below Crane Flat, and to mountaineers by way of Yosemite Creek basin and the head of the middle fork of the Tuolumne. [...]

The correspondence between the Hetch Hetchy walls in their trends, sculpture, physical structure, and general arrangement of the main rock-masses and those of the Yosemite Valley has excited the wondering admiration of every observer. We have seen that the El Capitan and Cathedral rocks occupy the same relative positions in both valleys; so also do their Yosemite points and North Domes. Again, that part of the Yosemite north wall immediately to the east of the Yosemite Fall has two horizontal benches, about 500 and 1500 feet above the floor, timbered with golden-cup oak. Two benches similarly situated and timbered occur on the same relative portion of the Hetch Hetchy north wall, to the east of Wapama Fall, and on no other. The Yosemite is bounded at the head by the great Half Dome. Hetch Hetchy is bounded in the same way, though its head rock is incomparably less wonderful and sublime in form.

The floor of the Valley is about three and a half miles long, and from a fourth to half a mile wide. The lower portion is mostly a level meadow about a mile long, with the trees restricted to the sides and the river banks, and partially separated from the main, upper, forested portion by a low bar of glacier-polished granite across which the river breaks in rapids. [...]

It appears, therefore, that Hetch Hetchy Valley, far from being a plain, common, rock-bound meadow, as many who have not seen it seem to suppose, is a grand landscape garden, one of Nature's rarest and most precious mountain temples. As in Yosemite, the sublime rocks of its walls seem to glow with life, whether leaning back in repose or standing erect in thoughtful attitudes, giving welcome to storms and calms alike, their brows in the sky, their feet set in the groves and gay flowery meadows, while birds, bees, and butterflies help the river and waterfalls to stir all the air into music—things frail and fleeting and types of permanence meeting here and blending, just as they do in Yosemite, to draw her lovers into close and confiding communion with her.

Sad to say, this most precious and sublime feature of the Yosemite National Park, one of the greatest of all our natural resources for the uplifting joy and peace and health of the people, is in danger of being dammed and made into a reservoir to help supply San Francisco with water and light, thus flooding it from wall to wall and burying its gardens and groves one or two hundred feet deep. This grossly destructive commercial scheme has long been planned and urged (though water as pure and abundant can be got from sources outside of the people's park, in a dozen different places), because of the comparative cheapness of the dam and of the territory which it is sought to divert from the great uses to which it was dedicated in the Act of 1890 establishing the Yosemite National Park.

The making of gardens and parks goes on with civilization all over the world, and they increase both in size and number as their value is recognized. Everybody needs beauty as well as bread, places to play in and pray in, where Nature may heal and cheer and give strength to body and soul alike. This natural beauty-hunger is made manifest in the little window-sill gardens of the poor, though perhaps only a geranium slip in a broken cup, as well as in the carefully tended rose and lily gardens of the rich, the thousands of spacious city parks and botanical gardens, and in our magnificent National parks—the Yellowstone, Yosemite, Sequoia, etc.—Nature's sublime wonderlands, the admiration and joy of the world. Nevertheless, like anything else worth while, from the very beginning, however well guarded, they have always been subject to attack by despoiling gain-seekers and mischief-makers of every degree from Satan to Senators, eagerly trying to make everything immediately and selfishly commercial, with schemes disguised in smug-smiling philanthropy, industriously, shampiously crying, "Conservation, conservation, panutilization," that man and beast may be fed and the dear Nation made great. Thus long ago a few enterprising merchants utilized the Jerusalem temple as a place of business instead of a place of prayer, changing money, buying and selling cattle and sheep and doves; and earlier still, the first forest reservation, including only one tree, was likewise despoiled. Ever since the establishment of the Yosemite National Park, strife has been going on around its borders and I suppose this will go on as part of the universal battle, between right and wrong, however much its boundaries may be shorn, or its wild beauty destroyed.

The first application to the Government by the San Francisco Supervisors for the commercial use of Lake Eleanor and the Hetch Hetchy Valley was made in 1903, and on December 22nd of that year it was denied by the Secretary of the Interior, Mr. Hitchcock, who truthfully said:

Presumably the Yosemite National Park was created such by law because of the natural objects of varying degrees of scenic importance located within its boundaries, inclusive alike of its beautiful small lakes, like Eleanor, and its majestic wonders, like Hetch Hetchy and Yosemite Valley. It is the aggregation of such natural scenic features that makes the Yosemite Park a wonderland which the Congress of the United States sought by law to reserve for all coming time as nearly as practicable in the condition fashioned by the hand of the Creator—a worthy object of National pride and a source of healthful pleasure and rest for the thousands of people who may annually sojourn there during the heated months.

In 1907 when Mr. Garfield became Secretary of the Interior the application was renewed and granted; but under his successor, Mr. Fisher, the matter has been referred to a Commission, which as this volume goes to press still has it under consideration. [...]

That any one would try to destroy such a place seems incredible; but sad experience shows that there are people good enough and bad enough for anything. The proponents of the dam scheme bring forward a lot of bad arguments to prove that the only righteous thing to do with the people's parks is to destroy them bit by bit as they are able. Their arguments are curiously like those of the devil, devised for the destruction of the first garden—so much of the very best Eden fruit going to waste; so much of the best Tuolumne water and Tuolumne scenery going to waste. Few of their statements are even partly true, and all are misleading.

Thus, Hetch Hetchy, they say, is a "low-lying meadow." On the contrary, it is a high-lying natural landscape garden, as the photographic illustrations show.

"It is a common minor feature, like thousands of others." On the contrary it is a very uncommon feature; after Yosemite, the rarest and in many ways the most important in the National Park.

"Damming and submerging it 175 feet deep would enhance its beauty by forming a crystal-clear lake." Landscape gardens, places of recreation and worship, are never made beautiful by destroying and burying them. The beautiful sham lake, forsooth, would be only an eyesore, a dismal blot on the landscape, like many others to be seen in the Sierra. For, instead of keeping it at the same level all the year, allowing Nature centuries of time to make new shores, it would, of course, be full only a month or two in the spring, when the snow is melting fast; then it would be gradually drained, exposing the slimy sides of the basin and shallower parts of the bottom, with the gathered drift and waste, death and decay of the upper basins, caught here instead of being swept on to decent natural burial along the banks of the river or in the sea. Thus the Hetch Hetchy dam-lake would be only a rough imitation of a natural lake for a few of the spring months, an open sepulcher for the others.

"Hetch Hetchy water is the purest of all to be found in the Sierra, unpolluted, and forever unpollutable." On the contrary, excepting that of the Merced below Yosemite, it is less pure than that of most of the other Sierra streams, because of the sewerage of camp grounds draining into it, especially of the Big Tuolumne Meadows camp ground, occupied by hundreds of tourists and mountaineers, with their animals, for months every summer, soon to be followed by thousands from all the world.

These temple destroyers, devotees of ravaging commercialism, seem to have a perfect contempt for Nature, and, instead of lifting their eyes to the God of the mountains, lift them to the Almighty Dollar.

Dam Hetch Hetchy! As well dam for water-tanks the people's cathedrals and churches, for no holier temple has ever been consecrated by the heart of man.

[TY]

Mary Harris "Mother" Jones, "Appeal to the Cause of Miners in the Paint Creek District" Speech

August 15, 1912

Mary Harris "Mother" Jones was best known for her work as a union organizer and her skills as an eloquent orator. A founding member of the Industrial Workers of the World (also known as "Wobblies"), Jones was an active and influential part of numerous labor movements, most notably the United Mine Workers and the Socialist Party of America. Jones delivered this speech on the front steps of the State Capitol building in Charleston, West Virginia, on August 15, 1912.

– Note by James Daley

THIS, MY FRIENDS, marks, in my estimation, the most remarkable move ever made in the State of West Virginia. It is a day that will mark history in the long ages to come. What is it? It is an uprising of the oppressed against the master class. [...]

I have worked, boys, I have worked with you for years. I have seen the suffering children, and in order to be convinced I went into the mines on the night shift and day shift and helped the poor wretches to load coal at times. We lay down at noon and we took our lunches and we talked our wrongs over, we gathered together at night and asked "How will we remedy things?" We organized secretly, and after a while held public meetings. We got our people together in those organized States. To-day the mine owners and the miners come together. They meet each other and shake hands, and have no more war in those States, and the workingmen are

107

becoming more intelligent. And I am one of those my friends, I don't care about your woman suffrage and the temperance brigade or any other of your class associations, I want women of the coming day to discuss and find out the cause of child crucifixion, that is what I want to find out.

I have worked in the factories of Georgia and Alabama, and these bloodhounds were tearing the hands off of children and working them 14 hours a day until I fought for them. They made them put up every Saturday money for missionary work in China. I know what I am talking about. I am not talking haphazard, I have the goods.

Go down, men of to-day, who rob and exploit, go down into hell and look at the ruins you have put there, look at the jails. We pay $6,000,000 a year to chain men like demons in a bastille—and we call ourselves civilized. Six million dollars a year we pay for jails, and nothing for education.

I have been in jail more than once, and I expect to go again. If you are too cowardly to fight, I will fight. You ought to be ashamed of yourselves, actually to the Lord you ought, just to see one old woman who is not afraid of all the bloodhounds. How scared those villains are when one woman 80 years old, with her head gray, can come in and scare hell out of the whole bunch. [*Laughter.*] We didn't scare them? The mine owners run down the street like a mad dog to-day. They ask who started this thing. I started it, I did it, and I am not afraid to tell you if you are here, and I will start more before I leave West Virginia. I started this mass meeting to-day, I had these banners written, and don't accuse anybody else of the job. [*Loud applause.*]

It is freedom or death, and your children will be free. We are not going to leave a slave class to the coming generation, and I want to say to you that the next generation will not charge us for what we have done; they will charge and condemn us for what we have left undone. [*Cries of "That is right."*]

You have got your bastille. Yes; we have no fears of them at all. I was put out at 12 o'clock at night—and landed with 5 cents in my pocket—by seven bayonets in the State of Colorado. The governor told me—he is a corporation rat, you know—he told me never to come back. A man is a fool, if he is a governor, to tell a woman not to do a thing. [*Loud applause, and cries of "Tell them again; tell them about it."*]

I went back next day and I have been back since the fight, and he hasn't bothered me. He has learned it won't do to tamper with women of the right metal. You have a few cats [*mocking*]—they are not women, they are what you call ladies. There is a difference between women and ladies. The modern parasites made ladies, but God Almighty made women. [*Applause and cries of "Tell us one more."*]

Now, my boys, you are mine; we have fought together, we have hungered together, we have marched together, but I can see victory in the Heavens for you. I can see the hand above you guiding and inspiring you to move onward and upward. No white flag—we can not raise it; we must not raise it. We must redeem the world.

Go into our factories, see how the conditions are there, see how women are ground up for the merciless money pirates, see how many of the poor wretches go to work with crippled bodies. I talked with a mother who had her small children working. She said to me, "Mother, they are not of age, but I had to say they were; I had to tell them they were of age so they could get a chance to help me to get something to eat." She said after they were there a little while, "I have saved $40, the first I ever saw. I put that into a cow and we had some milk for the little ones." In all the years her husband had put in the earth digging out wealth, he never got a glimpse of $40 until he had to take his infant boys that ought to go to school, and sacrifice them.

If there was no other reason that should stimulate every man and woman to fight this damnable system of commercial pirates. [*Cries of "Right, right."*] That alone should do it, my friends.

Is there a committee here? I want to take a committee of the well-fed fellows and well-dressed fellows; I want to present this to the governor. Be very polite. Don't get on your knees. Get off your knees and stand up. None of these fellows are better than you, they are only flesh and blood—that is the truth.

(Committee formed around "Mother" and start into the capitol building.) These fellows all want to go and see the king. [*Laughter.*]

I will give the press a copy of this resolution and this petition, which was given to the governor.

Now, my boys, guard rule and tyranny will have to go; there must be an end. I am going up Cabin Creek. I am going to hold meetings there. I am going to claim the right of an American citizen. I was on this earth before these operators were. I was in this country before these operators. I have been 74 years under this flag. I have got the right to talk. I have seen its onward march. I have seen the growth of oppression, and I want to say to you, my friends, I am going to claim my right as a citizen of this Nation. I won't violate the law; I will not kill anybody or starve anybody; but I will talk unsparingly of all the corporation bloodhounds we can bring to jail. [*Laughter.*]

I have no apologies to offer. I have seen your children murdered; I have seen you blown to death in the mines, and there was no redress. A fellow in Colorado says, "Why don't you prop the mines?" The operator said, "Oh, hell; Dagoes are cheaper than props!" Every miner is a Dago with the blood-sucking pirates, and they are cheaper than props, because if they kill a hundred of you, well, it was your fault; there must be a mine inspector kept there.

The night before the little Johnson boys were killed the mine inspector—John Laing is a mine owner; he wouldn't inspect them—the mine inspector went there and said the mines are propped securely. The next morning the little Johnson children went to work, and when they were found their hands were clasped in their dinner buckets with two biscuits.

You work for Laing day after day. He is a mine inspector, but he wouldn't be if I had anything to say about it. He would take a back seat.

Boys, I want to say to you, obey the law. Let me say to the governor and let me say to the mine owners—let me say to all people—that I will guarantee there will be no destruction of property.

In the first place, that is our property. It is inside where our jobs are. We have every reason to protect it. In the mines is where our jobs are. We are not out to destroy property; we are out to preserve and protect property, and I will tell you why. We are going to get more wages and we are going to stop the docking system. Put that down. Your day for docking is done. Stop it. If they don't stop it, we will. [*Cries of "Good!" "Good!"*]

We'll take care of the property; there will be no property destroyed [*Cries of "Not a bit!"*]

Not a bit; and if you want your property protected these miners will protect it for you, and they won't need a gun. [*Cries of "It is our interest to do so!"*]

We will protect it at the risk of our lives. I know the miners; I have marched with 10,000—20,000—and destroyed no property. We had 20,000 miners in Pennsylvania, but destroyed no property.

They used to do that years ago, but after we have educated them they saw that violence was not the idea. We stopped it; we organized; we brought them to school once again. I will tell you why we are not going to destroy your property, Mr. Governor: Because one of these days we are going to take over the mines. [*Loud applause.*]

That is what we are going to do; we are going to take over those mines. […]

[GSAW]

The World Wars

President Woodrow Wilson, First *Lusitania* Note

May 13, 1915

Through the efforts of President Wilson (1856–1924), the United States declared itself neutral in World War I. On May 7, 1915, however, a German submarine sank the British ship Lusitania, sailing from New York to London, on board of which were more than a hundred and twenty American civilians. This act nearly brought the United States into the war with the Allies against Germany. When German officials attempted to justify the sinking, Wilson wrote a second note, on June 7, 1915, insisting further on Germany's compliance in avoiding attacks on American ships and passengers. After a series of violations by Germany, Wilson persuaded Congress to declare war in the spring of 1917.

IN VIEW OF recent acts of the German authorities in violation of American rights on the high seas which culminated in the torpedoing and sinking of the British steamship *Lusitania* on May 7, 1915, by which over 100 American citizens lost their lives, it is clearly wise and desirable that the Government of the United States and the Imperial German Government should come to a clear and full understanding as to the grave situation which has resulted.

The sinking of the British passenger steamer *Falaba* by a German submarine on March 28, through which Leon C. Thrasher, an American citizen, was drowned; the attack on April 28 on the American vessel *Cushing* by a German aeroplane; the torpedoing on May 1 of the American vessel *Gulflight* by a German submarine, as a result of which two or more American citizens met their death; and, finally, the torpedoing and sinking of the steamship *Lusitania,* constitute a series of events which the Government of the United States has observed with growing concern, distress, and amazement.

Recalling the humane and enlightened attitude hitherto assumed by the Imperial German Government in matters of international right, and particularly with regard to the freedom of the seas; having learned to recognize the German views and the German influence in the field of international obligation as always engaged upon the side of justice and humanity; and having understood the instructions of the Imperial German Government to its naval commanders to be upon the same plane of humane action prescribed by the naval codes of other nations, the Government of the United States was loath to believe—it can not now bring itself to believe—that these acts, so absolutely contrary to the rules, the practices, and the spirit of modern warfare, could have the countenance or sanction of that great Government. It feels it to be its duty, therefore, to address the Imperial German Government concerning them with the utmost frankness and in the earnest hope that it is not mistaken in expecting action on the part of the Imperial German Government which will correct the unfortunate impressions which have been created and vindicate once more the position of that Government with regard to the sacred freedom of the seas.

The Government of the United States has been apprised that the Imperial German Government considered themselves to be obliged by the extraordinary circumstances of the present war and the measures adopted by their adversaries in seeking to cut Germany off from all commerce, to adopt methods of retaliation which go much beyond the ordinary methods of warfare at sea, in the proclamation of a war zone from which they have warned neutral ships to keep away. This Government has already taken occasion to inform the Imperial German Government that it cannot admit the adoption of such measures or such a warning of danger to operate as in any degree an abbreviation of the rights of American shipmasters or of American citizens bound on lawful errands as passengers on merchant ships of belligerent nationality; and that it must hold the Imperial German Government to a strict accountability for any infringement of those rights, intentional or incidental. It does not understand the Imperial German Government to question those rights. It assumes, on the contrary, that the Imperial Government accept, as of course, the rule that the lives of noncombatants, whether they be of neutral citizenship or citizens of one of the nations at war, can not lawfully or rightfully be put in jeopardy by the capture or destruction of an unarmed merchantman, and recognize also, as all other nations do, the obligation to take the usual precaution of visit and search to ascertain whether a suspected merchantmen is in fact of belligerent nationality or is in fact carrying contraband of war under a neutral flag.

The Government of the United States, therefore, desires to call the attention of the Imperial German Government with the utmost earnestness to the fact that the objection to their present method of attack against the trade of their enemies lies in the practical impossibility of employing submarines in the destruction of commerce without disregarding those rules of fairness, reason, justice, and humanity which all modern opinion regards as imperative. It is practically impossible for the officers of a submarine to visit a merchantman at sea and examine her papers and cargo. It is practically impossible for them to make a prize of her; and, if they can not put a prize crew on board of her, they can not sink her without leaving her crew and all on board of her to the mercy of the sea in her small boats. These facts it is understood the Imperial German Government frankly admit. We are informed that in the instances of which we have spoken time enough for even that poor measure of safety was not given, and in at least two of the cases cited not so much as a warning was received. Manifestly submarines can not be used against merchantmen, as the last few weeks have shown, without an inevitable violation of many sacred principles of justice and humanity.

American citizens act within their indisputable rights in taking their ships and in traveling wherever their legitimate business calls them upon the high seas, and exercise those rights in what should be the well-justified confidence that their lives will not be endangered by acts done in clear violation of universally acknowledged international obligations, and certainly in the confidence that their own Government will sustain them in the exercise of their rights.

There was recently published in the newspapers of the United States, I regret to inform the Imperial German Government, a formal warning, purporting to come from the Imperial German Embassy at Washington, addressed to the people of the United States, and stating, in effect, that any citizen of the United States who exercised his right of free travel upon the seas would do so at his peril if his journey should take him within the zone of waters within which the Imperial

German Navy was using submarines against the commerce of Great Britain and France, notwithstanding the respectful but very earnest protest of his Government, the Government of the United States. I do not refer to this for the purpose of calling the attention of the Imperial German Government at this time to the surprising irregularity of a communication from the Imperial German Embassy at Washington addressed to the people of the United States through the newspapers, but only for the purpose of pointing out that no warning that an unlawful and inhumane act will be committed can possibly be accepted as an excuse or palliation for that act or as an abatement of the responsibility for its commission.

Long acquainted as this Government has been with the character of the Imperial German Government and with the high principles of equity by which they have in the past been actuated and guided, the Government of the United States can not believe that the commanders of the vessels which committed these acts of lawlessness did so except under a misapprehension of the orders issued by the Imperial German naval authorities. It takes it for granted that, at least within the practical possibilities of every such case, the commanders even of submarines were expected to do nothing that would involve the lives of noncombatants or the safety of neutral ships, even at the cost of failing of their object of capture or destruction. It confidently expects, therefore, that the Imperial German Government will disavow the acts of which the Government of the United States complains, that they will make reparation so far as reparation is possible for injuries which are without measure, and that they will take immediate steps to prevent the recurrence of anything so obviously subversive of the principles of warfare for which the Imperial German Government have in the past so wisely and so firmly contended.

The Government and people of the United States look to the Imperial German Government for just, prompt, and enlightened action in this vital matter with the greater confidence because the United States and Germany are bound together not only by special ties of friendship but also by the explicit stipulations of the treaty of 1828 between the United States and the Kingdom of Prussia.

Expressions of regret and offers of reparation in case of the destruction of neutral ships sunk by mistake, while they may satisfy international obligations, if no loss of life results, can not justify or excuse a practice, the natural and necessary effect of which is to subject neutral nations and neutral persons to new and immeasurable risks.

The Imperial German Government will not expect the Government of the United States to omit any word or any act necessary to the performance of its sacred duty of maintaining the rights of the United States and its citizens and of safeguarding their free exercise and enjoyment.

[SAJ]

President Woodrow Wilson, Joint Address to Congress, "The Fourteen Points"

January 8, 1918

Wilson, anticipating the end of World War I, outlined, in his usual efficient and clear manner, his goals for America's and its allies' diplomatic enforcement of peace throughout Europe. He used some of his points to help negotiate the end of the war and the Treaty of Versailles a year later. The U.S. Senate, however, would not ratify the treaty as presented by Wilson.

GENTLEMEN OF THE CONGRESS: Once more, as repeatedly before, the spokesmen of the Central Empires have indicated their desire to discuss the objects of the war and the possible basis of a general peace. Parleys have been in progress at Brest-Litovsk between Russian representatives and representatives of the Central Powers to which the attention of all the belligerents has been invited for the purpose of ascertaining whether it may be possible to extend these parleys into a general conference with regard to terms of peace and settlement. The Russian representatives presented not only a perfectly definite statement of the principles upon which they would be willing to conclude peace, but also an equally definite program of the concrete application of those principles. The representatives of the Central Powers, on their part, presented an outline of settlement which, if much less definite, seemed susceptible of liberal interpretation until their specific program of practical terms was added. That program proposed no concessions at all, either to the sovereignty of Russia or to the preferences of the population with whose fortunes it dealt, but meant, in a word, that the Central Empire were to keep every foot of territory their armed forces had occupied—every province, every city, every point of vantage—as a permanent addition to their territories and their power. It is a reasonable conjecture that the gentle principles of settlement which they at first suggested originated with the more liberal statesmen of Germany and Austria, the men who have begun to feel the force their own people's thought and purpose, while the concrete terms of actual settlement came from the military leaders who have no thought but to keep what they have got. The negotiations have been broken off. The Russian representatives are sincere and in earnest. They cannot entertain such proposals of request and domination. [...]

We entered this war because violations of right had occurred which touched us to the quick and made the life of our own people impossible unless they were corrected and the world secured once for all against their recurrence. What we demand in this war, therefore, is nothing peculiar to ourselves. It is that the world be made fit and safe to live in; and particularly that it be made safe for every peace-loving nation which, like our own, wishes to live its own life, determine its own institutions, be assured of justice and fair dealings by the other people of the world, as against force and selfish aggression. All of the people of the world are in effect partners in this interest and for our own part we see very clearly that unless justice be done to others it will not be done to us.

The program of the world's peace, therefore, is our program, and that program, the only possible program, as we see it, is this:

I. Open covenants of peace must be arrived at, after which there will surely be no private international action or rulings of any kind, but diplomacy shall proceed always frankly and in the public view.

II. Absolute freedom of navigation upon the seas, outside territorial waters, alike in peace and in war, except as the seas may be closed in whole or in part by international action for the enforcement of international covenants.

III. The removal, so far as possible, of all economic barriers and the establishment of an equality of trade conditions among all the nations consenting to the peace and associating themselves for its maintenance.

IV. Adequate guaranties given and taken that national armaments will reduce to the lowest point consistent with domestic safety.

V. Free, open-minded, and absolutely impartial adjustment of all colonial claims, based upon a strict observance of the principle that in determining all such questions of sovereignty the interests of the population concerned must have equal weight with the equitable claims of the government whose title is to be determined.

VI. The evacuation of all Russian territory and such a settlement of all questions affecting Russia as will secure the best and freest cooperation of the other nations of the world in obtaining for her an unhampered and unembarrassed opportunity for the independent determination of her own political development and national policy, and assure her of a sincere welcome into the society of free nations under institutions of her own choosing; and, more than a welcome, assistance also of every kind that she may need and may herself desire. The treatment accorded Russia by her sister nations in the months to come will be the acid test of their good-will, of their comprehension of her needs as distinguished from their own interests, and of their intelligent and unselfish sympathy.

VII. Belgium, the whole world will agree, must be evacuated and restored, without any attempt to limit the sovereignty which she enjoys in common with all other free nations. No other single act will serve as this will serve to restore confidence among the nations in the laws which they have themselves let and determined for the government of their relations with one another. Without this healing act the whole structure and validity of international law is forever impaired.

VIII. All French territory should be freed and the invaded portions restored, and the wrong done to France by Prussia in 1871 in the matter of Alsace-Lorraine, which has unsettled the peace of the world for nearly fifty years, should be righted, in order that peace may once more be made secure in the interest of all.

IX. A readjustment of the frontiers of Italy should be effected along clearly recognizable lines of nationality.

X. The peoples of Austria-Hungary, whose place among the nations we wish to see safeguarded and assured, should be accorded the freest opportunity of autonomous development.

XI. Roumania, Serbia, and Montenegro should be evacuated; occupied territories restored; Serbia accorded free and secure access to the sea; and the relations of the several Balkan States to one another determined by friendly counsel along historically established lines of allegiance and nationality; and international guaranties of the political and economic independence and territorial integrity of the several Balkan States should be entered into.

XII. The Turkish portions of the present Ottoman Empire should be assured a secure sovereignty, but the other nationalities which are now under Turkish rule should be assured an undoubted security of life and an absolutely unmolested opportunity of autonomous development, and the Dardanelles should be permanently opened as a free passage to the ships and commerce of all nations under international guaranties.

XIII. An independent Polish state should be erected which should include the territories inhabited by indisputably Polish populations, which should be assured a free and secure access to the sea, and whose political and economic independence and territorial integrity should be guaranteed by international covenant.

XIV. A general association of nations must be formed under specific covenants for the purpose of affording mutual guaranties of political independence and territorial integrity to great and small states a like.

In regard to these essential rectifications of wrong and assertions of right, we feel ourselves to be intimate partners of all the Governments and peoples associated together against the imperialists. We cannot be separated in interest or divided in purpose. We stand together until the end.

For such arrangements and covenants we are willing to fight and to continue to fight until they are achieved; but only because we wish the right to prevail and desire a just and stable peace, such as can be secured only by removing the chief provocations to war, which this program does remove. We have no jealousy of German greatness and there is nothing in this program that impairs it. We grudge her no achievement or distinction of learning or of pacific enterprise such as have made her record very bright and very enviable. We do not wish to injure her or to block in any way her legitimate influence or power. We do not wish to fight her either with arms or with hostile arrangements of trade, if she is willing to associate herself with us and the other peace-loving nations of the world in covenants of justice and law and fair dealing. We wish her only to accept a place of equality among the peoples of the world—the new world in which we now live—instead of a place of mastery.

Neither do we presume to suggest to her any alteration or modification of her institutions. But it is necessary, we must frankly say, and necessary as a preliminary to any intelligent dealings with her on our part, that we should know whom her spokesmen speak for when they speak to us, whether for the Reichstag majority or for the military party and the men whose creed is imperial domination.

We have spoken now, surely, in terms too concrete to admit of any further doubt or question. An evident principle runs through the whole program I have outlined. It is the principle of justice to all peoples and nationalities, and their right to live on equal terms of liberty and safety with one another, whether they be strong or weak. Unless this principle be made its foundation, no part of the structure of international justice can stand. The people of the United States could act upon no other principle, and to the vindication of this principle they are ready to devote their lives, their honor, and everything that they possess. The moral climax of this, the culminating and final war for human liberty, has come, and they are ready to put their own strength, their own highest purpose, their own integrity and devotion to the test.

[WGS]

President Woodrow Wilson, Address in Support of the League of Nations

September 25, 1919

At the Peace Conference in Paris following World War I, Wilson made the opening presentation. It was the first time during a presidency that a U.S. President ever visited much less spoke in Europe. Wilson had his heart set on establishing America's participation in this international organization that he believed would prevent wars. He could not persuade his own Senate, which was suspicious of limits to American action, to go along with him, and the United States never joined the league, despite continued efforts even after his presidency ended.

MR. CHAIRMAN:—I consider it a distinguished privilege to be permitted to open the discussion in this Conference on the League of Nations. We have assembled for two purposes: to make the present settlements which have been rendered necessary by this war, and also to secure the peace of the world, not only by the present settlements, but by the arrangements we shall make at this Conference for its maintenance. The League of Nations seems to me to be necessary for both of these purposes. There are many complicated questions connected with the present settlements which perhaps cannot be successfully worked out to an ultimate issue by the decisions we shall arrive at here. I can easily conceive that many of these settlements will need subsequent consideration, that many of the decisions we make shall need subsequent alteration in some degree; for, if I may judge by my own study of some of these questions, they are not susceptible of confident judgments at present.

It is, therefore, necessary that we should set up some machinery by which the work of this Conference should be rendered complete. We have assembled here for the purpose of doing very much more than making the present settlements that are necessary. We are assembled under very peculiar conditions of world opinion. I may say, without straining the point, that we are not representatives of governments, but representatives of peoples. It will not suffice to satisfy governmental circles anywhere. It is necessary that we should satisfy the opinion of mankind. The burdens of this war have fallen in an unusual degree upon the whole population of the countries involved. I do not need to draw for you the picture of how the burden has been thrown back from the front upon the older men, upon the women, upon the children, upon the homes of the civilized world, and how the real strain of the war has come where the eye of government could not reach, but where the heart of humanity beat. We are bidden by these people to make a peace which will make them secure. We are bidden by these people to see to it that this strain does not come upon them, and I venture to say that it has been possible for them to bear this strain because they hoped that those who represented them could get together after this war and make such another sacrifice unnecessary.

It is a solemn obligation on our part, therefore, to make permanent arrangements that justice shall be rendered and peace maintained. This is the central object of our meeting. Settlements may be temporary, but the action of the nations in the interest of peace and justice must be permanent. We can set up permanent processes. We may not be able to set up permanent decisions. Therefore, it seems to me that we must take, so far as we can, a picture of the world into our minds.

Is it not a startling circumstance, for one thing, that the great discoveries of science, that the quiet studies of men in laboratories, that the thoughtful developments which have taken place in quiet lecture-rooms, have now been turned to the destruction of civilization? The powers of destruction have not so much multiplied as gained facility. The enemy whom we have just overcome had at his seats of learning some of the principal centers of scientific study and discovery, and he used them in order to make destruction sudden and complete and only the watchful, continuous cooperation of men can see to it that science, as well as armed men, is kept within the harness of civilization.

In a sense, the United States is less interested in this subject than the other nations here assembled. With her great territory and her extensive sea borders, it is less likely that the United States should suffer from the attack of enemies than that many of the other nations here should suffer; and the ardor of the United States—for it is a very deep and genuine ardor—for the society of nations is not an ardor springing out of fear or apprehension, but an ardor springing out of the ideals which have come to consciousness in this war. In coming into this war the United States never for a moment thought that she was intervening in the politics of Europe, or the politics of Asia, or the politics of any part of the world. Her thought was that the entire world had now become conscious that there was a single cause which turned upon the issues of this war. That was the cause of justice and of liberty for men of every kind and place. Therefore, the United States would feel that her part in this war had been played in vain if there ensued upon it a body of European settlements. She would feel that she could not take part in guaranteeing those European settlements unless the guaranty involved the continuous superintendence of the peace of the world by the associated nations of the world.

Therefore, it seems to me that we must concert our best judgment in order to make this League of Nations a vital thing—not merely formal thing, not an occasional thing, not a thing sometimes called into life to meet an exigency, but always functioning in watchful attendance upon the interests of the nations, and that its continuity should be a vital continuity; that it should have functions that are continuing functions, and that do not permit an intermission of its watchfulness and of its labor; that it should be the eye of the nations to keep watch upon the common interest, an eye that did not slumber, an eye that was everywhere watchful and attentive.

And if we do not make it vital, what shall we do? We shall disappoint the expectations of the peoples. This is what their thought centers upon. I have had the very delightful experience of visiting several nations since I came to this side of the water, and every time the voice of the body of the people reached me through any representative, at the front of the plea stood the hope for the League of Nations. Gentlemen, the select classes of mankind are no longer the governors of mankind. The fortunes of mankind are now in the hands of the plain people of the whole world. Satisfy them, and you have not only justified their confidence, but established peace. Fail to satisfy them, and no arrangement that you can make will either set up or steady the peace of the world.

You can imagine, gentlemen, I dare say, the sentiments and the purpose with which representatives of the United States support this great project for a League of Nations. We regard it as the keystone of the whole program which expressed our purposes and ideals in this war and which the associated nations accepted as the basis of the settlement. If we return to the United States without having made every effort in our power to realize this program, we should return to meet the merited scorn of our fellow-citizens. For they are a body that constitutes a great democracy. They expect their leaders to speak their thoughts and no private purpose of their own. They expect their representatives to be their servants. We have no choice but to obey their mandate. But it is with the greatest enthusiasm and pleasure that we accept that mandate; and because this is the keystone of the whole fabric, we have pledged our every purpose to it, as we have to every item of the fabric. We would not dare abate a single item of the program which constitutes our instruction. We would not dare compromise upon any matter as the champion of this thing—this peace of the world, this attitude of justice, this principle that we are the masters of no people, but are here to see that every people in the world shall choose its own masters and govern its own destinies, not as we wish but as it wishes. We are here to see, in short, that the very foundations of this war are swept away.

Those foundations were the private choice of small coteries of civil rulers and military staffs. Those foundations were the aggression of great powers upon small. Those foundations were the holding together of empires of unwilling subjects by the duress of arms. Those foundations were the power of small bodies of men to work their will and use mankind as pawns in a game. And nothing less than the emancipation of the world from these things will accomplish peace. You can see that the representatives of the United States are, therefore, never put to the embarrassment of choosing a way of expediency, because they have laid down for them the unalterable lines of principle. And, thank God, those lines have been accepted as the lines of settlement by all the high-minded men who have had to do with the beginnings of this great business.

I hope, Mr. Chairman, that when it is known, as I feel confident it will be known, that we have adopted the principles of the League of Nations and mean to work out that principle in effective action, we shall by that single thing have lifted a great part of the load of anxiety from the hearts of men everywhere. We stand in a peculiar case. As I go about the streets here I see everywhere the American uniform. Those men came into the war after they had uttered our purposes. They came as crusaders, not merely to win a war, but to win a cause; and I am responsible to them, for it fell to me to formulate the purposes for which I asked them to fight, and I, like them, must be a crusader for these things, whatever it costs and whatever it may be necessary to do, in honor, to accomplish the object for which they fought.

I have been glad to find from day to day that there is no question of our standing alone in this matter, for there are champions of this cause upon every hand. I am merely avowing this in order that you may understand why, perhaps, it fell to us, who are disengaged from the politics of this great continent and of the Orient, to suggest that this was the keystone of the arch, and why it occurred to the generous mind of our President to call upon me to open this debate. It is not because we alone represent this idea, but because it is our privilege to associate ourselves with you in representing it.

I have only tried in what I have said to give you the fountains of the enthusiasm which is within us for this thing, for those fountains spring, it seems to me, from all the ancient wrongs and sympathies of mankind, and the very pulse of the world seems to beat to the surface in this enterprise.

[WGS]

Nineteenth Amendment to the Constitution, Ratification of Women's Right to Vote

August 18, 1920

AMENDMENT XIX
Passed by Congress June 4, 1919. Ratified August 18, 1920.

THE RIGHT OF citizens of the United States to vote shall not be denied or abridged by the United States or by any State on account of sex.

Congress shall have power to enforce this article by appropriate legislation.

[ARCH]

Marcus Garvey, Speech, "The Handwriting is on the Wall"

August 31, 1921

Garvey's newspaper, The Negro World, *describes how, at the Second International Convention of Negroes of the World, at Liberty Hall, in Harlem, New York City, he rose before a cheering crowd to give this speech, "smiling and bowing to the right and then to the left like a black Napoleon." Garvey (1887–1940) was the charismatic Jamaican who in the late 1910s and early 1920s concentrated and sparked the energy of hundreds of thousands of African-Americans with the dream of African redemption. After serving a prison term for mail fraud, he was deported, and his power faded. He died in England.*

WE ARE ASSEMBLED here tonight to bring to a close our great convention of thirty-one days and thirty-one nights. Before we separate ourselves and take our departure to the different parts of the world from which we came, I desire to give you a message; one that you will, I hope, take home and propagate among the scattered millions of Africa's sons and daughters.

We have been here, sent here by the good will of the 400,000,000 Negroes of the world to legislate in their interests, and in the time allotted to us we did our best to enact laws and to frame laws that in our judgment, we hope, will solve the great problem that confronts us universally. The Universal Negro Improvement Association seeks to emancipate the Negro everywhere, industrially, educationally, politically and religiously. It also seeks a free and redeemed Africa. It has a great struggle ahead; it has a gigantic task to face. Nevertheless, as representatives of the Negro people of the world we have undertaken the task of freeing the 400,000,000 of our race, and of freeing our bleeding Motherland, Africa. We counseled with each other during the thirty-one days; we debated with each other during the thirty-one days, and out of all we did, and out of all we said, we have come to the one conclusion—that speedily Africa must be redeemed! [*Applause.*] We have come to the conclusion that speedily there must be an emancipated Negro race everywhere [*applause*]; and on going back to our respective homes we go with our determination to lay down, if needs be, the last drop of our blood for the defense of Africa and for the emancipation of our race.

The handwriting is on the wall. You see it as plain as daylight; you see it coming out of India, the tribes of India rising in rebellion against their overlords. You see it coming out of Africa, our dear motherland, Africa; the Moors rising in rebellion against their overlords, and defeating them at every turn. [*Applause.*] According to the last report flashed to this country from Morocco by the Associated Press, the Moors have again conquered and subdued the Spanish hordes. The same Associated Press flashes to us the news that there is a serious uprising in India, and the English people are marshaling their troops to subdue the spirit of liberty, of freedom, which is now permeating India. The news has come to us, and I have a cable in my pocket that comes from Ireland that the Irish are determined to have liberty and nothing less than liberty. [*Applause.*]

The handwriting is on the wall, and as we go back to our respective homes we shall serve notice upon the world that we also are coming; coming with a united effort; coming with a united determination, a determination that Africa shall be free from coast to coast. [*Applause.*] I have before me the decision of the League of Nations. Immediately after the war a Council of the League of Nations was called, and at that council they decided that the territories wrested from Germany in West Africa, taken from her during the conflict, should be divided between France and England—608,000 square miles—without even asking the civilized Negroes of the world what disposition shall be made of their own homeland, of their own country. An insult was hurled at the civilized Negroes of the world when they thus took upon themselves the right to parcel out and apportion as they pleased 608,000 square miles of our own land; for we never gave it up; we never sold it. It is still ours. [*Cries of "Yes!"*] They parceled it out between these two nations—England and France—gave away our property without consulting us, and we are aggrieved, and we desire to serve notice on civilization and on the world that 400,000,000 Negroes are aggrieved. [*Cries of "Yes!" and applause.*]

And we are the more aggrieved because of the lynch rope, because of segregation, because of the Jim Crowism that is used, practiced and exercised here in this country, and in other parts of the world by the White nations of the earth, wherever Negroes happen accidentally or otherwise to find themselves. If there is no safety for Negroes in the white world, 1 cannot see what right they have to parcel out the homeland, the country of Negroes, without consulting Negroes and asking their permission to do so. Therefore, we are aggrieved. This question of prejudice will be the downfall of civilization [*Applause*], and I warn the white race of this, and of their doom. I hope they will take heed, because the handwriting is on the wall. [*Applause.*] No portion of humanity, no group of humanity, has an abiding right, an everlasting right, an eternal right to oppress other sections or portions of humanity. God never gave them the right, and if there is such a right, man arrogated it to himself, and God in all ages has been displeased with the arrogance of man. I warn those nations which believe themselves above the law of God, above the commandments of God. I warn those nations that believe themselves above human justice. You cannot ignore the laws of God; you cannot long ignore the commandments of God; you cannot long ignore human justice, and exist. Your arrogance will destroy you, and I warn the races and the nations that have arrogated to themselves the right to oppress, the right to circumscribe, the right to keep down other races. I warn them that the hour is coming when the oppressed will rise in their might, in their majesty, and throw off the yoke of ages.

The world ought to understand that the Negro has come to life, possessed with a new conscience and a new soul. The old Negro is buried, and it is well the world knew it. It is not my purpose to deceive the world. I believe in righteousness; I believe in truth; I believe in honesty. That is why I warn a selfish world of the outcome of their actions towards the oppressed. There will come a day, Josephus Daniels wrote about it, a white statesman, and the world has talked about it, and I warn the world of it, that the day will come when the races of the world will marshal themselves in great conflict for the survival of the fittest. Men of the Universal Negro Improvement Association, I am asking you to prepare yourselves, and prepare your race the world over, because the conflict is coming, not because you will it, not because you desire it, because you will be forced into it. The conflict between the races is drawing nearer and nearer. You see it; I see it; I see it in the handwriting on the wall, as expressed in the uprising in India. You see the handwriting on the wall of Africa; you see it, the handwriting on the wall of Europe. It is coming; it is drawing nearer and nearer. Four hundred million Negroes of the world, I am asking you to prepare yourselves, so that you will not be found wanting when that day comes. Ah! What a sorry day it will be. I hope it will never come. But my hope, my wish, will not prevent its coming. All that I can do is to warn humanity everywhere, so that humanity may change its tactics, and warn them of the danger. I repeat: I warn the white world against the prejudice they are practicing against Negroes; I warn them against the segregation and injustice they mete out to us, for the perpetuation of these things will mean the ultimate destruction of the present civilization, and the building up of a new civilization founded upon mercy, justice, and equality.

I know that we have good men in all races living at the present time. We have good men of the black race, we have good men of the white race, good men of the yellow race, who are endeavoring to do the best they can to ward off this coming conflict. White men who have the vision, go ye back and warn your people of this coming conflict! Black men of vision, go ye to the four corners of the earth, and warn your people of this coming conflict. Yellow men, go ye out and warn your people of this coming conflict, because it is drawing nearer and nearer; nearer and nearer. Oh! if the world will only listen to the heart-throbs, to the soul-beats of those who have the vision, those who have God's love in their hearts.

I see before me white men, black men and yellow men working assiduously for the peace of the world; for the bringing together of this thing called human brotherhood; I see them working through their organizations. They have been working during the last fifty years. Some worked to bring about the emancipation, because they saw the danger of perpetual slavery. They brought about the liberation of 4,000,000 black people. They passed away, and others started to work, but the opposition against them is too strong; the opposition against them is weighing them down. The world has gone mad; the world has become too material; the world has lost its spirit of kinship with God, and man can see nothing else but prejudice, avarice and greed. Avarice and greed will destroy the world, and I am appealing to white, black and yellow whose hearts, whose souls are touched with the true spirit of humanity, with the true feeling of human brotherhood, to preach the doctrine of human love, more, to preach it louder, to preach it longer, because there is great need for it in the world at this time. Ah! if they could but see the danger—the conflict between the races—races fighting against each other. What a destruction, what a holocaust it will be! Can you imagine it?

Just take your idea from the last bloody war, wherein a race was pitted against itself (for the whole white races united as one from a common origin), the members of which, on both sides, fought so tenaciously that they killed off each other in frightful, staggering numbers. If a race pitted against itself could fight so tenaciously to kill itself without mercy, can you imagine the fury, can you imagine the mercilessness, the terribleness of the war that will come when all the races of the world will be on the battlefield, engaged in deadly combat for the destruction or overthrow of the one or the other, when beneath it and as a cause of it lies prejudice and hatred? Truly, it will be an ocean of blood; that is all it will be. So that if I can sound a note of warning now that will echo and reverberate around the world and thus prevent such a conflict, God help me to do it; for Africa, like Europe, like Asia, is preparing for that day. [*Great applause.*]

You may ask yourselves if you believe Africa is still asleep. Africa has been slumbering; but she was slumbering for a purpose. Africa still possesses her hidden mysteries; Africa has unused talents, and we are unearthing them now for the coming conflict. [*Applause.*] Oh, I hope it will never come; therefore, I hope the white world will change its attitude towards the weaker races of the world, for we shall not be weak everlastingly. Ah, history teaches us of the rise and fall of nations, races and empires. Rome fell in her majesty; Greece fell in her triumph; Babylon, Assyria, Carthage, Prussia, the German Empire—all fell in their pomp and power; the French Empire fell from the sway of the great Napoleon, from the dominion of the indomitable Corsican soldier. As they fell in the past, so will nations fall in the present age, and so will they fall in the future ages to come, the result of their unrighteousness.

I repeat, I warn the world, and I trust you will receive this warning as you go into the four corners of the earth. The white race should teach humanity. Out there is selfishness in the world. Let the white race teach humanity first, because we have been following the cause of humanity for three hundred years, and we have suffered much. If a change must come, it must not come from Negroes; it must come from the white race, for they are the ones who have brought about this estrangement between the races. The Negro never hated; at no time within the last five hundred years can they point to one single instance of Negro hatred. The Negro has loved even under the severest punishment. In slavery the Negro loved his master; he protected his master; he safeguarded his master's home. "Greater love hath no man than that he should lay down his life for another." We gave not only our services, our unrequited labor; we gave also our souls, we gave our hearts, we gave our all, to our oppressors.

But, after all, we are living in a material world, even though it is partly spiritual, and since we have been very spiritual in the past, we are going to take a part of the material now, and will give others the opportunity to practice the spiritual side of life. Therefore, I am not telling you to lead in humanity; I am not telling you to lead in the bringing about of the turning of humanity, because you have been doing that for three hundred years, and you have lost. But the compromise must come from the dominant races. We are warning them. We are not preaching a doctrine of hatred, and I trust you will not go back to your respective homes and preach such a doctrine. We are preaching, rather, a doctrine of humanity, a doctrine of human love. But we say love begins at home; "charity begins at home."

We are aggrieved because of this partitioning of Africa, because it seeks to deprive Negroes of the chance of higher national development; no chance, no opportunity, is given us to prove our fitness to govern, to dominate in our own behalf. They impute so many bad things against Haiti and against Liberia, that they themselves circumvented Liberia so as to make it impossible for us to demonstrate our ability for self-government. Why not be honest? Why not be straightforward? Having desired the highest development, as they avowed and professed, of the Negro, why not give him a fair chance, an opportunity to prove his capacity for governing? What better opportunity ever presented itself than the present, when the territories of Germany in Africa were wrested from her control by the Allies in the last war—what better chance ever offered itself for trying out the higher ability of Negroes to govern themselves than to have given those territories to the civilized Negroes, and thus give them a trial to exercise themselves in a proper system of government? Because of their desire to keep us down, because of their desire to keep us apart, they refuse us a chance. The chance that they did give us is the chance that we are going to take. [*Great applause.*] Hence tonight, before I take my seat, I will move a resolution, and I think it is befitting at this time to pass such a resolution as I will move, so that the League of Nations and the Supreme Council of the Nations will understand that Negroes are not asleep; that Negroes are not false to themselves; that Negroes are wide awake, and that Negroes intend to take a serious part in the future government of this world; that God Almighty created him and placed him in it. This world owes us a place, and we are going to occupy that place.

We have a right to a large part in the political horizon, and I say to you that we are preparing to occupy that part.

Go back to your respective corners of the earth and preach the real doctrine of the Universal Negro Improvement Association—the doctrine of universal emancipation for Negroes, the doctrine of a free and a redeemed Africa!*

[GSTC]

---

*The resolution protesting "against the distribution of the land of Africa by the Supreme Council and the League of Nations among the white nations of the world" followed and was carried "unanimously."

Margaret Sanger, Speech, "Morality of Birth Control"

November 18, 1921

A New York State native who had worked as a nurse, Sanger (1879–1966) was a women's rights activist who concerned herself with issues of women's health. Having organized the first American Birth Control Conference in New York City in 1921 (her American Birth Control League was a precursor to Planned Parenthood), Sanger was arrested at the closing meeting where she was to give this speech. After her release she gave the speech at another venue.

THE MEETING TONIGHT is a postponement of one which was to have taken place at the Town Hall last Sunday evening. It was to be a culmination of a three day conference, two of which were held at the Hotel Plaza, in discussing the birth control subject in its various and manifold aspects.

The one issue upon which there seems to be most uncertainty and disagreement exists in the moral side of the subject of birth control. It seemed only natural for us to call together scientists, educators, members of the medical profession and the theologians of all denominations to ask their opinion upon this uncertain and important phase of the controversy. Letters were sent to the most eminent men and women in the world. We asked in this letter, the following questions:—

1. Is over-population a menace to the peace of the world?

2. Would the legal dissemination of scientific birth control information through the medium of clinics by the medical profession be the most logical method of checking the problem of over-population?

3. Would knowledge of birth control change the moral attitude of men and women toward the marriage bond or lower the moral standards of the youth of the country?

4. Do you believe that knowledge which enables parents to limit the families will make for human happiness, and raise the moral, social and intellectual standards of population?

We sent such a letter not only to those who, we thought, might agree with us, but we sent it also to our known opponents. Most of these people answered. Everyone who answered did so with sincerity and courtesy, with the exception of one group whose reply to this important question as demonstrated at the Town Hall last Sunday evening was a disgrace to liberty-loving people, and to all traditions we hold dear in the United States. [*Applause.*] I believed that the discussion of the moral issue was one which did not solely belong to theologians and to scientists, but belonged to the people. [*Applause.*] And because I believed that the people of this country may and can discuss this subject with dignity and with intelligence I desired to bring them together, and to discuss it in the open.

When one speaks of moral, one refers to human conduct. This implies action of many kinds, which in turn depends upon the mind and the brain. So that in speaking of morals one must remember that there is a direct connection between morality and brain development. Conduct is said to be action in pursuit of ends, and if this is so, then we must hold the irresponsibility and recklessness in our action is immoral, while responsibility and forethought put into action for the benefit of the individual and the race becomes in the highest sense the finest kind of morality.

We know that every advance that woman has made in the last half century has been made with opposition, all of which has been based upon the grounds of immorality. When women fought for higher education, it was said that this would cause her to become immoral and she would lose her place in the sanctity of the home. When women asked for the franchise it was said that this would lower her standard of morals, that it was not fit that she should meet with and mix with the members of the opposite sex, but we notice that there was no objection to her meeting with the same members of the opposite sex when she went to church. The church has ever opposed the progress of woman on the ground that her freedom would lead to immorality. We ask the church to have more confidence in women. We ask the opponents of this movement to reverse the methods of the church, which aims to keep women moral by keeping them in fear and in ignorance, and to inculcate into them a higher and truer morality based upon knowledge. [*Applause*]. And ours is the morality of knowledge. If we cannot trust woman with the knowledge of her own body, then I claim that two thousand years of Christian teaching has proved to be a failure. [*Applause.*]

We stand on the principle that birth control should be available to every adult man and woman. We believe that every adult man and woman should be taught the responsibility and the right use of knowledge. We claim that woman should have the right over her own body and to say if she shall or if she shall not be a mother, as she sees fit. [*Applause.*] We further claim that the first right of a child is to be desired. [*Applause.*] While the second right is that it should be conceived in love, and the third, that it should have a heritage of sound health.

Upon these principles the birth control movement in America stands.

When it comes to discussing the methods of birth control, that is far more difficult. There are laws in this country which forbid the imparting of practical information to the mothers of the land. We claim that every mother in this country, either sick or well, has the right to the best, the safest, the most scientific information. This information should be disseminated directly to the mothers through clinics by members of the medical profession, registered nurses and registered midwives. [*Applause.*]

Our first step is to have the backing of the medical profession so that our laws may be changed, so that motherhood may be the function of dignity and choice, rather than one of ignorance and chance. [*Applause.*] Conscious control of offspring is now becoming the ideal and the custom in all civilized countries.

Those who oppose it claim that however desirable it may be on economic or social grounds, it may be abused and the morals of the youth of the country may be lowered. Such people should be reminded that there are two points to be considered. First, that such control is the inevitable advance in civilization. Every civilization involves an increasing forethought for others, even for those yet unborn. [*Applause.*] The reckless abandonment of the impulse of the moment and the careless regard for the consequences is not morality [*Applause*]. The selfish gratification of temporary desire at the expense of suffering to lives that will come may seem very beautiful to some, but it is not our conception of civilization, or is it our concept of morality. [*Applause.*]

In the second place, it is not only inevitable, but it is right to control the size of the family for by this control and adjustment we can raise the level and the standards of the human race. While Nature's way of reducing her numbers is controlled by disease, famine and war, primitive man has achieved the same results by infanticide, exposure of infants, the abandonment of children, and by abortion. But such ways of controlling population is no longer possible for us. We have attained high standards of life, and along the lines of science must we conduct such control. We must begin farther back and control the beginnings of life. We must control conception. This is a better method; it is a more civilized method, for it involves not only greater forethought for others, but finally a higher sanction for the value of life itself.

Society is divided into three groups. Those intelligent and wealthy members of the upper classes who have obtained knowledge of birth control and exercise it in regulating the size of their families. They have already benefited by this knowledge, and are today considered the most respectable and moral members of the community. They have only children when they desire and all society points to them as types that should perpetuate their kind.

The second group is equally intelligent and responsible. They desire to control the size of their families, but are unable to obtain knowledge or to put such available knowledge into practice.

The third are those irresponsible and reckless ones having little regard for the consequence of their acts, or whose religious scruples prevent their exercising control over their numbers. Many of this group are diseased, feeble-minded, and are of the pauper element dependent entirely upon the normal and fit members of society for their support. There is no doubt in the minds of all thinking people that the procreation of this group should be stopped. [*Applause.*] For if they are not able to support and care for themselves, they should certainly not be allowed to bring offspring into this world for others to look after. [*Applause.*] We do not believe that filling the earth with misery, poverty and disease is moral. And it is our desire and intention to carry on our crusade until the perpetuation of such conditions has ceased.

We desire to stop at its source the disease, poverty and feeble-mindedness and insanity which exist today, for these lower the standards of civilization and make for race deterioration. We know that the masses of people are growing wiser and are using their own minds to decide their individual conduct. The more people of this kind we have, the less immorality shall exist. For the more responsible people grow, the higher they do and shall they attain real morality. [*Applause.*]

[GSTC]

William W. Husband, Report of the Commissioner General of Immigration, The Per Centum Limit Act of 1921

June 30, 1923

In the country of immigrants, immigration has been a repeatedly debated issue. With the passing of the Immigration Act of 1891, there came official policies and new quota systems. The Bureau of Immigration moved into the Department of Labor in 1913 and eventually became the Immigration and Naturalization Service. William W. Husband (1871–1942), a former executive secretary of the U.S. Immigration Commission, became the Commissioner General of Immigration in 1921 and was responsible for this report in which recent immigration policy was reviewed: "Even a casual survey of congressional discussions of the immigration problem during the past quarter of a century demonstrates very clearly that while the law makers were deeply concerned with the mental, moral, and physical quality of immigrants, there developed as time went on an even greater concern as to the fundamental racial character of the constantly increasing numbers who came."

DEPARTMENT OF LABOR,
BUREAU OF IMMIGRATION,
Washington, June 30, 1923.

THE PER CENTUM LIMIT ACT OF 1921.

THE FISCAL YEAR just ended was the second during which the so-called per centum limit immigration act of May 19, 1921, was in operation, and because of this the statistical records of the Immigration Service are peculiarly interesting and significant. The law is still new, and there is so much evidence that its purpose and provisions are not fully understood that a brief discussion of what it is and of the events which led to its enactment by Congress may be appropriate at this time.

Perhaps it is not very generally realized that the per centum limit law marked the beginning of actual restriction or limitation of immigration to the United States from Europe, Africa, Australasia, and a considerable part of Asia. The Chinese exclusion act of 1882, the passport agreement with Japan which became effective in 1908, and the "barred zone" provision in the general immigration law of 1917 had already stopped or greatly reduced the influx of oriental peoples, but so far as others, and particularly Europeans, were concerned, all applicants who met the various tests prescribed in the general law were admitted. This general law, first enacted in 1882 and several times revised and strengthened, was and still is based on the principle of selection rather than of numerical restriction. It is probably true that the provision barring illiterate aliens front admission, which was added to the general law in 1917, was intended as a restrictive measure rather than a quality test, but in its practical effect it was only another addition to the already numerous class of alleged undesirables who were denied admission, and obviously could not be relied upon actually to limit the volume of immigration.

The immigration act of 1882, which, as already indicated, was the first general law upon the subject, provided for the exclusion from the United States of the following classes only: Convicts, lunatics, idiots, and persons likely to become a public charge. This law underwent more or less important revisions in 1891, 1893, 1903, 1907, and 1917, until the last-mentioned act, which is the present general immigration law, denies admission to many classes of aliens, including the following: Idiots, imbeciles, feeble-minded persons, epileptics, insane persons; persons who have had one or more attacks of insanity at any time previously; persons of constitutional psychopathic inferiority; persons with chronic alcoholism; paupers; professional beggars; vagrants; persons afflicted with tuberculosis in any form or with a loathsome or dangerous contagious disease; persons certified by the examining physician as being mentally or physically defective, such physical defect being of a nature which may affect the ability of the alien to earn a living; persons who have been convicted of or admit having committed a felony or other crime or misdemeanor involving moral turpitude; polygamists, or persons who practice polygamy or believe in or advocate the practice of polygamy; anarchists and similar classes; immoral persons and persons coming for an immoral purpose; contract laborers; persons likely to become a public charge; persons seeking admission within one year of date of previous debarment or deportation; persons whose ticket or passage is paid for with the money of another or who are assisted by others to come, unless it is affirmatively shown that such persons do not belong to one of the foregoing excluded classes; persons whose ticket or passage is paid for by any corporation, association, society, municipality, or foreign government, either directly or indirectly; stowaways; children under 10 years of age unless accompanied by one or both of their parents; persons who are natives of certain geographically defined territory; aliens over 16 years of age who are unable to read some language or dialect; certain accompanying aliens, as described in the last proviso of section 18 of the act; and persons who have arrived in Canada or Mexico by certain steamship lines. Persons who fail to meet certain passport requirements were added to the excluded classes in subsequent legislation.

Obviously it would be difficult to find, or even to invent, many other terms denoting individual undesirability which might be added to the foregoing list, but, as already pointed out, the general law is essentially selective in theory, for even its most rigid application with respect to the excludable classes above enumerated could not be depended upon to prevent the coming of unlimited numbers of aliens who were able to meet the tests imposed.

Even a casual survey of congressional discussions of the immigration problem during the past quarter of a century demonstrates very clearly that while the law makers were deeply concerned with the mental, moral, and physical quality of immigrants, there developed as time went on an even greater concern as to the fundamental racial character of the constantly increasing numbers who came. The record of alien arrivals year by year had shown a gradual falling off in the immigration of northwest European peoples, representing racial stocks which were common to America even in colonial days, and a rapid and remarkably large increase in the movement from southern and eastern European countries and Asiatic Turkey. Immigration from the last-named sources reached an annual average of about

750,000 and in some years nearly a million came, and there seems to have been a general belief in Congress that it would increase rather than diminish. At the same time no one seems to have anticipated a revival of the formerly large influx from the "old sources," as the countries of northwest Europe came to be known.

This remarkable change in the sources and racial character of our immigrants led to an almost continuous agitation of the immigration problem both in and out of Congress, and there was a steadily growing demand for restriction, particularly of the newer movement from the south and east of Europe. During the greater part of this period of agitation the so-called literacy test for aliens was the favorite weapon of the restrictionists, and its widespread popularity appears to have been based quite largely on a belief, or at least a hope, that it would reduce to some extent the stream of "new" immigration, about one-third of which was illiterate, without seriously interfering with the coming of the older type, among whom illiteracy was at a minimum.

Presidents Cleveland and Taft vetoed immigration bills because they contained a literacy test provision, and President Wilson vetoed two bills largely for the same reason. In 1917, however, Congress passed a general immigration bill which included the literacy provision over the President's veto, and, with certain exceptions, aliens who are unable to read are no longer admitted to the United States. At that time, however, the World War had already had the effect of reducing immigration from Europe to a low level, and our own entry into the conflict a few days before the law in question went into effect, practically stopped it altogether. Consequently, the value of the literacy provision as a means of restricting European immigration was never fairly tested under normal conditions.

The Congress, however, seemingly realized that even the comprehensive immigration law of 1917, including the literacy test, would afford only a frail barrier against the promised rush from the war-stricken countries of Europe, and in December, 1920, the House of Representatives, with little opposition, passed a bill to suspend practically all immigration for the time being. The per centum limit plan was substituted by the Senate, however, and the substitute prevailed in Congress, but it failed to become a law at the time because President Wilson withheld executive approval. Nevertheless, favorable action was not long delayed, for at the special session called at the beginning of the present administration the measure was quickly enacted, and, with President Harding's approval, became a law on May 19, 1921. This law expired by limitation June 30, 1922, but by the act of May 11, 1922, its life was extended to June 30, 1924, and some strengthening amendments were added.

The principal provisions of the per centum limit act, or the "quota law," as it is popularly known, are as follows:

The number of aliens of any nationality who may be admitted to the United States in any fiscal year shall not exceed 3 per cent of the number of persons of such nationality who were resident in the United States according to the census of 1910.

Monthly quotas are limited to 20 per cent of the annual quota.

For the purposes of the act, "nationality" is determined by country of birth.

The law does not apply to the following classes of aliens: Government officials; aliens in transit; aliens visiting the United States as tourists or temporarily for business or pleasure; aliens from countries immigration from which is regulated in accordance with treaties or agreement relating solely to immigration, otherwise China and Japan; aliens from the so-called Asiatic barred zone; aliens who have resided continuously for at least five years in Canada, Newfoundland, Cuba, Mexico, Central or South America, or adjacent islands; aliens under the age of 18 who are children of citizens of the United States.

Certain other classes of aliens who are counted against quotas are admissible after a quota is exhausted. The following are included in this category: Aliens returning from a temporary visit abroad; aliens who are professional actors, artists, lecturers, singers, ministers of any religious denomination, professors for colleges or seminaries, members of any recognized learned profession, or aliens employed as domestic servants.

So far as possible preference is given to the wives and certain near relatives of citizens of the United States, applicants for citizenship, and honorably discharged soldiers, eligible to citizenship, who served in the United States military or naval forces at any time between April 6, 1917, and November 11, 1918.

Transportation companies are liable to a fine of $200 for each alien brought to a United States port in excess of the quota and where such fine is imposed the amount paid for passage must be returned to the rejected alien.

The quota limit law is in addition to and not in substitution for the provisions of the immigration laws. [...]

[CGI]

William Jennings Bryan,
The Scopes "Monkey Trial"

July 16, 1925

In these excerpts from the fifth day's proceedings of the Scopes trial, the most famous American trial of the first half of the twentieth century, the lawyer William Jennings Bryan, former Secretary of State under Woodrow Wilson and three-time presidential candidate, defends the State of Tennessee's right to have made and to enforce laws banning the teaching of evolution in its public schools. He discusses not only the pervasive Christian belief of the state's citizens but the unwelcome interest and participation of outsiders at this trial. The debate he highlights between the teaching of science versus religious beliefs continues today: "The people of this state passed this law, the people of this state knew what they were doing when they passed the law, and they knew the dangers of the doctrine—that they did not want it taught to their children, and my friends." Bryan died only a few days after the trial ended.

IF THE COURT please we are now approaching the end of the first week of this trial and I haven't thought it proper until this time to take part in the discussions that have been dealing with phases of this question, or case, where the state laws and the state rules of practice were under discussion and I feel that those who are versed in the law of the state and who are used to the customs of the court might better take the burden of the case, but today we come to the discussion of a very important part of this case, a question so important that upon its decision will determine the length of this trial. If the court holds, as we believe the court should hold, that the testimony that the defense is now offering is not competent and not proper testimony, then I assume we are near the end of this trial and because the question involved is not confined to local questions, but is the broadest that will possibly arise, I have felt justified in submitting my views on the case for the consideration of the court. I have been tempted to speak at former times, but I have been able to withstand the temptation. I have been drawn into the case by, I think nearly all the lawyers on the other side. The principal attorney has often suggested that I am the arch-conspirator and that I am responsible for the presence of this case and I have almost been credited with leadership of the ignorance and bigotry which he thinks he could alone inspire a law like this. Then Mr. Malone has seen fit to honor me by quoting my opinion on religious liberty. I assume he means that that is the most important opinion on religious liberty that he has been able to find in this country and I feel complimented that I should be picked out from all the men living and dead as the one whose expressions are most vital to the welfare of our country. And this morning I was credited with being the cause of the presence of these so-called experts.

Mr. Hays says that before he got here he read that I said this was to be a duel to the death, between science—was it?—and revealed religion. I don't know who the other duelist was, but I was representing one of them and because of that they went to the trouble and the expense of several thousand dollars to bring down their witnesses. Well, my friend, if you said that this was important enough to be regarded as a duel between two great ideas or groups I certainly will be given credit for foreseeing what I could not then know and that is that this question is so important between religion and irreligion that even the invoking of the divine blessing upon it might seem partisan and partial. I think when we come to consider the importance of this question, that all of us who are interested as lawyers on either side, could claim what we—what your honor so graciously grants—a hearing. I have got down here for fear I might forget them, certain points that I desire to present for your honor's consideration.

In the first place, the statute—our position is that the statute is sufficient. The statute defines exactly what the people of Tennessee desired and intended and did declare unlawful and it needs no interpretation. The caption speaks of the evolutionary theory and the statute specifically states that teachers are forbidden to teach in the schools supported by taxation in this state, any theory of creation of man that denies the divine record of man's creation as found in the Bible, and that there might be no difference of opinion—there might be no ambiguity—that there might be no such confusion of thought as our learned friends attempt to inject into it, the legislature was careful to define what it meant by the first part of the statute. It says to teach that man is a descendant of any lower form of life—if that had not been there—if the first sentence had been the only sentence in the statute, then these gentlemen might come and ask to define what that meant or to explain whether the thing that was taught was contrary to the language of the statute in the first sentence, but the second sentence removes all doubt, as has been stated by my colleague. The second sentence points out specifically what is meant, and that is the teaching that man is the descendant of any lower form of life, and if the defendant taught that as we have proven by the textbook that he used and as we have proven by the students that went to hear him—if he taught that man is a descendant of any lower form of life, he violated that statute, and more than that we have his own confession that he knew he was violating the statute. We have the testimony here of Mr. White, the superintendent of schools, who says that Mr. Scopes told him he could not teach that book without violating the law. We have the testimony of Mr. Robertson—Robinson—the head of the Board of Education, who talked with Mr. Scopes just at the time the schools closed, or a day or two afterward, and Mr. Scopes told him that he had reviewed that book just before the school closed, and that he could not teach it without teaching evolution and without violating the law, and we have Mr. Robinson's statement that Mr. Scopes told him that he and one of the teachers, Mr. Ferguson, had talked it over after the law was passed and had decided that they could not teach it without the violation of the law, and yet while Mr. Scopes knew what the law was, and knew that it violated the law, he proceeded to violate the law.

That is the evidence before this court, and we do not need any expert to tell us what that law means. An expert cannot be permitted to come in here and try to defeat the enforcement of a law by testifying that it isn't a bad law and it isn't—I mean a bad doctrine—no matter how these people phrase the doctrine—no matter how they eulogize it. This is not the place to try to prove that the law ought never to have been passed. The place to prove that, or teach that, was to the legislature. If these people were so anxious to keep the state of Tennessee from disgracing itself, if they were so afraid that by this action taken by the legislature, the state would put itself before the people of the nation as ignorant people and bigoted people—if they had half the affection for Tennessee that you would think they had as they come here to testify, they would have come at a time when their testimony would have been valuable and not at this time to ask you to refuse to enforce a law because they did not think the law ought to have been passed.

And, my friends, if the people of Tennessee were to go into a state like New York—the one from which this impulse comes to resist this law, or go into any state—if they went into any state and tried to convince the people that a law they had passed ought not to be enforced, just because the people who went there didn't think it ought to have been passed, don't you think it would be resented as an impertinence?... The people of this state passed this law, the people of this state knew what they were doing when they passed the law, and they knew the dangers of the doctrine—that they did not want it taught to their children, and my friends. It isn't—Your Honor—it isn't proper to bring experts in here to try to defeat the purpose of the people of this state by trying to show that this thing that they denounce and outlaw is a beautiful thing that everybody ought to believe in.... These people want to come here with experts to make Your Honor believe that the law should never have been passed and because in their opinion it ought not to have been passed, it ought not to be enforced. It isn't a place for expert testimony. We have sufficient proof in the book—doesn't the book state the very thing that is objected to, and outlawed in this state? Who has a copy of that book?

The Court: Do you mean the Bible?

Mr. Bryan: No, sir; the biology. *(Laughter in the courtroom.)*

A Voice: Here it is; Hunter's Biology.

Mr. Bryan: No, not the Bible, you see in this state they cannot teach the Bible. They can only teach things that declare it to be a lie, according to the learned counsel. These people in the state—Christian people—have tied their hands by their constitution. They say we all believe in the Bible, for it is the overwhelming belief in the state, but we will not teach that Bible, which we believe, even to our children through teachers that we pay with our money. No, no, it isn't the teaching of the Bible, and we are not asking it. The question is can a minority in this state come in and compel a teacher to teach that the Bible is not true and make the parents of these children pay the expenses of the teacher to tell their children what these people believe is false and dangerous? Has it come to a time when, the minority can take charge of a state like Tennessee and compel the majority to pay their teachers while they take religion out of the heart of the children of the parents who pay the teachers?...

So, my friends, if that were true, if man and monkey were in the same class, called primates, it would mean they did not come up from the same order. It might mean that instead of one being the ancestor of the other they were all cousins. But it does not mean that they did not come up from the lower animals, if this is the only place they could come from, and the Christian believes man came from above, but the evolutionist believes he must have come from below...

Your Honor, I want to show you that we have evidence enough here, we do not need any experts to come in here and tell us about this thing. Here we have Mr. Hunter. Mr. Hunter is the author of this biology and this is the man who wrote the book Mr. Scopes was teaching. And here we have the diagram....

There is that book! There is the book they were teaching your children that man was a mammal and so indistinguishable among the mammals that they leave him there with thirty-four hundred and ninety-nine other mammals....

He tells the children to copy this, copy this diagram. In the note-book, children are to copy this diagram and take it home in their notebooks. To show their parents that you cannot find man. That is the great game to put in the public schools to find man among animals, if you can.

Tell me that the parents of this day have not any right to declare that children are not to be taught this doctrine? Shall not be taken down from the high plane upon which God put man? Shall be detached from the throne of God and be compelled to link their ancestors with the jungle, tell that to these children? Why, my friend, if they believe it, they go back to scoff at the religion of their parents! And the parents have a right to say that no teacher paid by their money shall rob their children of faith in God and send them back to their homes, skeptical, infidels, or agnostics, or atheists....

Your Honor, we first pointed out that we do not need any experts in science. Here is one plain fact, and the statute defines itself, and it tells the kind of evolution it does not want taught, and the evidence says that this is the kind of evolution that was taught, and no number of scientists could come in here, my friends, and override that statute or take from the jury its right to decide this question, so that all the experts that they could bring would mean nothing. And, when it comes to Bible experts, every member of the jury is as good an expert on the Bible as any man that they could bring, or that we could bring.... We have a book here that shows everything that is needed to make one understand evolution, and to show that the man violated the law. Then why should we prolong this case? We can bring our experts here for the Christians; for every one they can bring who does not believe in Christianity, we can bring more than one who believes in the Bible and rejects evolution, and our witnesses will be just as good experts as theirs on a question of that kind. We could have a thousand or a million witnesses, but this case as to whether evolution is true or not, is not going to be tried here, within this city; if it is carried to the state's courts, it will not be tried there, and if it is taken to the great court at Washington, it will not be tried there. No, my friends, no court or the law, and no jury, great or small, is going to destroy the issue between the believer and the unbeliever.

The Bible is the Word of God; the Bible is the only expression of man's hope of salvation.... That Bible is not going to be driven out of this court by experts who come hundreds of miles to testify that they can reconcile evolution, with its ancestor in the jungle, with man made by God in His image, and put here for purposes as a part of the divine plan.... Your court is an office of this state, and we who represent the state as counsel are officers of the state, and we cannot humiliate the great state of Tennessee by admitting for a moment that people can come from anywhere and protest against the enforcement of this state's laws on the ground that it does not conform with their ideas, or because it banishes from our schools a thing that they believe in and think ought to be taught in spite of the protest of those who employ the teacher and pay him his salary.

The facts are simple, the case is plain, and if those gentlemen want to enter upon a larger field of educational work on the subject of evolution, let us get through with this case and then convene a mock court, for it will deserve the title of mock court if its purpose is to banish from the hearts of the people the Word of God as revealed.

[IS]

The Sacco-Vanzetti Case, Bartolomeo Vanzetti, Statement to Court after Being Sentenced to Death

April 9, 1927

Nicola Sacco (1891–1927) and Bartolomeo Vanzetti (1888–1927) were Italian immigrants accused of murder in 1920 in Braintree, near Boston. Their trial ran for several weeks in 1921 and attracted national and international attention, as many believed they had been accused because of their political, that is, anarchist beliefs. They were executed on August 23, 1927.

What I say is that I am innocent. Everybody that knows these two arms knows very well that I did not need to go into the streets and kill a man or try to take money. I can live by my two hands and live well. But besides that, I can live even without work with my hands for other people. I have had plenty of chance to live independently and to live what the world conceives to be a higher life than to gain our bread with the sweat of our brow.

My father in Italy is in a good condition. I could have come back in Italy and he would have welcomed me every time with open arms. Even if I come back there with not a cent in my pocket, my father could have give me a position, not to work but to make business, or to oversee upon the land that he owns. He has wrote me many letters in that sense, and as another well-to-do relative has wrote me letters in that sense that I can produce.

Now, I should say that I am not only innocent of all these things, not only have I never committed a real crime in my life – though some sins but not crimes – not only have I struggled all my life to eliminate crimes, the crimes that the official law and the moral law condemns, but also the crime that the moral law and the official law sanction and sanctify, the exploitation and the oppression of the man by the man.

There is the best man I ever cast my eyes upon since I lived, a man that will last and will grow always more near to and more dear to the heart of the people, so long as admiration for goodness, for virtues, and for sacrifice will last. I mean Eugene Victor Debs. He has said that not even a dog that kills chickens would have found an American jury disposed to convict it with the proof that the Commonwealth has produced against us. That man was not with me in Plymouth or with Sacco where he was on the day of the crime. You can say that it is arbitrary, what we are saying from him, that he is good and he applied to the other his goodness, that he is incapable of crime, and he believed that everybody is incapable of crime.

He knew, and not only he knew, but every man of understanding in the world, not only in this country but also in other countries, men to whom we have provided a certain amount of the records of the case at times, they all know and still stick with us, the flower of mankind of Europe, the better writers, the greatest thinkers of Europe, have pleaded in our favor. The scientists, the greatest scientists, the greatest statesmen of Europe, have pleaded in our favor.

Is it possible that only a few, a handful of men of the jury, only two or three other men, who would shame their mother for worldly honor and for earthly fortune; is it possible that they are right against what the world, for the whole world has said that it is wrong and I know that it is wrong? If there is one that should know it, if it is right or if it is wrong, it is I and this man. You see it is seven years that we are in jail. What we have suffered during these seven years no human tongue can say, and yet you see me before you, not trembling, you see me looking you in your eyes straight, not blushing, not changing color, not ashamed or in fear.

We were tried during a time whose character has now passed into history. I mean by that, a time when there was a hysteria of resentment and hate against the people of our principles, against the foreigner, against slackers, and it seems to me – rather, I am positive of it, that both you and Mr. Katzmann have done all what it were in your power in order to work out, in order to agitate still more the passion of the juror, the prejudice of the juror, against us.

The jury were hating us because we were against the war, and the jury don't know that it makes any difference between a man that is against the war because he believes that the war is unjust, because he hate no country, because he is a cosmopolitan, and a man that is against the war because he is in favor of the other country that fights against the country in which he is, and therefore a spy, an enemy, and he commits any crime in the country in which he is in behalf of the other country in order to serve the other country. We are not men of that kind. Nobody can say that we are German spies or spies of any kind.

We believe more now than ever that the war was wrong, and we are against war more now than ever, and I am glad to be on the doomed scaffold if I can say to mankind, "Look out; you are in a catacomb of the flower of mankind. For what? All that they say to you, all that they have promised to you – it was a lie, it was an illusion, it was a cheat, it was a fraud, it was a crime. They promised you liberty. Where is liberty? They promised you prosperity. Where is prosperity?

I never committed a crime in my life – I have never stolen and I have never killed and I have never spilt blood, and I have fought against crime, and I have fought and I have sacrificed myself even to eliminate the crimes that the law and the church legitimate and sanctify.

This is what I say: I would not wish to a dog or to a snake, to the most low and misfortunate creature of the earth – I would not wish to any of them what I have had to suffer for things that I am not guilty of. I am suffering because I am a radical and indeed I am a radical; I have suffered because I was an Italian, and indeed I am an Italian; I have suffered more for my family and for my beloved than for myself; but I am so convinced to be right that you can only kill me once but if you could execute me two times, and if I could be reborn two other times, I would live again to do what I have done already.

[SI]

Alfred E. Smith, Speech, "Religious Prejudice and Politics"

September 20, 1928

As the Democratic nominee for the presidency of the United States, Smith (1873–1944), the governor of New York State, campaigned across the country. He was the first Roman Catholic nominee from a major party for the presidency, and he directly addressed this as an issue in the radio broadcast speech that follows. Herbert Hoover defeated him in the election on November 6.

I FEEL THAT I owe it to the Democratic Party to talk out plainly. If I had listened to the counselors that advised political expediency I would probably keep quiet, but I'm not by nature a quiet man. [*Laughter and applause.*]

I never keep anything to myself. I talk it out. And I feel I owe it, not only to the party, but I sincerely believe that I owe it to the country itself to drag this un-American propaganda out into the open.

Because this country, to my way of thinking, cannot be successful if it ever divides on sectarian lines. [*Applause.*] If there are any considerable number of our people that are going to listen to appeals to their passion and to their prejudice, if bigotry and intolerance and their sister vices are going to succeed, it is dangerous for the future life of the Republic, and the best way to kill anything un-American is to drag it out into the open; because anything un-American cannot live in the sunlight. [*Applause.*]

Where does all this propaganda come from? Who is paying for its distribution? One of the women leaders of North Carolina was talking to me in the executive chamber in Albany about two weeks ago, and she said: "Governor, I have some notion about the cost of distributing election material. The amount of it that has come into our state could not be printed and distributed for less than $1,000,000."

Where is the money coming from? I think we got the answer the other day when a woman went into the national committee in Washington and meekly walked up to the man in charge and said: "I want some literature on Governor Smith; I want the non-political kind." And he brought her down stairs, put her in an automobile and took her over to an office where a paper is published called 'The Fellowship Forum,' which, for a number of years, has been engaged in this senseless, foolish, stupid attack upon the Catholic Church and the members of the faith. [*Applause.*]

Prior to the convention the grand dragon of the Realm of Arkansas wrote to one of the delegates from Arkansas, and in the letter he advised the delegate that he not vote for me in the national convention, and he put it on the ground of upholding American ideals against institutions as established by our forefathers. Now, can you think of any man or any group of men banded together in what they call the Ku-Klux Klan, who profess to be 100 per cent Americans, and forget the great principle that Jefferson stood for, the equality of man, and forget that our forefathers in their wisdom, foreseeing probably such a sight as we look at today, wrote into the fundamental law of the country that at no time was religion to be regarded as a qualification for public office.

Just think of a man breathing the spirit of hatred against millions of his fellow citizens, proclaiming and subscribing at the same time to the doctrine of Jefferson, of Lincoln, of Roosevelt and of Wilson. Why, there is no greater mockery in this world today than the burning of the Cross, the emblem of faith, the emblem of salvation, the place upon which Christ Himself made the great sacrifice for all of mankind, by these people who are spreading this propaganda, while the Christ they are supposed to adore, love and venerate, during all of His lifetime on earth, taught the holy, sacred writ of brotherly love.

So much for him. (A voice: "That is plenty.")

Now we know there is another lie, or series of lies, being carefully put out around the country, and it is surprising to find the number of people who seem to believe it. I would have refrained from talking about this if it were not for the avalanche of letters that have poured into the national committee and have poured into my own office in the executive department at Albany asking for the facts. And that is the lie that has been spread around: that since I have been Governor of the State of New York nobody has ever been appointed to office but Catholics. (Loud noises.)

We are losing time on the radio. Please wait.

The cabinet of the governorship is made up of fourteen men. Three of them are Catholics, ten of them are Protestants and one of them is a Jew. [*Applause.*] Outside of the cabinet members, the Governor appoints two boards and commissions under the cabinet of twenty-six people. Twelve of them are Catholics, fourteen of them are Protestants. Aside from that of his boards and commissions, the Governor appoints 157. Thirty-five of them are Catholics, 106 of them are Protestants, twelve of them are Jews, and four I was unable to find out anything about. [*Laughter and applause.*]

"Judicial appointments, county appointments, and all positions in the various judicial and country districts of the state not directly related to the Executive Department, although appointed by the Governor to fill vacancies: Total number of appointments, 175; 64 Catholics, 90 Protestants, and 12 that we don't know anything about. [*Laughter and applause.*]

Now just another word and I am going to finish. Here is the meanest thing that I have seen in the whole campaign. This is the product of the lowest and most cunning mind that could train itself to do something mean and dirty. This was sent to me by a member of the Masonic order, a personal friend of mine. It purports to be a circular sent out under Catholic auspices to Catholic voters and tells how "We have control in New York, stick together and we'll get control of the country." And designedly it said to the roster of the Masonic order in my state, because so many of that order are friends of mine and have been voting for me for the last ten years. "Stand together."

Now, I disown that circular, the Democratic Party disowns it, and I have no right to talk for the Catholic Church, but I'll take a chance and say that nobody inside of the Catholic Church has been stupid enough to do a thing like that. [*Applause.*]

Let me make myself perfectly clear. I do not want any Catholic in the United States of America to vote for me on the 6th of November because I am a Catholic (applause). If any Catholic in this country believes that the welfare, the well-being, the prosperity, the growth and the expansion of the United States is best conserved and best promoted by the election of Hoover, I want him to vote for Hoover and not for me (applause).

But, on the other hand, I have the right to say that any citizen of this country that believes I can promote its welfare, that I am capable of steering the ship of state safely through the next four years and then votes against me because of my religion, he is not a real, pure, genuine American. [*Applause.*]

[GSTC]

President Herbert Hoover, Speech, "Rugged Individualism"

October 22, 1928

At the time of this speech, Herbert Hoover (1874–1964) was the Republican Presidential nominee. He had made a name for himself as an organizer of complicated relief efforts; during World War I as the head of the Food Administration, he arranged getting tons of food to the hungry civilians in the ravaged areas of Europe. Despite his having served as Secretary of Commerce under the last two presidents, his ardent anti-government sentiments resounded with the voters and helped him win the presidency in November. In 1929 the stock market crashed and brought on the Great Depression. Hoover lost the presidential election in 1932 to Franklin Delano Roosevelt. The most inspirational sections of his speech follow.

[...] AFTER THE WAR, when the Republican Party assumed administration of the country, we were faced with the problem of determination of the very nature of our national life. During 150 years we have built up a form of self-government and a social system which is peculiarly our own. It differs essentially from all others in the world. It is the American system. It is just as definite and positive a political and social system as has ever been developed on earth. It is founded upon a particular conception of self-government; in which decentralized local responsibility is the very base. Further than this, it is founded upon the conception that only through ordered liberty, freedom and equal opportunity to the individual will his initiative and enterprise spur on the march of progress. And in our insistence upon equality of opportunity has our system advanced beyond the entire world.

During the war we necessarily turned to the Government to solve every difficult economic problem. The Government having absorbed every energy of our people for war, there was no other solution. For the preservation of the State, the Federal Government became a centralized despotism which undertook unprecedented responsibilities, assumed autocratic powers, and took over the business of citizens. To a large degree we regimented our whole people temporarily into a socialistic state. However justified in time of war, if continued in peace time it would destroy not only our American system but with it our progress and freedom as well.

When the war closed, the most vital of all issues both in our own country and throughout the world was whether Governments should continue their wartime ownership and operation of many instrumentalities of production and distribution. We were challenged with a peace-time choice between the American system of rugged individualism and a European philosophy of diametrically opposed doctrines—doctrines of paternalism and state socialism. The acceptance of these ideas would have meant the destruction of self-government through centralization of government. It would have meant the undermining of the individual initiative and enterprise through which our people have grown to unparalleled greatness.

The Republican Party from the beginning resolutely turned its face away from these ideas and these war practices. A Republican Congress cooperated with the Democratic administration to demobilize many of our war activities. At that time the two parties were accord upon that point. When the Republican Party came into full power, it went at once resolutely back to our fundamental conception of the state and the rights and responsibilities of the individual. Thereby it restored confidence and hope in the American people, it freed and stimulated enterprise; it restored the Government to its position as an umpire instead of a player in the economic game. For these reasons the American people have gone forward in progress while the rest of the world has halted, and some countries have even gone backwards. If anyone will study the causes of retarded recuperation in Europe, he will find much of it due to the stifling of private initiative on one hand, and overloading of the Government with business on the other.

There has been revived in this campaign, however, a series of proposals which, if adopted, would be a long step toward the abandonment of our American system and surrender to the destructive operation of governmental conduct of commercial business. Because the country is faced with difficulty and doubt over certain national problems—that is, prohibition, farm relief and electrical power—our opponents propose that we must thrust government a long way into the businesses which give rise to these problems. In effect, they abandon the tenets of their own party and turn to state socialism as a solution for the difficulties presented by all three. It is proposed that we shall change from prohibition to the state purchase and sale of liquor. If their agricultural relief program means anything, it means that the Government shall directly or indirectly buy and sell and fix prices of agricultural products. And we are to go into the hydroelectric-power business. In other words, we are confronted with a huge program of government in business. [...]

The first problem of the government about to adventure in commercial business is to determine a method of administration. It must secure leadership and direction. Shall this leadership be chosen by political agencies or shall we make it elective? The hard practical fact is that leadership in business must come through the sheer rise in ability and character. That rise can only take place in the free atmosphere of competition. Competition is closed by bureaucracy. Political agencies are feeble channels through which to select able leaders to conduct commercial business.

Government, in order to avoid the possible incompetence, corruption and tyranny of too great authority in individuals entrusted with commercial business, inevitably turns to boards and commissions. To make sure that there are checks and balances, each member of such boards and commissions must have equal authority. Each has his separate responsibility to the public, and at once we have the conflict of ideas and the lack of decision which would ruin any commercial business. It has contributed greatly to the demoralization of our shipping business. Moreover, these commissions must be representative of different sections and different political parties, so that at once we have an entire blight upon coordinated action within their ranks which destroys any possibility of effective administration.

Moreover, our legislative bodies cannot in fact delegate their full authority to commissions or to individuals for the conduct of matters vital to the American people; for if we would preserve government by the people we must preserve the authority of our legislators in the activities of our government.

Thus every time the Federal Government goes into a commercial business, 531 Senators and Congressmen become the actual board of directors of that business. Every time a state government goes into business, one or two hundred state senators and legislators become the actual directors of that business. Even if they were supermen and if there were no politics in the United States, no body of such numbers could competently direct commercial activities; for that requires initiative, instant decision, and action. It took Congress six years of constant discussion to even decide what the method of administration of Muscle Shoals should be.

When the Federal Government undertakes to go into business, the state governments are at once deprived of control and taxation of that business; when a state government undertakes to go into business, it at once deprives the municipalities of taxation and control of that business. Municipalities, being local and close to the people, can, at times, succeed in business where Federal and State Governments must fail.

We have trouble enough with log rolling in legislative bodies today. It originates naturally from desires of citizens to advance their particular section or to secure some necessary service. It would be multiplied a thousand-fold were the Federal and state governments in these businesses.

The effect upon our economic progress would be even worse. Business progressiveness is dependent on competition. New methods and new ideas are the outgrowth of the spirit of adventure, of individual initiative and of individual enterprise. Without adventure there is no progress. No government administration can rightly take chances with taxpayers' money. [...]

The Government in commercial business does not tolerate amongst its customers the freedom of competitive reprisals to which private business is subject. Bureaucracy does not tolerate the spirit of independence; it spreads the spirit of submission into our daily life and penetrates the temper of our people not with the habit of powerful resistance to wrong but with the habit of timid acceptance of irresistible might.

Bureaucracy is ever desirous of spreading its influence and its power. You cannot extend the mastery of the government over the daily working life of a people without at the same time making it the master of the people's souls and thoughts. Every expansion of government in business means that government in order to protect itself from the political consequences of its errors and wrongs is driven irresistibly without peace to greater and greater control of the nations' press and platform. Free speech does not live many hours after free industry and free commerce die.

It is a false liberalism that interprets itself into the Government operation of commercial business. Every step of bureaucratizing of the business of our country poisons the very roots of liberalism—that is, political equality, free speech, free assembly, free press, and equality of opportunity. It is the road not to more liberty, but to less liberty. Liberalism should be found not striving to spread bureaucracy but striving to set bounds to it. True liberalism seeks all legitimate freedom first in the confident belief that without such freedom the pursuit of all other blessings and benefits is vain. That belief is the foundation of all American progress, political as well as economic.

Liberalism is a force truly of the spirit, a force proceeding from the deep realization that economic freedom cannot be sacrificed if political freedom is to be preserved. Even if governmental conduct of business could give us more efficiency instead of less efficiency, the fundamental objection to it would remain unaltered and unabated. It would destroy political equality. It would increase rather than decrease abuse and corruption. It would stifle initiative and invention. It would undermine the development of leadership. It would cramp and cripple the mental and spiritual energies of our people. It would extinguish equality and opportunity. It would dry up the spirit of liberty and progress. For these reasons primarily it must be resisted. For a hundred and fifty years liberalism has found its true spirit in the American system, not in the European systems.

I do not wish to be misunderstood in this statement. I am defining a general policy. It does not mean that our government is to part with one iota of its national resources without complete protection to the public interest. I have already stated that where the government is engaged in public works for purposes of flood control, of navigation, of irrigation, of scientific research or national defense, or in pioneering a new art, it will at times necessarily produce power or commodities as a by-product. But they must be a by-product of the major purpose, not the major purpose itself.

Nor do I wish to be misinterpreted as believing that the United States is free-for-all and devil-take-the-hind-most. The very essence of equality of opportunity and of American individualism is that there shall be no domination by any group or combination in this Republic, whether it be business or political. On the contrary, it demands economic justice as well as political and social justice. It is no system of laissez faire. [...]

One of the great problems of government is to determine to what extent the Government shall regulate and control commerce and industry and how much it shall leave it alone. No system is perfect. We have had many abuses in the private conduct of business. That every good citizen resents. It is just as important that business keep out of government as that government keep out of business.

Nor am I setting up the contention that our institutions are perfect. No human ideal is ever perfectly attained, since humanity itself is not perfect. The wisdom of our forefathers in their conception that progress can only be attained as the sum of the accomplishment of free individuals has been re-enforced by all of the great leaders of the country since that day. Jackson, Lincoln, Cleveland, McKinley, Roosevelt, Wilson, and Coolidge have stood unalterably for these principles.

And what have been the results of our American system? Our country has become the land of opportunity to those born without inheritance, not merely because of the wealth of its resources and industry but because of this freedom of initiative and enterprise. Russia has natural resources equal to ours. Her people are equally industrious, but she has not had the blessings of 150 years of our form of government and of our social system.

By adherence to the principles of decentralized self-government, ordered liberty, equal opportunity and freedom to the individual, our American experiment in human welfare has yielded a degree of well-being unparalleled in the entire world. It has come nearer to the abolition of poverty, to the abolition of fear of want, than humanity has ever reached before. Progress of the past seven years is the proof of it. This alone furnishes the answer to our opponents who ask us to introduce destructive elements into the system by which this has been accomplished. [...]

The foundations of progress and prosperity are dependent as never before upon the wise policies of government, for government now touches at a thousand points the intricate web of economic and social life. Under administration by the Republican Party in the last 7 1/2 years our country as a whole has made unparalleled progress and this has been in generous part reflected to this great city. Prosperity is no idle expression. It is a job for every worker; it is the safety and the safeguard of every business and every home. A continuation of the policies of the Republican Party is fundamentally necessary to the further advancement of this progress and to the further building up of this prosperity.

I have dwelt at some length on the principles of relationship between the Government and business. I make no apologies for dealing with this subject. The first necessity of any nation is the smooth functioning of the vast business machinery for employment, feeding, clothing, housing and providing luxuries and comforts to a people. Unless these basic elements are properly organized and function, there can be no progress in business in education, literature, music or art. There can be no advance in the fundamental ideals of a people. A people cannot make progress in poverty.

I have endeavored to present to you that the greatness of America has grown out of a political and social system and a method of control of economic forces distinctly its own—our American system—which has carried this great experiment in human welfare farther than ever before in all history. We are nearer today to the ideal of the abolition of poverty and fear from the lives of men and women than ever before in any land. And I again repeat that the departure from our American system by injecting principles destructive to it which our opponents propose will jeopardize the very liberty and freedom of our people, will destroy equality of opportunity not alone to ourselves but to our children.

To me the foundation of American life rests upon the home and the family. I read into these great economic forces, these intricate and delicate relations of the Government with business and with our political and social life, but one supreme end—that we reinforce the ties that bind together the millions of our families, that we strengthen the security, the happiness and the independence of every home.

My conception of America is a land where men and women may walk in ordered freedom in the independent conduct of their occupations; where they may enjoy the advantages of wealth, not concentrated in the hands of the few but spread through the lives of all, where they build and safeguard their homes, and give to their children the fullest advantages and opportunities of American life; where every man shall be respected in the faith that his conscience and his heart direct him to follow; where a contented and happy people, secure in their liberties, free from poverty and fear, shall have the leisure and impulse to seek a fuller life.

Some may ask where all this may lead beyond mere material progress. It leads to a release of the energies of men and women from the dull drudgery of life to a wider vision and a higher hope. It leads to the opportunity for greater and greater service, not alone from man to man in our own land, but from our country to the whole world. It leads to an America, healthy in body, healthy in spirit, unfettered, youthful, and eager—with a vision searching beyond the farthest horizons, with an open mind sympathetic and generous. It is to these higher ideals and for these purposes that I pledge myself and the Republican Party.

[MC]

President Franklin D. Roosevelt, First Inaugural Address

March 4, 1933

If Roosevelt knew one thing in 1932, it was his New Deal program had to be sold to the American public. He campaigned hard, traveling over 12,000 miles to every section of the country and giving over 200 speeches. The electorate responded. He won the presidency by 57.4% of the popular vote to 39.7% for the incumbent Herbert Hoover. The vote in the Electoral College was 472 to 59 with FDR winning forty-two of the forty-eight states. His inauguration as the thirty-second president was set for Saturday, March 4, 1933. The most dramatic incident in the months leading up to the inauguration was an assassination attempt at virtually point-blank range following a brief speech at Miami's Bay Front Park in February. Miraculously, the president-elect escaped unscathed, and from all accounts supremely untroubled; but the attack did take the life of another prominent Democrat, Mayor Anton Cermak of Chicago. Roosevelt's advisors took pains to reassure the nation that the incident was not part of a political plot to stifle the New Deal before it was launched—just the act of a single gunman driven by illness and personal demons. In due course, the perpetrator—who was captured at the scene—was tried, convicted and executed.

Economic conditions had worsened during the long Depression winter between the November election and the March inauguration. The most immediate problem confronting FDR as he took office concerned the banking system. Banks everywhere had failed, confidence in the nation's banking system was eroding, and depositors large and small worried about the safety of their funds. In a situation where panic tended to feed on itself, runs on banks intensified as people decided to hoard what gold and currency they had. The entire banking system was in free fall as inauguration Saturday

169

approached, with the governors of many states having issued proclamations shutting down banks over which they had control. The gravity of the situation was brought home to many visitors to Washington who had come to celebrate the inauguration when hotels there refused out-of-town checks, and wires for cash from home were limited to $100 because of the currency shortage. It was later reported that Eleanor Roosevelt had wondered how in these circumstances the large Roosevelt entourage would be able to pay for their accommodations at the Mayflower Hotel which, of course, included the presidential suite. After a few days, the major hotels realized it would benefit no one to keep their guests captive because they couldn't pay with local checks, and most of them relented.

With the Navy airship Akron *circling overhead and a crowd of 100,000 in attendance in front of the east portico of the Capitol, Roosevelt took the oath of office from Chief Justice Charles Evans Hughes. FDR's hand was on an old Dutch Bible which had been used by his family to record births and deaths for over 200 years, open to his favorite passage in Paul's First Epistle to the Corinthians: "And now abideth Faith, Hope, Charity, these three, but the greatest of these is Charity." Addressing the banking situation, Roosevelt outlined his plans only in the most general terms—except for announcing that he was about to call a special session of Congress because of the crisis at hand. "The only thing we have to fear is fear itself," was his memorable pronouncement in the opening segment of this first inaugural address. Eleanor Roosevelt told a reporter how she perceived the event a few days later: "It was very, very solemn," she said. "And a little terrifying." At one o'clock in the morning on Monday, March 6th—thirty-six hours into the new presidency—the White House issued a proclamation, based on powers FDR's legal advisors found vested in the president under a "World War One Trading with the Enemy Act" still on the books. The proclamation declared that a national bank holiday would begin that day, absolutely suspending all banking transactions throughout the country. The legal underpinnings of this move may have been improvisational, but the crisis was so grave, and the efforts of the preceding administration to deal with it so futile, that objections were few.*

— Note by John Grafton

I AM CERTAIN that my fellow Americans expect that on my induction into the Presidency I will address them with a candor and a decision which the present situation of our Nation impels. This is preeminently the time to speak the truth, the whole truth, frankly and boldly. Nor need we shrink from honestly facing conditions in our country today. This great Nation will endure as it has endured, will revive and will prosper. So, first of all, let me assert my firm belief that the only thing we have to fear is fear itself—nameless, unreasoning, unjustified terror which paralyzes needed efforts to convert retreat into advance. In every dark hour of our national life a leadership of frankness and vigor has met with that understanding and support of the people themselves which is essential to victory. I am convinced that you will again give that support to leadership in these critical days.

In such a spirit on my part and on yours we face our common difficulties. They concern, thank God, only material things. Values have shrunken to fantastic levels; taxes have risen; our ability to pay has fallen; government of all kinds is faced by serious curtailment of income; the means of exchange are frozen in the currents of trade; the withered leaves of industrial enterprise lie on every side; farmers find no markets for their produce; the savings of many years in thousands of families are gone.

More important, a host of unemployed citizens face the grim problem of existence, and an equally great number toil with little return. Only a foolish optimist can deny the dark realities of the moment.

Yet our distress comes from no failure of substance. We are stricken by no plague of locusts. Compared with the perils which our forefathers conquered because they believed and were not afraid, we have still much to be thankful for. Nature still offers her bounty and human efforts have multiplied it. Plenty is at our doorstep, but a generous use of it languishes in the very sight of the supply. Primarily this is because the rulers of the exchange of mankind's goods have failed, through their own stubbornness and their own incompetence, have admitted their failure, and abdicated. Practices of the unscrupulous money changers stand indicted in the court of public opinion, rejected by the hearts and minds of men.

True they have tried, but their efforts have been cast in the pattern of an outworn tradition. Faced by failure of credit they have proposed only the lending of more money. Stripped of the lure of profit by which to induce our people to follow their false leadership, they have resorted to exhortations, pleading tearfully for restored confidence. They know only the rules of a generation of self-seekers. They have no vision, and when there is no vision the people perish.

The money changers have fled from their high seats in the temple of our civilization. We may now restore that temple to the ancient truths. The measure of the restoration lies in the extent to which we apply social values more noble than mere monetary profit.

Happiness lies not in the mere possession of money; it lies in the joy of achievement, in the thrill of creative effort. The joy and moral stimulation of work no longer must be forgotten in the mad chase of evanescent profits. These dark days will be worth all they cost us if they teach us that our true destiny is not to be ministered unto but to minister to ourselves and to our fellow men.

Recognition of the falsity of material wealth as the standard of success goes hand in hand with the abandonment of the false belief that public office and high political position are to be valued only by the standards of pride of place and personal profit; and there must be an end to a conduct in banking and in business which too often has given to a sacred trust the likeness of callous and selfish wrongdoing. Small wonder that confidence languishes, for it thrives only on honesty, on honor, on the sacredness of obligations, on faithful protection, on unselfish performance; without them it cannot live.

Restoration calls, however, not for changes in ethics alone. This Nation asks for action, and action now.

Our greatest primary task is to put people to work. This is no unsolvable problem if we face it wisely and courageously. It can be accomplished in part by direct recruiting by the Government itself, treating the task as we would treat the emergency of a war, but at the same time, through this employment, accomplishing greatly needed projects to stimulate and reorganize the use of our natural resources.

Hand in hand with this we must frankly recognize the overbalance of population in our industrial centers and, by engaging on a national scale in redistribution, endeavor to provide a better use of the land for those best fitted for the land. The task can be helped by definite efforts to raise the values of agricultural products and with this the power to purchase the output of our cities. It can be helped by preventing realistically the tragedy of the growing loss through foreclosure of our small homes and our farms. It can be helped by insistence that the Federal, State, and local governments act forthwith on the demand that their cost be drastically reduced. It can be helped by the unifying of relief activities which today are often scattered, uneconomical, and unequal. It can be helped by national planning for and supervision of all forms of transportation and of communications and other utilities which have a definitely public character. There are many ways in which it can be helped, but it can never be helped merely by talking about it. We must act and act quickly.

Finally, in our progress toward a resumption of work we require two safeguards against a return of the evils of the old order; there must be a strict supervision of all banking and credits and investments; there must be an end to speculation with other people's money, and there must be provision for an adequate but sound currency.

These are the lines of attack. I shall presently urge upon a new Congress in special session detailed measures for their fulfillment, and I shall seek the immediate assistance of the several States.

Through this program of action we address ourselves to putting our own national house in order and making income balance outgo. Our international trade relations, though vastly important, are in point of time and necessity secondary to the establishment of a sound national economy. I favor as a practical policy the putting of first things first. I shall spare no effort to restore world trade by international economic readjustment, but the emergency at home cannot wait on that accomplishment.

The basic thought that guides these specific means of national recovery is not narrowly nationalistic. It is the insistence, as a first consideration, upon the interdependence of the various elements in all parts of the United States—a recognition of the old and permanently important manifestation of the American spirit of the pioneer. It is the way to recovery. It is the immediate way. It is the strongest assurance that the recovery will endure.

In the field of world policy I would dedicate this Nation to the policy of the good neighbor—the neighbor who resolutely respects himself and, because he does so, respects the rights of others—the neighbor who respects his obligations and respects the sanctity of his agreements in and with a world of neighbors.

If I read the temper of our people correctly, we now realize as we have never realized before our interdependence on each other; that we can not merely take but we must give as well; that if we are to go forward, we must move as a trained and loyal army willing to sacrifice for the good of a common discipline, because without such discipline no progress is made, no leadership becomes effective. We are, I know, ready and willing to submit our lives and property to such discipline, because it makes possible a leadership which aims at a larger good. This I propose to offer, pledging that the larger purposes will bind upon us all as a sacred obligation with a unity of duty hitherto evoked only in time of armed strife.

With this pledge taken, I assume unhesitatingly the leadership of this great army of our people dedicated to a disciplined attack upon our common problems.

Action in this image and to this end is feasible under the form of government which we have inherited from our ancestors. Our Constitution is so simple and practical that it is possible always to meet extraordinary needs by changes in emphasis and arrangement without loss of essential form. That is why our constitutional system has proved itself the most superbly enduring political mechanism the modern world has produced. It has met every stress of vast expansion of territory, of foreign wars, of bitter internal strife, of world relations.

It is to be hoped that the normal balance of executive and legislative authority may be wholly adequate to meet the unprecedented task before us. But it may be that an unprecedented demand and need for undelayed action may call for temporary departure from that normal balance of public procedure.

I am prepared under my constitutional duty to recommend the measures that a stricken nation in the midst of a stricken world may require. These measures, or such other measures as the Congress may build out of its experience and wisdom, I shall seek, within my constitutional authority, to bring to speedy adoption.

But in the event that the Congress shall fail to take one of these two courses, and in the event that the national emergency is still critical, I shall not evade the clear course of duty that will then confront me. I shall ask the Congress for the one remaining instrument to meet the crisis—broad Executive power to wage a war against the emergency, as great as the power that would be given to me if we were in fact invaded by a foreign foe.

For the trust reposed in me I will return the courage and the devotion that befit the time. I can do no less.

We face the arduous days that lie before us in the warm courage of the national unity; with the clear consciousness of seeking old and precious moral values; with the clean satisfaction that comes from the stern performance of duty by old and young alike. We aim at the assurance of a rounded and permanent national life.

We do not distrust the future of essential democracy. The people of the United States have not failed. In their need they have registered a mandate that they want direct, vigorous action. They have asked for discipline and direction under leadership. They have made me the present instrument of their wishes. In the spirit of the gift I take it.

In this dedication of a Nation we humbly ask the blessing of God. May He protect each and every one of us. May He guide me in the days to come.

[FDR]

President Franklin D. Roosevelt, Communications on American Official Recognition of the Union of Soviet Socialist Republics

November 16, 1933

Until this date, there had been no official recognition by the United States of the Union of Soviet Socialist Republics, the country and region which had come into being in 1922 after the civil war in Russia following the 1917 Revolution. On this date, in a series of negotiations with Maxim Litvinov, the People's Commissar for Foreign Affairs for the USSR, President Roosevelt also bargained for religious freedom for Americans living in the USSR.

The White House, Washington
November 16, 1933
My dear Mr. Litvinov:

I AM VERY happy to inform you that as a result of our conversations the Government of the United States has decided to establish normal diplomatic relations with the Government of the Union of Soviet Socialist Republics and to exchange ambassadors.

I trust that the relations now established between our peoples may forever remain normal and friendly, and that our Nations henceforth may cooperate for their mutual benefit and for the preservation of the peace of the world. I am, my dear Mr. Litvinov,

Very sincerely yours,
Franklin D. Roosevelt

The White House, Washington
November 16, 1933
My dear Mr. Litvinov:

I am glad to have received the assurance expressed in your note to me of this date that it will be the fixed policy of the Government of the Union of Soviet Socialist Republics:

1. To respect scrupulously the indisputable right of the United States to order its own life within its own jurisdiction in its own way and to refrain from interfering in any manner in the internal affairs of the United States, its territories or possessions.

2. To refrain, and to restrain all persons in Government service and all organizations of the Government or under its direct or indirect control, including organizations in receipt of any financial assistance from it, from any act overt or covert liable in any way whatsoever to injure the tranquility, prosperity, order, or security of the whole or any part of the United States, its territories or possessions, and, in particular, from any act tending to incite or encourage armed intervention, or any agitation or propaganda having as an aim, the violation of the territorial integrity of the United States, its territories or possessions, or the bringing about by force of a change in the political or social order of the whole or any part of the United States, its territories or possessions.

3. Not to permit the formation or residence on its territory of any organization or group—and to prevent the activity on its territory of any organization or group, or of representatives or officials of any organization or group—which makes claim to be the Government of, or makes attempt upon the territorial integrity of, the United States, its territories or possessions; not to form, subsidize, support or permit on its territory military organizations or groups having the aim of armed struggle against the United States, its territories or possessions, and to prevent any recruiting on behalf of such organizations and groups.

4. Not to permit the formation or residence on its territory of any organization or group—and to prevent the activity on its territory of any organization or group, or of representatives or officials of any organization or group—which has as an aim the overthrow or the preparation for the overthrow of, or the bringing about by force of a change in, the political or social order of the whole or any part of the United States, its territories or possessions.

It will be the fixed policy of the Executive of the United States within the limits of the powers conferred by the Constitution and the laws of the United States to adhere reciprocally to the engagements above expressed.

I am, my dear Mr. Litvinov,

Very sincerely yours,
Franklin D. Roosevelt

[APP]

United States v. One Book Called "Ulysses"

December 6, 1933

The most famous novel of the twentieth century, the Irish author James Joyce's Ulysses, *first published in 1922 in Paris, encountered censorship in America when a portion of it appeared in a literary magazine in 1922. The New York publishing company Random House decided to publish the book and challenged the designation of it as "pornographic" by the U.S. Customs Service. District Judge John M. Woolsey ruled in favor of the novel's entrance to America.*

[...] THE MOTION FOR a decree dismissing the libel herein is granted, and, consequently, of course, the government's motion for a decree of forfeiture and destruction is denied. Accordingly a decree dismissing the libel without costs may be entered herein. [...]

I. [...] It seems to me that a procedure of this kind is highly appropriate in libels such as this for the confiscation of books. It is an especially advantageous procedure in the instant case because, on account of the length of "Ulysses" and the difficulty of reading it, a jury trial would have been an extremely unsatisfactory, if not an almost impossible method of dealing with it.

II. I have read "Ulysses" once in its entirety and I have read those passages of which the government particularly complains several times. In fact, for many weeks, my spare time has been devoted to the consideration of the decision which my duty would require me to make in this matter.

"Ulysses" is not an easy book to read or to understand. But there has been much written about it, and in order properly to approach the consideration of it is advisable to read a number of other books which have now become its satellites. The study of "Ulysses" is, therefore, a heavy task.

III. The reputation of "Ulysses" in the literary world, however, warranted my taking such time as was necessary to enable me to satisfy myself as to the intent with which the book was written, for, of course, in any case where a book is claimed to be obscene it must first be determined, whether the intent with which it was written was what is called, according to the usual phrase, pornographic, that is, written for the purpose of exploiting obscenity.

If the conclusion is that the book is pornographic, that is the end of the inquiry and forfeiture must follow.

But in "Ulysses," in spite of its unusual frankness, I do not detect anywhere the leer of the sensualist. I hold, therefore, that it is not pornographic.

IV. In writing "Ulysses," Joyce sought to make a serious experiment in a new, if not wholly novel, literary genre. He takes persons of the lower middle class living in Dublin in 1904 and seeks, not only to describe what they did on a certain day early in June of that year as they went about the city bent on their usual occupations, but also to tell what many of them thought about the while.

Joyce has attempted — it seems to me, with astonishing success — to show how the screen of consciousness with its ever-shifting kaleidoscopic impressions carries, as it were on a plastic palimpsest, not only what is in the focus of each man's observation of the actual things about him, but also in a penumbral zone residua of past impressions, some recent and some drawn up by association from the domain of the subconscious. He shows how each of these impressions affects the life and behavior of the character which he is describing.

What he seeks to get is not unlike the result of a double or, if that is possible, a multiple exposure on a cinema film, which would give a clear foreground with a background visible but somewhat blurred and out of focus in varying degrees.

To convey by words an effect which obviously lends itself more appropriately to a graphic technique, accounts, it seems to me, for much of the obscurity which meets a reader of "Ulysses." And it also explains another aspect of the book, which I have further to consider, namely, Joyce's sincerity and his honest effort to show exactly how the minds of his characters operate.

If Joyce did not attempt to be honest in developing the technique which he has adopted in "Ulysses," the result would be psychologically misleading and thus unfaithful to his chosen technique. Such an attitude would be artistically inexcusable.

It is because Joyce has been loyal to his technique and has not funked its necessary implications, but has honestly attempted to tell fully what his characters think about, that he has been the subject of so many attacks and that his purpose has been so often misunderstood and misrepresented. For his attempt sincerely and honestly to realize his objective has required him incidentally to use certain words which are generally considered dirty words and has led at times to what many think is a too poignant preoccupation with sex in the thoughts of his characters.

The words which are criticized as dirty are old Saxon words known to almost all men and, I venture, to many women, and are such words as would be naturally and habitually used, I believe, by the types of folk whose life, physical and mental, Joyce is seeking to describe. In respect of the recurrent emergence of the theme of sex in the minds of his characters, it must always be remembered that his locale was Celtic and his season spring.

Whether or not one enjoys such a technique as Joyce uses is a matter of taste on which disagreement or argument is futile, but to subject that technique to the standards of some other technique seems to me to be little short of absurd.

Accordingly, I hold that "Ulysses" is a sincere and honest book, and I think that the criticisms of it are entirely disposed of by its rationale.

V. Furthermore, "Ulysses" is an amazing tour de force when one considers the success which has been in the main achieved with such a difficult objective as Joyce set for himself. As I have stated, "Ulysses" is not an easy book to read. It is brilliant and dull, intelligible and obscure, by turns. In many places it seems to me to be disgusting, but although it contains, as I have mentioned above, many words usually considered dirty, I have not found anything that I consider to be dirt for dirt's sake. Each word of the book contributes like a bit of mosaic to the detail of the picture which Joyce is seeking to construct for his readers.

If one does not wish to associate with such folk as Joyce describes, that is one's own choice. In order to avoid indirect contact with them one may not wish to read "Ulysses"; that is quite understandable. But when such a great artist in words, as Joyce undoubtedly is, seeks to draw a true picture of the lower middle class in a European city, ought it to be impossible for the American public legally to see that picture?

To answer this question it is not sufficient merely to find, as I have found above, that Joyce did not write "Ulysses" with what is commonly called pornographic intent, I must endeavor to apply a more objective standard to his book in order to determine its effect in the result, irrespective of the intent with which it was written.

VI. The statute under which the libel is filed only denounces, in so far as we are here concerned, the importation into the United States from any foreign country of "any obscene book." [...] It does not marshal against books the spectrum of condemnatory adjectives found, commonly, in laws dealing with matters of this kind. I am, therefore, only required to determine whether "Ulysses" is obscene within the legal definition of that word.

The meaning of the word "obscene" as legally defined by the courts is: Tending to stir the sex impulses or to lead to sexually impure and lustful thoughts. [...]

Whether a particular book would tend to excite such impulses and thoughts must be tested by the court's opinion as to its effect on a person with average sex instincts — what the French would call *l'homme moyen sensuel* — who plays, in this branch of legal inquiry, the same role of hypothetical reagent as does the "reasonable man" in the law of torts and "the man learned in the art" on questions of invention in patent law.

The risk involved in the use of such a reagent arises from the inherent tendency of the trier of facts, however fair he may intend to be, to make his reagent too much subservient to his own idiosyncrasies. Here, I have attempted to avoid this, if possible, and to make my reagent herein more objective than he might otherwise be, by adopting the following course:

After I had made my decision in regard to the aspect of "Ulysses," now under consideration, I checked my impressions with two friends of mine who in my opinion answered to the above-stated requirement for my reagent.

These literary assessors — as I might properly describe them — were called on separately, and neither knew that I was consulting the other. They are men whose opinion on literature and on life I value most highly. They had both read "Ulysses," and, of course, were wholly unconnected with this cause.

Without letting either of my assessors know what my decision was, I gave to each of them the legal definition of obscene and asked each whether in his opinion "Ulysses" was obscene within that definition.

I was interested to find that they both agreed with my opinion: That reading "Ulysses" in its entirety, as a book must be read on such a test as this, did not tend to excite sexual impulses or lustful thoughts, but that its net effect on them was only that of a somewhat tragic and very powerful commentary on the inner lives of men and women.

It is only with the normal person that the law is concerned. Such a test as I have described, therefore, is the only proper test of obscenity in the case of a book like "Ulysses" which is a sincere and serious attempt to devise a new literary method for the observation and description of mankind.

I am quite aware that owing to some of its scenes "Ulysses" is a rather strong draught to ask some sensitive, though normal, persons to take. But my considered opinion, after long reflection, is that, whilst in many places the effect of "Ulysses" on the reader undoubtedly is somewhat emetic, nowhere does it tend to be an aphrodisiac.

"Ulysses" may, therefore, be admitted into the United States.

[DAH]

Social Security Act

August 14, 1935

ONE OF THE most significant changes brought to American life during President Franklin D. Roosevelt's first term was the creation of the Committee on Economic Security in 1934. That committee developed a comprehensive insurance system focusing on unemployment and old age; after negotiations by President Roosevelt with Congress, the bill brought into being the Social Security Board (so named until 1946, when it became known as the Social Security Administration).

An Act to provide for the general welfare by establishing a system of Federal old-age benefits, and by enabling the several States to make more adequate provision for aged persons, blind persons, dependent and crippled children, maternal and child welfare, public health, and the administration of their unemployment compensation laws; to establish a Social Security Board; to raise revenue; and for other purposes.

Be it enacted by the Senate and House of Representatives of the United States of America in Congress assembled,

TITLE I—GRANTS TO STATES FOR OLD AGE ASSISTANCE

APPROPRIATION

SECTION 1. For the purpose of enabling each State to furnish financial assistance, as far as practicable under the conditions in such State, to aged needy individuals, there is hereby authorized to be appropriated for the fiscal year ending June 30, 1936, the sum of

$49,750,000, and there is hereby authorized to be appropriated for each fiscal year thereafter a sum sufficient to carry out the purposes of this title. The sums made available under this section shall be used for making payments to States which have submitted, and had approved by the Social Security Board established by Title VII, State plans for old-age assistance.

STATE OLD–AGE ASSISTANCE PLANS

SEC. 2. (a) A State plan for old-age assistance must (1) provide that it shall be in effect in all political subdivisions of the State, and, if administered by them, be mandatory upon them; (2) provide for financial participation by the State; (3) either provide for the establishment or designation of a single State agency to administer the plan, or provide for the establishment or designation of a single State agency to supervise the administration of the plan; (4) provide for granting to any individual, whose claim for old-age assistance is denied, an opportunity for a fair hearing before such State agency; (5) provide such methods of administration (other than those relating to selection, tenure of office, and compensation of personnel) as are found by the Board to be necessary for the efficient operation of the plan; (6) provide that the State agency will make such reports, in such form and containing such information, as the Board may from time to time require, and comply with such provisions as the Board may from time to time find necessary to assure the correctness and verification of such reports; and (7) provide that, if the State or any of its political subdivisions collects from the estate of any recipient of old-age assistance any amount with respect to old-age assistance furnished him under the plan, one-half of the net amount so collected shall be promptly paid to the United States. Any payment so made shall be deposited in the Treasury to the credit of the appropriation for the purposes of this title.

(b) The Board shall approve any plan which fulfills the conditions specified in subsection (a), except that it shall not approve any plan which imposes, as a condition of eligibility for old-age assistance under the plan—

(1) An age requirement of more than sixty-five years, except that the plan may impose, effective until January 1, 1940, an age requirement of as much as seventy years; or

(2) Any residence requirement which excludes any resident of the State who has resided therein five years during the nine years

immediately preceding the application for old-age assistance and has resided therein continuously for one year immediately preceding the application; or

(3) Any citizenship requirement which excludes any citizen of the United States. […]

TITLE II—FEDERAL OLD–AGE BENEFITS

OLD-AGE RESERVE ACCOUNT

SECTION 201. (a) There is hereby created an account in the Treasury of the United States to be known as the "Old-Age Reserve Account." […]

OLD-AGE BENEFIT PAYMENTS

SEC. 202. (a) Every qualified individual shall be entitled to receive, with respect to the period beginning on the date he attains the age of sixty-five, or on January 1, 1942, whichever is the later, and ending on the date of his death, an old–age benefit (payable as nearly as practicable in equal monthly installments) […..]

PAYMENTS UPON DEATH

SEC. 203. (a) If any individual dies before attaining the age of sixty–five, there shall be paid to his estate an amount equal to 3½ per centum of the total wages determined by the Board to have been paid to him, with respect to employment after December 31, 1936. […]

PAYMENTS TO AGED INDIVIDUALS NOT QUALIFIED FOR BENEFITS

SEC. 204. (a) There shall be paid in a lump sum to any individual who, upon attaining the age of sixty-five, is not a qualified individual, an amount equal to 3½ per centum of the total wages determined by the Board to have been paid to him, with respect to employment after December 31, 1936, and before he attained the age of sixty-five.

(b) After any individual becomes entitled to any payment under subsection (a), no other payment shall be made under this title in any manner measured by wages paid to him, except that any part of any payment under subsection (a) which is not paid to him before his death shall be paid to his estate. [...]

Sec. 210. [...]

(b) The term "employment" means any service, of whatever nature, performed within the United States by an employee for his employer, except—

(1) Agricultural labor;

(2) Domestic service in a private home;

(3) Casual labor not in the course of the employer's trade or business;

(4) Service performed as an officer or member of the crew of a vessel documented under the laws of the United States or of any foreign country;

(5) Service performed in the employ of the United States Government or of an instrumentality of the United States;

(6) Service performed in the employ of a State, a political subdivision thereof, or an instrumentality of one or more States or political subdivisions;

(7) Service performed in the employ of a corporation, community chest, fund, or foundation, organized and operated exclusively for religious, charitable, scientific, literary, or educational purposes, or for the prevention of cruelty to children or animals, no part of the net earnings of which inures to the benefit of any private shareholder or individual. [...]

[DAH]

President Franklin D. Roosevelt, State of the Union Message, "The Four Freedoms"

January 6, 1941

The military-political context of the debate over Lend-Lease in the winter of 1940–41 was the Battle of Britain raging night after night in the sky above England, with reports from the scene of that conflict appearing every day in American newspapers and newsreels. There is little question that sympathy with the British in this vital struggle for survival aided the fight for public opinion in support of Lend-Lease in America. Whatever may have been his private thoughts on the matter—many historians have written what now seems obvious, that by this time FDR could hardly have still believed that the Axis powers could be overthrown without the direct military intervention of the United States—he was still able to argue that making war materiel available to the British through Lend-Lease was the only way to avoid sending American soldiers to fight overseas. Winston Churchill got on the same bandwagon during this debate when in a broadcast to America he simply promised, "Give us the tools and we will finish the job." The American public largely agreed, and after a few months of debate, Lend-Lease passed Congress by healthy majorities: 260 to 165 in the House, 60 to 31 in the Senate.

On January 6, 1941, the week after his "Arsenal of Democracy" Fireside Chat, while the Lend-Lease debate was in its early stages, Roosevelt delivered his State of the Union message to Congress. In it, he reiterated his position on the need to aid the world's democracies in the struggle against fascism, and beyond that, outlined the philosophical basis of his position as head of a nation confronting the possibility of world war: "In future days," he said, "which we seek to make secure, we look forward to a world founded upon four essential human freedoms." These were freedom of speech, freedom of worship, freedom from want, and freedom from fear. It was reported that applause in Congress was strong but somewhat subdued, not because anyone disagreed with the idea of the "Four Freedoms"—as this philosophical program became known—but because FDR's words had brought home to his audience the gravity of the situation at that moment.

— Note by John Grafton

Mr. Speaker, members of the 77th Congress:

I ADDRESS YOU, the members of this new Congress, at a moment unprecedented in the history of the union. I use the word "unprecedented" because at no previous time has American security been as seriously threatened from without as it is today.

Since the permanent formation of our government under the Constitution in 1789, most of the periods of crisis in our history have related to our domestic affairs. And, fortunately, only one of these—the four-year war between the States—ever threatened our national unity. Today, thank God, 130,000,000 Americans in forty-eight States have forgotten points of the compass in our national unity.

It is true that prior to 1914 the United States often has been disturbed by events in other continents. We have even engaged in two wars with European nations and in a number of undeclared wars in the West Indies, in the Mediterranean and in the Pacific, for the maintenance of American rights and for the Principles of peaceful commerce. But in no case has a serious threat been raised against our national safety or our continued independence.

What I seek to convey is the historic truth that the United States as a nation has at all times maintained opposition—clear, definite opposition—to any attempt to lock us in behind an ancient Chinese wall while the procession of civilization went past. Today, thinking of our children and of their children, we oppose enforced isolation for ourselves or for any other part of the Americas.

That determination of ours, extending over all these years, was proved, for example, in the early days during the quarter century of wars following the French Revolution. While the Napoleonic struggle did threaten interests of the United States because of the French foothold in the West Indies and in Louisiana, and while we engaged in the War of 1812 to vindicate our right to peaceful trade, it is nevertheless clear that neither France nor Great Britain nor any other nation was aiming at domination of the whole world.

And in like fashion, from 1815 to 1914—ninety-nine years—no single war in Europe or in Asia constituted a real threat against our future or against the future of any other American nation.

Except in the Maximilian interlude in Mexico, no foreign power sought to establish itself in this hemisphere. And the strength of the British fleet in the Atlantic has been a friendly strength; it is still a friendly strength. Even when the World War broke out in 1914 it seemed to contain only small threat of danger to our own American future. But as time went on, as we remember, the American people began to visualize what the downfall of democratic nations might mean to our own democracy.

We need not overemphasize imperfections in the peace of Versailles. We need not harp on failure of the democracies to deal with problems of world reconstruction. We should remember that the peace of 1919 was far less unjust than the kind of pacification which began even before Munich, and which is being carried on under the new order of tyranny that seeks to spread over every continent today. The American people have unalterably set their faces against that tyranny. I suppose that every realist knows that the democratic way of life is at this moment being directly assailed in every part of the world—assailed either by arms or by secret spreading of poisonous propaganda by those who seek to destroy unity and promote discord in nations that are still at peace.

During sixteen long months this assault has blotted out the whole pattern of democratic life in an appalling number of independent nations, great and small. And the assailants are still on the march, threatening other nations, great and small. Therefore, as your President, performing my constitutional duty to "give to the Congress information of the state of the union," I find it unhappily necessary to report that the future and the safety of our country and of our democracy are overwhelmingly involved in events far beyond our borders.

Armed defense of democratic existence is now being gallantly waged in four continents. If that defense fails, all the population and all the resources of Europe and Asia, Africa and Australia will be dominated by conquerors. And let us remember that the total of those populations in those four continents, the total of those populations and their resources greatly exceeds the sum total of the population and the resources of the whole of the Western Hemisphere—yes, many times over.

In times like these it is immature—and, incidentally, untrue—for anybody to brag that an unprepared America, single-handed and with one hand tied behind its back, can hold off the whole world. No realistic American can expect from a dictator's peace international generosity, or return of true independence, or world disarmament, or freedom of expression, or freedom of religion—or even good business. Such a peace would bring no security for us or for our neighbors. Those who would give up essential liberty to purchase a little temporary safety deserve neither liberty nor safety.

As a nation we may take pride in the fact that we are soft-hearted; but we cannot afford to be soft-headed. We must always be wary of those who with sounding brass and a tinkling cymbal preach the ism of appeasement. We must especially beware of that small group of selfish men who would clip the wings of the American eagle in order to feather their own nests. I have recently pointed out how quickly the tempo of modern warfare could bring into our very midst the physical attack which we must eventually expect if the dictator nations win this war.

There is much loose talk of our immunity from immediate and direct invasion from across the seas. Obviously, as long as the British Navy retains its power, no such danger exists. Even if there were no British Navy, it is not probable that any enemy would be stupid enough to attack us by landing troops in the United States from across thousands of miles of ocean, until it had acquired strategic bases from which to operate. But we learn much from the lessons of the past years in Europe—particularly the lesson of Norway, whose essential seaports were captured by treachery and surprise built up over a series of years.

The first phase of the invasion of this hemisphere would not be the landing of regular troops. The necessary strategic points would be occupied by secret agents and by their dupes—and great numbers of them are already here and in Latin America. As long as the aggressor nations maintain the offensive they, not we, will choose the time and the place and the method of their attack. And that is why the future of all the American Republics is today in serious danger. That is why this annual message to the Congress is unique in our history. That is why every member of the executive branch of the government and every member of the Congress face great responsibility—great accountability.

The need of the moment is that our actions and our policy should be devoted primarily—almost exclusively—to meeting this foreign peril. For all our domestic problems are now a part of the great emergency. Just as our national policy in internal affairs has been based upon a decent respect for the rights and the dignity of all of our fellow men within our gates, so our national policy in foreign affairs has been based on a decent respect for the rights and the dignity of all nations, large and small. And the justice of morality must and will win in the end.

Our national policy is this: First, by an impressive expression of the public will and without regard to partisanship, we are committed to all-inclusive national defense. Second, by an impressive expression of the public will and without regard to partisanship, we are committed to full support of all those resolute people everywhere who are resisting aggression and are thereby keeping war away from our hemisphere. By this support we express our determination that the democratic cause shall prevail, and we strengthen the defense and the security of our own nation.

Third, by an impressive expression of the public will and without regard to partisanship, we are committed to the proposition that principle of morality and considerations for our own security will never permit us to acquiesce in a peace dictated by aggressors and sponsored by appeasers. We know that enduring peace cannot be bought at the cost of other people's freedom. In the recent national election there was no substantial difference between the two great parties in respect to that national policy. No issue was fought out on the line before the American electorate. And today it is abundantly evident that American citizens everywhere are demanding and supporting speedy and complete action in recognition of obvious danger.

Therefore, the immediate need is a swift and driving increase in our armament production. Leaders of industry and labor have responded to our summons. Goals of speed have been set. In some cases these goals are being reached ahead of time. In some cases we are on schedule; in other cases there are slight but not serious delays. And in some cases—and, I am sorry to say, very important cases—we are all concerned by the slowness of the accomplishment of our plans. The Army and Navy, however, have made substantial progress during the past year. Actual experience is improving and speeding up our methods of production with every passing day. And today's best is not good enough for tomorrow.

I am not satisfied with the progress thus far made. The men in charge of the program represent the best in training, in ability and in patriotism. They are not satisfied with the progress thus far made. None of us will be satisfied until the job is done. No matter whether the original goal was set too high or too low, our objective is quicker and better results. Tρ give you two illustrations: We are behind schedule in turning out finished airplanes. We are working day and night to solve the innumerable problems and to catch up.

We are ahead of schedule in building warships, but we are working to get even further ahead of that schedule. To change a whole nation from a basis of peacetime production of implements of peace to a basis of wartime production of implements of war is no small task. The greatest difficulty comes at the beginning of the program, when new tools, new plant facilities, new assembly lines, new shipways must first be constructed before the actual material begins to flow steadily and speedily from them.

The Congress of course, must rightly keep itself informed at all times of the progress of the program. However, there is certain information, as the Congress itself will readily recognize, which, in the interests of our own security and those of the nations that we are supporting, must of needs be kept in confidence. New circumstances are constantly begetting new needs for our safety. I shall ask this Congress for greatly increased new appropriations and authorizations to carry on what we have begun.

I also ask this Congress for authority and for funds sufficient to manufacture additional munitions and war supplies of many kinds, to be turned over to those nations which are now in actual war with aggressor nations. Our most useful and immediate role is to act as an arsenal for them as well as for ourselves. They do not need manpower, but they do need billions of dollars' worth of the weapons of defense. The time is near when they will not be able to pay for them all in ready cash. We cannot, and we will not, tell them that they must surrender merely because of present inability to pay for the weapons which we know they must have.

I do not recommend that we make them a loan of dollars with which to pay for these weapons—a loan to be repaid in dollars. I recommend that we make it possible for those nations to continue to obtain war materials in the United States, fitting their orders into our own program. And nearly all of their material would, if the time ever came, be useful in our own defense. Taking counsel of expert military and naval authorities, considering what is best for our own security, we are free to decide how much should be kept here and how much should be sent abroad to our friends who, by their determined and heroic resistance, are giving us time in which to make ready our own defense.

For what we send abroad we shall be repaid, repaid within a reasonable time following the close of hostilities, repaid in similar materials, or at our option in other goods of many kinds which they can produce and which we need. Let us say to the democracies: "We Americans are vitally concerned in your defense of freedom. We are putting forth our energies, our resources and our organizing powers to give you the strength to regain and maintain a free world. We shall send you in ever-increasing numbers, ships, planes, tanks, guns. That is our purpose and our pledge."

In fulfillment of this purpose we will not be intimidated by the threats of dictators that they will regard as a breach of international law or as an act of war our aid to the democracies which dare to resist their aggression. Such aid is not an act of war, even if a dictator should unilaterally proclaim it so to be.

And when the dictators—if the dictators—are ready to make war upon us, they will not wait for an act of war on our part.

They did not wait for Norway or Belgium or the Netherlands to commit an act of war. Their only interest is in a new one-way international law which lacks mutuality in its observance and therefore becomes an instrument of oppression. The happiness of future generations of Americans may well depend on how effective and how immediate we can make our aid felt. No one can tell the exact character of the emergency situations that we may be called upon to meet. The nation's hands must not be tied when the nation's life is in danger.

Yes, and we must prepare, all of us prepare, to make the sacrifices that the emergency—almost as serious as war itself—demands. Whatever stands in the way of speed and efficiency in defense, in defense preparations at any time, must give way to the national need.

A free nation has the right to expect full cooperation from all groups. A free nation has the right to look to the leaders of business, of labor and of agriculture to take the lead in stimulating effort, not among other groups but within their own groups.

The best way of dealing with the few slackers or trouble-makers in our midst is, first, to shame them by patriotic example, and if that fails, to use the sovereignty of government to save government.

As men do not live by bread alone, they do not fight by armaments alone. Those who man our defenses and those behind them who build our defenses must have the stamina and the courage which come from unshakeable belief in the manner of life which they are defending. The mighty action that we are calling for cannot be based on a disregard of all the things worth fighting for.

The nation takes great satisfaction and much strength from the things which have been done to make its people conscious of their individual stake in the preservation of democratic life in America. Those things have toughened the fiber of our people, have renewed their faith and strengthened their devotion to the institutions we make ready to protect. Certainly this is no time for any of us to stop thinking about the social and economic problems which are the root cause of the social revolution which is today a supreme factor in the world. For there is nothing mysterious about the foundations of a healthy and strong democracy.

The basic things expected by our people of their political and economic systems are simple. They are:

Equality of opportunity for youth and for others.

Jobs for those who can work.

Security for those who need it.

The ending of special privilege for the few.

The preservation of civil liberties for all.

The enjoyment of the fruits of scientific progress in a wider and constantly rising standard of living.

These are the simple, the basic things that must never be lost sight of in the turmoil and unbelievable complexity of our modern world. The inner and abiding strength of our economic and political systems is dependent upon the degree to which they fulfill these expectations. Many subjects connected with our social economy call for immediate improvement. As examples:

We should bring more citizens under the coverage of old-age pensions and unemployment insurance.

We should widen the opportunities for adequate medical care.

We should plan a better system by which persons deserving or needing gainful employment may obtain it.

I have called for personal sacrifice, and I am assured of the willingness of almost all Americans to respond to that call. A part of the sacrifice means the payment of more money in taxes. In my budget message I will recommend that a greater portion of this great defense program be paid for from taxation than we are paying for today. No person should try, or be allowed to get rich out of the program, and the principle of tax payments in accordance with ability to pay should be constantly before our eyes to guide our legislation.

If the congress maintains these principles the voters, putting patriotism ahead of pocketbooks, will give you their applause.

In the future days which we seek to make secure, we look forward to a world founded upon four essential human freedoms.

The first is freedom of speech and expression—everywhere in the world.

The second is freedom of every person to worship God in his own way—everywhere in the world.

The third is freedom from want, which, translated into world terms, means economic understandings which will secure to every nation a healthy peacetime life for its inhabitants—everywhere in the world.

The fourth is freedom from fear, which, translated into world terms, means a world-wide reduction of armaments to such a point and in such a thorough fashion that no nation will be in a position to commit an act of physical aggression against any neighbor—anywhere in the world.

That is no vision of a distant millennium. It is a definite basis for a kind of world attainable in our own time and generation. That kind of world is the very antithesis of the so-called "new order" of tyranny which the dictators seek to create with the crash of a bomb.

To that new order we oppose the greater conception—the moral order. A good society is able to face schemes of world domination and foreign revolutions alike without fear. Since the beginning of our American history we have been engaged in change, in a perpetual, peaceful revolution, a revolution which goes on steadily, quietly, adjusting itself to changing conditions without the concentration camp or the quicklime in the ditch. The world order which we seek is the cooperation of free countries, working together in a friendly, civilized society.

This nation has placed its destiny in the hands, heads and hearts of its millions of free men and women, and its faith in freedom under the guidance of God. Freedom means the supremacy of human rights everywhere. Our support goes to those who struggle to gain those rights and keep them. Our strength is our unity of purpose.

To that high concept there can be no end save victory.

[FDR]

President Franklin D. Roosevelt and Prime Minister of the United Kingdom Winston Churchill, Joint Declaration, "The Atlantic Charter"

August 14, 1941

After President Franklin D. Roosevelt and British Prime Minister Winston S. Churchill met on August 9–10 on the U.S.S. Augusta in Placentia Bay, Newfoundland, they agreed on this statement of their countries' aims in World War II and for the post-war. While important, it was not a binding treaty. The United States was still not officially intervening in the war, despite producing supplies for England.

THE PRESIDENT OF the United States of America and the Prime Minister, Mr. Churchill, representing His Majesty's Government in the United Kingdom, being met together, deem it right to make known certain common principles in the national policies of their respective countries on which they base their hopes for a better future for the world.

First, their countries seek no aggrandizement, territorial or other;

Second, they desire to see no territorial changes that do not accord with the freely expressed wishes of the peoples concerned;

Third, they respect the right of all peoples to choose the form of government under which they will live; and they wish to see sovereign rights and self government restored to those who have been forcibly deprived of them;

Fourth, they will endeavor, with due respect for their existing obligations, to further the enjoyment by all States, great or small, victor or vanquished, of access, on equal terms, to the trade and to the raw materials of the world which are needed for their economic prosperity;

Fifth, they desire to bring about the fullest collaboration between all nations in the economic field with the object of securing, for all, improved labor standards, economic advancement and social security;

Sixth, after the final destruction of the Nazi tyranny, they hope to see established a peace which will afford to all nations the means of dwelling in safety within their own boundaries, and which will afford assurance that all the men in all the lands may live out their lives in freedom from fear and want;

Seventh, such a peace should enable all men to traverse the high seas and oceans without hindrance;

Eighth, they believe that all of the nations of the world, for realistic as well as spiritual reasons must come to the abandonment of the use of force. Since no future peace can be maintained if land, sea or air armaments continue to be employed by nations which threaten, or may threaten, aggression outside of their frontiers, they believe, pending the establishment of a wider and permanent system of general security, that the disarmament of such nations is essential. They will likewise aid and encourage all other practicable measures which will lighten for peace-loving peoples the crushing burden of armaments.

Franklin D. Roosevelt
Winston S. Churchill

[ACF]

Charles Lindbergh, Speech, "America First"

September 11, 1941

The famous American aviator (1902–1974) was criticized for accepting awards and recognition from the Nazis for his accomplishments as a pilot and flight engineer. As a well-known member of the America First organization, he led rallies against the United States' preparations for involvement in World War II. He delivered this occasionally anti-Semitic speech at a rally in Des Moines, Iowa.

It is now two years since this latest European war began. From that day in September 1939, until the present moment, there has been an over-increasing effort to force the United States into the conflict.

That effort has been carried on by foreign interests, and by a small minority of our own people; but it has been so successful that, today, our country stands on the verge of war.

At this time, as the war is about to enter its third winter, it seems appropriate to review the circumstances that have led us to our present position. Why are we on the verge of war? Was it necessary for us to become so deeply involved? Who is responsible for changing our national policy from one of neutrality and independence to one of entanglement in European affairs?

Personally, I believe there is no better argument against our intervention than a study of the causes and developments of the present war. I have often said that if the true facts and issues were placed before the American people, there would be no danger of our involvement.

Here, I would like to point out to you a fundamental difference between the groups who advocate foreign war, and those who believe in an independent destiny for America.

If you will look back over the record, you will find that those of us who oppose intervention have constantly tried to clarify facts and issues; while the interventionists have tried to hide facts and confuse issues.

We ask you to read what we said last month, last year, and even before the war began. Our record is open and clear, and we are proud of it.

We have not led you on by subterfuge and propaganda. We have not resorted to steps short of anything, in order to take the American people where they did not want to go.

What we said before the elections, we say [illegible] and again, and again today. And we will not tell you tomorrow that it was just campaign oratory. Have you ever heard an interventionist, or a British agent, or a member of the administration in Washington ask you to go back and study a record of what they have said since the war started? Are their self-styled defenders of democracy willing to put the issue of war to a vote of our people? Do you find these crusaders for foreign freedom of speech, or the removal of censorship here in our own country?

The subterfuge and propaganda that exists in our country is obvious on every side. Tonight, I shall try to pierce through a portion of it, to the naked facts which lie beneath.

When this war started in Europe, it was clear that the American people were solidly opposed to entering it. Why shouldn't we be? We had the best defensive position in the world; we had a tradition of independence from Europe; and the one time we did take part in a European war left European problems unsolved, and debts to America unpaid.

National polls showed that when England and France declared war on Germany, in 1939, less than 10 percent of our population favored a similar course for America. But there were various groups of people, here and abroad, whose interests and beliefs necessitated the involvement of the United States in the war. I shall point out some of these groups tonight, and outline their methods of procedure. In doing this, I must speak with the utmost frankness, for in order to counteract their efforts, we must know exactly who they are.

The three most important groups who have been pressing this country toward war are the British, the Jewish and the Roosevelt administration.

Behind these groups, but of lesser importance, are a number of capitalists, Anglophiles, and intellectuals who believe that the future of mankind depends upon the domination of the British Empire. Add to these the Communistic groups who were opposed to intervention until a few weeks ago, and I believe I have named the major war agitators in this country.

I am speaking here only of war agitators, not of those sincere but misguided men and women who, confused by misinformation and frightened by propaganda, follow the lead of the war agitators.

As I have said, these war agitators comprise only a small minority of our people; but they control a tremendous influence. Against the determination of the American people to stay out of war, they have marshaled the power of their propaganda, their money, their patronage.

Let us consider these groups, one at a time.

First, the British: It is obvious and perfectly understandable that Great Britain wants the United States in the war on her side. England is now in a desperate position. Her population is not large enough and her armies are not strong enough to invade the continent of Europe and win the war she declared against Germany.

Her geographical position is such that she cannot win the war by the use of aviation alone, regardless of how many planes we send her. Even if America entered the war, it is improbable that the Allied armies could invade Europe and overwhelm the Axis powers. But one thing is certain. If England can draw this country into the war, she can shift to our shoulders a large portion of the responsibility for waging it and for paying its cost.

As you all know, we were left with the debts of the last European war; and unless we are more cautious in the future than we have been in the past, we will be left with the debts of the present case. If it were not for her hope that she can make us responsible for the war financially, as well as militarily, I believe England would have negotiated a peace in Europe many months ago, and be better off for doing so.

England has devoted, and will continue to devote every effort to get us into the war. We know that she spent huge sums of money in this country during the last war in order to involve us. Englishmen have written books about the cleverness of its use.

We know that England is spending great sums of money for propaganda in America during the present war. If we were Englishmen, we would do the same. But our interest is first in America; and as Americans, it is essential for us to realize the effort that British interests are making to draw us into their war.

The second major group I mentioned is the Jewish.

It is not difficult to understand why Jewish people desire the overthrow of Nazi Germany. The persecution they suffered in Germany would be sufficient to make bitter enemies of any race.

No person with a sense of the dignity of mankind can condone the persecution of the Jewish race in Germany. But no person of honesty and vision can look on their pro-war policy here today without seeing the dangers involved in such a policy both for us and for them. Instead of agitating for war, the Jewish groups in this country should be opposing it in every possible way for they will be among the first to feel its consequences.

Tolerance is a virtue that depends upon peace and strength. History shows that it cannot survive war and devastations. A few far-sighted Jewish people realize this and stand opposed to intervention. But the majority still does not.

Their greatest danger to this country lies in their large ownership and influence in our motion pictures, our press, our radio and our government.

I am not attacking either the Jewish or the British people. Both races, I admire. But I am saying that the leaders of both the British and the Jewish races, for reasons which are as understandable from their viewpoint as they are inadvisable from ours, for reasons which are not American, wish to involve us in the war.

We cannot blame them for looking out for what they believe to be their own interests, but we also must look out for ours. We cannot allow the natural passions and prejudices of other peoples to lead our country to destruction.

The Roosevelt administration is the third powerful group which has been carrying this country toward war. Its members have used the war emergency to obtain a third presidential term for the first time in American history. They have used the war to add unlimited billions to a debt which was already the highest we have ever known. And they have just used the war to justify the restriction of congressional power, and the assumption of dictatorial procedures on the part of the president and his appointees.

The power of the Roosevelt administration depends upon the maintenance of a wartime emergency. The prestige of the Roosevelt administration depends upon the success of Great Britain to whom the president attached his political future at a time when most people thought that England and France would easily win the war. The danger of the Roosevelt administration lies in its subterfuge. While its members have promised us peace, they have led us to war heedless of the platform upon which they were elected.

In selecting these three groups as the major agitators for war, I have included only those whose support is essential to the war party. If any one of these groups—the British, the Jewish, or the administration—stops agitating for war, I believe there will be little danger of our involvement.

I do not believe that any two of them are powerful enough to carry this country to war without the support of the third. And to these three, as I have said, all other war groups are of secondary importance.

When hostilities commenced in Europe in 1939, it was realized by these groups that the American people had no intention of entering the war. They knew it would be worse than useless to ask us for a declaration of war at that time. But they believed that this country could be entered into the war in very much the same way we were entered into the last one.

They planned: first, to prepare the United States for foreign war under the guise of American defense; second, to involve us in the war, step by step, without our realization; third, to create a series of incidents which would force us into the actual conflict. These plans were of course, to be covered and assisted by the full power of their propaganda.

Our theaters soon became filled with plays portraying the glory of war. Newsreels lost all semblance of objectivity. Newspapers and magazines began to lose advertising if they carried anti-war articles. A smear campaign was instituted against individuals who opposed intervention. The terms "fifth columnist," "traitor," "Nazi," "anti-Semitic" were thrown ceaselessly at any one who dared to suggest that it was not to the best interests of the United States to enter the war. Men lost their jobs if they were frankly anti-war. Many others dared no longer speak.

Before long, lecture halls that were open to the advocates of war were closed to speakers who opposed it. A fear campaign was inaugurated. We were told that aviation, which has held the British fleet off the continent of Europe, made America more vulnerable than ever before to invasion. Propaganda was in full swing.

There was no difficulty in obtaining billions of dollars for arms under the guise of defending America. Our people stood united on a program of defense. Congress passed appropriation after appropriation for guns and planes and battleships, with the approval of the overwhelming majority of our citizens. That a large portion of these appropriations was to be used to build arms for Europe, we did not learn until later. That was another step.

To use a specific example; in 1939, we were told that we should increase our air corps to a total of 5,000 planes. Congress passed the necessary legislation. A few months later, the administration told us that the United States should have at least 50,000 planes for our national safety. But almost as fast as fighting planes were turned out from our factories, they were sent abroad, although our own air corps was in the utmost need of new equipment; so that today, two years after the start of war, the American army has a few hundred thoroughly modern bombers and fighters—less in fact, than Germany is able to produce in a single month.

Ever since its inception, our arms program has been laid out for the purpose of carrying on the war in Europe, far more than for the purpose of building an adequate defense for America.

Now at the same time we were being prepared for a foreign war, it was necessary, as I have said, to involve us in the war. This was accomplished under that now famous phrase "steps short of war."

England and France would win if the United States would only repeal its arms embargo and sell munitions for cash, we were told. And then [illegible] began, a refrain that marked every step we took toward war for many months—"the best way to defend America and keep out of war," we were told, was "by aiding the Allies."

First, we agreed to sell arms to Europe; next, we agreed to loan arms to Europe; then we agreed to patrol the ocean for Europe; then we occupied a European island in the war zone. Now, we have reached the verge of war.

The war groups have succeeded in the first two of their three major steps into war. The greatest armament program in our history is under way.

We have become involved in the war from practically every standpoint except actual shooting. Only the creation of sufficient "incidents" yet remains; and you see the first of these already taking place, according to plan [illegible]... a plan that was never laid before the American people for their approval.

Men and women of Iowa; only one thing holds this country from war today. That is the rising opposition of the American people. Our system of democracy and representative government is on test today as it has never been before. We are on the verge of a war in which the only victor would be chaos and prostration.

We are on the verge of a war for which we are still unprepared, and for which no one has offered a feasible plan for victory—a war which cannot be won without sending our soldiers across the ocean to force a landing on a hostile coast against armies stronger than our own.

We are on the verge of war, but it is not yet too late to stay out. It is not too late to show that no amount of money, or propaganda, or patronage can force a free and independent people into war against its will. It is not yet too late to retrieve and to maintain the independent American destiny that our forefathers established in this new world.

The entire future rests upon our shoulders. It depends upon our action, our courage, and our intelligence. If you oppose our intervention in the war, now is the time to make your voice heard.

Help us to organize these meetings; and write to your representatives in Washington. I tell you that the last stronghold of democracy and representative government in this country is in our house of representatives and our senate.

There, we can still make our will known. And if we, the American people, do that, independence and freedom will continue to live among us, and there will be no foreign war.

[IS]

President Franklin D. Roosevelt, War Message to Congress

December 8, 1941

Roosevelt received news of the Japanese attack on Pearl Harbor at 1:50 P.M. on Sunday, December 7, 1941, while lunching at the White House with political advisor, Harry Hopkins. It came in the form of a telephone call from the Secretary of the Navy, Frank Knox. Within a few hours the dimensions of the disaster were clear: 2,403 killed, over 1,000 more wounded, nineteen ships damaged or sunk, almost 200 airplanes destroyed—mostly on the ground. Although a great deal of Japanese military activity had been monitored in the weeks leading up to Pearl Harbor—codes had been broken and messages intercepted—American military commanders on the scene had obviously been caught by surprise as the attacking Japanese task force had penetrated undetected to within a few hundred miles of Honolulu.

The diplomatic background to the attack centered on the oil embargo then in force by America against Japan in retaliation for Japanese aggression in Indochina. The oil embargo was part of a total suspension of trade between America and Japan, and the freezing of Japanese economic assets in America which had been enforced earlier in the year. Diplomatic talks to ease the tensions between America and Japan were ongoing at the time of Pearl Harbor, but were not in a productive mode at the decisive moment. While the diplomats were talking, the Japanese military was considering many factors which spurred them to attack when they did. Weather patterns seemed to give the Japanese the choice of attacking in December or waiting until spring. In December, 1941, they still had oil, enough for another year and a half of war, and they knew that months later their oil situation would probably be worse. An American naval buildup authorized by Congress after the fall of France in June, 1940 had not yet produced much effect, and in December, 1941, the Japanese fleet still dominated the Pacific. The Japanese naval commanders knew that a year or so later, that might no longer be true.

After receiving news of the attack on Pearl Harbor, FDR spoke on the telephone with Winston Churchill, and then met with his cabinet and Vice-President Henry Wallace in the same room of the White House where Lincoln had met with his cabinet when the Civil War began. FDR decided to deliver a concise War Message to Congress the following day, and drafted the seven-minute speech himself with some suggestions from Hopkins. The compelling phrase, "a date which will live in infamy," was an afterthought, penciled in by Roosevelt just before he spoke on December 8th. Although isolationists would still complain about his handling of events, the Pearl Harbor speech to a packed joint session of Congress was punctuated by great applause; and the Congress which had kept Woodrow Wilson hanging for a week in 1917 took only thirty-three minutes to pass the resolution declaring war on Japan in 1941. The vote was 88–0 in the Senate and 388–1 in the House, the only negative vote coming from Jeannette Rankin, Republican of Montana who—as a pacifist—had also voted against war in 1917. On December 11th, Germany and Italy as Japan's allies, declared war on America, and Congress promptly reciprocated. The long and bitter debate over isolationism and America's role on the world stage had finally been overtaken by events. – Note by John Grafton

MR. VICE PRESIDENT, Mr. Speaker, members of the Senate and the House of Representatives:

Yesterday, December 7, 1941—a date which will live in infamy—the United States of America was suddenly and deliberately attacked by naval and air forces of the empire of Japan.

The United States was at peace with that nation, and, at the solicitation of Japan, was still in conversation with its government and its Emperor looking toward the maintenance of peace in the Pacific.

Indeed, one hour after Japanese air squadrons had commenced bombing in the American island of Oahu, the Japanese Ambassador to the United States and his colleague delivered to our Secretary of State a formal reply to a recent American message. And, while this reply stated that it seemed useless to continue the existing diplomatic negotiations, it contained no threat or hint of war or of armed attack.

It will be recorded that the distance of Hawaii from Japan makes it obvious that the attack was deliberately planned many days or even weeks ago. During the intervening time the Japanese

Government has deliberately sought to deceive the United States by false statements and expressions of hope for continued peace.

The attack yesterday on the Hawaiian Islands has caused severe damage to American naval and military forces. I regret to tell you that very many American lives have been lost. In addition, American ships have been reported torpedoed on the high seas between San Francisco and Honolulu.

Yesterday the Japanese Government also launched an attack against Malaya.

Last night Japanese forces attacked Hong Kong.

Last night Japanese forces attacked Guam.

Last night Japanese forces attacked the Philippine Islands.

Last night Japanese forces attacked Wake Island.

And this morning the Japanese attacked Midway Island.

Japan has therefore undertaken a surprise offensive extending through the Pacific Area. The facts of yesterday and today speak for themselves. The people of the United States have already formed their opinions and well understand the implications to the very life and safety of our nation.

As Commander in Chief of the Army and Navy I have directed that all measures be taken for our defense, that always will our whole nation remember the character of the onslaught against us.

No matter how long it may take us to overcome this premeditated invasion, the American people, in their righteous might, will win through absolute victory.

I believe that I interpret the will of the Congress and of the people when I assert that we will not only defend ourselves to the uttermost but will make it very certain that this form of treachery shall never again endanger us.

Hostilities exist. There is no blinking at the fact that our people, our territory and our interests are in grave danger.

With confidence in our armed forces, with the unbounding determination of our people, we will gain the inevitable triumph. So help us God.

I ask that the Congress declare that since the unprovoked and dastardly attack by Japan on Sunday, December 7, 1941, a state of war has existed between the United States and the Japanese Empire.

[FDR]

President Franklin D. Roosevelt, Japanese Relocation Order

February 19, 1942

In the aftermath of the bombing of Pearl Harbor in Hawaii, President Roosevelt's War Department pressed him to allow it to "relocate," which meant essentially imprisoning, for the duration of the war, 112,000 Japanese American citizens and immigrants ("alien enemies") most of whom had been living in California, and impounding their property. This order counts as one of the disgraces of American domestic policy.

Executive Order No. 9066
The President
Executive Order
Authorizing the Secretary of War to Prescribe Military Areas

Whereas the successful prosecution of the war requires every possible protection against espionage and against sabotage to national-defense material, national-defense premises, and national-defense utilities as defined in Section 4, Act of April 20, 1918, 40 Stat. 533, as amended by the Act of November 30, 1940, 54 Stat. 1220, and the Act of August 21, 1941, 55 Stat. 655 (U.S.C., Title 50, Sec. 104);

Now, therefore, by virtue of the authority vested in me as President of the United States, and Commander in Chief of the Army and Navy, I hereby authorize and direct the Secretary of War, and the Military Commanders whom he may from time to time designate, whenever he or any designated Commander deems such action necessary or desirable, to prescribe military areas in such places and of such extent as he or the appropriate Military Commander may determine, from which any or all persons may be excluded, and with respect to which, the right of any person to enter, remain in, or leave shall be subject to whatever restrictions the Secretary of War or the appropriate Military Commander may impose in his discretion. The Secretary of War is hereby authorized to provide for residents of any such area who are excluded therefrom, such transportation, food, shelter, and other accommodations as may be necessary, in the judgment of the Secretary of War or the said Military Commander, and until other arrangements are made, to accomplish the purpose of this order. The designation of military areas in any region or locality shall supersede designations of prohibited and restricted areas by the Attorney General under the Proclamations of December 7 and 8, 1941, and shall supersede the responsibility and authority of the Attorney General under the said Proclamations in respect of such prohibited and restricted areas.

I hereby further authorize and direct the Secretary of War and the said Military Commanders to take such other steps as he or the appropriate Military Commander may deem advisable to enforce compliance with the restrictions applicable to each Military area hereinabove authorized to be designated, including the use of Federal troops and other Federal Agencies, with authority to accept assistance of state and local agencies.

I hereby further authorize and direct all Executive Departments, independent establishments and other Federal Agencies, to assist the Secretary of War or the said Military Commanders in carrying out this Executive Order, including the furnishing of medical aid, hospitalization, food, clothing, transportation, use of land, shelter, and other supplies, equipment, utilities, facilities, and services.

This order shall not be construed as modifying or limiting in any way the authority heretofore granted under Executive Order No. 8972, dated December 12, 1941, nor shall it be construed as limiting or modifying the duty and responsibility of the Federal Bureau of Investigation, with respect to the investigation of alleged acts of sabotage or the duty and responsibility of the Attorney General and the Department of Justice under the Proclamations of December 7 and 8, 1941, prescribing regulations for the conduct and control of

alien enemies, except as such duty and responsibility is superseded
by the designation of military areas hereunder.

Franklin D. Roosevelt
The White House,
February 19, 1942.

[NARA]

President Franklin D. Roosevelt, Fireside Chat on the Fifth War Loan Drive

June 12, 1944

When FDR went on the radio on the evening of June 5, 1944, to an-
nounce that the Fifth Army had captured Rome, he knew what only a
handful of people in the Western Hemisphere knew at that moment, that
the first wave of paratroopers had already been dropped behind enemy lines
in France, and the huge D-Day invasion force was on its way across the
English Channel to the Normandy beaches. With uncertain weather condi-
tions and German defenses of unknown strength, the next several days
represented an uneasy period in Washington as the Allies put a million
soldiers and the necessary equipment ashore. This was the background for
FDR's June 12th speech on behalf of the Fifth World War II Loan Drive
then getting under way. For the Commander in Chief, the war not only had
to be won, it had to be paid for. Taxes raised less than half of the $321
billion cost of World War II (in 1940s dollars), and their collection in those
wartime years did add one new feature to the American fiscal landscape—the
withholding of federal income taxes that went into effect in 1943. Money
not raised by taxes had to be borrowed, and as war bonds were sold, the
national debt rose from $49 billion in 1941 to more than five times that
figure by 1945.

— Note by John Grafton

Ladies and gentlemen:

ALL OUR FIGHTING men overseas today have their appointed stations
on the far-flung battlefronts of the world. We at home have ours

too. We need, we are proud of, our fighting men—most decidedly. But, during the anxious times ahead, let us not forget that they need us too.

It goes almost without saying that we must continue to forge the weapons of victory—the hundreds of thousands of items, large and small, essential to the waging of the war. This has been the major task from the very start, and it is still a major task. This is the very worst time for any war worker to think of leaving his machine or to look for a peacetime job.

And it goes almost without saying, too, that we must continue to provide our Government with the funds necessary for waging war not only by the payment of taxes—which, after all, is an obligation of American citizenship—but also by the purchase of War Bonds—an act of free choice which every citizen has to make for himself under the guidance of his own conscience.

Whatever else any of us may be doing, the purchase of War Bonds and stamps is something all of us can do and should do to help win the war. I am happy to report tonight that it is something which—something nearly everyone seems to be doing. Although there are now approximately sixty-seven million persons who have or earn some form of income (including the armed forces), eighty-one million persons or their children have already bought war bonds. They have bought more than six hundred million individual bonds. Their purchases have totaled more than thirty-two billion dollars. These are the purchases of individual men, women and children. Anyone who would have said this was possible a few years ago would have been put down as a starry-eyed visionary. But of such visions is the stuff of America fashioned.

Of course, there are always pessimists with us everywhere, a few here and a few there. I am reminded of the fact that after the fall of France in 1940 I asked the Congress for the money for the production by the United States of fifty thousand airplanes per year. Well, I was called crazy—it was said that the figure was fantastic; that it could not be done. And yet today we are building airplanes at the rate of one hundred thousand a year.

There is a direct connection between the Bonds you have bought and the stream of men and equipment now rushing over the English Channel for the liberation of Europe. There is a direct connection between your War Bonds and every part of this global war today.

Tonight, therefore on the opening of this Fifth War Loan Drive, it is appropriate for us to take a broad look at this panorama of world war, for the success or the failure of the drive is going to have so much to do with the speed with which we can accomplish victory and the peace.

While I know that the chief interest tonight is centered on the English Channel and on the beaches and farms and the cities of Normandy, we should not lose sight of the fact that our armed forces are engaged on other battlefronts all over the world, and that no one front can be considered alone without its proper relation to all.

It is worth while, therefore, to make over-all comparisons with the past. Let us compare today with just two years ago—June, 1942. At that time Germany was in control of practically all of Europe, and was steadily driving the Russians back toward the Ural Mountains. Germany was practically in control of North Africa and the Mediterranean, and was beating at the gates of the Suez Canal and the route to India. Italy was still an important military and supply factor—as subsequent, long campaigns have proved.

Japan was in control of the western Aleutian Islands; and in the South Pacific was knocking at the gates of Australia and New Zealand—and also was threatening India. Japan had seized control of nearly one half of the Central Pacific.

American armed forces on land and sea and in the air were still very definitely on the defensive, and in the building-up stage. Our Allies were bearing the heat and the brunt of the attack.

In 1942 Washington heaved a sigh of relief that the first War Bond issue had been cheerfully over-subscribed by the American people. Way back in those days, two years ago, America was still hearing from many "amateur strategists" and political critics, some of whom were doing more good for Hitler than for the United States—two years ago.

But today we are on the offensive all over the world—bringing the attack to our enemies.

In the Pacific, by relentless submarine and naval attacks, and amphibious thrusts, and ever-mounting air attacks, we have deprived the Japs of the power to check the momentum of our ever-growing and ever-advancing military forces. We have reduced the Japs' shipping by more than three million tons. We have overcome their original advantage in the air. We have cut off from a return to the homeland, cut off from that return, tens of thousands of beleaguered

Japanese troops who now face starvation or ultimate surrender. And we have cut down their naval strength, so that for many months they have avoided all risk of encounter with our naval forces.

True, we still have a long way to go to Tokyo. But, carrying out our original strategy of eliminating our European enemy first and then turning all our strength to the Pacific, we can force the Japanese to unconditional surrender or to national suicide much more rapidly than has been thought possible.

Turning now to our enemy who is first on the list for destruction—Germany has her back against the wall—in fact three walls at once!

In the south—we have broken the German hold on central Italy. On June fourth, the city of Rome fell to the Allied armies. And allowing the enemy no respite, the Allies are now pressing hard on the heels of the Germans as they retreat northwards in ever-growing confusion.

On the east—our gallant Soviet Allies have driven the enemy back from the lands which were invaded three years ago. The great Soviet armies are now initiating crushing blows.

Overhead—vast Allied air fleets of bombers and fighters have been waging a bitter air war over Germany and Western Europe. They have had two major objectives: to destroy German war industries which maintain the German armies and air forces; and to shoot the German Luftwaffe out of the air. As a result German production has been whittled down continuously, and the German fighter forces now have only a fraction of their former power.

This great air campaign, strategic and tactical, is going to continue—with increasing power.

And on the west—the hammer blow which struck the coast of France last Tuesday morning, less than a week ago, was the culmination of many months of careful planning and strenuous preparation.

Millions of tons of weapons and supplies, hundreds of thousands of men assembled in England, are now being poured into the great battle in Europe.

I think that from the standpoint of our enemy we have achieved the impossible. We have broken through their supposedly impregnable wall in Northern France. But the assault has been costly in men and costly in materials. Some of our landings were desperate adventures; but from advices received so far, the losses were lower than our commanders had estimated would occur. We have established a firm foothold. We are now prepared to meet the inevitable counter-attacks of the Germans—with power and with confidence. And we all pray that we will have far more, soon, than a firm foothold.

Americans have all worked together to make this day possible.

The liberation forces now streaming across the Channel, and up the beaches and through the fields and the forests of France are using thousands and thousands of planes and ships and tanks and heavy guns. They are carrying with them many thousands of items needed for their dangerous, stupendous undertaking. There is a shortage of nothing—nothing! And this must continue.

What has been done in the United States since those days of 1940—when France fell—in raising and equipping and transporting our fighting forces, and in producing weapons and supplies for war, has been nothing short of a miracle. It was largely due to American teamwork—teamwork among capital and labor and agriculture, between the armed forces and the civilian economy—indeed among all of them.

And every one—every man or woman or child—who bought a War Bond helped—and helped mightily!

There are still many people in the United States who have not bought War Bonds, or who have not bought as many as they can afford. Everyone knows for himself whether he falls into that category or not. In some cases his neighbors know too. To the consciences of those people, this appeal by the President of the United States is very much in order.

For all of the things which we use in this war, everything we send to our fighting Allies, costs money—a lot of money. One sure way every man, woman and child can keep faith with those who have given, and are giving, their lives, is to provide the money which is needed to win the final victory.

I urge all Americans to buy War Bonds without stint. Swell the mighty chorus to bring us nearer to victory!

[FDR]

Into the Cold War

President Harry S. Truman Message to Congress, "The Truman Doctrine"

March 12, 1947

The president's speech advocated aid for Greece and Turkey in the aftermath of World War II. Great Britain, which had been financially supporting both countries, could no longer do so. Truman saw the danger of intervention and take-over in these and other countries by the Soviet Union and explained: "One of the primary objectives of the foreign policy of the United States is the creation of conditions in which we and other nations will be able to work out a way of life free from coercion. This was a fundamental issue in the war with Germany and Japan. Our victory was won over countries which sought to impose their will, and their way of life, upon other nations."

Mr. President, Mr. Speaker, Members of the Congress of the United States:

THE GRAVITY OF the situation which confronts the world today necessitates my appearance before a joint session of the Congress. The foreign policy and the national security of this country are involved.

One aspect of the present situation, which I wish to present to you at this time for your consideration and decision, concerns Greece and Turkey.

The United States has received from the Greek Government an urgent appeal for financial and economic assistance. Preliminary reports from the American Economic Mission now in Greece and reports from the American Ambassador in Greece corroborate the statement of the Greek Government that assistance is imperative if Greece is to survive as a free nation.

I do not believe that the American people and the Congress wish to turn a deaf ear to the appeal of the Greek Government.

Greece is not a rich country. Lack of sufficient natural resources has always forced the Greek people to work hard to make both ends meet. Since 1940, this industrious and peace loving country has suffered invasion, four years of cruel enemy occupation, and bitter internal strife.

When forces of liberation entered Greece they found that the retreating Germans had destroyed virtually all the railways, roads, port facilities, communications, and merchant marine. More than a thousand villages had been burned. Eighty-five per cent of the children were tubercular. Livestock, poultry, and draft animals had almost disappeared. Inflation had wiped out practically all savings.

As a result of these tragic conditions, a militant minority, exploiting human want and misery, was able to create political chaos which, until now, has made economic recovery impossible.

Greece is today without funds to finance the importation of those goods which are essential to bare subsistence. Under these circumstances the people of Greece cannot make progress in solving their problems of reconstruction. Greece is in desperate need of financial and economic assistance to enable it to resume purchases of food, clothing, fuel and seeds. These are indispensable for the subsistence of its people and are obtainable only from abroad. Greece must have help to import the goods necessary to restore internal order and security, so essential for economic and political recovery.

The Greek Government has also asked for the assistance of experienced American administrators, economists and technicians to insure that the financial and other aid given to Greece shall be used effectively in creating a stable and self-sustaining economy and in improving its public administration.

The very existence of the Greek state is today threatened by the terrorist activities of several thousand armed men, led by Communists, who defy the government's authority at a number of points, particularly along the northern boundaries. A Commission appointed by the United Nations security Council is at present investigating disturbed conditions in northern Greece and alleged border violations along the frontier between Greece on the one hand and Albania, Bulgaria, and Yugoslavia on the other.

Meanwhile, the Greek Government is unable to cope with the situation. The Greek army is small and poorly equipped. It needs supplies and equipment if it is to restore the authority of the government throughout Greek territory. Greece must have assistance if it is to become a self-supporting and self-respecting democracy.

The United States must supply that assistance. We have already extended to Greece certain types of relief and economic aid but these are inadequate.

There is no other country to which democratic Greece can turn.

No other nation is willing and able to provide the necessary support for a democratic Greek government.

The British Government, which has been helping Greece, can give no further financial or economic aid after March 31. Great Britain finds itself under the necessity of reducing or liquidating its commitments in several parts of the world, including Greece.

We have considered how the United Nations might assist in this crisis. But the situation is an urgent one requiring immediate action and the United Nations and its related organizations are not in a position to extend help of the kind that is required.

It is important to note that the Greek Government has asked for our aid in utilizing effectively the financial and other assistance we may give to Greece, and in improving its public administration. It is of the utmost importance that we supervise the use of any funds made available to Greece; in such a manner that each dollar spent will count toward making Greece self-supporting, and will help to build an economy in which a healthy democracy can flourish.

No government is perfect. One of the chief virtues of a democracy, however, is that its defects are always visible and under democratic processes can be pointed out and corrected. The Government of Greece is not perfect. Nevertheless it represents eighty-five per cent of the members of the Greek Parliament who were chosen in an election last year. Foreign observers, including 692 Americans, considered this election to be a fair expression of the views of the Greek people.

The Greek Government has been operating in an atmosphere of chaos and extremism. It has made mistakes. The extension of aid by this country does not mean that the United States condones everything that the Greek Government has done or will do. We have condemned in the past, and we condemn now, extremist measures of the right or the left. We have in the past advised tolerance, and we advise tolerance now.

Greece's neighbor, Turkey, also deserves our attention.

The future of Turkey as an independent and economically sound state is clearly no less important to the freedom-loving peoples of the world than the future of Greece. The circumstances in which Turkey finds itself today are considerably different from those of Greece. Turkey has been spared the disasters that have beset Greece. And during the war, the United States and Great Britain furnished Turkey with material aid.

Nevertheless, Turkey now needs our support.

Since the war Turkey has sought financial assistance from Great Britain and the United States for the purpose of effecting that modernization necessary for the maintenance of its national integrity.

That integrity is essential to the preservation of order in the Middle East.

The British government has informed us that, owing to its own difficulties can no longer extend financial or economic aid to Turkey.

As in the case of Greece, if Turkey is to have the assistance it needs, the United States must supply it. We are the only country able to provide that help.

I am fully aware of the broad implications involved if the United States extends assistance to Greece and Turkey, and I shall discuss these implications with you at this time.

One of the primary objectives of the foreign policy of the United States is the creation of conditions in which we and other nations will be able to work out a way of life free from coercion. This was a fundamental issue in the war with Germany and Japan. Our victory was won over countries which sought to impose their will, and their way of life, upon other nations.

To ensure the peaceful development of nations, free from coercion, the United States has taken a leading part in establishing the United Nations, The United Nations is designed to make possible lasting freedom and independence for all its members. We shall not realize our objectives, however, unless we are willing to help free peoples to maintain their free institutions and their national integrity against aggressive movements that seek to impose upon them totalitarian regimes. This is no more than a frank recognition that totalitarian regimes imposed on free peoples, by direct or indirect aggression, undermine the foundations of international peace and hence the security of the United States.

The peoples of a number of countries of the world have recently had totalitarian regimes forced upon them against their will. The Government of the United States has made frequent protests against coercion and intimidation, in violation of the Yalta agreement, in Poland, Rumania, and Bulgaria. I must also state that in a number of other countries there have been similar developments.

At the present moment in world history nearly every nation must choose between alternative ways of life. The choice is too often not a free one.

One way of life is based upon the will of the majority, and is distinguished by free institutions, representative government, free elections, guarantees of individual liberty, freedom of speech and religion, and freedom from political oppression.

The second way of life is based upon the will of a minority forcibly imposed upon the majority. It relies upon terror and oppression, a controlled press and radio; fixed elections, and the suppression of personal freedoms.

I believe that it must be the policy of the United States to support free peoples who are resisting attempted subjugation by armed minorities or by outside pressures.

I believe that we must assist free peoples to work out their own destinies in their own way.

I believe that our help should be primarily through economic and financial aid which is essential to economic stability and orderly political processes.

The world is not static, and the status quo is not sacred. But we cannot allow changes in the status quo in violation of the Charter of the United Nations by such methods as coercion, or by such subterfuges as political infiltration. In helping free and independent nations to maintain their freedom, the United States will be giving effect to the principles of the Charter of the United Nations.

It is necessary only to glance at a map to realize that the survival and integrity of the Greek nation are of grave importance in a much wider situation. If Greece should fall under the control of an armed minority, the effect upon its neighbor, Turkey, would be immediate and serious. Confusion and disorder might well spread throughout the entire Middle East.

Moreover, the disappearance of Greece as an independent state would have a profound effect upon those countries in Europe whose peoples are struggling against great difficulties to maintain their freedoms and their independence while they repair the damages of war.

It would be an unspeakable tragedy if these countries, which have struggled so long against overwhelming odds, should lose that victory for which they sacrificed so much. Collapse of free institutions and loss of independence would be disastrous not only for them but for the world. Discouragement and possibly failure would quickly be the lot of neighboring peoples striving to maintain their freedom and independence.

Should we fail to aid Greece and Turkey in this fateful hour, the effect will be far reaching to the West as well as to the East.

We must take immediate and resolute action.

I therefore ask the Congress to provide authority for assistance to Greece and Turkey in the amount of $400,000,000 for the period ending June 30, 1948. In requesting these funds, I have taken into consideration the maximum amount of relief assistance which would be furnished to Greece out of the $350,000,000 which I recently requested that the Congress authorize for the prevention of starvation and suffering in countries devastated by the war.

In addition to funds, I ask the Congress to authorize the detail of American civilian and military personnel to Greece and Turkey, at the request of those countries, to assist in the tasks of reconstruction, and for the purpose of supervising the use of such financial and material assistance as may be furnished. I recommend that authority also be provided for the instruction and training of selected Greek and Turkish personnel.

Finally, I ask that the Congress provide authority which will permit the speediest and most effective use, in terms of needed commodities, supplies, and equipment, of such funds as may be authorized.

If further funds, or further authority, should be needed for purposes indicated in this message, I shall not hesitate to bring the situation before the Congress. On this subject the Executive and Legislative branches of the Government must work together.

This is a serious course upon which we embark.

I would not recommend it except that the alternative is much more serious. The United States contributed $341,000,000,000 toward winning World War II. This is an investment in world freedom and world peace.

The assistance that I am recommending for Greece and Turkey amounts to little more than 1 tenth of 1 per cent of this investment. It is only common sense that we should safeguard this investment and make sure that it was not in vain.

The seeds of totalitarian regimes are nurtured by misery and want. They spread and grow in the evil soil of poverty and strife. They reach their full growth when the hope of a people for a better life has died. We must keep that hope alive.

The free peoples of the world look to us for support in maintaining their freedoms.

If we falter in our leadership, we may endanger the peace of the world—and we shall surely endanger the welfare of our own nation.

Great responsibilities have been placed upon us by the swift movement of events.

I am confident that the Congress will face these responsibilities squarely.

[NARA – AVA]

Secretary of State George C. Marshall, Speech, "The Marshall Plan"

June 5, 1947

George C. Marshall (1880–1959), the Army Chief of Staff from 1939 through 1945, had been recently appointed by President Truman to serve as the Secretary of State when he spoke at Harvard University's commencement exercises about the economic crisis and famine in post-war Europe. The significance of the points he made in the speech resulted in the Economic Cooperation Act of 1948.

MR. PRESIDENT, DR. CONANT, members of the board of overseers, ladies and gentlemen, I'm profoundly grateful and touched by the distinction and honor and great compliment accorded me by the authorities of Harvard this morning. I'm overwhelmed, as a matter of fact, and I'm rather fearful of my inability to maintain such a high rating as you've been generous enough to accord to me. In these historic and lovely surroundings, this perfect day, and this very wonderful assembly, it is a tremendously impressive thing to an individual in my position.

I need not tell you gentlemen that the world situation is very serious. That must be apparent to all intelligent people. I think one difficulty is that the problem is one of such enormous complexity that the very mass of facts presented to the public by press and radio make it exceedingly difficult for the man in the street to reach a clear appraisement of the situation. Furthermore, the people of this country are distant from the troubled areas of the earth and it is hard for them to comprehend the plight and consequent reactions of the long-suffering peoples, and the effect of those reactions on their governments in connection with our efforts to promote peace in the world.

In considering the requirements for the rehabilitation of Europe, the physical loss of life, the visible destruction of cities, factories, mines and railroads was correctly estimated, but it has become obvious during recent months that this visible destruction was probably less serious than the dislocation of the entire fabric of European economy. For the past ten years conditions have been highly abnormal. The feverish preparation for war and the more feverish maintenance of the war effort engulfed all aspects of national economies. Machinery has fallen into disrepair or is entirely obsolete. Under the arbitrary and destructive Nazi rule, virtually every possible enterprise was geared into the German war machine. Long-standing commercial ties, private institutions, banks, insurance companies and shipping companies disappeared, through loss of capital, absorption through nationalization or by simple destruction. In many countries, confidence in the local currency has been severely shaken. The breakdown of the business structure of Europe during the war was complete. Recovery has been seriously retarded by the fact those two years after the close of hostilities a peace settlement with Germany and Austria has not been agreed upon. But even given a more prompt solution of these difficult problems, the rehabilitation of the economic structure of Europe quite evidently will require a much longer time and greater effort than had been foreseen.

There is a phase of this matter which is both interesting and serious. The farmer has always produced the foodstuffs to exchange with the city dweller for the other necessities of life. This division of labor is the basis of modern civilization. At the present time it is threatened with breakdown. The town and city industries are not producing adequate goods to exchange with the food-producing farmer. Raw materials and fuel are in short supply. Machinery is lacking or worn out. The farmer or the peasant cannot find the goods for sale which he desires to purchase. So the sale of his farm produce for money which he cannot use seems to him an unprofitable transaction. He, therefore, has withdrawn many fields from crop cultivation and is using them for grazing. He feeds more grain to stock and finds for himself and his family an ample supply of food, however short he may be on clothing and the other ordinary gadgets of civilization. Meanwhile people in the cities are short of food and fuel. So the governments are forced to use their foreign money and credits to procure these necessities abroad. This process exhausts funds which are urgently needed for reconstruction. This very serious situation is rapidly developing which bodes no good for the world. The modern system of the division of labor upon which the exchange of products is based is in danger of breaking down.

The truth of the matter is that Europe's requirements for the next three or four years of foreign food and other essential products— principally from America—are so much greater than her present ability to pay that she must have substantial additional help, or face economic, social and political deterioration of a very grave character.

The remedy lies in breaking the vicious circle and restoring the confidence of the European people in the economic future of their own countries and of Europe as a whole. The manufacturer and the farmer throughout wide areas must be able and willing to exchange their products for currencies the continuing value of which is not open to question.

Aside from the demoralizing effect on the world at large and the possibilities of disturbances arising as a result of the desperation of the people concerned, the consequences to the economy of the United States should be apparent to all. It is logical that the United States should do whatever it is able to do to assist in the return of normal economic health in the world, without which there can be no political stability and no assured peace. Our policy is directed not against any country or doctrine but against hunger, poverty, desperation and chaos. Its purpose should be the revival of a working economy in the world so as to permit the emergence of political and social conditions in which free institutions can exist. Such assistance, I am convinced, must not be on a piece-meal basis as various crises develop. Any assistance that this Government may render in the future should provide a cure rather than a mere palliative. Any government that is willing to assist in the task of recovery will find full cooperation, I am sure, on the part of the United States Government. Any government which maneuvers to block the recovery of other countries cannot expect help from us. Furthermore, governments, political parties or groups which seek to perpetuate human misery in order to profit therefrom politically or otherwise will encounter the opposition of the United States.

It is already evident that, before the United States Government can proceed much further in its efforts to alleviate the situation and help start the European world on its way to recovery, there must be some agreement among the countries of Europe as to the

requirements of the situation and the part those countries themselves will take in order to give proper effect to whatever action
might be undertaken by this Government. It would be neither fitting nor efficacious for this Government to undertake to draw up
unilaterally a program designed to place Europe on its feet economically. This is the business of the Europeans. The initiative, I
think, must come from Europe. The role of this country should
consist of friendly aid in the drafting of a European program and of
later support of such a program so far as it may be practical for us
to do so. The program should be a joint one, agreed to by a number, if not all European nations.

An essential part of any successful action on the part of the
United States is an understanding on the part of the people of
America of the character of the problem and the remedies to be
applied. Political passion and prejudice should have no part. With
foresight, and a willingness on the part of our people to face up to
the vast responsibility which history has clearly placed upon our
country, the difficulties I have outlined can and will be overcome.

I am sorry that on occasion I have said something publicly in
regard to our international situation; I've been forced by the necessities of the case to enter into rather technical discussions. But to
my mind, it is of vast importance that our people reach some general understanding of what the complications really are, rather than
react from a passion or a prejudice or an emotion of the moment.
As I said more formally a moment ago, we are remote from the
scene of these troubles. It is virtually impossible at this distance
merely by reading, or listening, or even seeing photographs or motion pictures, to grasp at all the real significance of the situation.
And yet the whole world of the future hangs on a proper judgment.
It hangs, I think, to a large extent on the realization of the American people, of just what are the various dominant factors. What are
the reactions of the people? What are the justifications of those
reactions? What are the sufferings? What is needed? What can best
be done? What must be done? Thank you very much.

[GCM]

Senator Joseph R. McCarthy, Address to the Republican Women's Club of Wheeling, West Virginia, "Enemies from Within"

February 9, 1950

Joseph R. McCarthy (1908–1957), a Wisconsin Senator from 1946 to 1957, made himself notorious by indulging in America's paranoia about communists. He bullied and intimidated the government and its representatives for several years, until the blindness of his accusations and the relentlessness of his persecutions proved for the most part only his own disreputableness. He never produced the "list of 205" Communist Party members, he mentions herein, but for the next four years menaced or threatened to menace thousands of innocent Americans.

LADIES AND GENTLEMEN, tonight as we celebrate the one hundred forty-first birthday of one of the greatest men in American history, I would like to be able to talk about what a glorious day today is in the history of the world. As we celebrate the birth of this man who with his whole heart and soul hated war, I would like to be able to speak of peace in our time—of war being outlawed—and of world-wide disarmament. These would be truly appropriate things to be able to mention as we celebrate the birthday of Abraham Lincoln.

Five years after a world war has been won, men's hearts should anticipate a long peace—and men's minds should be free from the heavy weight that comes with war. But this is not such a period—for this is not a period of peace. This is a time of "the cold war." This is a time when the entire world is split into two vast, increasingly hostile, armed camps—a time of a great armament race.

Today we can almost physically hear the mutterings and rumblings of an invigorated god of war. You can see it, feel it, and hear it all the way from the Indochina hills, from the shores of Formosa, right over into the very heart of Europe itself.

The one encouraging thing is that the "mad moment" has not yet arrived for the firing of the gun or the exploding of the bomb which will set civilization about the final task of destroying itself. There is still a hope for peace if we finally decide that no longer can we safely blind our eyes and close our ears to those facts which are shaping up more and more clearly—and that is that we are now engaged in a show-down fight—not the usual war between nations for land areas or other material gains, but a war between two diametrically opposed ideologies.

The great difference between our western Christian world and the atheistic Communist world is not political, gentlemen, it is moral. For instance, the Marxian idea of confiscating the land and factories and running the entire economy as a single enterprise is momentous. Likewise, Lenin's invention of the one-party police state as a way to make Marx's idea work is hardly less momentous.

Stalin's resolute putting across of these two ideas, of course, did much to divide the world. With only these differences, however, the east and the west could most certainly still live in peace.

The real, basic difference, however, lies in the religion of immoralism—invented by Marx, preached feverishly by Lenin, and carried to unimaginable extremes by Stalin. This religion of immoralism, if the Red half of the world triumphs—and well it may, gentlemen—this religion of immoralism will more deeply wound and damage mankind than any conceivable economic or political system.

Karl Marx dismissed God as a hoax, and Lenin and Stalin have added in clear-cut, unmistakable language their resolve that no nation, no people who believe in a god, can exist side by side with their communistic state.

Karl Marx, for example, expelled people from his Communist Party for mentioning such things as love, justice, humanity or morality. He called this "soulful ravings" and "sloppy sentimentality."

While Lincoln was a relatively young man in his late thirties, Karl Marx boasted that the Communist specter was haunting

Europe. Since that time, hundreds of millions of people and vast areas of the world have come under Communist domination. Today, less than 100 years after Lincoln's death, Stalin brags that this Communist specter is not only haunting the world, but is about to completely subjugate it.

Today we are engaged in a final, all-out battle between communistic atheism and Christianity. The modern champions of communism have selected this as the time, and ladies and gentlemen, the chips are down—they are truly down.

Lest there be any doubt that the time has been chosen, let us go directly to the leader of communism today—Joseph Stalin. Here is what he said—not back in 1928, not before the war, not during the war—but 2 years after the last war was ended: "To think that the Communist revolution can be carried out peacefully, within the framework of a Christian democracy, means one has either gone out of one's mind and lost all normal understanding, or has grossly and openly repudiated the Communist revolution."

This is what was said by Lenin in 1919—and quoted with approval by Stalin in 1947:

"We are living," says Lenin, "not merely in a state, but in a system of states, and the existence of the Soviet Republic side by side with Christian states for a long time is unthinkable. One or the other must triumph in the end. And before that end supervenes, a series of frightful collisions between the Soviet Republic and the bourgeois states will be inevitable."

Ladies and gentlemen, can there be anyone tonight who is so blind as to say that the war is not on? Can there be anyone who fails to realize that the Communist world has said the time is now?—that this is the time for the showdown between the democratic Christian world and the communistic atheistic world?

Unless we face this fact, we shall pay the price that must be paid by those who wait too long.

Six years ago, at the time of the first conference to map out the peace, there was within the Soviet orbit, 180,000,000 people. Lined up on the anti-totalitarian side there were in the world at that time, roughly 1,625,000,000 people. Today, only 6 years later, there are 80,000,000,000 people under the absolute domination of Soviet Russia—an increase of over 400 percent. On our side, the figure has shrunk to around 500,000. In other words, in less than 6 years, the odds have changed from 9 to 1 in our favor to 8 to 1 against us.

This indicates the swiftness of the tempo of Communist victories and American defeats in the cold war. As one of our outstanding historical figures once said, "When a great democracy is destroyed, it will not be from enemies from without, but rather because of enemies from within."

The truth of this statement is becoming terrifyingly clear as we see this country each day losing on every front.

At war's end we were physically the strongest nation on earth and at least potentially the most powerful intellectually and morally. Ours could have been the honor of being a beacon in the desert of destruction—shining proof that civilization was not yet ready to destroy itself. Unfortunately, we have failed miserably and tragically to arise to the opportunity.

The reason why we find ourselves in a position of impotency is not because our only powerful potential enemy has sent men to invade our shores—but rather because of the traitorous actions of those who have been treated so well by this Nation. It has not been the less fortunate, or members of minority groups who have been traitorous to this Nation—but rather those who have had all the benefits that the wealthiest Nation on earth has had to offer—the finest homes, the finest college education and the finest jobs in government we can give.

This is glaringly true in the State Department. There the bright young men who are born with silver spoons in their mouths are the ones who have been most traitorous.

Now I know it is very easy for anyone to condemn a particular bureau or department in general terms. Therefore, I would like to cite some specific cases.

When Chiang Kai-shek was fighting our war, the State Department had in China a young man named John Service. His task, obviously, was not to work for communization of China. However, strangely, he sent official reports back to the State Department urging that we torpedo our ally Chiang Kai-shek—and stating in unqualified terms (and I quote) that "communism was the only hope of China."

Later, this man—John Service—and please remember that name, ladies and gentlemen, was picked up by the Federal Bureau of Investigation for turning over to the Communists secret State Department information. Strangely, however, he was never prosecuted. However, John Grew, the Under Secretary of State, who insisted on his prosecution, was forced to resign. Two days after, his successor, Dean Acheson, took over as Under Secretary of State. This man, John Service, who had been picked up by the FBI and who had previously urged that communism was the only hope of China, was not only reinstated in the State Department, but promoted—and finally, under Acheson, placed in charge of all placements and promotions. Today, ladies and gentlemen, this man Service is on his way to represent the State Department and Acheson in Calcutta, by far and away the most important listening post in the Far East.

That's one case. Let's go to another—Gustavo Duran, who was labeled as (I quote) "a notorious international Communist," was made assistant to the Assistant Secretary of State in charge of Latin American affairs. He was taken into the State Department from his job as a lieutenant colonel in the Communist International Brigade. Finally, after intense congressional pressure and criticism, he re-signed in 1946 from the State Department. And, ladies and gentle-men, where do you think he is now? He took over a high-salaried job, as Chief of Cultural Activities Section in the office of the As-sistant Secretary General of the United Nations.

Then there was a Mrs. Mary Jane Kenney, from the Board of Economic Warfare in the State Department, who was named in a FBI report and in a House committee report as a courier for the Communist Party while working for the Government. And where do you think Mrs. Mary Jane is—she is now an editor in the United Nations Document Bureau.

Then there was Julian H. Wadleigh, economist in the Trade Agreements Section of the State Department for 11 years. And who was sent to Turkey and Italy and other countries as United States representative. After the statute of limitations had run so he could not be prosecuted for treason, he openly and brazenly not only admitted but proclaimed that he had been a member of the Com-munist Party—that while working for the State Department he stole a vast number of secret documents—and furnished these documents to the Russian spy ring of which he was a part.

And, ladies and gentlemen, while I cannot take the time to name all the men in the State Department who have been named as active members of the Communist Party and members of a spy ring, I have here in my hand a list of 205—a list of names that were made known to the Secretary of State as being members of the

Communist Party and who nevertheless are still working and shaping policy in that State Department.

One thing to remember in discussing the Communists in our Government is that we are not dealing with spies who get 30 pieces of silver to steal the blueprints of a new weapon. We are dealing with a far more sinister type of activity because it permits the enemy to guide and shape our policy.

In that connection I would like to read to you very briefly from the testimony of Larry E. Kerley, a man who was with the Counterespionage Section of the FBI for 8 years. And keep in mind as I read this to you that at the time he is speaking there was in the State Department Alger Hiss (the convicted traitor), John Service (the man whom the FBI picked up for espionage), Julian Wadleigh (who brazenly admitted he was a spy and wrote newspaper articles in regard thereto).

Here is what the FBI man said: "In accordance with instructions of the State Department to the Federal Bureau of Investigation, the FBI was not even permitted to open an espionage case against any Russian suspect without State Department approval."

And some further questions:

MR. ARENS. "Did the State Department ever withhold from the Justice Department the right to intern suspects?"

KERLEY. "They withheld the right to get out process for them which, in effect, kept them from being arrested, as in the case of Schevchenko and others."

ARENS. "In how many instances did the State Department decline to permit process to be served on Soviet agents?"

KERLEY. "Do you mean how many Soviet agents were affected?"

ARENS. "Yes."

KERLEY. "That would be difficult to say because there were so many people connected in one espionage ring, whether or not they were directly conspiring with the ring."

ARENS. "Was that order applicable to all persons?"

KERLEY. "Yes, all persons in the Soviet espionage organization."

ARENS. "What did you say the order was as you understood it or as it came to you?"

KERLEY. "That no arrests of any suspects in the Russian espionage activities in the United States were to be made without the prior approval of the State Department."

Now the reason for the State Department's opposition to arresting any of this spy ring is made rather clear in the next question and answer.

SENATOR O'CONNOR. "Did you understand that that was to include also American participants?"

KERLEY. "Yes, because if they were arrested that would disclose the whole apparatus, you see."

In other words they could not afford to let the whole ring which extended to the State Department, be shown.

This brings us down to the case of one Alger Hiss who is important not as an individual any more, but rather because he is so representative of a group in the State Department. It is unnecessary to go over the sordid events showing how he sold out the Nation which had given him so much. Those are rather fresh in all of our minds.

However, it should be remembered that the facts in regard to his connection with this international Communist spy ring were made known to the then Under Secretary of State Berle three days after Hitler and Stalin signed the Russo German Alliance Pact. At that time one Wittaker Chambers—who was also part of the spy ring—apparently decided that with Russia on Hitler's side he could no longer betray our Nation. He gave Under Secretary of State Berle—and this is all a matter of record—practically all, if not more, of the facts upon which Hiss' conviction was based.

Under Secretary Berle promptly contacted Dean Acheson and received word in return that Acheson (and I quote) "could vouch for Hiss absolutely"—at which time the matter was dropped. And this, you understand, was at a time when Russia was an ally of Germany. These conditions existed while Russia and Germany were invading and dismembering Poland, and while the Communist groups here were screaming "warmonger" at the United States for their support of the Allied nations.

Again in 1943 the FBI had occasion to investigate the facts surrounding Hiss. But even after that FBI report was submitted, nothing was done.

Then late in 1948—on August 5—when the Un-American Activities Committee called Alger Hiss to give an accounting, President Truman and the left-wing press commenced a systematic program of vilification of that committee. On the day that Truman labeled the Hiss investigation a "red herring," on that same day (and listen to this, ladies and gentlemen) President Truman also issued a Presidential directive ordering all Government agencies to refuse to turn over any information whatsoever in regard to the Communist activities of any Government employee to a congressional committee.

Incidentally, even after Hiss was convicted it is interesting to note that the President still labeled the exposé of Hiss as a "red herring."

If time permitted, it might be well to go into detail about the fact that Hiss was Roosevelt's chief advisor at Yalta when Roosevelt was admittedly in ill health and tired physically and mentally—and when, according to the Secretary of State, Hiss and Gromiko drafted the report on the conference.

According to the then Secretary of State, here are some of the things that Hiss helped to decide at Yalta. (1) The establishment of a European High Commission; (2) the treatment of Germany—this you will recall was the conference at which it was decided that we would occupy Berlin with Russia occupying an area completely circling the city, which, as you know, resulted in the Berlin air lift which cost 31 American lives; (3) the Polish question; (4) the relationship between UNRRA and the Soviet; (5) the rights of Americans on control commissions of Rumania, Bulgaria and Hungary: (6) Iran; (7) China—here's where we gave away Manchuria; (8) Turkish Straits question; (9) international trusteeship; (10) Korea.

Of the results of this conference, Arthur Bliss Lane of the State Department had this to say: "As I glanced over the document, I could not believe my eyes. To me, almost every line spoke of a surrender to Stalin."

As you hear this story of high treason, I know that you are saying to yourself—well, why doesn't the Congress do something about it. Actually, ladies and gentlemen, the reason for the graft, the corruption, the dishonesty, the disloyalty, the treason in high government positions—the reason this continues is because of a lack of moral uprising on the part of the 140,000,000 American people. In the light of history, however, this is not hard to explain.

It is the result of an emotional hangover and a temporary moral lapse which follows every war. It is the apathy to evil which people who have been subjected to the tremendous evils of war feel. As the people of the world see mass murder, the destruction of defenseless and innocent people, and all of the crime and lack of morals which go with war, they become numb and apathetic. It has always been thus after war.

However, the morals of our people have not been destroyed. They still exist. This cloak of numbness and apathy has only needed a spark to rekindle them. Happily, this has finally been supplied.

As you know, very recently the Secretary of State proclaimed his loyalty to a man guilty of what has always been considered as the most abominable of all crimes—being a traitor to the people who gave him a position of trust—high treason. The Secretary of State in attempting to justify his continued devotion to the man who sold out the Christian world to the atheistic world, referred to Christ's Sermon on the Mount as a justification and reason therefore.

And the reaction of the American people to this would have made the heart of Abraham Lincoln happy.

Thus this pompous diplomat in striped pants, with a phony British accent, tells the American people that Christ on the Mount endorsed communism, high treason, and betrayal of a sacred trust, this blasphemy was just great enough to awaken the dormant, inherent decency indignation of the American people.

He has lighted the spark which is resulting in a moral uprising and will end only when the whole sorry mess of twisted, warped thinkers is swept from the national scene so that we may have a new birth of honesty and decency in government.

[IS]

Senator Margaret Chase Smith, Speech to the Senate, "Declaration of Conscience"

June 1, 1950

A career politician from Maine, Smith (1897–1995) distinguished herself in the era of the Red Scare by bravely rising to challenge her fellow senators for their political persecution of innocent and patriotic Americans.

I WOULD LIKE to speak briefly and simply about a serious national condition. It is a national feeling of fear and frustration that could result in national suicide and the end of everything that we Americans hold dear. It is a condition that comes from the lack of effective leadership in either the Legislative Branch or the Executive Branch of our Government.

That leadership is so lacking that serious and responsible proposals are being made that national advisory commission be appointed to provide such critically needed leadership.

I speak as briefly as possible because too much harm has already been done with irresponsible words of bitterness and selfish political opportunism. I speak as simply as possible because the issue is too great to be obscured by eloquence. I speak simply and briefly in the hope that my words will be taken to heart.

I speak as a Republican. I speak as a woman. I speak as a United States Senator. I speak as an American.

The United States Senate has long enjoyed worldwide respect as the greatest deliberative body in the world. But recently that deliberative character has too often been debased to the level of a forum of hate and character assassination sheltered by the shield of congressional immunity.

It is ironical that we Senators can in debate in the Senate directly or indirectly, by any form of words, impute to any American who is not a Senator any conduct or motive unworthy or unbecoming an American—and without that non-Senator American having any legal redress against us—yet if we say the same thing in the Senate about our colleagues we can be stopped on the grounds of being out of order.

It is strange that we can verbally attack anyone else without restraint and with full protection and yet we hold ourselves above the same type of criticism here on the Senate Floor. Surely the United States Senate is big enough to take self-criticism and self-appraisal. Surely we should be able to take the same kind of character attacks that we "dish out" to outsiders.

I think that it is high time for the United States Senate and its members to do some soul-searching—for us to weigh our consciences—on the manner in which we are performing our duty to the people of America—on the manner in which we are using or abusing our individual powers and privileges.

I think that it is high time that we remembered that we have sworn to uphold and defend the Constitution. I think that it is high time that we remembered that the Constitution, as amended, speaks not only of the freedom of speech but also of trial by jury instead of trial by accusation.

Whether it be a criminal prosecution in court or a character prosecution in the Senate, there is little practical distinction when the life of a person has been ruined.

Those of us who shout the loudest about Americanism in making character assassinations are all too frequently those who, by our own words and acts, ignore some of the basic principles of Americanism:

The right to criticize;

The right to hold unpopular beliefs;

The right to protest;

The right of independent thought.

The exercise of these rights should not cost one single American citizen his reputation or his right to a livelihood nor should he be in danger of losing his reputation or livelihood merely because he happens to know someone who holds unpopular beliefs. Who of us doesn't? Otherwise none of us could call our souls our own. Otherwise thought control would have set in.

The American people are sick and tired of being afraid to speak their minds lest they be politically smeared as "Communists" or "Fascists" by their opponents. Freedom of speech is not what it used to be in America. It has been so abused by some that it is not exercised by others.

The American people are sick and tired of seeing innocent people smeared and guilty people whitewashed. But there have been enough proved cases such as the Amerasia case, the Hiss case, the Coplon case, the Gold case, to cause nationwide distrust and suspicion that there may be something to the unproved, sensational accusations.

As a Republican, I say to my colleagues on this side of the aisle that the Republican Party faces a challenge today that is not unlike the challenge that it faced back in Lincoln's day. The Republican Party so successfully met that challenge that it emerged from the Civil War as the champion of a united nation—in addition to being a Party that unrelentingly fought loose spending and loose programs.

Today our country is being psychologically divided by the confusion and the suspicions that are bred in the United States Senate to spread like cancerous tentacles of "know nothing, suspect everything" attitudes. Today we have a Democratic Administration that has developed a mania for loose spending and loose programs. History is repeating itself—and the Republican Party again has the opportunity to emerge as the champion of unity and prudence.

The record of the present Democratic Administration has provided us with sufficient campaign issues without the necessity to resorting to political smears. America is rapidly losing its position as leader of the world simply because the Democratic Administration has pitifully failed to provide effective leadership.

The Democratic Administration has completely confused the American people by its daily contradictory grave warnings and optimistic assurances—that show the people that our Democratic Administration has no idea of where it is going.

The Democratic Administration has greatly lost the confidence of the American people by its complacency to the threat of communism here at home and the leak of vital secrets to Russia through key officials of the Democratic Administration. There are enough proved cases to make this point without diluting our criticism with unproved charges.

Surely these are sufficient reasons to make it clear to the American people that it is time for a change and that a Republican victory is necessary to the security of this country. Surely it is clear that this nation will continue to suffer as long as it is governed by the present ineffective Democratic Administration.

Yet to displace it with a Republican regime embracing a philosophy that lacks political integrity or intellectual honesty would prove equally disastrous to this nation. The nation sorely needs a Republican victory. But I don't want to see the Republican Party ride to political victory on the Four Horsemen of Calumny—Fear, Ignorance, Bigotry, and Smear.

I doubt if the Republican Party could—simply because I don't believe the American people will uphold any political party that puts political exploitation above national interest. Surely we Republicans aren't that desperate for victory. '

I don't want to see the Republican Party win that way. While it might be a fleeting victory for the Republican Party, it would be a more lasting defeat for the American people. Surely it would ultimately be suicide for the Republican Party and the two-party system that has protected our American liberties from the dictatorship of a one-party system.

As members of the Minority Party, we do not have the primary authority to formulate the policy of our Government. But we do have the responsibility of rendering constructive criticism, of clarifying issues, of allaying fears by acting as responsible citizens.

As a woman, I wonder how the mothers, wives, sisters, and daughters feel about the way in which members of their families have been politically mangled in Senate debate—and I use the word "debate" advisedly.

As a United States Senator, I am not proud of the way in which the Senate has been made a publicity platform for irresponsible sensationalism. I am not proud of the reckless abandon in which unproved charges have been hurled from this side of the aisle. I am not proud of the obviously staged, undignified countercharges that have been attempted in retaliation from the other side of the aisle.

I don't like the way the Senate has been made a rendezvous for vilification, for selfish political gain at the sacrifice of individual reputations and national unity. I am not proud of the way we smear outsiders from the Floor of the Senate and hide behind the cloak of congressional immunity and still place ourselves beyond criticism on the Floor of the Senate.

As an American, I am shocked at the way Republicans and Democrats alike are playing directly into the Communist design of "confuse, divide, and conquer." As an American, I don't want a Democratic Administration "whitewash" or "coverup" any more than I want a Republican smear or witch hunt.

As an American, I condemn a Republican "Fascist" just as much as I condemn a Democrat "Communist." I condemn a Democrat "Fascist" just as much as I condemn a Republican "Communist." They are equally dangerous to you and me and to our country. As an American, I want to see our nation recapture the strength and unity it once had when we fought the enemy instead of ourselves.

It is with these thoughts that I have drafted what I call a "Declaration of Conscience." I am gratified that Senator Tobey, Senator Aiken, Senator Morse, Senator Ives, Senator Thye, and Senator Hendrickson have concurred in that declaration and have authorized me to announce their concurrence.

[GSTC]

President Harry S. Truman, Statement on the Korean War

June 27, 1950

When North Korea, the post-World War II government sponsored by the Soviet Union and China, attacked South Korea, President Truman issued this press release. The United States, as part of the United Nations forces, defended South Korea. The war continued until an armistice was signed in the summer of 1953.

IN KOREA THE Government forces, which were armed to prevent border raids and to preserve internal security, were attacked by invading forces from North Korea. The Security Council of the United Nations called upon the invading troops to cease hostilities and to withdraw to the 38th parallel. This they have not done, but on the contrary have pressed the attack. The Security Council called upon all members of the United Nations to render every assistance to the United Nations in the execution of this resolution. In these circumstances I have ordered United States air and sea forces to give the Korean Government troops cover and support.

The attack upon Korea makes it plain beyond all doubt that communism has passed beyond the use of subversion to conquer independent nations and will now use armed invasion and war. It has defied the orders of the Security Council of the United Nations issued to preserve international peace and security. In these circumstances the occupation of Formosa by Communist forces would be a direct threat to the security of the Pacific area and to United States forces performing their lawful and necessary functions in that area.

Accordingly I have ordered the 7th Fleet to prevent any attack on Formosa. As a corollary of this action I am calling upon the ·Chinese Government on Formosa to cease all air and sea operations against the mainland. The 7th Fleet will see that this is done. The determination of the future status of Formosa must await the restoration of security in the Pacific, a peace settlement with Japan, or consideration by the United Nations.

I have also directed that United States Forces in the Philippines be strengthened and that military assistance to the Philippine Government be accelerated.

I have similarly directed acceleration in the furnishing of military assistance to the forces of France and the Associated States in Indochina and the dispatch of a military mission to provide close working relations with those forces.

I know that all members of the United Nations will consider carefully the consequences of this latest aggression in Korea in defiance of the Charter of the United Nations. A return to the rule of force in international affairs would have far-reaching effects. The United States will continue to uphold the rule of law.

I have instructed Ambassador Austin, as the representative of the United States to the Security Council, to report these steps to the Council.

[APP]

President Harry S. Truman, Address about Policy in the Far East and the Recall of General Douglas MacArthur

April 11, 1951

The World War II hero General Douglas MacArthur (1880–1964) was leading the United Nations forces in the Korean War when President Truman "recalled" him. The primary cause of the firing was MacArthur's repeated public pronouncements about the need to extend the war against North Korea into China, a policy directly counter to the Truman Administration's. Truman explained his policy and the firing in a broadcast speech to the country, saying, "We are trying to prevent a Third World War."

I WANT TO talk plainly to you tonight about what we are doing in Korea and about our policy in the Far East.

In the simplest terms, what we are doing in Korea is this: We are trying to prevent a Third World War.

I think most people in this country recognized that fact last June. And they warmly supported the decision of the Government to help the Republic of Korea against the communist aggressors. Now, many persons, even some who applauded our decision to defend Korea, have forgotten the basic reason for our action.

It is right for us to be in Korea. It was right last June. It is right today. I want to remind you why this is true.

The communists in the Kremlin are engaged in a monstrous conspiracy to stamp out freedom all over the world. If they were to succeed, the United States would be numbered among their principal victims. It must be clear to everyone that the United States cannot and will not – sit idly by and await foreign conquest. The only question is: When is the best time to meet the threat and how?

The best time to meet the threat is in the beginning. It is easier to put out a fire in the beginning when it is small than after it has become a roaring blaze.

And the best way to meet the threat of aggression is for the peace-loving nations to act together. If they don't act together, they are likely to be picked off, one by one.

If they had followed the right policies in the 1930's – if the free countries had acted together, to crush the aggression of the dictators, and if they had acted in the beginning, when the aggression was small – there probably would have been no World War II. If history has taught us anything, it is that aggression anywhere in the world is a threat to peace everywhere in the world. When that aggression is supported by the cruel and selfish rulers of a powerful nation who are bent on conquest, it becomes a clear and present danger to the security and independence of every free nation.

This is a lesson that most people in this country have learned thoroughly. This is the basic reason why we joined in creating the United Nations. And, since the end of World War II, we have been putting that lesson into practice—we have been working with other free nations to check the aggressive designs of the Soviet Union before they can result in a third world war.

That is what we did in Greece, when that nation was threatened by the aggression of international communism.

The attack against Greece could have led to general war. But this country came to the aid of Greece. The United Nations supported Greek resistance. With our help, the determination and efforts of the Greek people defeated the attack on the spot.

Another big communist threat to peace was the Berlin blockade. That too could have led to war. But again it was settled because free men would not back down in an emergency.

The aggression against Korea is the boldest and most dangerous move the communists have yet made.

The attack on Korea was part of a greater plan for conquering all of Asia. I would like to read to you from a secret intelligence report which came to us after the attack. It is a report of a speech a communist army officer in North Korea gave to a group of spies and saboteurs last May, one month before South Korea was invaded. The report shows in great detail how this invasion was part of a carefully prepared plot. Here is part of what the communist officer, who had been trained in Moscow, told his men: "Our forces," he said, "are scheduled to attack South Korean forces about the middle of June. The coming attack on South Korea marks the first step toward the liberation of Asia." Notice that he used the word "liberation." That is communist double-talk meaning "conquest."

I have another secret intelligence report here. This one tells what another communist officer in the Far East told his men several months before the invasion of Korea. Here is what he said: "In order to successfully undertake the long awaited world revolution, we must first unify Asia. ... Java, Indo-China, Malaya, India, Tibet, Thailand, Philippines, and Japan are our ultimate targets. The United States is the only obstacle on our road for the liberation of all countries in Southeast Asia. In other words, we must unify the people of Asia and crush the United States."

That is what the communist leaders are telling their people, and that is what they have been trying to do.

They want to control all Asia from the Kremlin.

This plan of conquest is in flat contradiction to what we believe. We believe that Korea belongs to the Koreans, that India belongs to the Indians – that all the nations of Asia should be free to work out their affairs in their own way. This is the basis of peace in the Far East and everywhere else.

The whole communist imperialism is back of the attack on peace in the Far East. It was the Soviet Union that trained and equipped the North Koreans for aggression. The Chinese communists massed 44 well-trained and well-equipped divisions on the Korean frontier. These were the troops they threw into battle when the North Korean communists were beaten.

The question we have had to face is whether the communist plan of conquest can be stopped without general war. Our Government and other countries associated with us in the United Nations believe that the best chance of stopping it without general war is to meet the attack in Korea and defeat it there.

That is what we have been doing. It is a difficult and bitter task. But so far it has been successful.

So far, we have prevented World War III.

So far, by fighting a limited war in Korea, we have prevented aggression from succeeding, and bringing on a general war. And the ability of the whole free world to resist communist aggression has been greatly improved.

We have taught the enemy a lesson. He has found out that aggression is not cheap or easy. Moreover, men all over the world who want to remain free have been given new courage and new hope. They know now that the champions of freedom can stand up and fight and that they will stand up and fight.

Our resolute stand in Korea is helping the forces of freedom now fighting in Indo-China and other countries in that part of the world. It has already slowed down the timetable of conquest.

In Korea itself, there are signs that the enemy is building up his ground forces for a new mass offensive. We also know that there have been large increases in the enemy's available air forces.

If a new attack comes, I feel confident it will be turned back. The United Nations fighting forces are tough and able, and well equipped. They are fighting for a just cause. They are proving to all the world that the principle of collective security will work. We are proud of all these forces for the magnificent job they have done against heavy odds. We pray that their efforts may succeed, for upon their success may hinge the peace of the world.

The communist side must now choose its course of action. The communist rulers may press the attack against us. They may take further action which will spread the conflict. They have that choice, and with it the awful responsibility for what may follow. The communists also have the choice of a peaceful settlement which could lead to a general relaxation of tensions in the Far East. The decision is theirs, because the forces of the United Nations will strive to limit the conflict if possible.

We do not want to see the conflict in Korea extended. We are trying to prevent a world war – not to start one. The best way to do that is to make it plain that we and the other free countries will continue to resist the attack.

But you may ask why we can't take other steps to punish the aggressor. Why don't we bomb Manchuria and China itself? Why don't we assist Chinese Nationalists troops to land on the mainland of China?

If we were to do these things, we would be running a very grave risk of starting a general war. If that were to happen, we would have brought about the exact situation we are trying to prevent.

If we were to do these things, we would become entangled in a vast conflict on the continent of Asia and our task would become immeasurably more difficult all over the world.

What would suit the ambitions of the Kremlin better than for our military forces to be committed to a full scale war with Red China?

It may well be that, in spite of our best efforts; the communists may spread the war. But it would be wrong – tragically wrong – for us to take the initiative in extending the war. The dangers are great. Make no mistake about it. Behind the North Koreans and Chinese communists in the front lines stand additional millions of Chinese soldiers. And behind the Chinese stand the tanks, the planes, the submarines, the soldiers, and the scheming rulers of the Soviet Union.

Our aim is to avoid the spread of the conflict.

The course we have been following is the one best calculated to avoid an all out war. It is the course consistent with our obligation to do all we can to maintain international peace and security. Our experience in Greece and Berlin shows that it is the most effective course of action we can follow.

First of all, it is clear that our efforts in Korea can blunt the will of the Chinese communists to continue the struggle. The United Nations forces have put up a tremendous fight in Korea and have inflicted very heavy casualties on the enemy. Our forces are stronger now than they have been before. These are plain facts which may discourage the Chinese communists from continuing their attack.

Second, the free world as a whole is growing in military strength every day. In the United States, in Western Europe, and throughout the world, free men are alert to the Soviet threat and are building their defenses. This may discourage the communist rulers from continuing the war in Korea – and from undertaking new acts of aggression elsewhere.

If the communist authorities realize that they cannot defeat us in Korea, if they realize it would be foolhardy to widen the hostilities beyond Korea, then they may recognize the folly of continuing their aggression. A peaceful settlement may then be possible. The door is always open.

Then we may achieve a settlement in Korea which will not compromise the principles and purposes of the United Nations.

I have thought long and hard about this question of extending the war in Asia. I have discussed it many times with the ablest military advisers in the country. I believe with all my heart that the course we are following is the best course.

I believe that we must try to limit the war to Korea for these vital reasons: to make sure that the precious lives of our fighting men are not wasted; to see that the security of our country and the free world is not needlessly jeopardized; and to prevent a third world war.

A number of events have made it evident that General MacArthur did not agree with that policy. I have therefore considered it essential to relieve General MacArthur so that there would be no doubt or confusion as to the real purpose and aim of our policy.

It was with the deepest personal regret that I found myself compelled to take this action. General MacArthur is one of our greatest military commanders. But the cause of world peace is more important than any individual.

The change in commands in the Far East means no change whatever in the policy of the United States. We will carry on the fight in Korea with vigor and determination in an effort to bring the war to a speedy and successful conclusion.

We are ready, at any time, to negotiate for a restoration of peace in the area. But we will not engage in appeasement. We are only interested in real peace.

Real peace can be achieved through a settlement based on the following factors:

One: the fighting must stop.

Two: concrete steps must be taken to insure that the fighting will not break out again.

Three: there must be an end to the aggression.

A settlement founded upon these elements would open the way for the unification of Korea and the withdrawal of all foreign forces.

In the meantime, I want to be clear about our military objective. We are fighting to resist an outrageous aggression in Korea. We are trying to keep the Korean conflict from spreading to other areas. But at the same time we must conduct our military activities so as to insure the security of our forces. This is essential if they are to continue the fight until the enemy abandons its ruthless attempt to destroy the Republic of Korea.

That is our military objective—to repel attack and to restore peace. In the hard fighting in Korea, we are proving that collective action among nations is not only a high principle but a workable means of resisting aggression. Defeat of aggression in Korea may be the turning point in the world's search for a practical way of achieving peace and security.

The struggle of the United Nations in Korea is a struggle for peace. The free nations have united their strength in an effort to prevent a third world war.

That war can come if the communist rulers want it to come. But this Nation and its allies will not be responsible for its coming.

We do not want to widen the conflict. We will use every effort to prevent that disaster. And in so doing, we know that we are following the great principles of peace, freedom, and justice.

[AE]

Secretary of State John Foster Dulles, Speech before the Council on Foreign Relations, "The Strategy of Massive Retaliation"

January 12, 1954

John Foster Dulles (1888–1959) brought into common discourse the fearsome idea of "massive retaliation," whereby threats by the USSR or China would be answered by the United States with a nuclear attack. Dulles served as President Dwight D. Eisenhower's Secretary of State from the beginning of Eisenhower's first term until shortly before his own death. President Kennedy's administration abandoned this policy.

IT IS NOW nearly a year since the Eisenhower administration took office. During that year I have often spoken of various parts of our foreign policies. Tonight I should like to present an overall view of those policies which relate to our security.

First of all, let us recognize that many of the preceding foreign policies were good. Aid to Greece and Turkey had checked the Communist drive to the Mediterranean. The European Recovery Program [Marshall Plan] had helped the peoples of Western Europe to pull out of the postwar morass. The Western powers were steadfast in Berlin and overcame the blockade with their airlift. As a loyal member of the United Nations, we had reacted with force to repel the Communist attack in Korea. When that effort exposed our military weakness, we rebuilt rapidly our military establishment. We also sought a quick build up of armed strength in Western Europe.

These were the acts of a nation which saw the danger of Soviet communism; which realized that its own safety was tied up with that of others; which was capable of responding boldly and promptly to emergencies. These are precious values to be acclaimed. Also, we can pay tribute to congressional bipartisanship which puts the nation above politics.

But we need to recall that what we did was in the main emergency action, imposed on us by our enemies. ... We live in a world where emergencies are always possible, and our survival may depend upon our capacity to meet emergencies. Let us pray that we shall always have that capacity. But, having said that, it is necessary also to say that emergency measures – however good for the emergency – do not necessarily make good permanent policies. Emergency measures are costly; they are superficial; and they imply that the enemy has the initiative. They cannot be depended on to serve our long-time interests.

This "long time" factor is of critical importance. The Soviet Communists are planning for what they call "an entire historical era," and we should do the same. They seek, through many types of maneuvers, gradually to divide and weaken the free nations by overextending them in efforts which, as Lenin put it, are "beyond their strength, so that they come to practical bankruptcy." Then, said Lenin, "our victory is assured." Then, said Stalin, will be "the moment for the decisive blow." In the face of this strategy, measures cannot be judged adequate merely because they ward off an immediate danger. It is essential to do this, but it is also essential to do so without exhausting ourselves.

When the Eisenhower administration applied this test, we felt that some transformations were needed. It is not sound military strategy permanently to commit U.S. land forces to Asia to a degree that leaves us no strategic reserves. It is not sound economics, or good foreign policy to support permanently other countries, for in the long run, that creates as much ill will as good will. Also, it is not sound to become permanently committed to military expenditures so vast that they lead to "practical bankruptcy."

Change was imperative to assure the stamina needed for permanent security. But it was equally imperative that change should be accompanied by understanding of our true purposes. Sudden and spectacular change had to be avoided. Otherwise, there might have been a panic among our friends and miscalculated aggression by our enemies. We can, I believe, make a good report in these respects. We need allies and collective security. Our purpose is to make these relations more effective, less costly. This can be done by placing more reliance on deterrent power and less dependence on local defensive power.

This is accepted practice so far as local communities are concerned. We keep locks on our doors, but we do not have an armed guard in every home. We rely principally on a community security system so well equipped to punish any who break in and steal that, in fact, would-be aggressors are generally deterred. That is the modern way of getting maximum protection at a bearable cost. What the Eisenhower administration seeks is a similar international security system. We want, for ourselves and the other free nations, a maximum deterrent at a bearable cost.

Local defense will always be important. But there is no local defense which alone will contain the mighty land power of the Communist world. Local defenses must be reinforced by the further deterrent of massive retaliatory power. A potential aggressor must know that he cannot always prescribe battle conditions that suit him. Otherwise, for example, a potential aggressor, who is glutted with manpower, might be tempted to attack in confidence that resistance would be confined to manpower. He might be tempted to attack in places where his superiority was decisive.

The way to deter aggression is for the free community to be willing and able to respond vigorously at places and with means of its own choosing. So long as our basic policy concepts were unclear, our military leaders could not be selective in building our military power. If an enemy could pick his time and place and method of warfare – and if our policy was to remain the traditional one of meeting aggression by direct and local opposition – then we needed to be ready to fight in the Arctic and in the Tropics; in Asia, the Near East, and in Europe; by sea, by land, and by air; with old weapons and with new weapons. ...

But before military planning could be changed, the President and his advisers, as represented by the National Security Council, had to take some basic policy decisions. This has been done. The basic decision was to depend primarily upon a great capacity to retaliate, instantly, by means and at places of our choosing. Now the

Department of Defense and the Joint Chiefs of Staff can shape our military establishment to fit what is our policy, instead of having to try to be ready to meet the enemy's many choices. That permits of a selection of military means instead of a multiplication of means. As a result, it is now possible to get, and share, more basic security at less cost. ...

[FP]

Supreme Court, Brown v. Board of Education

May 17, 1954, and April 11, 1955

More than fifty years after Plessy v. Ferguson *legitimized the "separate but equal" doctrine of segregation, separate schools for blacks and whites were the norm in much of the country, with seventeen states requiring educational segregation, and only sixteen states prohibiting the practice. Linda Brown was a third grader in Topeka, Kansas, who had to walk six blocks to catch a bus to her segregated black school over a mile away, while there was a white school only six blocks from her home. When Linda's father, Oliver Brown, attempted to enroll her at the more convenient white school, he was refused and directed back to the segregated black school. Thus, with the backing of the NAACP and along with eleven other plaintiffs, Brown filed a class action suit in the U.S. District Court against the Board of Education of Topeka, Kansas. When that case failed, due to the judges' citation of the Supreme Court's* Plessy v. Ferguson *decision, Brown et al. appealed to the U.S. Supreme Court. In taking up* Brown v. Board *of Ed., the Supreme Court decided to combine it with four other NAACP-sponsored cases on similar issues, so as to hear and decide on all five of them together. These other cases were:* Briggs v. Elliott, Davis et al. v. County School Board of Prince Edward County, Virginia, et al., Gebhart et al. v. Belton et al., *and* Boiling v. Sharp.

The Court's decision was delivered in two parts: the first, delivered on May 17, 1954, refuted the "separate but equal" doctrine in education, stating that segregation was inherently unequal and thus a violation of the Fourteenth Amendment; the second part, delivered on April 11, 1955, directed the lower courts to see to it that schools be desegregated "with all deliberate speed." This case was the first of many that, over the next twenty years, eradicated nearly all legally sanctioned discrimination against blacks in the United States.

– Note by James Daley

U.S. SUPREME COURT

Brown v. Board of Education, 347 U.S. 483
(1954) 347 U.S. 483
Brown et al. v. Board of Education of Topeka et al.
Appeal from the United States District Court for the
District of Kansas. *No. 1.
Argued December 9, 1952; Reargued December 8, 1953.
Decided May 17, 1954.

SEGREGATION OF WHITE and Negro children in the public schools of a State solely on the basis of race, pursuant to state laws permitting or requiring such segregation, denies to Negro children the equal protection of the laws guaranteed by the Fourteenth Amendment—even though the physical facilities and other "tangible" factors of white and Negro schools may be equal. Pp. 486–496.

(a) The history of the Fourteenth Amendment is inconclusive as to its intended effect on public education. Pp. 489–490.

(b) The question presented in these cases must be determined, not on the basis of conditions existing when the Fourteenth Amendment was adopted, but in the light of the full development of public education and its present place in American life throughout the Nation. Pp. 492–493.

(c) Where a State has undertaken to provide an opportunity for an education in its public schools, such an opportunity is a right which must be made available to all on equal terms. P. 493.

(d) Segregation of children in public schools solely on the basis of race deprives children of the minority group of equal educational opportunities, even though the physical facilities and other "tangible" factors may be equal. Pp. 493–494.

---

*Together with No. 2, Briggs et al. v. Elliott et al., on appeal from the United States District Court for the Eastern District of South Carolina, argued December 9–10, 1952, reargued December 7–8, 1953; No. 4, Davis et al. v. County School Board of Prince Edward County, Virginia, et al., on appeal from the United States District Court for the Eastern District of Virginia, argued December 10, 1952, reargued December 7–8, 1953; and No. 10, Gephardt et al. v. Belton et al., on certiorari to the Supreme Court of Delaware, argued December 11, 1952, reargued December 9, 1953.

(e) The "separate but equal" doctrine adopted in Plessy v. Ferguson, 163 U.S. 537, has no place in the field of public education. P. 495. [347 U.S. 483, 484]

(f) The cases are restored to the docket for further argument on specified questions relating to the forms of the decrees. Pp. 495–496. […]

MR. CHIEF JUSTICE WARREN delivered the opinion of the Court.

These cases come to us from the States of Kansas, South Carolina, Virginia, and Delaware. They are premised on different facts and different local conditions, but a common legal question justifies their consideration together in this consolidated opinion.[1] [347 U.S. 483, 487]

---

[1] In the Kansas case, Brown v. Board of Education, the plaintiffs are Negro children of elementary school age residing in Topeka. They brought this action in the United States District Court for the District of Kansas to enjoin enforcement of a Kansas statute which permits, but does not require, cities of more than 15,000 populations to maintain separate school facilities for Negro and white students. Kan. Gen. Stat. 72–1724 (1949). Pursuant to that authority, the Topeka Board of Education elected to establish segregated elementary schools. Other public schools in the community, however, are operated on a nonsegregated basis. The three-judge District Court, convened under 28 U.S.C. 2281 and 2284, found that segregation in public education has a detrimental effect upon Negro children, but denied relief on the ground that the Negro and white schools were substantially equal with respect to buildings, transportation, curricula, and educational qualifications of teachers. 98 F. Supp. 797. The case is here on direct appeal under 28 U.S.C. 1253. In the South Carolina case, Briggs v. Elliott, the plaintiffs are Negro children of both elementary and high school age residing in Clarendon County. They brought this action in the United States District Court for the Eastern District of South Carolina to enjoin enforcement of provisions in the state constitution and statutory code which require the segregation of Negroes and whites in public schools. S. C. Const., Art. XI, 7; S. C. Code 5377 (1942). The three-judge District Court, convened under 28 U.S.C. 2281 and 2284, denied the requested relief. The court found that the Negro schools were inferior to the white schools and ordered the defendants to begin immediately to equalize the facilities. But the court sustained the validity of the contested provisions and denied the plaintiff's admission [347 U.S. 483, 487] to the white schools during the equalization program. 98 F. Supp. 529. This Court vacated the District Court's judgment and remanded the case for the purpose of obtaining the court's views on a report filed by the defendants concerning the progress made in the equalization program. 342 U.S. 350. On remand, the District Court found that substantial equality had been achieved except for buildings and that the defendants were proceeding to rectify this inequality as well. 103 F. Supp. 920. The case is again here on direct appeal under 28 U.S.C. 1253. In the Virginia case, Davis v. County School Board, the plaintiffs are Negro

In each of the cases, minors of the Negro race, through their legal representatives, seek the aid of the courts in obtaining admission to the public schools of their community on a nonsegregated basis. In each instance, [347 U.S. 483, 488] they had been denied admission to schools attended by white children under laws requiring or permitting segregation according to race. This segregation was alleged to deprive the plaintiffs of the equal protection of the laws under the Fourteenth Amendment. In each of the cases other than the Delaware case, a three-judge federal district court denied relief to the plaintiffs on the so-called "separate but equal" doctrine announced by this Court in Plessy v. Ferguson, 163 U.S. 537. Under that doctrine, equality of treatment is accorded when the races are provided substantially equal facilities, even though these facilities be separate. In the Delaware case, the Supreme Court of Delaware adhered to that

children of high school age residing in Prince Edward county. They brought this action in the United States District Court for the Eastern District of Virginia to enjoin enforcement of provisions in the state constitution and statutory code which require the segregation of Negroes and whites in public schools. Va. Const., 140; Va. Code 22–221 (1950). The three-judge District Court, convened under 28 U.S.C. 2281 and 2284, denied the requested relief. The court found the Negro school inferior in physical plant, curricula, and transportation, and ordered the defendants forthwith to provide substantially equal curricula and transportation and to "proceed with all reasonable diligence and dispatch to remove" the inequality in physical plant. But, as in the South Carolina case, the court sustained the validity of the contested provisions and denied the plaintiffs admission to the white schools during the equalization program. 103 F. Supp. 337. The case is here on direct appeal under 28 U.S.C. 1253. In the Delaware case, Gebhart v. Belton, the plaintiffs are Negro children of both elementary and high school age residing in New Castle County. They brought this action in the Delaware Court of Chancery to enjoin enforcement of provisions in the state constitution and statutory code which require the segregation of Negroes and whites in public schools. Del. Const., Art. X, 2; Del. Rev. Code 2631 (1935). The Chancellor gave judgment for the plaintiffs and ordered their immediate admission to schools previously attended only by white children, on the ground that the Negro schools were inferior with respect to teacher training, pupil-teacher ratio, extracurricular activities, physical plant, and time and distance involved [347 U.S. 483, 488] in travel. 87 A. 2d 862. The Chancellor also found that segregation itself results in an inferior education for Negro children (see note 10, infra), but did not rest his decision on that ground. Id., at 865. The Chancellor's decree was affirmed by the Supreme Court of Delaware, which intimated, however, that the defendants might be able to obtain a modification of the decree after equalization of the Negro and white schools had been accomplished. 91 A. 2d 137, 152. The defendants, contending only that the Delaware courts had erred in ordering the immediate admission of the Negro plaintiffs to the white schools, applied to this Court for certiorari. The writ was granted, 344 U.S. 891. The plaintiffs, who were successful below, did not submit a cross-petition.

doctrine, but ordered that the plaintiffs be admitted to the white schools because of their superiority to the Negro schools.

The plaintiffs contend that segregated public schools are not "equal" and cannot be made "equal," and that hence they are deprived of the equal protection of the laws. Because of the obvious importance of the question presented, the Court took jurisdiction. Argument was heard in the 1952 Term, and reargument was heard this Term on certain questions propounded by the Court. [347 U.S. 483, 489]

Reargument was largely devoted to the circumstances surrounding the adoption of the Fourteenth Amendment in 1868. It covered exhaustively consideration of the Amendment in Congress, ratification by the states, then existing practices in racial segregation, and the views of proponents and opponents of the Amendment. This discussion and our own investigation convince us that, although these sources cast some light, it is not enough to resolve the problem with which we are faced. At best, they are inconclusive. The most avid proponents of the post-War Amendments undoubtedly intended them to remove all legal distinctions among "all persons born or naturalized in the United States." Their opponents, just as certainly, were antagonistic to both the letter and the spirit of the Amendments and wished them to have the most limited effect. What others in Congress and the state legislatures had in mind cannot be determined with any degree of certainty.

An additional reason for the inconclusive nature of the Amendment's history, with respect to segregated schools, is the status of public education at that time. In the South, the movement toward free common schools, supported [347 U.S. 483, 490] by general taxation, had not yet taken hold. Education of white children was largely in the hands of private groups. Education of Negroes was almost nonexistent, and practically all of the race were illiterate. In fact, any education of Negroes was forbidden by law in some states. Today, in contrast, many Negroes have achieved outstanding success in the arts and sciences as well as in the business and professional world. It is true that public school education at the time of the Amendment had advanced further in the North, but the effect of the Amendment on Northern States was generally ignored in the congressional debates. Even in the North, the conditions of public education did not approximate those existing today. The curriculum was usually rudimentary; ungraded schools were common in rural areas; the school term was but three months a year in many states;

and compulsory school attendance was virtually unknown. As a consequence, it is not surprising that there should be so little in the history of the Fourteenth Amendment relating to its intended effect on public education.

In the first cases in this Court construing the Fourteenth Amendment, decided shortly after its adoption, the Court interpreted it as proscribing all state-imposed discriminations against the Negro race. The doctrine of [347 U.S. 483, 491] "separate but equal" did not make its appearance in this Court until 1896 in the case of Plessy v. Ferguson, supra, involving not education but transportation. American courts have since labored with the doctrine for over half a century. In this Court, there have been six cases involving the "separate but equal" doctrine in the field of public education. [...]

In none of these cases was it necessary to re-examine the doctrine to grant relief to the Negro plaintiff. And in Sweatt v. Painter, supra, the Court expressly reserved decision on the question whether Plessy v. Ferguson should be held inapplicable to public education.

In the instant cases, that question is directly presented. Here, unlike Sweatt v. Painter, there are findings below that the Negro and white schools involved have been equalized, or are being equalized, with respect to buildings, curricula, qualifications and salaries of teachers, and other "tangible" factors. Our decision, therefore, cannot turn on merely a comparison of these tangible factors in the Negro and white schools involved in each of the cases. We must look instead to the effect of segregation itself on public education.

In approaching this problem, we cannot turn the clock back to 1868 when the Amendment was adopted, or even to 1896 when Plessy v. Ferguson was written. We must consider public education in the light of its full development and its present place in American life throughout [347 U.S. 483, 493] the Nation. Only in this way can it be determined if segregation in public schools deprives these plaintiffs of the equal protection of the laws.

Today, education is perhaps the most important function of state and local governments. Compulsory school attendance laws and the great expenditures for education both demonstrate our recognition of the importance of education to our democratic society. It is required in the performance of our most basic public responsibilities, even service in the armed forces. It is the very foundation of good citizenship. Today it is a principal instrument in awakening the child to cultural values, in preparing him for later professional training, and in helping him to adjust normally to his environment. In these days, it is doubtful that any child may reasonably be expected to succeed in life if he is denied the opportunity of an education. Such an opportunity, where the state has undertaken to provide it, is a right which must be made available to all on equal terms.

We come then to the question presented: Does segregation of children in public schools solely on the basis of race, even though the physical facilities and other "tangible" factors may be equal, deprive the children of the minority group of equal educational opportunities? We believe that it does.

In Sweatt v. Painter, supra, in finding that a segregated law school for Negroes could not provide them equal educational opportunities, this Court relied in large part on "those qualities which are incapable of objective measurement but which make for greatness in a law school." In McLaurin v. Oklahoma State Regents, supra, the Court, in requiring that a Negro admitted to a white graduate school be treated like all other students, again resorted to intangible considerations: "... his ability to study, to engage in discussions and exchange views with other students, and, in general, to learn his profession." [347 U.S. 483, 494] Such considerations apply with added force to children in grade and high schools. To separate them from others of similar age and qualifications solely because of their race generates a feeling of inferiority as to their status in the community that may affect their hearts and minds in a way unlikely ever to be undone. The effect of this separation on their educational opportunities was well stated by a finding in the Kansas case by a court which nevertheless felt compelled to rule against the Negro plaintiffs:

> "Segregation of white and colored children in public schools has a detrimental effect upon the colored children. The impact is greater when it has the sanction of the law; for the policy of separating the races is usually interpreted as denoting the inferiority of the negro group. A sense of inferiority affects the motivation of a child to learn. Segregation with the sanction of law, therefore, has a tendency to [retard] the educational and mental development of negro children and to deprive them of some of the benefits they would receive in a racial[ly] integrated school system."

Whatever may have been the extent of psychological knowledge at the time of Plessy v. Ferguson, this finding is amply supported by modern authority. Any language [347 U.S. 483, 495] in Plessy v. Ferguson contrary to this finding is rejected.

We conclude that in the field of public education the doctrine of "separate but equal" has no place. Separate educational facilities are inherently unequal. Therefore, we hold that the plaintiffs and others similarly situated for whom the actions have been brought are, by reason of the segregation complained of, deprived of the equal protection of the laws guaranteed by the Fourteenth Amendment. This disposition makes unnecessary any discussion whether such segregation also violates the Due Process Clause of the Fourteenth Amendment.

Because these are class actions, because of the wide applicability of this decision, and because of the great variety of local conditions, the formulation of decrees in these cases presents problems of considerable complexity. On reargument, the consideration of appropriate relief was necessarily subordinated to the primary question—the constitutionality of segregation in public education. We have now announced that such segregation is a denial of the equal protection of the laws. In order that we may have the full assistance of the parties in formulating decrees, the cases will be restored to the docket, and the parties are requested to present further argument on Questions 4 and 5 previously propounded by the Court for the reargument this Term. The Attorney General [347 U.S. 483, 496] of the United States is again invited to participate. The Attorneys General of the states requiring or permitting segregation in public education will also be permitted to appear as amici curiae upon request to do so by September 15, 1954, and submission of briefs by October 1, 1954.

It is so ordered.

U.S. SUPREME COURT

Brown v. Board of Education,
349 U.S. 294 (1955) 349 U.S. 294
Brown et al. v. Board of Education of Topeka et al.
Appeal from the United States District
Court for the District of Kansas.

No. 1. Reargued on the question of relief April 11–14, 1955. Opinion and judgments announced May 31, 1955.

1. Racial discrimination in public education is unconstitutional, 347 U.S. 483, 497, and all provisions of federal, state or local law

requiring or permitting such discrimination must yield to this principle. P. 298. [...]

MR. CHIEF JUSTICE WARREN delivered the opinion of the Court.

These cases were decided on May 17, 1954. The opinions of that date, declaring the fundamental principle that racial discrimination in public education is unconstitutional, are incorporated herein by reference. All provisions of federal, state, or local law requiring or permitting such discrimination must yield to this principle. There remains for consideration the manner in which relief is to be accorded.

Because these cases arose under different local conditions and their disposition will involve a variety of local problems, we requested further argument on the question of relief. In view of the nationwide importance of the decision, we invited the Attorney General of the United [349 U.S. 294, 299] States and the Attorneys General of all states requiring or permitting racial discrimination in public education to present their views on that question. The parties, the United States, and the States of Florida, North Carolina, Arkansas, Oklahoma, Maryland, and Texas filed briefs and participated in the oral argument.

These presentations were informative and helpful to the Court in its consideration of the complexities arising from the transition to a system of public education freed of racial discrimination. The presentations also demonstrated that substantial steps to eliminate racial discrimination in public schools have already been taken, not only in some of the communities in which these cases arose, but in some of the states appearing as amici curiae, and in other states as well. Substantial progress has been made in the District of Columbia and in the communities in Kansas and Delaware involved in this litigation. The defendants in the cases coming to us from South Carolina and Virginia are awaiting the decision of this Court concerning relief.

Full implementation of these constitutional principles may require solution of varied local school problems. School authorities have the primary responsibility for elucidating, assessing, and solving these problems; courts will have to consider whether the action of school authorities constitutes good faith implementation of the governing constitutional principles. Because of their proximity to local conditions and the possible need for further hearings, the courts which originally heard these cases can best perform this judicial appraisal. Accordingly, we believe it appropriate to remand the cases to those courts. [349 U.S. 294, 300]

In fashioning and effectuating the decrees, the courts will be guided by equitable principles. Traditionally, equity has been characterized by a practical flexibility in shaping its remedies and by a facility for adjusting and reconciling public and private needs. These cases call for the exercise of these traditional attributes of equity power. At stake is the personal interest of the plaintiffs in admission to public schools as soon as practicable on a nondiscriminatory basis. To effectuate this interest may call for elimination of a variety of obstacles in making the transition to school systems operated in accordance with the constitutional principles set forth in our May 17, 1954, decision. Courts of equity may properly take into account the public interest in the elimination of such obstacles in a systematic and effective manner. But it should go without saying that the vitality of these constitutional principles cannot be allowed to yield simply because of disagreement with them.

While giving weight to these public and private considerations, the courts will require that the defendants make a prompt and reasonable start toward full compliance with our May 17, 1954, ruling. Once such a start has been made, the courts may find that additional time is necessary to carry out the ruling in an effective manner. The burden rests upon the defendants to establish that such time is necessary in the public interest and is consistent with good faith compliance at the earliest practicable date. To that end, the courts may consider problems related to administration, arising from the physical condition of the school plant, the school transportation system, personnel, revision of school districts and attendance areas into compact units to achieve a system of determining admission to the public schools [349 U.S. 294, 301] on a nonracial basis, and revision of local laws and regulations which may be necessary in solving the foregoing problems. They will also consider the adequacy of any plans the defendants may propose to meet these problems and to effectuate a transition to a racially nondiscriminatory school system. During this period of transition, the courts will retain jurisdiction of these cases.

The judgments below, except that in the Delaware case, are accordingly reversed and the cases are remanded to the District Courts to take such proceedings and enter such orders and decrees consistent with this opinion as are necessary and proper to admit to public schools on a racially nondiscriminatory basis with all deliberate speed the parties to these cases. The judgment in the Delaware case—ordering the immediate admission of the plaintiffs to schools previously attended only by white children—is affirmed on the basis of the principles stated in our May 17, 1954, opinion, but the case is remanded to the Supreme Court of Delaware for such further proceedings as that Court may deem necessary in light of this opinion.

It is so ordered.

[LD]

President Dwight D. Eisenhower, Address to the American People on the Situation in Little Rock

September 24, 1957

President Dwight D. Eisenhower (1890–1969) spoke on radio and televisions from Washington, D.C., about the racist and violent resistance to school integration in Arkansas. Several southern states resisted the federal law resulting from Brown v. Board of Education (1954, 1955).

Good Evening, My Fellow Citizens:

FOR A FEW minutes this evening I want to speak to you about the serious situation that has arisen in Little Rock. To make this talk I have come to the President's office in the White House. I could have spoken from Rhode Island, where I have been staying recently, but I felt that, in speaking from the house of Lincoln, of Jackson and of Wilson, my words would better convey both the sadness I feel in the action I was compelled today to take and the firmness with which I intend to pursue this course until the orders of the Federal Court at Little Rock can be executed without unlawful interference.

In that city, under the leadership of demagogic extremists, disorderly mobs have deliberately prevented the carrying out of proper orders from a Federal Court. Local authorities have not eliminated that violent opposition and, under the law, I yesterday issued a Proclamation calling upon the mob to disperse.

This morning the mob again gathered in front of the Central High School of Little Rock, obviously for the purpose of again preventing the carrying out of the Court's order relating to the admission of Negro children to that school.

Whenever normal agencies prove inadequate to the task and it becomes necessary for the Executive Branch of the Federal Government to use its powers and authority to uphold Federal Courts, the President's responsibility is inescapable.

In accordance with that responsibility, I have today issued an Executive Order [No. 10730] directing the use of troops under Federal authority to aid in the execution of Federal law at Little Rock, Arkansas. This became necessary when my Proclamation of yesterday was not observed, and the obstruction of justice still continues.

It is important that the reasons for my action be understood by all our citizens.

As you know, the Supreme Court of the United States has decided that separate public educational facilities for the races are inherently unequal and therefore compulsory school segregation laws are unconstitutional.

Our personal opinions about the decision have no bearing on the matter of enforcement; the responsibility and authority of the Supreme Court to interpret the Constitution are very clear. Local Federal Courts were instructed by the Supreme Court to issue such orders and decrees as might be necessary to achieve admission to public schools without regard to race—and with all deliberate speed.

During the past several years, many communities in our Southern States have instituted public school plans for gradual progress in the enrollment and attendance of school children of all races in order to bring themselves into compliance with the law of the land.

They thus demonstrated to the world that we are a nation in which laws, not men, are supreme.

I regret to say that this truth—the cornerstone of our liberties—was not observed in this instance.

It was my hope that this localized situation would be brought under control by city and State authorities. If the use of local police powers had been sufficient, our traditional method of leaving the problems in those hands would have been pursued. But when large gatherings of obstructionists made it impossible for the decrees of the Court to be carried out, both the law and the national interest demanded that the President take action.

Here is the sequence of events in the development of the Little Rock school case.

In May of 1955, the Little Rock School Board approved a moderate plan for the gradual desegregation of the public schools in that city. It provided that a start toward integration would be made at the present term in the high school, and that the plan would be in full operation by 1963. Here I might say that in a number of communities in Arkansas integration in the schools has already started and without violence of any kind. Now this Little Rock plan was challenged in the courts by some who believed that the period of time as proposed in the plan was too long.

The United States Court at Little Rock, which has supervisory responsibility under the law for the plan of desegregation in the public schools, dismissed the challenge, thus approving a gradual rather than an abrupt change from the existing system. The court found that the school board had acted in good faith in planning for a public school system free from racial discrimination.

Since that time, the court has on three separate occasions issued orders directing that the plan be carried out. All persons were instructed to refrain from interfering with the efforts of the school board to comply with the law.

Proper and sensible observance of the law then demanded the respectful obedience which the nation has a right to expect from all its people. This, unfortunately, has not been the case at Little Rock. Certain misguided persons, many of them imported into Little Rock by agitators, have insisted upon defying the law and have sought to bring it into disrepute. The orders of the court have thus been frustrated.

The very basis of our individual fights and freedoms rests upon the certainty that the President and the Executive Branch of Government will support and insure the carrying out of the decisions of the Federal Courts, even, when necessary with all the means at the President's command.

Unless the President did so, anarchy would result.

There would be no security for any except that which each one of us could provide for himself.

The interest of the nation in the proper fulfillment of the law's requirements cannot yield to opposition and demonstrations by some few persons.

Mob rule cannot be allowed to override the decisions of our courts.

Now, let me make it very clear that Federal troops are not being used to relieve local and state authorities of their primary duty to preserve the peace and order of the community. Nor are the troops there for the purpose of taking over the responsibility of the School Board and the other responsible local officials in running Central High School. The running of our school system and the maintenance of peace and order in each of our States are strictly local affairs and the Federal Government does not interfere except in a very few special cases and when requested by one of the several States. In the present case the troops are there, pursuant to law, solely for the purpose of preventing interference with the orders of the Court.

The proper use of the powers of the Executive Branch to enforce the orders of a Federal Court is limited to extraordinary and compelling circumstances. Manifestly, such an extreme situation has been created in Little Rock. This challenge must be met and with such measures as will preserve to the people as a whole their lawfully-protected rights in a climate permitting their free and fair exercise.

The overwhelming majority of our people in every section of the country are united in their respect for observance of the law—even in those cases where they may disagree with that law.

They deplore the call of extremists to violence.

The decision of the Supreme Court concerning school integration, of course, affects the South more seriously than it does other sections of the country. In that region I have many warm friends, some of them in the city of Little Rock. I have deemed it a great personal privilege to spend in our Southland tours of duty while in the military service and enjoyable recreational periods since that time.

So from intimate personal knowledge, I know that the overwhelming majority of the people in the South—including those of Arkansas and of Little Rock—are of good will, united in their efforts to preserve and respect the law even when they disagree with it.

They do not sympathize with mob rule. They, like the rest of our nation, have proved in two great wars their readiness to sacrifice for America.

A foundation of our American way of life is our national respect for law.

In the South, as elsewhere, citizens are keenly aware of the tremendous disservice that has been done to the people of Arkansas in the eyes of the nation, and that has been done to the nation in the eyes of the world.

At a time when we face grave situations abroad because of the hatred that Communism bears toward a system of government based on human rights, it would be difficult to exaggerate the harm that is being done to the prestige and influence, and indeed to the safety, of our nation and the world.

Our enemies are gloating over this incident and using it everywhere to misrepresent our whole nation. We are portrayed as a violator of those standards of conduct which the peoples of the world united to proclaim in the Charter of the United Nations. There they affirmed "faith in fundamental human rights" and "in the dignity and worth of the human person" and they did so "without distinction as to race, sex, language or religion."

And so, with deep confidence, I call upon the citizens of the State of Arkansas to assist in bringing to an immediate end all interference with the law and its processes. If resistance to the Federal Court orders ceases at once, the further presence of Federal troops will be unnecessary and the City of Little Rock will return to its normal habits of peace and order and a blot upon the fair name and high honor of our nation in the world will be removed.

Thus will be restored the image of America and of all its parts as one nation, indivisible, with liberty and justice for all.

Good night, and thank you very much.

[APP]

President John F. Kennedy, Inaugural Address

January 20, 1961

Kennedy [born on May 29, 1917] defeated Republican Vice President Richard M. Nixon to become the nation's first Catholic president. The morning of his inauguration, Kennedy attended Holy Trinity Catholic Church in Georgetown before traveling with President Eisenhower to the Capitol. The oath of office was administered by Chief Justice Earl Warren, after which Robert Frost read one of his poems. President Kennedy served for a little less than three years before his assassination in Dallas on November 22, 1963.

– Note by James Daley.

VICE PRESIDENT JOHNSON, Mr. Speaker, Mr. Chief Justice, President Eisenhower, Vice President Nixon, President Truman, reverend clergy, fellow-citizens, we observe today not a victory of party, but a celebration of freedom—symbolizing an end, as well as a beginning—signifying renewal, as well as change. For I have sworn before you and Almighty God the same solemn oath our forebears prescribed nearly a century and three quarters ago.

The world is very different now. For man holds in his mortal hands the power to abolish all forms of human poverty and all forms of human life. And yet the same revolutionary beliefs for which our forebears fought are still at issue around the globe—the belief that the rights of man come not from the generosity of the state, but from the hand of God.

We dare not forget today that we are the heirs of that first revolution. Let the word go forth from this time and place, to friend and foe alike, that the torch has been passed to a new generation of Americans—born in this century, tempered by war, disciplined by a hard and bitter peace, proud of our ancient heritage—and unwilling to witness or permit the slow undoing of those human rights to which this Nation has always been committed, and to which we are committed today at home and around the world.

Let every nation know, whether it wishes us well or ill, that we shall pay any price, bear any burden, meet any hardship, support any friend, oppose any foe, in order to assure the survival and the success of liberty.

This much we pledge—and more.

To those old allies whose cultural and spiritual origins we share, we pledge the loyalty of faithful friends. United, there is little we cannot do in a host of cooperative ventures. Divided, there is little we can do—for we dare not meet a powerful challenge at odds and split asunder.

To those new States whom we welcome to the ranks of the free, we pledge our word that one form of colonial control shall not have passed away merely to be replaced by a far more iron tyranny. We shall not always expect to find them supporting our view. But we shall always hope to find them strongly supporting their own freedom—and to remember that, in the past, those who foolishly sought power by riding the back of the tiger ended up inside.

To those peoples in the huts and villages across the globe struggling to break the bonds of mass misery, we pledge our best efforts to help them help themselves, for whatever period is required—not because the Communists may be doing it, not because we seek their votes, but because it is right. If a free society cannot help the many who are poor, it cannot save the few who are rich.

To our sister republics south of our border, we offer a special pledge—to convert our good words into good deeds—in a new alliance for progress—to assist free men and free governments in casting off the chains of poverty. But this peaceful revolution of hope cannot become the prey of hostile powers. Let all our neighbors know that we shall join with them to oppose aggression or subversion anywhere in the Americas. And let every other power know that this Hemisphere intends to remain the master of its own house.

To that world assembly of sovereign states, the United Nations, our last best hope in an age where the instruments of war have far outpaced the instruments of peace, we renew our pledge of support—to prevent it from becoming merely a forum for invective—to strengthen its shield of the new and the weak—and to enlarge the area in which its writ may run.

Finally, to those nations who would make themselves our adversary, we offer not a pledge but a request: that both sides begin anew the quest for peace, before the dark powers of destruction unleashed by science engulf all humanity in planned or accidental self-destruction.

We dare not tempt them with weakness. For only when our arms are sufficient beyond doubt can we be certain beyond doubt that they will never be employed.

But neither can two great and powerful groups of nations take comfort from our present course—both sides overburdened by the cost of modern weapons, both rightly alarmed by the steady spread of the deadly atom, yet both racing to alter that uncertain balance of terror that stays the hand of mankind's final war.

So let us begin anew—remembering on both sides that civility is not a sign of weakness, and sincerity is always subject to proof. Let us never negotiate out of fear. But let us never fear to negotiate.

Let both sides explore what problems unite us instead of belaboring those problems which divide us.

Let both sides, for the first time, formulate serious and precise proposals for the inspection and control of arms—and bring the absolute power to destroy other nations under the absolute control of all nations.

Let both sides seek to invoke the wonders of science instead of its terrors. Together let us explore the stars, conquer the deserts, eradicate disease, tap the ocean depths, and encourage the arts and commerce.

Let both sides unite to heed in all corners of the earth the command of Isaiah—to "undo the heavy burdens . . . and to let the oppressed go free."

And if a beachhead of cooperation may push back the jungle of suspicion, let both sides join in creating a new endeavor, not a new balance of power, but a new world of law, where the strong are just and the weak secure and the peace preserved.

All this will not be finished in the first 100 days. Nor will it be finished in the first 1,000 days, nor in the life of this Administration, nor even perhaps in our lifetime on this planet. But let us begin.

In your hands, my fellow-citizens, more than in mine, will rest the final success or failure of our course. Since this country was founded, each generation of Americans has been summoned to give testimony to its national loyalty. The graves of young Americans who answered the call to service surround the globe.

Now the trumpet summons us again—not as a call to bear arms, though arms we need; not as a call to battle, though embattled we are—but a call to bear the burden of a long twilight struggle, year in and year out, "rejoicing in hope, patient in tribulation"—a struggle against the common enemies of man: tyranny, poverty, disease, and war itself.

Can we forge against these enemies a grand and global alliance, North and South, East and West, that can assure a more fruitful life for all mankind? Will you join in that historic effort?

In the long history of the world, only a few generations have been granted the role of defending freedom in its hour of maximum danger. I do not shrink from this responsibility—I welcome it. I do not believe that any of us would exchange places with any other people or any other generation. The energy, the faith, the devotion which we bring to this endeavor will light our country and all who serve it—and the glow from that fire can truly light the world.

And so, my fellow Americans: ask not what your country can do for you—ask what you can do for your country.

My fellow-citizens of the world: ask not what America will do for you, but what together we can do for the freedom of man.

Finally, whether you are citizens of America or citizens of the world, ask of us the same high standards of strength and sacrifice which we ask of you. With a good conscience our only sure reward, with history the final judge of our deeds, let us go forth to lead the land we love, asking His blessing and His help, but knowing that here on earth God's work must truly be our own.

[GIA]

President John F. Kennedy, Special Message to the Congress on Urgent National Needs (Americans in Space)

May 25, 1961

At the end of this speech that he delivered in person, President Kennedy discussed various crises and then, in the ninth and next-to-last section of his address, turned his and America's attention to "landing a man on the moon." A little more than eight years later, two American astronauts walked on the moon.

Mr. Speaker, Mr. Vice President, my copartners in Government, gentlemen—and ladies:

THE CONSTITUTION IMPOSES upon me the obligation to "from time to time give to the Congress information of the State of the Union." While this has traditionally been interpreted as an annual affair, this tradition has been broken in extraordinary times.

These are extraordinary times. And we face an extraordinary challenge. Our strength as well as our convictions have imposed upon this nation the role of leader in freedom's cause.

No role in history could be more difficult or more important. We stand for freedom. That is our conviction for us—that is our only commitment to others. No friend, no neutral and no adversary should think otherwise. We are not against any man—or any nation—or any system—except as it is hostile to freedom. Nor am I here to present a new military doctrine, bearing any one name or aimed at any one area. I am here to promote the freedom doctrine.

The great battleground for the defense and expansion of freedom today is the whole southern half of the globe—Asia, Latin America, Africa and the Middle East—the lands of the rising peoples. Their revolution is the greatest in human history. They seek an end to injustice, tyranny, and exploitation. More than an end, they seek a beginning.

And theirs is a revolution which we would support regardless of the Cold War, and regardless of which political or economic route they should choose to freedom. [...]

Finally, if we are to win the battle that is now going on around the world between freedom and tyranny, the dramatic achievements in space which occurred in recent weeks should have made clear to us all, as did the Sputnik in 1957, the impact of this adventure on the minds of men everywhere, who are attempting to make a determination of which road they should take. Since early in my term, our efforts in space have been under review. With the advice of the Vice President, who is Chairman of the National Space Council, we have examined where we are strong and where we are not, where we may succeed and where we may not. Now it is time to take longer strides—time for a great new American enterprise—time for this nation to take a clearly leading role in space achievement, which in many ways may hold the key to our future on earth.

I believe we possess all the resources and talents necessary. But the facts of the matter are that we have never made the national decisions or marshaled the national resources required for such leadership. We have never specified long-range goals on an urgent time schedule, or managed our resources and our time so as to insure theft fulfillment.

Recognizing the head start obtained by the Soviets with their large rocket engines, which gives them many months of lead-time, and recognizing the likelihood that they will exploit this lead for some time to come in still more impressive successes, we nevertheless are required to make new efforts on our own. For while we cannot guarantee that we shall one day be first, we can guarantee that any failure to make this effort will make us last. We take an additional risk by making it in full view of the world, but as shown by the feat of astronaut Shepard, this very risk enhances our stature when we are successful. But this is not merely a race. Space is open to us now; and our eagerness to share its meaning is not governed by the efforts of others. We go into space because whatever mankind must undertake, free men must fully share.

I therefore ask the Congress, above and beyond the increases I have earlier requested for space activities, to provide the funds which are needed to meet the following national goals:

First, I believe that this nation should commit itself to achieving the goal, before this decade is out, of landing a man on the moon and returning him safely to the earth. No single space project in this period will be more impressive to mankind or more important for the long-range exploration of space; and none will be so difficult or expensive to accomplish. We propose to accelerate the development of the appropriate lunar space craft. We propose to develop alternate liquid and solid fuel boosters, much larger than any now being developed, until certain which is superior. We propose additional funds for other engine development and for unmanned explorations—explorations which are particularly important for one purpose which this nation will never overlook: the survival of the man who first makes this daring flight. But in a very real sense, it will not be one man going to the moon—if we make this judgment affirmatively, it will be an entire nation. For all of us must work to put him there.

Secondly, an additional 23 million dollars, together with 7 million dollars already available, will accelerate development of the Rover nuclear rocket. This gives promise of some day providing a means for even more exciting and ambitious exploration of space, perhaps beyond the moon, perhaps to the very end of the solar system itself.

Third, an additional 50 million dollars will make the most of our present leadership, by accelerating the use of space satellites for world-wide communications.

Fourth, an additional 75 million dollars—of which 53 million dollars is for the Weather Bureau—will help give us at the earliest possible time a satellite system for world-wide weather observation.

Let it be clear—and this is a judgment which the Members of the Congress must finally make—let it be clear that I am asking the Congress and the country to accept a firm commitment to a new course of action—a course which will last for many years and carry very heavy costs: 531 million dollars in fiscal '62—an estimated seven to nine billion dollars additional over the next five years.

If we are to go only halfway, or reduce our sights in the face of difficulty, in my judgment it would be better not to go at all.

Now this is a choice which this country must make, and I am confident that under the leadership of the Space Committees of the Congress, and the Appropriating Committees, that you will consider the matter carefully.

It is a most important decision that we make as a nation. But all of you have lived through the last four years and have seen the significance of space and the adventures in space, and no one can predict with certainty what the ultimate meaning will be of mastery of space.

I believe we should go to the moon. But I think every citizen of this country as well as the Members of the Congress should consider the matter carefully in making their judgment, to which we have given attention over many weeks and months, because it is a heavy burden, and there is no sense in agreeing or desiring that the United States take an affirmative position in outer space, unless we are prepared to do the work and bear the burdens to make it successful. If we are not, we should decide today and this year.

This decision demands a major national commitment of scientific and technical manpower, materiel and facilities, and the possibility of their diversion from other important activities where they are already thinly spread. It means a degree of dedication, organization and discipline which have not always characterized our research and development efforts. It means we cannot afford undue work stoppages, inflated costs of material or talent, wasteful interagency rivalries, or a high turnover of key personnel.

New objectives and new money cannot solve these problems. They could in fact, aggravate them further—unless every scientist, every engineer, every serviceman, every technician, contractor, and civil servant gives his personal pledge that this nation will move forward, with the full speed of freedom, in the exciting adventure of space.

[APP]

President John F. Kennedy, Proclamation 3504, Interdiction of the Delivery of Offensive Weapons to Cuba

October 23, 1962

From before the beginning of Kennedy's term of office that began in 1961, the revolutionary leader Fidel Castro of Cuba had been challenging American intervention. The Cuban Missile Crisis was the most difficult of President Kennedy's challenges; it brought the Soviet Union, which had been supplying Cuba with arms and funding and was building nuclear missile sites on the island, and the United States to the brink of a nuclear war. Five days after this proclamation, the premier of the Soviet Union, Nikita Khrushchev, agreed to President Kennedy's demands to dismantle the sites.

By the President of the United States of America
A Proclamation

Whereas the peace of the world and the security of the United States and of all American States are endangered by reason of the establishment by the Sino-Soviet powers of an offensive military capability in Cuba, including bases for ballistic missiles with a potential range covering most of North and South America;

Whereas by a Joint Resolution passed by the Congress of the United States and approved on October 3, 1962, it was declared that the United States is determined to prevent by whatever means may be necessary, including the use of arms, the Marxist-Leninist regime in Cuba from extending, by force or the threat of force, its aggressive or subversive activities to any part of this hemisphere, and to prevent in Cuba the creation or use of an externally supported military capability endangering the security of the United States; and

Whereas the Organ of Consultation of the American Republics meeting in Washington on October 23, 1962, recommended that the Member States, in accordance with Articles 6 and 8 of the Inter-American Treaty of Reciprocal Assistance, take all measures, individually and collectively, including the use of armed force, which they may deem necessary to ensure that the Government of Cuba cannot continue to receive from the Sino–Soviet powers military material and related supplies which may threaten the peace and security of the Continent and to prevent the missiles in Cuba with offensive capability from ever becoming an active threat to the peace and security of the Continent:

Now, Therefore, I, John F. Kennedy, President of the United States of America, acting under and by virtue of the authority conferred upon me by the Constitution and statutes of the United States, in accordance with the aforementioned resolutions of the United States Congress and of the Organ of Consultation of the American Republics, and to defend the security of the United States, do hereby proclaim that the forces under my command are ordered, beginning at 2:00 p.m. Greenwich time October 24, 1962, to interdict, subject to the instructions herein contained, the delivery of offensive weapons and associated materiel to Cuba.

For the purposes of this Proclamation, the following are declared to be prohibited materiel:

Surface-to-surface missiles; bomber aircraft; bombs, air-to-surface rockets and guided missiles; warheads for any of the above weapons; mechanical or electronic equipment to support or operate the above items; and any other classes of materiel hereafter designated by the Secretary of Defense for the purpose of effectuating this Proclamation.

To enforce this order, the Secretary of Defense shall take appropriate measures to prevent the delivery of prohibited materiel to Cuba, employing the land, sea and air forces of the United States in cooperation with any forces that may be made available by other American States.

The Secretary of Defense may make such regulations and issue such directives as he deems necessary to ensure the effectiveness of this order, including the designation, within a reasonable distance of Cuba, of prohibited or restricted zones and of prescribed routes.

Any vessel or craft which may be proceeding toward Cuba may be intercepted and may be directed to identify itself, its cargo, equipment and stores and its ports of call, to stop, to lie to, to submit to visit and search, or to proceed as directed. Any vessel or craft which fails or refuses to respond to or comply with directions shall be subject to being taken into custody. Any vessel or craft which it is believed is en route to Cuba and may be carrying prohibited materiel or may itself constitute such materiel shall, wherever possible, be directed to proceed to another destination of its own choice and shall be taken into custody if it fails or refuses to obey such directions. All vessels or craft taken into custody shall be sent into a port of the United States for appropriate disposition.

In carrying out this order, force shall not be used except in case of failure or refusal to comply with directions, or with regulations or directives of the Secretary of Defense issued hereunder, after reasonable efforts have been made to communicate them to the vessel or craft, or in case of self-defense. In any case, force shall be used only to the extent necessary.

In Witness Whereof, I have hereunto set my hand and cause the seal of the United States of America to be affixed.

Done in the City of Washington this twenty-third day of October in the year of our Lord, nineteen hundred and sixty-two, and of the Independence of the United States of America the one hundred and eighty seventh.

[APP]

Governor of Alabama George C. Wallace, Inaugural Address "Segregation Forever"

January 14, 1963

The four-term Governor of Alabama was a blunt proponent of racial segregation in the early 1960s. Later, however, after an assassination attempt in 1972, Wallace (1919–1998) repented of his fight against integration. In this, his first speech as governor of Alabama, he audaciously argues that whites, controlling at this time every aspect of political power and big business in America, Europe, and half of the rest of the world, face persecution: "As the national racism of Hitler's Germany persecuted a national minority to the whim of a national majority... so the international racism of the liberals seek to persecute the international white minority to the whim of the international colored majority."

GOVERNOR PATTERSON, GOVERNOR Barnette, from one of the greatest states in this nation, Mississippi, Judge Brown, representing Governor Hollings of South Carolina,... members of the Alabama Congressional Delegation, members of the Alabama Legislature, distinguished guests, fellow Alabamians:

Before I begin my talk with you, I want to ask you for a few minutes patience while I say something that is on my heart: I want to thank those home folks of my county who first gave an anxious country boy his opportunity to serve in State politics. I shall always owe a lot to those who gave me that *first* opportunity to serve.

I will never forget the warm support and close loyalty at the folks of Suttons, Haigler's Mill, Eufaula, Beat 6 and Beat 14, Richards

Cross Roads and Gammage Beat...at Baker Hill, Beat 8, and Comer, Spring Hill, Adams Chapel and Mount Andrew...White Oak, Baxter's Station, Clayton, Louisville and Cunnigham Place; Horns Crossroads, Texas Ville and Blue Springs, where the vote was 304 for Wallace and 1 for the opposition...and the dear little lady whom I heard had made that one vote against me...by mistake...because she couldn't see too well...and she had pulled the wrong lever...Bless her heart. At Clio, my birthplace, and Elamville. I shall never forget them. May God bless them.

And I shall forever remember that election day morning as I waited...and suddenly at ten o'clock that morning the first return of a box was flashed over this state: it carried the message...Wallace 15, opposition zero; and it came from the Hamrick Beat at Putman's Mountain where the great hill people of our state live. May God bless the mountain man...his loyalty is unshakeable; he'll do to walk down the road with.

I hope you'll forgive me these few moments of remembering... but I wanted them...and you...to know, that I shall never forget.

And I wish I could shake hands and thank all of you in this state who voted for me...and those of you who did not...for I know you voted your honest convictions...and now, we must stand together and move the great State of Alabama forward.

I would be remiss, this day, if I did not thank my wonderful wife and fine family for their patience, support and loyalty...and there is no man living who does not owe more to his mother than he can ever repay, and I want my mother to know that I realize my debt to her.

This is the day of my Inauguration as Governor of the State of Alabama. And on this day I feel a deep obligation to renew my pledges, my covenants with you...the people of this great state.

General Robert E. Lee said that "duty" is the sublimest word on the English language and I have come, increasingly, to realize what he meant. I SHALL do my duty to you, God helping...to every man, to every woman...yes, to every child in this state. I shall fulfill my duty toward honesty and economy in our State government so that no man shall have a part of his livelihood cheated and no child shall have a bit of his future stolen away.

I have said to you that I would eliminate the liquor agents in this state and that the money saved would be returned to our citizens...I am happy to report to you that I am now filling orders for several hundred one-way tickets and stamped on them are these words..."for liquor agents...destination:...out of Alabama." I am happy to report to you that the big-wheeling cocktail-party boys have gotten the word that their free whiskey and boat rides are over...that the farmer in the field, the worker in the factory, the businessman in his office, the housewife in her home, have decided that the money can be better spent to help our children's education and our older citizens...and they have put a man in office to see that it is done. It shall be done. Let me say one more time... No more liquor drinking in your governor's mansion.

I shall fulfill my duty in working hard to bring industry into our state, not only by maintaining an honest, sober and free-enterprise climate of government in which industry can have confidence...but in going out and getting it...so that our people can have industrial jobs in Alabama and provide a better life for their children.

I shall not forget my duty to our senior citizens...so that their lives can be lived in dignity and enrichment of the golden years, nor to our sick, both mental and physical...and they will know we have not forsaken them. I want the farmer to feel confident that in this State government he has a partner who will work with him in raising his income and increasing his markets. And I want the laboring man to know he has a friend who is sincerely striving to better his field of endeavor.

I want to assure every child that this State government is not afraid to invest in their future through education, so that they will not be handicapped on every threshold of their lives.

Today I have stood, where once Jefferson Davis stood, and took an oath to my people. It is very appropriate then that from this Cradle of the Confederacy, this very Heart of the Great Anglo-Saxon Southland, that today we sound the drum for freedom as have our generations of forebears before us done, time and time again through history. Let us rise to the call of freedom-loving blood that is in us and send our answer to the tyranny that clanks its chains upon the South. In the name of the greatest people that have ever trod this earth, I draw the line in the dust and toss the gauntlet before the feet of tyranny...and I say...segregation today...segregation tomorrow...segregation forever.

The Washington, D.C., school riot report is disgusting and revealing. We will not sacrifice our children to any such type school system—and you can write that down. The federal troops in

Mississippi could be better used guarding the safety of the citizens of Washington, D.C., where it is even unsafe to walk or go to a ballgame—and that is the nation's capitol. I was safer in a B-29 bomber over Japan during the war in an air raid, than the people of Washington are walking to the White House neighborhood. A closer example is Atlanta. The city officials fawn for political reasons over school integration and *then* build barricades to stop residential integration—what hypocrisy!

Let us send this message back to Washington by our representatives who are with us today...that from this day we are standing up, and the heel of tyranny does not fit the neck of an upright man... that we intend to take the offensive and carry our fight for freedom across the nation, wielding the balance of power we know we possess in the Southland...that *we,* not the insipid bloc of voters of some sections...will determine in the next election who shall sit in the White House of these United States... That from this day, from this hour...from this minute...we give the word of a race of honor that we will tolerate their boot in our face no longer...and let those certain judges put *that* in their opium pipes of power and smoke it for what it is worth.

Hear me, Southerners! You sons and daughters who have moved north and west throughout this nation...we call on you from your native soil to join with us in national support and vote...and we know...wherever you are...away from the hearths of the Southland...that you will respond, for though you may live in the farthest reaches of this vast country...your heart has never left Dixieland.

And you native sons and daughters of old New England's rock-ribbed patriotism...and you sturdy natives of the great Mid-West...and you descendants of the far West flaming spirit of pioneer freedom...we invite you to come and be with us...for you are of the Southern spirit...and the Southern philosophy...you are Southerners too and brothers with us in our fight.

What I have said about segregation goes double this day...and what I have said to or about some federal judges goes *triple* this day.

Alabama has been blessed by God as few states in this Union have been blessed. Our state owns ten percent of all the natural resources of all the states in our country. Our inland waterway system is second to none...and has the potential of being the greatest waterway transport system in the entire world. We possess over thirty minerals in usable quantities and our soil is rich and varied, suited to a wide variety of plants. Our native pine and forestry system produces timber faster than we can cut it and yet we have only pricked the surface of the great lumber and pulp potential.

With ample rainfall and rich grasslands our live stock industry is in the infancy of a giant future that can make us a center of the big and growing meat packing and prepared foods marketing. We have the favorable climate, streams, woodlands, beaches, and natural beauty to make us a recreational mecca in the booming tourist and vacation industry. Nestled in the great Tennessee Valley, we possess the rocket center of the world and the keys to the space frontier.

While the tirade with a developing Europe built the great port cities of the east coast, our own fast developing port of Mobile faces as a magnetic gateway to the great continent of South America, well over twice as large and hundreds of times richer in resources, even now awakening to the growing probes of enterprising capital with a potential of growth and wealth beyond any present dream for our port development and corresponding results throughout the connecting waterways that thread our state.

And while the manufacturing industries of free enterprise have been coming to our state in increasing numbers, attracted by our bountiful natural resources, our growing numbers of skilled workers and our favorable conditions, their present rate of settlement here can be increased from the trickle they now represent to a stream of enterprise and endeavor, capital and expansion that can join us in our work of development and enrichment of the educational futures of our children, the opportunities of our citizens and the fulfillment of our talents as God has given them to us. To realize our ambitions and to bring to fruition our dreams, we as Alabamians must take cognizance of the world about us. We must re-define our heritage, re-school our thoughts in the lessons our forefathers knew so well, first hand, in order to function and to grow and to prosper. We can no longer hide our head in the sand and tell ourselves that the ideology of our free fathers is not being attacked and is not being threatened by another idea...for it is. We are faced with an idea that if a centralized government assume enough authority, enough power over its people, that it can provide a Utopian life...that if given the power to dictate, to forbid, to require, to demand, to distribute, to edict and to judge what is best and enforce that will produce only "good"...and it shall be our father...and our God. It is an idea of government that encourages our fears and destroys our faith...for where there is faith, there is no fear, and where there is fear, there is no faith. In encouraging our fears of economic insecurity it demands we place that economic management and control with government; in encouraging our fear of educational development it demands we place that education and the minds of our children under management and control of government, and even in feeding our fears of physical infirmities and declining years, it offers and demands to father us through it all and even into the grave. It is a government that claims to us that it is bountiful as it buys its power from us with the fruits of its rapaciousness of the wealth that free men before it have produced and builds on crumbling credit without responsibilities to the debtors... our children. It is an ideology of government erected on the encouragement of fear and fails to recognize the basic law of our fathers that governments do not produce wealth...people produce wealth...free people; and those people become less free...as they learn there is little reward for ambition...that it requires faith to risk...and they have none...as the government must restrict and penalize and tax incentive and endeavor and must increase its expenditures of bounties...then this government must assume more and more police powers and we find we are become government-fearing people...not God-fearing people. We find we have replaced faith with fear...and though we may give lip service to the Almighty...in reality, government has become our god. It is, therefore, a basically ungodly government and its appeal to the pseudo-intellectual and the politician is to change their status from servant of the people to master of the people...to play at being God...without faith in God...and without the wisdom of God. It is a system that is the very opposite of Christ for it feeds and encourages everything degenerate and base in our people as it assumes the responsibilities that we ourselves should assume. Its pseudo-liberal spokesmen and some Harvard advocates have never examined the logic of its substitution of what it calls "human rights" for individual rights, for its propaganda play on words has appeal for the unthinking. Its logic is totally material and irresponsible as it runs the full gamut of human desires...including the theory that everyone has voting rights without the spiritual responsibility of preserving freedom. Our founding fathers recognized those rights...but only within the framework of those spiritual responsibilities. But the strong, simple faith and sane reasoning of our founding fathers has long since been forgotten as the so-called "progressives" tell us that our Constitution was written for "horse and buggy" days...so were the Ten Commandments.

Not so long ago men stood in marvel and awe at the cities, the buildings, the schools, the autobahns that the government of Hitler's Germany had built...just as centuries before they stood in wonder of Rome's building...but it could not stand...for the system that built it had rotted the souls of the builders...and in turn...rotted the foundation of what God meant that men should be. Today that same system on an international scale is sweeping the world. It is the "changing world" of which we are told...it is called "new" and "liberal." It is as old as the oldest dictator. It is degenerate and decadent. As the *national* racism of Hitler's Germany persecuted a *national* minority to the whim of a national majority...so the *international* racism of the liberals seek to persecute the *international* white minority to the whim of the *international* colored majority...so that we are footballed about according to the favor of the Afro-Asian bloc. But the Belgian survivors of the Congo cannot present their case to a war crimes commission... nor the Portuguese of Angola...nor the survivors of Castro...nor the citizens of Oxford, Mississippi.

It is this theory of international power politic that led a group of men on the Supreme Court for the first time in American history to issue an edict, based not on legal precedent, but upon a volume, the editor of which said our Constitution is outdated and must be changed and the writers of which, some had admittedly belonged to as many as half a hundred communist-front organizations. It is this theory that led this same group of men to briefly bare the ungodly core of that philosophy in forbidding little school children to say a prayer. And we find the evidence of that ungodliness even in the removal of the words "in God we trust" from some of our dollars, which was placed there as like evidence by our founding fathers as the faith upon which this system of government was built. It is the spirit of power thirst that caused a President in Washington to take up Caesar's pen and with one stroke of it make a law. A law which the law making body of Congress refused to pass...a law that tells us that we can or cannot buy or sell our very homes, except by his conditions...and except at *his* discretion. It is the spirit of power thirst that led the same President to launch a full offensive of twenty-five thousand troops against a university...of all places...in his own country...and against his own people, when this nation maintains only six thousand troops in the beleaguered city of Berlin. We have witnessed such acts of "might makes right" over the world as men yielded to the temptation to play God...but we have never before witnessed it in America. We reject such acts as free men. We do not defy, for there is nothing to defy...since as free men we do not recognize any government right to give freedom...or deny freedom. No government erected by man has that right. As Thomas Jefferson said, "The God who gave us life, gave us liberty at the same time; no King holds the right of liberty in his hands." Nor does any ruler in American government.

We intend, quite simply, to practice the free heritage as bequeathed to us as sons of free fathers. We intend to re-vitalize the truly new and progressive form of government that is less that two hundred years old...a government first founded in this nation simply and purely on faith...that there is a personal God who rewards good and punishes evil...that hard work will receive its just deserts... that ambition and ingenuity and incentiveness...and profit of such... are admirable traits and goals...that the individual is encouraged in his spiritual growth and from that growth arrives at a character that enhances his charity toward others and from that character and that charity so is influenced business, and labor and farmer and government. We intend to renew our faith as God-fearing men...*not* government-fearing men nor any other kind of fearing-men. We intend to roll up our sleeves and pitch in to develop this full bounty God has given us...to live full and useful lives and in absolute freedom from all fear. Then can we enjoy the full richness of the Great American Dream.

We have placed this sign, "In God We Trust," upon our State Capitol on this Inauguration Day as physical evidence of determination to renew the faith of our fathers and to practice the free heritage they bequeathed to us. We do this with the clear and solemn knowledge that such physical evidence is evidently a direct violation of the logic of that Supreme Court in Washington D.C., and if they or their spokesmen in this state wish to term this defiance...I say...then let them make the most of it.

This nation was never meant to be a unit of one...but a united of the many...that is the exact reason our freedom loving forefathers established the states, so as to divide the rights and powers among the states, insuring that no central power could gain master government control.

In united effort we were meant to live under this government...
whether Baptist, Methodist, Presbyterian, Church of Christ, or whatever one's denomination or religious belief...each respecting the other's right to a separate denomination...each, by working to develop his own, enriching the total of all our lives through united effort. And so it was meant in our political lives...whether Republican, Democrat, Prohibition, or whatever political party...each striving from his separate political station...respecting the rights of others to be separate and work from within their political frame work...and each separate political station making its contribution to our lives....

And so it was meant in our racial lives...each race, within its own framework has the freedom to teach...to instruct...to develop...to ask for and receive deserved help from others of separate racial stations. This is the great freedom of our American founding fathers... but if we amalgamate into the one unit as advocated by the communist philosophers...then the enrichment of our lives...the freedom for our development...is gone forever. We become, therefore, a mongrel unit of one under a single all-powerful government...and we stand for everything...and for nothing.

The true brotherhood of America, of respecting the separateness of others...and uniting in effort...has been so twisted and distorted from its original concept that there is a small wonder that communism is winning the world.

We invite the Negro citizens of Alabama to work with us from his separate racial station...as we will work with him...to develop, to grow in individual freedom and enrichment. We want jobs and a good future for *both* races...the tubercular and the infirm. This is the basic heritage of my religion, if which I make full practice...for we are all the handiwork of God.

But we warn those, of any group, who would follow the false doctrine of communistic amalgamation that we will not surrender our system of government...our freedom of race and religion...that freedom was won at a hard price and if it requires a hard price to retain it...we are able...and quite willing to pay it.

The liberals' theory that poverty, discrimination and lack of opportunity is the cause of communism is a false theory...if it were true the South would have been the biggest single communist bloc in the western hemisphere long ago...for after the great War Between the States, our people faced a desolate land of burned universities, destroyed crops and homes, with manpower depleted and crippled, and even the mule, which was required to work the land, was so scarce that whole communities shared one animal to make the spring plowing. There were no government handouts, no Marshall Plan aid, no coddling to make sure that *our* people would not suffer; instead the South was set upon by the vulturous carpetbagger and federal troops, all loyal Southerners were denied the vote at the point of bayonet, so that the infamous, illegal 14th Amendment might be passed. There was no money, no food and no hope of either. But our grandfathers bent their knee only in church and bowed their head only to God.

Not for a single instant did they ever consider the easy way of federal dictatorship and amalgamation in return for fat bellies. They fought. They dug sweet roots from the ground with their bare hands and boiled them in iron pots...they gathered poke salad from the woods and acorns from the ground. They fought. They followed no false doctrine...they knew what they wanted...and they fought for freedom! They came up from their knees in the greatest display of sheer nerve, grit and guts that has ever been set down in the pages of written history...and they won! The great writer Rudyard Kipling wrote of them that: "There in the Southland of the United States of America, lives the greatest fighting breed of man...in all the world!"

And that is why today, I stand ashamed of the fat, well-fed whimpers who say that it is inevitable...that our cause is lost. I am ashamed *of* them...and I am ashamed *for* them. They do not represent the people of the Southland.

And may we take note of one other fact, with all trouble with communists that some sections of this country have...there are not enough native communists in the South to fill up a telephone booth...and *that* is a matter of public FBI record.

We remind all within hearing of this Southland that a *Southerner,* Peyton Randolph, presided over the Continental Congress in our nation's beginning...that a *Southerner,* Thomas Jefferson, wrote the Declaration of Independence, that a *Southerner,* George Washington, is the Father of our country...that a *Southerner,* James Madison, authored our Constitution, that a *Southerner,* George Mason, authored the Bill of Rights and it was a Southerner who said, "Give me liberty...or give me death," Patrick Henry.

Southerners played a most magnificent part in erecting this great divinely inspired system of freedom...and as God is our witness, Southerners will save it.

Let us, as Alabamians, grasp the hand of destiny and walk out of the shadow of fear...and fill our divine destination. Let us not simply defend...but let us assume the leadership of the fight and carry our leadership across this nation. God has placed us here in this crisis...let us not fail in this...our most historical moment.

You are here today, present in this audience, and to you over this great state, wherever you are in sound of my voice, I want to humbly and with all sincerity, thank you for your faith in me.

I promise you that I will try to make you a good governor. I promise you that, as God gives me the wisdom and the strength, I will be sincere with you. I will be honest with you.

I will apply the old sound rule of our fathers, that anything worthy of our defense is worthy of one hundred percent of our defense. I have been taught that freedom meant freedom from any threat or fear of government. I was born in that freedom; I was raised in that freedom...I intend to live in that freedom...and God willing, when I die, I shall leave that freedom to my children...as my father left it to me.

My pledge to you...to "Stand up for Alabama," is a stronger pledge today than it was the first day I made that pledge. I shall "Stand up for Alabama," as Governor of our State...you stand with me...and we together, can give courageous leadership to millions of people throughout this nation who look to the South for their hope in this fight to win and preserve our freedoms and liberties.

So help me God.

And my prayer is that the Father who reigns above us will bless all the people of this great sovereign State and nation, both white and black.

I thank you.

[IS]

Martin Luther King, Jr., Speech, "I Have a Dream"

August 28, 1963

As president of the Southern Christian Leadership Conference, the Baptist pastor Dr. King (1929–1968) spoke at the Lincoln Memorial to the participants of the civil rights march on Washington, D.C. A native of Atlanta, King earned his undergraduate degree at Morehouse College and his Ph.D. at Boston University. He was an inspiring speaker as he advocated for racial justice and peace. In 1968, the Nobel Peace Prize winner was assassinated in Memphis.

I AM HAPPY to join with you today in what will go down in history as the greatest demonstration for freedom in the history of our nation.

Five score years ago, a great American, in whose symbolic shadow we stand, signed the Emancipation Proclamation. This momentous decree came as a great beacon light of hope to millions of Negro slaves who had been seared in the flames of withering injustice. It came as a joyous daybreak to end the long night of captivity.

But one hundred years later, we must face the tragic fact that the Negro is still not free. One hundred years later, the life of the Negro is still sadly crippled by the manacles of segregation and the chains of discrimination. One hundred years later, the Negro lives on a lonely island of poverty in the midst of a vast ocean of material prosperity. One hundred years later the Negro is still languishing in the corners of American society and finds himself an exile in his own land. So we have come here today to dramatize an appalling condition.

In a sense we have come to our nation's Capital to cash a check. When the architects of our republic wrote the magnificent words of the Constitution and the Declaration of Independence, they were signing a promissory note to which every American was to fall heir. This note was a promise that all men would be guaranteed the unalienable rights of life, liberty, and the pursuit of happiness.

It is obvious today that America has defaulted on this promissory note insofar as her citizens of color are concerned. Instead of honoring this sacred obligation, America has given the Negro people a bad check; a check which has come back marked "insufficient funds." But we refuse to believe that the bank of justice is bankrupt. We refuse to believe that there are insufficient funds in the great vaults of opportunity of this nation. So we have come to cash this check—a check that will give us upon demand the riches of freedom and the security of justice. We have also come to this hallowed spot to remind America of the fierce urgency of *now*. This is no time to engage in the luxury of cooling off or to take the tranquilizing drug of gradualism. *Now* is the time to make real the promise of Democracy. *Now* is the time to rise from the dark and desolate valley of segregation to the sunlit path of racial justice. *Now* is the time to open the doors of opportunity to all of God's children. *Now* is the time to lift our nation from the quicksands of racial injustice to the solid rock of brotherhood.

It would be fatal for the nation to overlook the urgency of the moment and to underestimate the determination of the Negro. This sweltering summer of the Negro's legitimate discontent will not pass until there is an invigorating autumn of freedom and equality. 1963 is not an end, but a beginning. Those who hope that the Negro needed to blow off steam and will now be content will have a rude awakening if the Nation returns to business as usual. There will be neither rest nor tranquility in America until the Negro is granted his citizenship rights. The whirlwinds of revolt will continue to shake the foundations of our Nation until the bright day of justice emerges.

But there is something that I must say to my people who stand on the warm threshold which leads into the palace of justice. In the process of gaining our rightful place we must not be guilty of wrongful deeds. Let us not seek to satisfy our thirst for freedom by drinking from the cup of bitterness and hatred. We must forever conduct our struggle on the high plane of dignity and discipline. We must not allow our creative protest to degenerate into physical violence. Again and again we must rise to the majestic heights of meeting physical force with soul force. The marvelous new militancy which has engulfed the Negro community must not lead us to a distrust of all white people, for many of our white brothers, as evidenced by their presence here today, have come to realize that their destiny is tied up with our destiny and their freedom is inextricably bound to our freedom. We cannot walk alone.

And as we walk, we must make the pledge that we shall march ahead. We cannot turn back. There are those who are asking the devotees of civil rights, "When will you be satisfied?" We can never be satisfied as long as the Negro is the victim of the unspeakable horrors of police brutality. We can never be satisfied as long as our bodies, heavy with the fatigue of travel, cannot gain lodging in the motels of the highways and the hotels of the cities. We cannot be satisfied as long as the Negro's basic mobility is from a smaller ghetto to a larger one. We can never be satisfied as long as a Negro in Mississippi cannot vote and a Negro in New York believes he has nothing for which to vote. No, no, we are not satisfied, and we will not be satisfied until justice rolls down like waters and righteousness like a mighty stream.

I am not unmindful that some of you have come here out of great trials and tribulations. Some of you have come fresh from narrow jail cells. Some of you have come from areas where your quest for freedom left you battered by the storms of persecution and staggered by the winds of police brutality. You have been the veterans of creative suffering. Continue to work with the faith that unearned suffering is redemptive.

Go back to Mississippi, go back to Alabama, go back to South Carolina, go back to Georgia, go back to Louisiana, go back to the slums and ghettos of our modern cities, knowing that somehow this situation can and will be changed. Let us not wallow in the valley of despair.

I say to you today, my friends, that in spite of the difficulties and frustrations of the moment I still have a dream. It is a dream deeply rooted in the American dream.

I have a dream that one day this nation will rise up and live out the true meaning of its creed: "We hold these truths to be self-evident; that all men are created equal."

I have a dream that one day on the red hills of Georgia the sons of former slaves and the sons of former slave-owners will be able to sit down together at the table of brotherhood.

I have a dream that one day even the state of Mississippi, a desert state sweltering with the heat of injustice and oppression, will be transformed into an oasis of freedom and justice.

I have a dream that my four little children will one day live in a nation where they will not be judged by the color of their skin but by the content of their character.

I have a dream today.

I have a dream that one day the state of Alabama, whose governor's lips are presently dripping with the words of interposition and nullification, will be transformed into a situation where little black boys and black girls will be able to join hand with little white boys and white girls and walk together as sisters and brothers.

I have a dream today.

I have a dream that one day every valley shall be exalted, every hill and mountain shall be made low, the rough places will be made plains, and the crooked places will be made straight, and the glory of the Lord shall be revealed, and all flesh shall see it together.

This is our hope. This is the faith with which I return to the South. With this faith we will be able to hew out of the mountain of despair a stone of hope. With this faith we will be able to transform the jangling discords of our nation into a beautiful symphony of brotherhood. With this faith we will be able to work together, to pray together, to struggle together, to go to jail together, to stand up for freedom together, knowing that we will be free one day.

This will be the day when all of God's children will be able to sing with new meaning "My country 'tis of thee, sweet land of liberty, of thee I sing. Land where my fathers died, land of the pilgrim's pride, from every mountainside, let freedom ring."

And if America is to be a great nation this must become true. So let freedom ring from the prodigious hilltops of New Hampshire. Let freedom ring from the mighty mountains of New York. Let freedom ring from the heightening Alleghenies of Pennsylvania!

Let freedom ring from the snowcapped Rockies of Colorado!

Let freedom ring from the curvaceous peaks of California!

But not only that; let freedom ring from Stone Mountain of Georgia!

Let freedom ring from Lookout Mountain of Tennessee!

Let freedom ring from every hill and mole hill of Mississippi. From every mountainside, let freedom ring.

When we let freedom ring, when we let it ring from every village and every hamlet, from every state and every city, we will be able to speed up that day when all of God's children, black men and white men, Jews and Gentiles, Protestants and Catholics, will be able to join hands and sing in the words of the old Negro spiritual, "Free at last! Free at last! Thank God almighty, we are free at last!"

[GSTC]

Malcolm X, Speech,
The Black Revolution

April 8, 1964

Malcolm Little was born in Omaha, Nebraska, on May 19, 1925. A drop-out from school at fifteen, he was convicted of burglary and sent to prison in his twenty-first year. While in prison he was converted to the National of Islam (Black Muslims), and upon his release in 1952 adopted the name Malcolm X and became a leading figure in the movement. In 1963 he was suspended from his post as Minister of the New York Muslim temple. Following his suspension, he made two trips to Africa and the Middle East. Returning to the United States, Malcolm X began to organize a new movement called the Organization of Afro-American Unity. He dropped the Muslim religious ideology, but maintained the concept of Black Nationalism and rejected non-violence. On February 21, 1965, he was assassinated in the Audubon Ballroom in upper Harlem. At the time of his death, he was becoming the most dynamic leader of the Black Revolution. The following is part of a speech he delivered on "The Black Revolution" at a meeting sponsored by the Militant Labor Forum, a socialist organization, at Palm Gardens in New York City.
– Note by Lewis Copeland

JUST AS WE can see that all over the world one of the main problems facing the West is race, likewise here in America today, most of your Negro leaders as well as the whites agree that 1964 itself appears to be one of the most explosive years yet in the history of America on the racial front, on the racial scene. Not only is this racial explosion probably to take place in America, but all of the ingredients for this racial explosion in America to blossom into a world-wide racial explosion present themselves right here in front of us. America's racial powder keg, in short, can actually fuse or ignite a world-wide powder keg.

There are whites in this country who are still complacent when they see the possibilities of racial strife getting out of hand. You are complacent simply because you think you outnumber the racial minority in this country; what you have to bear in mind is wherein you might outnumber us in this country, you don't outnumber us all over the earth.

Any kind of racial explosion that takes place in this country today, in 1964, is not a racial explosion that can be confined to the shores of America. It is a racial explosion that can ignite the racial powder keg that exists all over the planet that we call earth. I think that nobody would disagree that the dark masses of Africa and Asia and Latin America are already seething with bitterness, animosity, hostility, unrest, and impatience with the racial intolerance that they themselves have experienced at the hands of the white West.

And just as they have the ingredients of hostility toward the West in general, here we also have 22 million African-Americans, black, brown, red, and yellow people, in this country who are also seething with bitterness and impatience and hostility and animosity at the racial intolerance not only of the white West but of white America in particular.

And by the hundreds of thousands today we find our own people have become impatient, turning away from your white nationalism, which you call democracy, toward the militant, uncompromising policy of nationalism. I point out right here that as soon as we announced we were going to start a black nationalist party in this country, we received from coast to coast, especially from young people at the college level, the university level, who expressed complete sympathy and support and a desire to take an active part in any kind of political action based on black nationalism, designed to correct or eliminate immediately evils that our people have suffered here for 400 years.

The black nationalists to many of you may represent only a minority in the community. And therefore you might have a tendency to classify them as something insignificant. But just as the fuse is the smallest part or smallest piece in the powder keg, it is yet that little fuse that ignites the entire powder keg. The black nationalists to you may represent a small minority in the so-called Negro community. But they just happen to be composed of the type of ingredient necessary to fuse or ignite the entire black community.

And this is one thing that whites—whether you call yourselves liberals or conservatives or racists or whatever else you might choose to be—one thing that you have to realize is, where the black community is concerned, although the large majority you come in contact with may impress you as being moderate and patient and loving and long-suffering and all that kind of stuff, the minority who you consider to be Muslims or nationalists happen to be made of the type of ingredient that can easily spark the black community. This should be understood. Because to me a powder keg is nothing without a fuse.

1964 will be America's hottest year; her hottest year yet; a year of much racial violence and much racial bloodshed. But it won't be blood that's going to flow only on one side. The new generation of black people that have grown up in this country during recent years are already forming the opinion, and it's a just opinion, that if there is to be bleeding, it should be reciprocal—bleeding on both sides.

It should also be understood that the racial sparks that are ignited here in America today could easily turn into a flaming fire abroad, which means it could engulf all the people of this earth into a giant race war. You cannot confine it to one little neighborhood, or one little community, or one little country. What happens to a black man in America today happens to a black man in Africa. What happens to a black man in America and Africa happens to the black man in Asia and to the man down in Latin America. What happens to one of us today happens to all of us. And when this is realized, I think that the whites—who are intelligent even if they aren't moral or aren't just or aren't impressed by legalities—those who are intelligent will realize that when they touch this one, they are touching all of them, and this in itself will have a tendency to be a checking factor.

The seriousness of this situation must be faced up to. I was in Cleveland last night, Cleveland, Ohio. In fact I was there Friday, Saturday and yesterday. Last Friday the warning was given that this is a year of bloodshed, that the black man has ceased to turn the other cheek, that he has ceased to be nonviolent, that he has ceased to feel that he must be confined by all these restraints that are put upon him by white society in struggling for what white society says he was supposed to have had a hundred years ago.

So today, when the black man starts reaching out for what America says are his rights, the black man feels that he is within his rights—when he becomes the victim of brutality by those who are depriving him of his rights—to do whatever is necessary to protect himself. An example of this was taking place last night at this same time in Cleveland, where the police were putting water hoses on our people there and also throwing tear gas at them—and they met a hail of stones, a hail of rocks, a hail of bricks. A couple of weeks ago in Jacksonville, Florida, a young teen-age Negro was throwing Molotov cocktails.

Well, Negroes didn't do this ten years ago. But what you should learn from this is that they are waking up. It was stones yesterday, Molotov cocktails today; it will be hand grenades tomorrow and what-ever else is available the next day. The seriousness of this situation must be faced up to. You should not feel that I am inciting someone to vio-lence. I'm only warning of a powder-keg situation. You can take it or leave it. If you take the warning, perhaps you can still save yourself. But if you ignore it or ridicule it, well, death is already at your doorstep. There are 22 million African-Americans who are ready to fight for independence right here. When I say fight for independence right here, I don't mean any non-violent fight, or turn-the-other-cheek fight. Those days are gone. Those days are over.

If George Washington didn't get independence for this country non-violently, and if Patrick Henry didn't come up with a nonvio-lent statement, and you taught me to look upon them as patriots and heroes, then it's time for you to realize that I have studied your books well. . . .

1964 will see the Negro revolt evolve and merge into the world-wide black revolution that has been taking place on this earth since 1945. The so-called revolt will become a real black revolution. Now the black revolution has been taking place in Africa and Asia and Latin America; when I say black, I mean non-white—black, brown, red or yellow. Our brothers and sisters in Asia, who were colonized by the Europeans, our brothers and sisters in Africa, who were colonized by the Europeans, and in Latin America, the peas-ants, who were colonized by the Europeans, have been involved in a struggle since 1945 to get the colonialists, or the colonizing pow-ers, the Europeans, off their land, out of their country.

This is a real revolution. Revolution is always based on land. Revolution is never based on begging somebody for an integrated cup of coffee. Revolutions are never fought by turning the other cheek. Revolutions are never based upon love-your-enemy and pray-for-those-who-spitefully-use-you. And revolutions are never waged singing "We Shall Overcome." Revolutions are based upon bloodshed. Revolutions are never compromising. Revolutions are never based upon negotiations. Revolutions are never based upon any kind of tokenism whatsoever. Revolutions are never even based upon that which is begging a corrupt society or a corrupt system to accept us into it. Revolutions overturn systems. And there is no system on this earth which has proven itself more corrupt, more criminal, than this system that in 1964 colonizes 22 million African-Americans, still enslaves 22 million Afro-Americans.

There is no system more corrupt than a system that represents itself as the example of freedom, the example of democracy, and can go all over this earth telling other people how to straighten out their house, when you have citizens of this country who have to use bullets if they want to cast a ballot.

The greatest weapon the colonial powers have used in the past against our people have always been divide-and-conquer. America is a colonial power. She has colonized 22 million Afro-Americans by depriving us of first-class citizenship, by depriving us of civil rights, actually by depriving us of human rights. She has not only deprived us of the right to be a citizen, she has deprived us of the right to be human beings, the right to be recognized and respected as men and women. In this country the black can be fifty years old and he is still a "boy."

I grew up with white people. I was integrated before they even invented the word and I have never met white people yet—if you are around them long enough—who won't refer to you as a "boy" or a "gal," no matter how old you are or what school you come out of, no matter what your intellectual or professional level is. In this society we remain "boys."

So America's strategy is the same strategy as that which was used in the past by the colonial powers: divide and conquer. She plays one Negro leader against the other. She plays one Negro organization against the other. She makes us think we have different objectives, different goals. As soon as one Negro says something, she runs to this Negro and asks him, "What do you think about what he said?" Why, anybody can see through that today—except some of the Negro leaders.

All of our people have the same goals, the same objective. That objective is freedom, justice, equality. All of us want recognition and respect as human beings. We don't want to be integrationists. Nor do we want to be separationists. We want to be human beings. Integration is only a method that is used by some groups to obtain freedom, justice, equality and respect as human beings. Separation is only a method that is used by other groups to obtain freedom, justice, equality or human dignity.

Our people have made the mistake of confusing the methods with the objectives. As long as we agree on objectives, we should never fall out with each other just because we believe in different methods or tactics or strategy to reach a common objective.

We have to keep in mind at all times that we are not fighting for integration, nor are we fighting for separation. We are fighting for recognition as human beings. We are fighting for the right to live as free humans in this society. In fact, we are actually fighting for rights that are even greater than civil rights and that is human rights. . . .

[WGS]

President Lyndon B. Johnson, Speech, "The Great Society"

May 22, 1964

Lyndon Baines Johnson (1908–1973) became the president of the United States after John F. Kennedy's assassination on November 22, 1963. The Texas Democrat would run for election as president in November of 1964 against the Republican nominee Barry Goldwater. He spoke here at Ann Arbor to Michigan state officials and the University of Michigan graduating class of 1964. He had previously announced the equally famous plan for a "war on poverty" and was at the moment leaning on Congress to approve the Civil Rights Act, which was finally signed into law in June.

[...] I HAVE COME today from the turmoil of your Capital to the tranquility of your campus to speak about the future of your country.

The purpose of protecting the life of our Nation and preserving the liberty of our citizens is to pursue the happiness of our people. Our success in that pursuit is the test of our success as a Nation.

For a century we labored to settle and to subdue a continent. For half a century we called upon unbounded invention and untiring industry to create an order of plenty for all of our people.

The challenge of the next half century is whether we have the wisdom to use that wealth to enrich and elevate our national life, and to advance the quality of our American civilization.

Your imagination, your initiative, and your indignation will determine whether we build a society where progress is the servant of our needs, or a society where old values and new visions are buried under unbridled growth. For in your time we have the opportunity to move not only toward the rich society and the powerful society, but upward to the Great Society.

The Great Society rests on abundance and liberty for all. It demands an end to poverty and racial injustice, to which we are totally committed in our time. But that is just the beginning.

The Great Society is a place where every child can find knowledge to enrich his mind and to enlarge his talents. It is a place where leisure is a welcome chance to build and reflect, not a feared cause of boredom and restlessness. It is a place where the city of man serves not only the needs of the body and the demands of commerce but the desire for beauty and the hunger for community.

It is a place where man can renew contact with nature. It is a place which honors creation for its own sake and for what it adds to the understanding of the race. It is a place where men are more concerned with the quality of their goals than the quantity of their goods.

But most of all, the Great Society is not a safe harbor, a resting place, a final objective, a finished work. It is a challenge constantly renewed, beckoning us toward a destiny where the meaning of our lives matches the marvelous products of our labor.

So I want to talk to you today about three places where we begin to build the Great Society—in our cities, in our countryside, and in our classrooms.

Many of you will live to see the day, perhaps 50 years from now, when there will be 400 million Americans four-fifths of them in urban areas. In the remainder of this century urban population will double, city land will double, and we will have to build homes, highways, and facilities equal to all those built since this country was first settled. So in the next 40 years we must rebuild the entire urban United States.

Aristotle said: "Men come together in cities in order to live, but they remain together in order to live the good life." It is harder and harder to live the good life in American cities today.

The catalog of ills is long: there is the decay of the centers and the despoiling of the suburbs. There is not enough housing for our people or transportation for our traffic. Open land is vanishing and old landmarks are violated.

Worst of all expansion is eroding the precious and time honored values of community with neighbors and communion with nature. The loss of these values breeds loneliness and boredom and indifference.

Our society will never be great until our cities are great. Today the frontier of imagination and innovation is inside those cities and not beyond their borders.

New experiments are already going on. It will be the task of your generation to make the American city a place where future generations will come, not only to live but to live the good life.

I understand that if I stayed here tonight I would see that Michigan students are really doing their best to live the good life.

This is the place where the Peace Corps was started. It is inspiring to see how all of you, while you are in this country, are trying so hard to live at the level of the people.

A second place where we begin to build the Great Society is in our countryside. We have always prided ourselves on being not only America the strong and America the free, but America the beautiful. Today that beauty is in danger. The water we drink, the food we eat, the very air that we breathe, are threatened with pollution. Our parks are overcrowded, our seashores overburdened. Green fields and dense forests are disappearing.

A few years ago we were greatly concerned about the "Ugly American." Today we must act to prevent an ugly America.

For once the battle is lost, once our natural splendor is destroyed, it can never be recaptured. And once man can no longer walk with beauty or wonder at nature his spirit will wither and his sustenance be wasted.

A third place to build the Great Society is in the classrooms of America. There your children's lives will be shaped. Our society will not be great until every young mind is set free to scan the farthest reaches of thought and imagination. We are still far from that goal.

Today, 8 million adult Americans, more than the entire population of Michigan, have not finished 5 years of school. Nearly 20 million have not finished 8 years of school. Nearly 54 million—more than one-quarter of all America—have not even finished high school.

Each year more than 100,000 high school graduates, with proved ability, do not enter college because they cannot afford it. And if we cannot educate today's youth, what will we do in 1970 when elementary school enrollment will be 5 million greater than 1960?

And high school enrollment will rise by 5 million. College enrollment will increase by more than 3 million.

In many places, classrooms are overcrowded and curricula are outdated. Most of our qualified teachers are underpaid, and many of our paid teachers are unqualified. So we must give every child a place to sit and a teacher to learn from. Poverty must not be a bar to learning, and learning must offer an escape from poverty.

But more classrooms and more teachers are not enough. We must seek an educational system which grows in excellence as it grows in size. This means better training for our teachers. It means preparing youth to enjoy their hours of leisure as well as their hours of labor. It means exploring new techniques of teaching, to find new ways to stimulate the love of learning and the capacity for creation.

These are three of the central issues of the Great Society. While our Government has many programs directed at those issues, I do not pretend that we have the full answer to those problems.

But I do promise this: We are going to assemble the best thought and the broadest knowledge from all over the world to find those answers for America. I intend to establish working groups to prepare a series of White House conferences and meetings—on the cities, on natural beauty, on the quality of education, and on other emerging challenges. And from these meetings and from this inspiration and from these studies we will begin to set our course toward the Great Society.

The solution to these problems does not rest on a massive program in Washington, nor can it rely solely on the strained resources of local authority. They require us to create new concepts of cooperation, a creative federalism, between the National Capital and the leaders of local communities.

Woodrow Wilson once wrote: "Every man sent out from his university should be a man of his Nation as well as a man of his time."

Within your lifetime powerful forces, already loosed, will take us toward a way of life beyond the realm of our experience, almost beyond the bounds of our imagination.

For better or for worse, your generation has been appointed by history to deal with those problems and to lead America toward a new age. You have the chance never before afforded to any people in any age. You can help build a society where the demands of morality, and the needs of the spirit, can be realized in the life of the Nation.

So, will you join in the battle to give every citizen the full equality which God enjoins and the law requires, whatever his belief, or race, or the color of his skin?

Will you join in the battle to give every citizen an escape from the crushing weight of poverty?

Will you join in the battle to make it possible for all nations to live in enduring peace—as neighbors and not as mortal enemies?

Will you join in the battle to build the Great Society, to prove that our material progress is only the foundation on which we will build a richer life of mind and spirit?

There are those timid souls who say this battle cannot be won; that we are condemned to a soulless wealth. I do not agree. We have the power to shape the civilization that we want. But we need your will, your labor, your hearts, if we are to build that kind of society.

Those who came to this land sought to build more than just a new country. They sought a new world. So I have come here today to your campus to say that you can make their vision our reality. So let us from this moment begin our work so that in the future men will look back and say: It was then, after a long and weary way, that man turned the exploits of his genius to the full enrichment of his life.

Thank you. Goodby.

[APP]

President Lyndon B. Johnson, On Vietnam and on the Decision Not to Seek Reelection

March 31, 1968

In this dramatic televised speech, President Johnson surprised the nation with his announcement that he would not run again for president. "Nineteen sixty-eight," he later wrote, "was one of the most agonizing years any president ever spent in the White House. I sometimes felt that I was living in a continuous nightmare."

GOOD EVENING, MY fellow Americans.

Tonight I want to speak to you of peace in Vietnam and Southeast Asia.

No other question so preoccupies our people. No other dream so absorbs the 250 million human beings who live in that part of the world. No other goal motivates American policy in Southeast Asia.

For years, representatives of our Government and others have traveled the world seeking to find a basis for peace talks.

Since last September they have carried the offer that I made public at San Antonio. And that offer was this:

That the United States would stop its bombardment of North Vietnam when that would lead promptly to productive discussions—and that we would assume that North Vietnam would not take military advantage of our restraint.

Hanoi denounced this offer, both privately and publicly. Even while the search for peace was going on, North Vietnam rushed their preparations for a savage assault on the people, the Government and the allies of South Vietnam.

Their attack—during the Tet holidays—failed to achieve its principal objectives.

It did not collapse the elected Government of South Vietnam or shatter its army—as the Communists had hoped. It did not produce a "general uprising" among the people of the cities, as they had predicted.

The Communists were unable to maintain control of any of the more than 30 cities that they attacked, and they took very heavy casualties.

But they did compel the South Vietnamese and their allies to move certain forces from the countryside into the cities.

They caused widespread disruption and suffering. Their attacks, and the battles that followed, made refugees of half a million human beings.

The Communists may renew their attack any day. They are, it appears, trying to make 1968 the year of decision in South Vietnam—the year that brings, if not final victory or defeat, at least a turning point in the struggle.

This much is clear: If they do mount another round of heavy attacks, they will not succeed in destroying the fighting power of South Vietnam and its allies.

But tragically, this is also clear: Many men—on both sides of the struggle—will be lost. A nation that has already suffered 20 years of warfare will suffer once again. Armies on both sides will take new casualties. And the war will go on.

There is no need for this to be so. There is no need to delay the talks that could bring an end to this long and this bloody war.

Tonight, I renew the offer I made last August: to stop the bombardment of North Vietnam. We ask that talks begin promptly, that they be serious talks on the substance of peace. We assume that during those talks Hanoi will not take advantage of our restraint.

We are prepared to move immediately toward peace through negotiations. So tonight, in the hope that this action will lead to early talks, I am taking the first step to de-escalate the conflict. We are reducing—substantially reducing—the present level of hostilities, and we are doing so unilaterally and at once.

Tonight I have ordered our aircraft and our naval vessels to make no attacks on North Vietnam except in the area north of the de-militarized zone where the continuing enemy build-up directly threatens allied forward positions and where the movement of their troops and supplies are clearly related to that threat.

Even this very limited bombing of the North could come to an early end—if our restraint is matched by restraint in Hanoi. But I cannot in good conscience stop all bombing so long as to do so would immediately and directly endanger the lives of our men and our allies. Whether a complete bombing halt becomes possible in the future will be determined by events.

And tonight I call upon the United Kingdom and I call upon the Soviet Union—as co-chairman of the Geneva conferences and as permanent members of the United Nations Security Council—to do all they can to move from the unilateral act of de-escalation that I have just announced toward genuine peace in Southeast Asia.

The South Vietnamese know that further efforts are going to be required to expand their own armed forces; to move back into the countryside as quickly as possible; to increase their taxes; to select the very best men they have for civil and military responsibility; to achieve a new unity within their constitutional government, and to include in the national effort all those groups who wish to preserve South Vietnam's control over its own destiny.

President Thieu told his people last week, and I quote:

We must make greater efforts; we must accept more sacri-fices, because as I have said many times, this is our country. The existence of our nation is at stake, and this is mainly a Vietnamese responsibility.

On many occasions I have told the American people that we would send to Vietnam those forces that are required to accomplish our mission there. So with that as our guide we have previously authorized a force level of approximately 525,000.

In order that these forces may reach maximum combat effective-ness, the Joint Chiefs of Staff have recommended to me that we should prepare to send during the next five months the support troops totaling approximately 13,500 men.

A portion of these men will be made available from our active forces. The balance will come from reserve component units, which will be called up for service.

Now let me give you my estimate of the chances for peace—the peace that will one day stop the bloodshed in South Vietnam. That will—all the Vietnamese people will be permitted to rebuild and develop their land. That will permit us to turn more fully to our own tasks here at home.

I cannot promise that the initiative that I have announced tonight will be completely successful in achieving peace any more than the 30 others that we have undertaken and agreed to in recent years.

One day, my fellow citizens, there will be peace in Southeast Asia. It will come because the people of Southeast Asia want it—those whose armies are at war tonight; those who, though threatened, have thus far been spared.

Peace will come because Asians were willing to work for it and to sacrifice for it—and to die by the thousands for it.

But let it never be forgotten: peace will come also because America sent her sons to help secure it.

It has not been easy—far from it. During the past four and a half years, it has been my fate and my responsibility to be Commander in Chief. I have lived daily and nightly with the cost of this war. I know the pain that it has inflicted. I know perhaps better than anyone the misgivings it has aroused.

This I believe very deeply. Throughout my entire public career I have followed the personal philosophy that I am a free man, an American, a public servant and a member of my party—in that order—always and only.

For 37 years in the service of our nation, first as a Congressman, as a Senator and as Vice President, and now as your President, I have put the unity of the people first. I have put it ahead of any divisive partisanship. And in these times, as in times before, it is true that a house divided against itself by the spirit of faction, of party, of region, of religion, of race, is a house that cannot stand.

There is division in the American house now. There is divisiveness among us all tonight. And holding the trust that is mine, as President of all the people, I cannot disregard the peril of the progress of the American people and the hope and the prospect of peace for all peoples, so I would ask all Americans whatever their personal interest or concern to guard against divisiveness and all of its ugly consequences.

Fifty-two months and ten days ago, in a moment of tragedy and trauma, the duties of this office fell upon me.

I asked then for your help, and God's, that we might continue America on its course binding up our wounds, healing our history, moving forward in new unity, to clear the American agenda and to keep the American commitment for all of our people.

United we have kept that commitment. And united we have enlarged that commitment. And through all time to come I think America will be a stronger nation, a more just society, a land of greater opportunity and fulfillment because of what we have all done together in these years of unparalleled achievement.

Our reward will come in the life of freedom and peace and hope that our children will enjoy through ages ahead.

What we won when all of our people united just must not now be lost in suspicion and distrust and selfishness and politics among any of our people. And believing this as I do I have concluded that I should not permit the Presidency to become involved in the partisan divisions that are developing in this political war.

With American sons in the fields far away, with America's future under challenge right here at home, with our hopes and the world's hopes for peace in the balance every day, I do not believe that I should devote an hour or a day of my time to any personal partisan causes or to any duties other than the awesome duties of this office—the Presidency of your country.

Accordingly, I shall not seek, and I will not accept, the nomination of my party for another term as your President. But let men everywhere know, however, that a strong and a confident and a vigilant America stands ready tonight to seek an honorable peace; and stands ready tonight to defend an honored cause, whatever the price, whatever the burden, whatever the sacrifice that duty may require.

Thank you for listening. Good night and God bless all of you.

[GSTC]

Congressperson Shirley Chisholm, Speech, The Equal Rights Amendment

May 21, 1969

The Brooklyn native Shirley Chisholm (1924–2005) served in the House of Representatives from 1969 to 1983, the first African-American woman to be elected to Congress. She entered the primaries for the Democratic nomination for the presidency in 1972.

MR. SPEAKER, WHEN a young woman graduates from college and starts looking for a job, she is likely to have a frustrating and even demeaning experience ahead of her. If she walks into an office for an interview, the first question she will be asked is, "Do you type?"

There is a calculated system of prejudice that lies unspoken behind that question. Why is it acceptable for women to be secretaries, librarians, and teachers, but totally unacceptable for them to be managers, administrators, doctors, lawyers, and Members of Congress?

The unspoken assumption is that women are different. They do not have executive ability, orderly minds, stability, leadership skills, and they are too emotional.

It has been observed before, that society, for a long time, discriminated against another minority, the blacks, on the same basis—that they were different and inferior. The happy little homemaker and the contented "old darkey" on the plantation were both produced by prejudice.

As a black person, I am no stranger to race prejudice. But the truth is that in the political world I have been far oftener discriminated against because I am a woman than because I am black.

Prejudice against blacks is becoming unacceptable although it will take years to eliminate it. But it is doomed because, slowly, white America is beginning to admit that it exists. Prejudice against women is still acceptable. There is very little understanding yet of the immorality involved in double pay scales and the classification of most of the better jobs as "for men only."

More than half of the population of the United States is female. But women occupy only two percent of the managerial positions. They have not even reached the level of tokenism yet. No women sit on the AFL-CIO council or Supreme Court. There have been only two women who have held Cabinet rank, and at present there are none. Only two women now hold ambassadorial rank in the diplomatic corps. In Congress, we are down to one Senator and ten Representatives.

Considering that there are about three and a half million more women in the United States than men, this situation is outrageous.

It is true that part of the problem has been that women have not been aggressive in demanding their rights. This was also true of the black population tor many years. They submitted to oppression and even cooperated with it. Women have done the same thing. But now there is an awareness of this situation particularly among the younger segment of the population.

As in the field of equal rights for blacks, Spanish-Americans, the Indians, and other groups, laws will not change such deep-seated problems overnight, but they can be used to provide protection for those who are most abused, and to begin the process of evolutionary change by compelling the insensitive majority to reexamine its unconscious attitudes.

It is for this reason that I wish to introduce today a proposal that has been before every Congress for the last forty years and that sooner or later must become part of the basic law of the land—the equal rights amendment.

Let me note and try to refute two of the commonest arguments that are offered against this amendment. One is that women are already protected under the law and do not need legislation. Existing laws are not adequate to secure equal rights for women. Sufficient

proof of this is the concentration of women in lower paying, me-
nial, unrewarding jobs and their incredible scarcity in the upper
level jobs. If women are already equal, why is it such an event
whenever one happens to be elected to Congress?

It is obvious that discrimination exists. Women do not have the
opportunities that men do. And women that do not conform to the
system, who try to break with the accepted patterns, are stigmatized
as "odd" and "unfeminine." The fact is that a woman who aspires
to be chairman of the board, or a Member of the House, does so
for exactly the same reasons as any man. Basically, these are that she
thinks she can do the job and she wants to try.

A second argument often heard against the equal rights amendment is that it would eliminate legislation that many States and the
Federal Government have enacted giving special protection to
women and that it would throw the marriage and divorce laws into
chaos.

As for the marriage laws, they are due for a sweeping reform, and
an excellent beginning would be to wipe the existing ones off the
books. Regarding special protection for working women, I cannot
understand why it should be needed. Women need no protection
that men do not need. What we need are laws to protect working
people, to guarantee them fair pay, safe working conditions, protection against sickness and layoffs, and provision for dignified, comfortable retirement. Men and women need these things equally. That
one sex needs protection more than the other is a male supremacist
myth as ridiculous and unworthy of respect as the white supremacist
myths that society is trying to cure itself of at this time.

[GSTC]

Apollo 11, Astronaut Narratives ("First Men on the Moon")

July 16–24, 1969

The first earthlings to ever set foot on the moon were Americans. The crew of the Apollo 11 was made up of the commander Neil A. Armstrong (1930–2012), the lunar module pilot Edwin E. "Buzz" Aldrin (b. 1930), and the command module pilot Michael Collins (b. 1930). The narrative below of the vehicle's launch, landing and return is from Edgar M. Cortright's thrilling Apollo: Expeditions to the Moon *(1975).*

THE SPLASHDOWN MAY 26, 1969, of Apollo 10 cleared the way for the first formal attempt at a manned lunar landing. Six days before, the Apollo 11 launch vehicle and spacecraft half crawled from the VAB and trundled at 0.9 mph to Pad 39-A. A successful countdown test ending on July 3 showed the readiness of machines, systems, and people. The next launch window (established by lighting conditions at the landing site on Mare Tranquillitatis) opened at 9:32 AM EDT on July 16, 1969. The crew for Apollo 11, all of whom had already flown in space during Gemini, had been intensively training as a team for many months. The following mission account makes use of crew members' own words, from books written by two of them, supplemented by space-to-ground and press-conference transcripts.

ALDRIN: At breakfast early on the morning of the launch. Dr. Thomas Paine, the Administrator of NASA, told us that concern for our own safety must govern all our actions, and if anything looked wrong we were to abort the mission. He then made a most surprising and unprecedented statement: if we were forced to abort, we would be immediately recycled and assigned to the next landing attempt. What he said and how he said it was very reassuring.

We were up early, ate, and began to suit up—a rather laborious and detailed procedure involving many people, which we would repeat once again, alone, before entering the LM for our lunar landing.

While Mike and Neil were going through the complicated business of being strapped in and connected to the spacecraft's life-support system, I waited near the elevator on the floor below. I waited alone for fifteen minutes in a sort of serene limbo. As far as I could see there were people and cars lining the beaches and highways. The surf was just beginning to rise out of an azure-blue ocean. I could see the massiveness of the Saturn V rocket below and the magnificent precision of Apollo above. I savored the wait and marked the minutes in my mind as something I would always want to remember.

COLLINS: I am everlastingly thankful that I have flown before, and that this period of waiting atop a rocket is nothing new. I am just as tense this time, but the tenseness comes mostly from an appreciation of the enormity of our undertaking rather than from the unfamiliarity of the situation. I am far from certain that we will be able to fly the mission as planned. I think we will escape with our skins, or at least I will escape with mine, but I wouldn't give better than even odds on a successful landing and return. There are just too many things that can go wrong. Fred Haise [the backup astronaut who had checked command-module switch positions] has run through a checklist 417 steps long, and I have merely a half dozen minor chores to take care of— nickel and dime stuff. In between switch throws I have plenty of time to think, if not daydream. Here I am a white male, age thirty-eight, height 5 feet 11 inches, weight 165 pounds, salary $17,000 per annum, resident of a Texas suburb, with black spot on my roses, state of mind unsettled, about to be shot off to the Moon. Yes, to the Moon.

At the moment, the most important control is over on Neil's side, just outboard of his left knee. It is the abort handle, and now it has power to it, so if Neil rotates it 30 counterclockwise, three solid rockets above us will fire and yank the CM free of the service module and everything below it. It is only to be used in extremes. A large bulky pocket has been added to Neil's left suit leg, and it looks as though if he moves his leg slightly, it's going to snag on the abort handle. I quickly point this out to Neil, and he grabs the pocket and pulls it as far over to the inside of his thigh as he can, but it still doesn't look secure to either one of us. Jesus, I can see the headlines now: "MOONSHOT FALLS INTO OCEAN. Mistake by crew, program officials intimate. Last transmission from Armstrong prior to leaving the pad reportedly was 'Oops.'"

ARMSTRONG: The flight started promptly, and I think that was characteristic of all events of the flight. The Saturn gave us one magnificent ride, both in Earth orbit and on a trajectory to the Moon. Our memory of that differs little from the reports you have heard from the previous Saturn V flights.

ALDRIN: For the thousands of people watching along the beaches of Florida and the millions who watched on television, our liftoff was ear shattering. For us there was a slight increase in the amount of background noise, not at all unlike the sort one notices taking off in a commercial airliner, and in less than a minute we were traveling ahead of the speed of sound.

COLLINS: This beast is best felt. Shake, rattle, and roll. We are thrown left and right against our straps in spasmodic little jerks. It is steering like crazy, like a nervous lady driving a wide car down a narrow alley, and I just hope it knows where it's going, because for the first ten seconds we are perilously close to that umbilical tower.

ALDRIN: A busy eleven minutes later we were in Earth orbit. The Earth didn't look much different from the way it had during my first flight, and yet I kept looking at it. From space it has an almost benign quality. Intellectually one could realize there were wars underway, but emotionally it was impossible to understand such things. The thought reoccurred that wars are generally fought for territory or are disputes over borders; from space the arbitrary borders established on Earth cannot be seen. After one and a half orbits a preprogrammed sequence fired the Saturn to send us out of Earth orbit and on our way to the Moon. [...]

ARMSTRONG: Hey Houston, Apollo 11. This Saturn gave us a magnificent ride. We have no complaints with any of the three stages on that ride. It was beautiful.

COLLINS: We started the burn at 100 miles altitude, and had reached only 180 at cutoff, but we are climbing like a dingbat. In nine hours, when we are scheduled to make our first midcourse correction, we will be 57,000 miles out. At the instant of shutdown, Buzz recorded our velocity as 35,579 feet per second, more than enough to escape from the Earth's gravitational field. As we proceed outbound, this number will get smaller and smaller until the tug of the Moon's gravity exceeds that of the Earth's and then we will start speeding up again. It's hard to believe that we are on our way to the Moon, at 1200 miles altitude now, less than three hours after liftoff, and I'll bet the launch-day crowd down at the Cape is still bumper to bumper, straggling back to the motels and bars.

ALDRIN: Mike's next major task, with Neil and me assisting, was to separate our command module Columbia from the Saturn third stage, turn around and connect with the lunar module Eagle, which was stored in the third stage. Eagle, by now, was exposed; its four enclosing panels had automatically come off and were drifting away. This of course was a critical maneuver in the flight plan. If the separation and docking did not work, we would return to Earth. There was also the possibility of an in-space collision and the subsequent decompression of our cabin, so we were still in our spacesuits as Mike separated us from the Saturn third stage. Critical as the maneuver is, I felt no apprehension about it, and if there was the slightest inkling of concern it disappeared quickly as the entire separation and docking proceeded perfectly to completion. The nose of Columbia was now connected to the top of the Eagle and heading for the Moon as we watched the Saturn third stage venting, a propulsive maneuver causing it to move slowly away from us.

Fourteen hours after liftoff, at 10:30 PM by Houston time, the three astronauts fasten covers over the windows of the slowly rotating command module and go to sleep. Days 2 and 3 are devoted to housekeeping chores, a small midcourse velocity correction, and TV transmissions back to Earth. In one news digest from Houston, the astronauts are amused to hear that Pravda has referred to Armstrong as "the czar of the ship."

ALDRIN: In our preliminary flight plan I wasn't scheduled to go to the LM until the next day in lunar orbit, but I had lobbied successfully to go earlier. My strongest argument was that I'd have ample time to make sure that the frail LM and its equipment had suffered no damage during the launch and long trip. By that time neither Neil nor I had been in the LM for about two weeks.

THE MOST AWESOME SPHERE

COLLINS: Day 4 has a decidedly different feel to it. Instead of nine hours' sleep, I get seven—and fitful ones at that. Despite our concentrated effort to conserve our energy on the way to the Moon, the pressure is overtaking us (or me at least), and I feel that all of us are aware that the honeymoon is over and we are about to lay our little pink bodies on the line. Our first shock comes as we stop our spinning motion and swing ourselves around so as to bring the Moon into view. We have not been able to see the Moon for nearly a day now, and the change is electrifying. The Moon I have known all my life, that two-dimensional small yellow disk in the sky, has gone away somewhere, to be replaced by the most awesome sphere I have ever seen. To begin with it is huge, completely filling our window. Second, it is three-dimensional. The belly of it bulges out toward us in such a pronounced fashion that I almost feel I can reach out and touch it. To add to the dramatic effect, we can see the stars again. We are in the shadow of the Moon now, and the elusive stars have reappeared.

As we ease around on the left side of the Moon, I marvel again at the precision of our path. We have missed hitting the Moon by a paltry 300 nautical miles, at a distance of nearly a quarter of a million miles from Earth, and don't forget that the Moon is a moving target and that we are racing through the sky just ahead of its leading edge. When we launched the other day the Moon was nowhere near where it is now; it was some 40 degrees of arc, or nearly 200,000 miles, behind where it is now, and yet those big computers in the basement in Houston didn't even whimper but belched out super-accurate predictions.

As we pass behind the Moon, we have just over eight minutes to go before the burn. We are super-careful now, checking and rechecking each step several times. When the moment finally arrives, the big engine instantly springs into action and reassuringly plasters us back in our seats. The acceleration is only a fraction of one G but it feels good nonetheless. For six minutes we sit there peering intent as hawks at our instrument panel, scanning the important dials and gauges, making sure that the proper thing is being done to us. When the engine shuts down, we discuss the matter with our computer and I read out the results: "Minus one, plus one, plus one." The accuracy of the overall system is phenomenal: out of a total of nearly three thousand feet per second, we have velocity errors in our body axis coordinate system of only a tenth of one foot per second in each of the three directions. That is one accurate burn, and even Neil acknowledges the fact.

ALDRIN: The second burn to place us in closer circular orbit of the Moon, the orbit from which Neil and I would separate from the Columbia and continue on to the Moon, was critically important. It had to be made in exactly the right place and for exactly the correct length of time. If we overburned for as little as two seconds we'd be on an impact course for the other side of the Moon. Through a complicated and detailed system of checks and balances, both in Houston and in lunar orbit, plus star checks and detailed platform alignments, two hours after our first lunar orbit we made our second burn, in an atmosphere of nervous and intense concentration. It, too, worked perfectly.

ASLEEP IN LUNAR ORBIT

We began preparing the LM. It was scheduled to take three hours, but because I had already started the checkout, we were completed a half hour ahead of schedule. Reluctantly we returned to the Columbia as planned. Our fourth night we were to sleep in lunar orbit. Although it was not in the flight plan, before covering the windows and dousing the lights, Neil and I carefully prepared all the equipment and clothing we would need in the morning, and mentally ran through the many procedures we would follow.

COLLINS: "Apollo 11, Apollo 11, good morning from the Black Team." Could they be talking to me? It takes me twenty seconds to fumble for the microphone button and answer groggily, I guess I have only been asleep five hours or so; I had a tough time getting to sleep, and now I'm having trouble waking up. Neil, Buzz, and I all putter about fixing breakfast and getting various items ready for transfer into the LM. [Later] I stuff Neil and Buzz into the LM along with an armload of equipment. Now I have to do the tunnel bit again, closing hatches, installing drogue and probe, and disconnecting the electrical umbilical. I am on the radio constantly now, running through an elaborate series of joint checks with Eagle. I check progress with Buzz: "I have five minutes and fifteen seconds since we started. Attitude is holding very well." "Roger, Mike, just hold it a little bit longer." "No sweat, I can hold it all day. Take your sweet time. How's the czar over there? He's so quiet." Neil chimes in, "Just hanging on—and punching." Punching those computer buttons, I guess he means. "All I can say is, beware the revolution," and then, getting no answer, I formally

bid them goodbye. "You cats take it easy on the lunar surface...."
"O.K., Mike," Buzz answers cheerily, and I throw the switch
which releases them. With my nose against the window and the
movie camera churning away, I watch them go. When they are
safely clear of me, I inform Neil, and he begins a slow pirouette in
place, allowing me a look at his outlandish machine and its four
extended legs. "The Eagle has wings" Neil exults.

It doesn't look like any eagle I have ever seen. It is the
weirdest-looking contraption ever to invade the sky, floating there
with its legs awkwardly jutting out above a body which has neither
symmetry nor grace. I make sure all four landing gears are down
and locked, report that fact, and then lie a little, "I think you've got
a fine-looking flying machine there, Eagle, despite the fact you're
upside down." "Somebody's upside down," Neil retorts. "O.K.,
Eagle. One minute . . . you guys take care." Neil answers, "See you
later." I hope so. When the one minute is up, I fire my thrusters
precisely as planned and we begin to separate, checking distances
and velocities as we go. This burn is a very small one, just to give
Eagle some breathing room. From now on it's up to them, and they
will make two separate burns in reaching the lunar surface. The first
one will serve to drop Eagle's perilune to fifty thousand feet. Then,
when they reach this spot over the eastern edge of the Sea of Tranquility, Eagle's descent engine will be fired up for the second and
last time, and Eagle will lazily arc over into a 12-minute
computer-controlled descent to some point at which Neil will take
over for a manual landing.

ALDRIN: We were still 60 miles above the surface when we
began our first burn. Neil and I were harnessed into the LM in a
standing position. [Later] at precisely the right moment the engine
ignited to begin the 12-minute powered descent. Strapped in by
the system of belts and cables not unlike shock absorbers, neither of
us felt the initial motion. We looked quickly at the computer to
make sure we were actually functioning as planned. After 26 seconds the engine went to full throttle and the motion became no-
ticeable. Neil watched his instruments while I looked at our
primary computer and compared it with our second computer,
which was part of our abort guidance system.

I then began a computer read-out sequence to Neil which was
also being transmitted to Houston. I had helped develop it. It
sounded as though I was chattering like a magpie. It also sounded

as though I was doing all the work. During training we had discussed the possibility of making the communication only between Neil and myself, but Mission Control liked the idea of hearing our communications with each other. Neil had referred to it once as "that damned open mike of yours," and I tried to make as little an issue of it as possible.

A Yellow Caution Light

At six thousand feet above the lunar surface a yellow caution light came on and we encountered one of the few potentially serious problems in the entire flight, a problem which might have caused us to abort, had it not been for a man on the ground who really knew his job.

COLLINS: At five minutes into the burn, when I am nearly directly overhead, Eagle voices its first concern. "Program Alarm," barks Neil, "It's a 1202." What the hell is that? I don't have the alarm numbers memorized for my own computer, much less for the LM's. I jerk out my own checklist and start thumbing through it, but before I can find 1202, Houston says, "Roger, we're GO on that alarm." No problem, in other words. My checklist says 1202 is an "executive overflow," meaning simply that the computer has been called upon to do too many things at once and is forced to postpone some of them.

A little farther along, at just three thousand feet above the surface, the computer flashes 1201, another overflow condition, and again the ground is superquick to respond with reassurances.

ALDRIN: Back in Houston, not to mention on board the Eagle, hearts shot up into throats while we waited to learn what would happen. We had received two of the caution lights when Steve Bales the flight controller responsible for LM computer activity, told us to proceed, through Charlie Duke, the capsule communicator. We received three or four more warnings but kept on going. When Mike, Neil, and I were presented with Medals of Freedom by President Nixon, Steve also received one. He certainly deserved it, because without him we might not have landed.

ARMSTRONG: In the final phases of the descent after a number of program alarms, we looked at the landing area and found a very large crater. This is the area we decided we would not go into; we extended the range downrange. The exhaust dust was kicked up by the engine and this caused some concern in that it degraded our ability to determine not only our altitude in the final phases but also our translational velocities over the ground. It's quite important not to stub your toe during the final phases of touchdown.

From the space-to-ground tapes:
EAGLE: 540 feet, down at 30 [feet per second] . . . down at 15 . . . 400 feet down at 9 . . . forward . . . 350 feet, down at 4 . . . 300 feet, down 3½ . . . 47 forward . . . 1½ down . . . 13 forward . . . 11 forward? coming down nicely . . . 200 feet, 4½ down . . . 5½ down . . . 5 percent . . . 75 feet . . . 6 forward . . . lights on . . . down 2½ . . . 40 feet? down 2½, kicking up some dust . . . 30 feet, 2½ down . . . faint shadow . . . 4 forward . . . 4 forward . . . drifting to right a little . . . O.K. . . .

HOUSTON: 30 seconds [fuel remaining].

EAGLE: Contact light! O.K., engine stop . . . descent engine command override off. . .

HOUSTON: We copy you down, Eagle.

EAGLE: Houston, Tranquility Base here. The Eagle has landed!

HOUSTON: Roger, Tranquility. We copy you on the ground. You've got a bunch of guys about to turn blue. We're breathing again. Thanks a lot.

TRANQUILITY: Thank you . . . That may have seemed like a very long final phase. The auto targeting was taking us right into a football-field-sized crater, with a large number of big boulders and rocks for about one or two crater-diameters around it, and it required flying manually over the rock field to find a reasonably good area.

HOUSTON: Roger, we copy. It was beautiful from here, Tranquility. Over.

TRANQUILITY: We'll get to the details of what's around here, but it looks like a collection of just about every variety of shape, angularity, granularity, about every variety of rock you could find.

HOUSTON: Roger, Tranquility. Be advised there's lots of smiling faces in this room, and all over the world.

TRANQUILITY: There are two of them up here.

COLUMBIA: And don't forget one in the command module.

ARMSTRONG: Once [we] settled on the surface, the dust settled immediately and we had an excellent view of the area surrounding the LM. We saw a crater surface, pockmarked with craters up to 15, 20, 30 feet, and many smaller craters down to a diameter of 1 foot and, of course, the surface was very fine-grained. There were a surprising number of rocks of all sizes.

A number of experts had, prior to the flight, predicted that a good bit of difficulty might be encountered by people due to the variety of strange atmospheric and gravitational characteristics. This didn't prove to be the case and after landing we felt very comfortable in the lunar gravity. It was, in fact, in our view preferable both to weightlessness and to the Earth's gravity.

When we actually descended the ladder it was found to be very much like the lunar-gravity simulations we had performed here on Earth. No difficulty was encountered in descending the ladder. The last step was about 3 ½ feet from the surface, and we were somewhat concerned that we might have difficulty in reentering the LM at the end of our activity period. So we practiced that before bringing the camera down.

ALDRIN: We opened the hatch and Neil, with me as his navigator, began backing out of the tiny opening. It seemed like a small eternity before I heard Neil say, "That's one small step for man . . . one giant leap for mankind." In less than fifteen minutes I was backing awkwardly out of the hatch and onto the surface to join Neil, who, in the tradition of all tourists, had his camera ready to photograph my arrival.

I felt buoyant and full of goose pimples when I stepped down on the surface. I immediately looked down at my feet and became intrigued with the peculiar properties of the lunar dust. If one kicks sand on a beach, it scatters in numerous directions with some grains traveling farther than others. On the Moon the dust travels exactly and precisely as it goes in various directions, and every grain of it lands nearly the same distance away.

THE BOY IN THE CANDY STORE

ARMSTRONG: There were a lot of things to do, and we had a hard time getting them finished. We had very little trouble, much less trouble than expected, on the surface. It was a pleasant operation. Temperatures weren't high. They were very comfortable. The little EMU, the combination of spacesuit and backpack that sustained our life on the surface, operated magnificently. The primary difficulty was just far too little time to do the variety of things we would have liked. We had the problem of the five-year-old boy in a candy store.

ALDRIN: I took off jogging to test my maneuverability. The exercise gave me an odd sensation and looked even more odd when I later saw the films of it. With bulky suits on, we seemed to be moving in slow motion. I noticed immediately that my inertia seemed much greater. Earth-bound, I would have stopped my run in just one step, but I had to use three of four steps to sort of wind down. My Earth weight, with the big backpack and heavy suit, was 360 pounds. On the Moon I weighed only 60 pounds.

At one point I remarked that the surface was "Beautiful, beautiful. Magnificent desolation." I was struck by the contrast between the starkness of the shadows and the desert-like barrenness of the rest of the surface. It ranged from dusty gray to light tan and was unchanging except for one startling sight: our LM sitting there with its black, silver and bright yellow-orange thermal coating shining brightly in the otherwise colorless landscape. I had seen Neil in his suit thousands of times before, but on the Moon the unnatural whiteness of it seemed unusually brilliant. We could also look around and see the Earth, which, though much larger than the Moon the Earth was seeing, seemed small—a beckoning oasis shining far away in the sky.

As the sequence of lunar operations evolved, Neil had the camera most of the time and the majority of pictures taken on the Moon that include an astronaut are of me. It wasn't until we were back on Earth and in the Lunar Receiving Laboratory looking over the pictures that we realized there were few pictures of Neil. My fault perhaps, but we had never simulated this in our training.

COAXING THE FLAG TO STAND

During a pause in experiments, Neil suggested we proceed with the flag. It took both of us to set it up and it was nearly a disaster. Public Relations obviously needs practice just as everything else does. A small telescoping arm was attached to the flagpole to keep the flag extended and perpendicular. As hard as we tried, the telescope wouldn't fully extend. Thus the flags which should have been flat, had its own unique permanent wave. Then to our dismay the staff of the pole wouldn't go far enough into the lunar surface to support itself in an upright position. After much struggling we finally coaxed it to remain upright, but in a most precarious position. I dreaded the possibility of the American flag collapsing into the lunar dust in front of the television camera.

COLLINS: [On his fourth orbital pass above] "How's it going?" "The EVA is progressing beautifully. I believe they're setting up the flag now." Just let things keep going that way, and no surprises, please. Neil and Buzz sound good, with no huffing and puffing to indicate they are overexerting themselves. But one surprise at least is in store. Houston comes on the air, not the slightest bit ruffled, and announces that the President of the United States would like to talk to Neil and Buzz. "That would be an honor," says Neil, with characteristic dignity.

The President's voice smoothly fills the air waves with the unaccustomed cadence of the speechmaker, trained to convey inspiration, or at least emotion, instead of our usual diet of numbers and reminders. "Neil and Buzz, I am talking to you by telephone from the Oval Office at the White House, and this certainly has to be the most historic telephone call ever made . . . Because of what you have done, the heavens have become a part of man's world. As you talk to us from the Sea of Tranquility, it inspires us to redouble our efforts to bring peace and tranquility to Earth ..." My God, I never thought of all this bringing peace and tranquility to anyone. As far as I am concerned, this voyage is fraught with hazards for the three of us—and especially two of us—and that is about as far as I have gotten in my thinking.

Neil, however, pauses long enough to give as well as he receives. "It's a great honor and privilege for us to be here, representing not only the United States but men of peace of all nations, and with interest and a curiosity and a vision for the future." [Later] Houston cuts off the White House and returns to business as usual, with a long string of numbers for me to copy for future use. My God, the juxtaposition of the incongruous—roll, pitch, and yaw; prayers, peace, and tranquility. What will it be like if we really carry this off and return to Earth in one piece, with our boxes full of rocks and our heads full of new perspectives for the planet? I have a little time to ponder this as I zing off out of sight of the White House and the Earth.

ALDRIN: We had a pulley system to load on the boxes of rocks. We found the process more time-consuming and dust-scattering than anticipated. After the gear and both of us were inside, our first chore was to pressure the LM cabin and begin stowing the rock boxes, film magazines, and anything else we wouldn't need until we were connected once again with the Columbia. We removed our boots and the big backpacks, opened the LM hatch, and threw these items onto the lunar surface, along with a bagful of empty food packages and the LM urine bags. The exact moment we tossed every thing out was measured back on Earth—the seismometer we had put out was even more sensitive than we had expected.

Before beginning liftoff procedures [we] settled down for our fitful rest. We didn't sleep much at all. Among other things we were elated—and also cold. Liftoff from the Moon, after a stay totaling twenty-one hours, was exactly on schedule and fairly uneventful. The ascent stage of the LM separated, sending out a shower of brilliant insulation particles which had been ripped off from the thrust of the ascent engine. There was no time to sightsee. I was concentrating on the computers, and Neil was studying the attitude indicator, but I looked up long enough to see the flag fall over . . . Three hours and ten minutes later we were connected once again with the Columbia.

COLLINS: I can look out through my docking reticle and see that they are steady as a rock as they drive down the center line of that final approach path. I give them some numbers. "I have 0.7 mile and I got you at 31 feet per second." We really are going to carry this off. For the first time since I was assigned to this incredible flight, I feel that it is going to happen. Granted, we are a long way from home, but from here on it should be all downhill. Within a few seconds Houston joins the conversation, with a tentative little call. "Eagle and Columbia, Houston standing by." They want to know what the hell is going on, but they don't want to interrupt us if we are in a crucial spot in our final maneuvering. Good heads! However, they needn't worry, and Neil lets them know it. "Roger, we're stationkeeping."

ALL SMILES AND GIGGLES

COLLINS: [After docking] it's time to hustle down into the tunnel and remove hatch, probe, and drogue, so Neil and Buzz can get through. Thank God, all the claptrap works beautifully in this its final workout. The probe and drogue will stay with the LM and be abandoned with it, for we will have no further need of them and don't want them cluttering up the command module. The first one through is Buzz, with a big smile on his face. I grab his head, a hand on each temple, and am about to give him a smooch on the forehead, as a parent might greet an errant child; but then, embarrassed, I think better of it and grab his hand, and then Neil's. We cavort about a little bit, all smiles and giggles over our success, and then it's back to work as usual.

Excerpts from a TV program broadcast by the Apollo 11 astronauts on the last evening of the flight the day before splashdown in the Pacific:

COLLINS: ". . . The Saturn V rocket which put us in orbit is an incredibly complicated piece of machinery, every piece of which worked flawlessly. This computer above my head has a 38,000-word vocabulary, each word of which has been carefully chosen to be of the utmost value to us. The SPS engine, our large rocket engine on the aft end of our service module, must have performed flawlessly or we would have been stranded in lunar orbit. The parachutes up above my head must work perfectly tomorrow or we will plummet into the ocean. We have always had confidence that this equipment will work properly. All this is possible only through the blood, sweat, and tears of a number of people. First, the American workmen who put these pieces of machinery together in the factory. Second, the painstaking work done by various test teams during the assembly and retest after assembly. And finally, the people at the Manned Spacecraft Center, both in management, in mission planning, in flight control, and last but not least, in crew training. This operation is somewhat like the periscope of a submarine. All you see is the three of us, but beneath the surface are thousands and thousands of others, and to all of those, I would like to say, 'Thank you very much.'"

ALDRIN: ". . . This has been far more than three men on a mission to the Moon; more, still, than the efforts of a government and industry team; more, even, than the efforts of one nation. We feel that this stands as a symbol of the insatiable curiosity of all mankind to explore the unknown. Today I feel we're really fully capable of accepting expanded roles in the exploration of space. In retrospect, we have all been particularly pleased with the call signs that we very laboriously chose for our spacecraft, Columbia and Eagle. We've been pleased with the emblem of our flight, the eagle carrying an olive branch, bringing the universal symbol of peace from the planet Earth to the Moon. Personally, in reflecting on the events of the past several days, a verse from Psalms comes to mind. 'When I consider the heavens, the work of Thy fingers, the Moon and the stars, which Thou hast ordained; What is man that Thou art mindful of him?'"

ARMSTRONG: "The responsibility for this flight lies first with history and with the giants of science who have preceded this effort; next with the American people, who have, through their will, indicated their desire; next with four administrations and their Congresses, for implementing that will; and then, with the agency and industry teams that built our spacecraft, the Saturn, the Columbia, the Eagle, and the little EMU, the spacesuit and backpack that was our small spacecraft out on the lunar surface. We would like to give special thanks to all those Americans who built the spacecraft; who did the construction, design, the tests, and put their hearts and all their abilities into those craft. To those people tonight, we give a special thank you, and to all the other people that are listening and watching tonight, God bless you. Good night from Apollo 11."

[AEM]

Supreme Court, Papers and Decisions on Roe v. Wade

January 22, 1973

In March of 1970, an unmarried and pregnant Norma L. McCorvey (aka "Jane Roe") filed suit in the U.S. District Court for the Northern District of Texas, naming Dallas County district attorney Henry B. Wade as the defendant. In this suit, McCorvey requested that the court declare the Texas abortion statutes—which permitted abortions only when necessary to save the life of the mother—to be unconstitutional, and thus grant an injunction to cease their enforcement. James Hubert Hallford, a licensed physician with three pending abortion violations, was permitted by the court to intervene and terminate her pregnancy. Contemporaneously, a childless married couple, "Jane and John Doe" filed a similar suit, claiming that due to the wife's mental illness, they would seek an abortion should she become pregnant in the future. A three-judge panel consolidated these two cases, ruling that the Texas law was in fact unconstitutional, though denying Roe's requested injunction. Failing to win the injunction, both Roe and the Does appealed their case to the U.S. Supreme Court.

The Supreme Court found, most notably, that the Ninth Amendment's guarantee of privacy protects a woman's choice of whether or not to end her own pregnancy. The court went on to rule on a number of other facets of the case, which further defined the individual's rights, while laying out the role of the legislature in regulating abortion. Though Roe v. Wade remains one of the most contentious and challenged decisions in the history of the Supreme Court, it has yet to be overturned or significantly revised.

— Note by James Daley

A PREGNANT SINGLE woman (Roe) brought a class action challenging the constitutionality of the Texas criminal abortion laws, which proscribe procuring or attempting an abortion except on medical advice for the purpose of saving the mother's life. A licensed physician (Hallford), who had two state abortion prosecutions pending against him, was permitted to intervene. A childless married couple (the Does), the wife not being pregnant, separately attacked the laws, basing alleged injury on the future possibilities of contraceptive failure, pregnancy, unpreparedness for parenthood, and impairment of the wife's health. A three-judge District Court, which consolidated the actions, held that Roe and Hallford, and members of their classes, had standing to sue and presented justiciable controversies. Ruling that declaratory, though not injunctive, relief was warranted, the court declared the abortion statutes void as vague and over-broadly infringing those plaintiffs' Ninth and Fourteenth Amendment rights. The court ruled the Does' complaint not justiciable. Appellants directly appealed to this Court on the injunctive rulings, and appellee cross-appealed from the District Court's grant of declaratory relief to Roe and Hallford. […]

We forthwith acknowledge our awareness of the sensitive and emotional nature of the abortion controversy, of the vigorous opposing views, even among physicians, and of the deep and seemingly absolute convictions that the subject inspires. One's philosophy, one's experiences, one's exposure to the raw edges of human existence, one's religious training, one's attitudes toward life and family and their values, and the moral standards one establishes and seeks to observe, are all likely to influence and to color one's thinking and conclusions about abortion.

In addition, population growth, pollution, poverty, and racial overtones tend to complicate and not to simplify the problem.

Our task, of course, is to resolve the issue by constitutional measurement, free of emotion and of predilection. We seek earnestly to do this, and, because we do, we [410 U.S. 113, 117] have inquired into, and in this opinion place some emphasis upon, medical and medical-legal history and what that history reveals about man's attitudes toward the abortion procedure over the centuries. We bear in mind too, Mr. Justice Holmes' admonition in his now-vindicated dissent in Lochner v. New York, 198 U.S. 45, 76 (1905):

"[The Constitution] is made for people of fundamentally differing views and the accident of our finding certain opinions natural and familiar or novel and even shocking ought not to conclude our judgment upon the question whether statutes embodying them conflict with the Constitution of the United States."

I.

The Texas statutes that concern us here are Arts. 1191–1194 and 1196 of the State's Penal Code. These make it a crime to "procure an abortion," as therein [410 U.S. 113,118] defined, or to attempt one, except with respect to "an abortion procured or attempted by medical advice for the purpose of saving the life of the mother." Similar statutes are in existence in a majority of the States. [410 U.S. 113, 119]. Texas first enacted a criminal abortion statute in 1854. […]

II.

Jane Roe, a single woman who was residing in Dallas County, Texas, instituted this federal action in March 1970 against the District Attorney of the county. She sought a declaratory judgment that the Texas criminal abortion statutes were unconstitutional on their face, and an injunction restraining the defendant from enforcing the statutes.

Roe alleged that she was unmarried and pregnant; that she wished to terminate her pregnancy by an abortion "performed by a competent, licensed physician, under safe, clinical conditions"; that she was unable to get a "legal" abortion in Texas because her life did not appear to be threatened by the continuation of her pregnancy; and that she could not afford to travel to another jurisdiction in order to secure a legal abortion under safe conditions. She claimed that the Texas statutes were unconstitutionally vague and that they abridged her right of personal privacy, protected by the First, Fourth, Fifth, Ninth, and Fourteenth Amendments. By an amendment to her complaint Roe purported to sue "on behalf of herself and all other women" similarly situated.

James Hubert Hallford, a licensed physician, sought and was granted leave to intervene in Roe's action. In his complaint he alleged that he had been arrested previously for violations of the Texas abortion statutes and [410 U.S. 113, 121] that two such prosecutions were pending against him. He described conditions of patients who came to him seeking abortions, and he claimed that for many cases he, as a physician, was unable to determine whether they fell within or outside the exception recognized by Article 1196. He alleged that, as a consequence, the statutes were vague and uncertain, in violation of the Fourteenth Amendment, and that they violated his own and his patients' rights to privacy in the doctor-patient relationship and his own right to practice medicine, rights he claimed were guaranteed by the First, Fourth, Fifth, Ninth, and Fourteenth Amendments.

John and Mary Doe, a married couple, filed a companion complaint to that of Roe. They also named the District Attorney as defendant, claimed like constitutional deprivations, and sought declaratory and injunctive relief. The Does alleged that they were a childless couple; that Mrs. Doe was suffering from a "neural-chemical" disorder; that her physician had "advised her to avoid pregnancy until such time as her condition has materially improved" (although a pregnancy at the present time would not present "a serious risk" to her life); that, pursuant to medical advice, she had discontinued use of birth control pills; and that if she should become pregnant, she would want to terminate the pregnancy by an abortion performed by a competent, licensed physician under safe, clinical conditions. By an amendment to their complaint, the Does purported to sue "on behalf of themselves and all couples similarly situated."

The two actions were consolidated and heard together by a duly convened three-judge district court. The suits thus presented the situations of the pregnant single woman, the childless couple, with the wife not pregnant, [410 U.S. 113,122] and the licensed practicing physician, all joining in the attack on the Texas criminal abortion statutes. Upon the filing of affidavits, motions were made for dismissal and for summary judgment. The court held that Roe and members of her class, and Dr. Hallford, had standing to sue and presented justiciable controversies, but that the Does had failed to allege facts sufficient to state a present controversy and did not have standing. It concluded that, with respect to the requests for a declaratory judgment, abstention was not warranted. On the merits, the District Court held that the "fundamental right of single women and married persons to choose whether to have children is protected by the Ninth Amendment, through the Fourteenth Amendment," and that the Texas criminal abortion statutes were void on their face because they were both unconstitutionally vague and constituted an overbroad infringement of the plaintiffs' Ninth Amendment rights. The court then held that abstention was warranted with respect to the requests for an injunction. It therefore dismissed the Does' complaint, declared the abortion statutes void, and dismissed the application for injunctive relief. [...]

VI.

It perhaps is not generally appreciated that the restrictive criminal abortion laws in effect in a majority of States today are of relatively recent vintage. Those laws, generally proscribing abortion or its attempt at anytime during pregnancy except when necessary to preserve the pregnant woman's life, are not of ancient or even of common-law origin. Instead, they derive from statutory changes effected, for the most part, in the latter half of the 19th century. [410 U.S. 113, 130]

1. Ancient attitudes. These are not capable of precise determination. We are told that at the time of the Persian Empire abortifacients were known and that criminal abortions were severely punished. We are also told, however, that abortion was practiced in Greek times as well as in the Roman Era, and that "it was resorted to without scruple." The Ephesian, Soranos, often described as the greatest of the ancient gynecologists, appears to have been generally opposed to Rome's prevailing free-abortion practices. He found it necessary to think first of the life of the mother, and he resorted to abortion when, upon this standard, he felt the procedure advisable. Greek and Roman law afforded little protection to the unborn. If abortion was prosecuted in some places, it seems to have been based on a concept of a violation of the father's right to his offspring. Ancient religion did not bar abortion.

2. The Hippocratic Oath. What then of the famous Oath that has stood so long as the ethical guide of the medical profession and that bears the name of the great Greek (460(?)–377(?) B.C.), who has been described [410 U.S. 113, 131] as the Father of Medicine, the "wisest and the greatest practitioner of his art," and the "most important and most complete medical personality of antiquity," who dominated the medical schools of his time, and who typified the sum of the medical knowledge of the past? The Oath varies somewhat according to the particular translation, but in any translation the content is clear: "I will give no deadly medicine to anyone if asked, nor suggest any such counsel; and in like manner I will not give to a woman a pessary to

produce abortion," or "I will neither give a deadly drug to anybody if asked for it, nor will I make a suggestion to this effect. Similarly, I will not give to a woman an abortive remedy."

Although the Oath is not mentioned in any of the principal briefs in this case or in Doe v. Bolton, post, p. 179, it represents the apex of the development of strict ethical concepts in medicine, and its influence endures to this day. Why did not the authority of Hippocrates dissuade abortion practice in his time and that of Rome? The late Dr. Edelstein provides us with a theory: The Oath was not uncontested even in Hippocrates' day; only the Pythagorean school of philosophers frowned upon the related act of suicide. Most Greek thinkers, on the other hand, commended abortion, at least prior to viability. See Plato, Republic, V, 461; Aristotle, Politics, VII, 1335b 25. For the Pythagoreans, however, it was a matter of dogma. For them the embryo was animate from the moment of conception, and abortion meant destruction of a living being. The abortion clause of the Oath, therefore, "echoes Pythagorean doctrines," [410 U.S. 113, 132] and "[i]n no other stratum of Greek opinion were such views held or proposed in the same spirit of uncompromising austerity."

Dr. Edelstein then concludes that the Oath originated in a group representing only a small segment of Greek opinion and that it certainly was not accepted by all ancient physicians. He points out that medical writings down to Galen (A.D. 130–200) "give evidence of the violation of almost every one of its injunctions." But with the end of antiquity a decided change took place. Resistance against suicide and against abortion became common. The Oath came to be popular. The emerging teachings of Christianity were in agreement with the Pythagorean ethic. The Oath "became the nucleus of all medical ethics" and "was applauded as the embodiment of truth." Thus, suggests Dr. Edelstein, it is "a Pythagorean manifesto and not the expression of an absolute standard of medical conduct."

This, it seems to us, is a satisfactory and acceptable explanation of the Hippocratic Oath's apparent rigidity. It enables us to understand, in historical context, a long-accepted and revered statement of medical ethics.

3. The common law. It is undisputed that at common law, abortion performed before "quickening"—the first recognizable movement of the fetus in utero, appearing usually from the 16th to the 18th week of pregnancy—was not an indictable offense. [...]

6. The position of the American Medical Association. The anti-abortion mood prevalent in this country in the late 19th

century was shared by the medical profession. Indeed, the attitude of the profession may have played a significant role in the enactment of stringent criminal abortion legislation during that period.

An AMA Committee on Criminal Abortion was appointed in May 1857. It presented its report, 12 Trans. of the Am. Med. Assn. 73–78 (1859), to the Twelfth Annual Meeting. That report observed that the Committee had been appointed to investigate criminal abortion "with a view to its general suppression." It deplored abortion and its frequency and it listed three causes of "this general demoralization":

> "The first of these causes is a wide-spread popular ignorance of the true character of the crime—a belief, even among mothers themselves, that the fetus is not alive till after the period of quickening.
>
> "The second of the agents alluded to is the fact that the profession themselves are frequently supposed careless of foetal life ....
>
> "The third reason of the frightful extent of this crime is found in the grave defects of our laws, both common and statute, as regards the independent and actual existence of the child before birth, as a living being. These errors, which are sufficient in most instances to prevent conviction, are based, and only based, upon mistaken and exploded medical dogmas. With strange inconsistency, the law fully acknowledges the foetus in utero and its inherent rights, for civil purposes; while personally and as criminally affected, it fails to recognize it, [410 U.S. 113, 142] and to its life as yet denies all protection." Id., at 75–76.

The Committee then offered, and the Association adopted, resolutions protesting "against such unwarrantable destruction of human life," calling upon state legislatures to revise their abortion laws, and requesting the cooperation of state medical societies "in pressing the subject." Id., at 28, 78.

In 1871 a long and vivid report was submitted by the Committee on Criminal Abortion. It ended with the observation, "We had to deal with human life. In a matter of less importance we could entertain no compromise. An honest judge on the bench would call things by their proper names. We could do no less." 22 Trans. of the Am. Med. Assn. 258 (1871). It proffered resolutions, adopted by the Association, id., at 38–39, recommending, among other things, that it "be unlawful and unprofessional for any physician to induce abortion or premature labor, without the concurrent opinion of at least one respectable consulting physician, and then always with a view to the safety of the child—if that be possible," and calling "the attention of the clergy of all denominations to the perverted views of morality entertained by a large class of females—aye, and men also, on this important question."

Except for periodic condemnation of the criminal abortionist, no further formal AMA action took place until 1967. In that year, the Committee on Human Reproduction urged the adoption of a stated policy of opposition to induced abortion, except when there is "documented medical evidence" of a threat to the health or life of the mother or that the child "may be born with incapacitating physical deformity or mental deficiency," or that a pregnancy "resulting from legally established statutory or forcible rape or incest may constitute a threat to the mental or physical health of the [410 U.S. 113, 143] patient," two other physicians "chosen because of their recognized professional competence have examined the patient and have concurred in writing," and the procedure "is performed in a hospital accredited by the Joint Commission on Accreditation of Hospitals." The providing of medical information by physicians to state legislatures in their consideration of legislation regarding therapeutic abortion was "to be considered consistent with the principles of ethics of the American Medical Association." This recommendation was adopted by the House of Delegates. Proceedings of the AMA House of Delegates 40–51 June 1967). [...]

VIII.

The Constitution does not explicitly mention any right of privacy. In a line of decisions, however, going back perhaps as far as Union Pacific R. Co. v. Botsford, 141 U.S. 250, 251 (1891), the Court has recognized that a right of personal privacy, or a guarantee of certain areas or zones of privacy, does exist under the Constitution. In varying contexts, the Court or individual Justices have, indeed, found at least the roots of that right in the First Amendment, Stanley v. Georgia, 394 U.S. 557, 564 (1969); in the Fourth and Fifth Amendments, Terry v. Ohio, 392 U.S. 1, 8–9 (1968), Katz v. United States, 389 U.S. 347, 350 (1967), Boyd v. United States,

116 U.S. 616 (1886), see Olmstead v. United States, 277 U.S. 438, 478 (1928) (Brandeis, J., dissenting); in the penumbras of the Bill of Rights, Griswold v. Connecticut, 381 U.S., at 484–485; in the Ninth Amendment, id., at 486 (Goldberg, J., concurring); or in the concept of liberty guaranteed by the first section of the Fourteenth Amendment, see Meyer v. Nebraska, 262 U.S. 390, 399 (1923). These decisions make it clear that only personal rights that can be deemed "fundamental" or "implicit in the concept of ordered liberty," Palko v. Connecticut, 302 U.S. 319, 325 (1937), are included in this guarantee of personal privacy. They also make it clear that the right has some extension to activities relating to marriage, Loving v. Virginia, 388 U.S. 1, 12 (1967); procreation, Skinner v. Oklahoma, 316 U.S. 535, 541–542 (1942); contraception, Eisenstadt v. Baird, 405 U.S., at 453–454; id., at 460, 463–465 [410 U.S. 113, 153] (WHITE, J., concurring in result); family relationships, Prince v. Massachusetts, 321 U.S. 158, 166 (1944); and child rearing and education, Pierce v. Society of Sisters, 268 U.S. 510, 535 (1925), Meyer v. Nebraska, supra.

This right of privacy, whether it be founded in the Fourteenth Amendment's concept of personal liberty and restrictions upon state action, as we feel it is, or, as the District Court determined, in the Ninth Amendment's reservation of rights to the people, is broad enough to encompass a woman's decision whether or not to terminate her pregnancy. The detriment that the State would impose upon the pregnant woman by denying this choice altogether is apparent. Specific and direct harm medically diagnosable even in early pregnancy may be involved. Maternity, or additional offspring, may force upon the woman a distressful life and future. Psychological harm may be imminent. Mental and physical health may be taxed by child care. There is also the distress, for all concerned, associated with the unwanted child, and there is the problem of bringing a child into a family already unable, psychologically and otherwise, to care for it. In other cases, as in this one, the additional difficulties and continuing stigma of unwed motherhood may be involved. All these are factors the woman and her responsible physician necessarily will consider in consultation.

On the basis of elements such as these, appellant and some amici argue that the woman's right is absolute and that she is entitled to terminate her pregnancy at whatever time, in whatever way, and for whatever reason she alone chooses. With this we do not agree.

Appellant's arguments that Texas either has no valid interest at all in regulating the abortion decision, or no interest strong enough to support any limitation upon the woman's sole determination, are unpersuasive. The [410 U.S. 113, 154] Court's decisions recognizing a right of privacy also acknowledge that some state regulation in areas protected by that right is appropriate. As noted above, a State may properly assert important interests in safeguarding health, in maintaining medical standards, and in protecting potential life. At some point in pregnancy, these respective interests become sufficiently compelling to sustain regulation of the factors that govern the abortion decision. The privacy right involved, therefore, cannot be said to be absolute. In fact, it is not clear to us that the claim asserted by some amici that one has an unlimited right to do with one's body as one pleases bears a close relationship to the right of privacy previously articulated in the Court's decisions. The Court has refused to recognize an unlimited right of this kind in the past. Jacobson v. Massachusetts, 197 U.S. 11 (1905) (vaccination); Buck v. Bell, 274 U.S. 200 (1927) (sterilization).

IX

We, therefore, conclude that the right of personal privacy includes the abortion decision, but that this right is not unqualified and must be considered against important state interests in regulation. [...]

Texas urges that, apart from the Fourteenth Amendment, life begins at conception and is present throughout pregnancy, and that, therefore, the State has a compelling interest in protecting that life from and after conception. We need not resolve the difficult question of when life begins. When those trained in the respective disciplines of medicine, philosophy, and theology are unable to arrive at any consensus, the judiciary, at this point in the development of man's knowledge, is not in a position to speculate as to the answer. [410 U.S. 113, 160]

It should be sufficient to note briefly the wide divergence of thinking on this most sensitive and difficult question. There has always been strong support for the view that life does not begin until live birth. This was the belief of the Stoics. It appears to be the predominant, though not the unanimous, attitude of the Jewish faith. It may be taken to represent also the position of a large segment of the Protestant community, insofar as that can be ascertained; organized groups that have taken a formal position on the abortion issue have generally regarded abortion as a matter for the conscience of the individual and her family. As we have noted, the common law found greater significance in quickening. Physicians and their scientific colleagues have regarded that event with less interest and have tended to focus either upon conception, upon live birth, or upon the interim point at which the fetus becomes "viable," that is, potentially able to live outside the mother's womb, albeit with artificial aid. Viability is usually placed at about seven months (28 weeks) but may occur earlier, even at 24 weeks. The Aristotelian theory of "mediate animation," that held sway throughout the Middle Ages and the Renaissance in Europe, continued to be official Roman Catholic dogma until the 19th century, despite opposition to this "ensoulment" theory from those in the Church who would recognize the existence of life from [410 U.S. 113, 161] the moment of conception. The latter is now, of course, the official belief of the Catholic Church. As one brief amicus discloses, this is a view strongly held by many non-Catholics as well, and by many physicians. Substantial problems for precise definition of this view are posed, however, by new embryological data that purport to indicate that conception is a "process" over time, rather than an event, and by new medical techniques such as menstrual extraction, the "morning-after" pill, implantation of embryos, artificial insemination, and even artificial wombs.

In areas other than criminal abortion, the law has been reluctant to endorse any theory that life, as we recognize it, begins before live birth or to accord legal rights to the unborn except in narrowly defined situations and except when the rights are contingent upon live birth. For example, the traditional rule of tort law denied recovery for prenatal injuries even though the child was born alive. That rule has been changed in almost every jurisdiction. In most States, recovery is said to be permitted only if the fetus was viable, or at least quick, when the injuries were sustained, though few [410 US. 113, 162] courts have squarely so held. In a recent development, generally opposed by the commentators, some States permit the parents of a stillborn child to maintain an action for wrongful death because of prenatal injuries. Such an action, however, would appear to be one to vindicate the parents' interest and is thus consistent with the view that the fetus, at most, represents only the potentiality of life. Similarly, unborn children have been recognized as acquiring rights or interests by way of inheritance or other devolution of property, and have been represented by guardians ad litem.

Perfection of the interests involved, again, has generally been contingent upon live birth. In short, the unborn have never been recognized in the law as persons in the whole sense.

X.

In view of all this, we do not agree that, by adopting one theory of life, Texas may override the rights of the pregnant woman that are at stake. We repeat, however, that the State does have an important and legitimate interest in preserving and protecting the health of the pregnant woman, whether she be a resident of the State or a nonresident who seeks medical consultation and treatment there, and that it has still another important and legitimate interest in protecting the potentiality of human life. These interests are separate and distinct. Each grows in substantiality as the woman approaches [410 U.S. 113, 163] term and, at a point during pregnancy, each becomes "compelling." [...]

Measured against these standards, Art. 1196 of the Texas Penal Code, in restricting legal abortions to those "procured or attempted by medical advice for the purpose of saving the life of the mother," sweeps too broadly. The statute makes no distinction between abortions performed early in pregnancy and those performed later, and it limits to a single reason, "saving" the mother's life, the legal justification for the procedure. The statute therefore, cannot survive the constitutional attack made upon it here. [...]

XI.

To summarize and to repeat:

1. A state criminal abortion statute of the current Texas type, that excepts from criminality only a life-saving procedure on behalf of the mother, without regard to pregnancy stage and without recognition of the other interests involved, is violative of the Due Process Clause of the Fourteenth Amendment.

(a) For the stage prior to approximately the end of the first trimester, the abortion decision and its effectuation must be left to the medical judgment of the pregnant woman's attending physician.

(b) For the stage subsequent to approximately the end of the first trimester, the State, in promoting its interest in the health of the mother, may, if it chooses, regulate the abortion procedure in ways that are reasonably related to maternal health.

(c) For the stage subsequent to viability, the State in promoting its interest in the potentiality of human life [410 U.S. 113, 165] may, if it chooses, regulate, and even proscribe, abortion except where it is necessary, in appropriate medical judgment, for the preservation of the life or health of the mother.

2. The State may define the term "physician," as it has been employed in the preceding paragraphs of this Part XI of this opinion, to mean only a physician currently licensed by the State, and may proscribe any abortion by a person who is not a physician as so defined.

In Doe v. Bolton, post, p. 179, procedural requirements contained in one of the modern abortion statutes are considered. That opinion and this one, of course, are to be read together.

This holding, we feel, is consistent with the relative weights of the respective interests involved, with the lessons and examples of medical and legal history, with the lenity of the common law, and with the demands of the profound problems of the present day. The decision leaves the State free to place increasing restrictions on abortion as the period of pregnancy lengthens, so long as those restrictions are tailored to the recognized state interests. The decision vindicates the right of the physician to administer medical treatment according to his professional judgment up to the points where important [410 U.S. 113, 166] state interests provide compelling justifications for intervention. Up to those points, the abortion decision in all its aspects is inherently, and primarily, a medical decision, and basic responsibility for it must rest with the physician. If an individual practitioner abuses the privilege of exercising proper medical judgment, the usual remedies, judicial and intra-professional, are available.

XII

Our conclusion that Art. 1196 is unconstitutional means, of course, that the Texas abortion statutes, as a unit, must fall. The exception of Art. 1196 cannot be struck down separately, for then the State would be left with a statute proscribing all abortion procedures no matter how medically urgent the case.

Although the District Court granted appellant Roe declaratory relief, it stopped short of issuing an injunction against enforcement of the Texas statutes. The Court has recognized that different considerations enter into a federal court's decision as to declaratory relief, on the one hand, and injunctive relief, on the other. Zwickler v. Koota, 389 U.S. 241, 252–255 (1967); Dombrowski v. Pfister, 380 U.S. 479 (1965). We are not dealing with a statute that, on its face, appears to abridge free expression, an area of particular concern under Dombrowski and refined in Younger v. Harris, 401 U.S., at 50.

We find it unnecessary to decide whether the District Court erred in withholding injunctive relief, for we assume the Texas prosecutorial authorities will give full credence to this decision that the present criminal abortion statutes of that State are unconstitutional.

The judgment of the District Court as to intervenor Hallford is reversed, and Dr. Hallford's complaint in intervention is dismissed. In all other respects, the judgment [410 U.S. 113, 167] of the District Court is affirmed. Costs are allowed to the appellee.

It is so ordered.

[For concurring opinion of MR. CHIEF JUSTICE BURGER, see post, p. 207.]

[For concurring opinion of MR. JUSTICE DOUGLAS, see post, p. 209.]

[For dissenting opinion of MR. JUSTICE WHITE, see post, p. 221.]

[LD]

President Richard M. Nixon Speech, "Watergate"

April 30, 1973

The Republican Richard M. Nixon (1913–1994), the 37th President of the United States, served as Dwight D. Eisenhower's vice president in the 1950s. He narrowly lost the presidential election in 1960 to John F. Kennedy, but defeated his Democratic presidential rivals Hubert Humphrey in 1968 and George McGovern in 1972. The Watergate scandal revolved around his involvement in the cover-up of a break-in of Democratic National Committee offices in the Watergate office complex in Washington, D.C. "In any organization, the man at the top must bear the responsibility," he declares here. "That responsibility, therefore, belongs here, in this office. I accept it." Two weeks later a Senate Committee commenced public hearings on the case. Nixon officially resigned from office, with impeachment proceedings looming in Congress, on August 9, 1974.

Good evening:

I WANT TO talk to you tonight from my heart on a subject of deep concern to every American.

In recent months, members of my Administration and officials of the Committee for the Re-Election of the President—including some of my closest friends and most trusted aides—have been charged with involvement in what has come to be known as the Watergate affair. These include charges of illegal activity during and preceding the 1972 Presidential election and charges that responsible officials participated in efforts to cover up that illegal activity.

The inevitable result of these charges has been to raise serious questions about the integrity of the White House itself. Tonight I wish to address those questions.

Last June 17, while I was in Florida trying to get a few days rest after my visit to Moscow, I first learned from news reports of the Watergate break-in. I was appalled at this senseless, illegal action, and I was shocked to learn that employees of the Re-Election Committee were apparently among those guilty. I immediately ordered an investigation by appropriate Government authorities. On September 15, as you will recall, indictments were brought against seven defendants in the case.

As the investigations went forward, I repeatedly asked those conducting the investigation whether there was any reason to believe that members of my Administration were in any way involved. I received repeated assurances that there were not. Because of these continuing reassurances, because I believed the reports I was getting, because I had faith in the persons from whom I was getting them, I discounted the stories in the press that appeared to implicate members of my Administration or other officials of the campaign committee.

Until March of this year, I remained convinced that the denials were true and that the charges of involvement by members of the White House Staff were false. The comments I made during this period, and the comments made by my Press Secretary in my behalf, were based on the information provided to us at the time we made those comments. However, new information then came to me which persuaded me that there was a real possibility that some of these charges were true, and suggesting further that there had been an effort to conceal the facts both from the public, from you, and from me.

As a result, on March 21, I personally assumed the responsibility for coordinating intensive new inquiries into the matter, and I personally ordered those conducting the investigations to get all the facts and to report them directly to me, right here in this office.

I again ordered that all persons in the Government or at the Re-Election Committee should cooperate fully with the FBI, the prosecutors, and the grand jury. I also ordered that anyone who refused to cooperate in telling the truth would be asked to resign from Government service. And, with ground rules adopted that would preserve the basic constitutional separation of powers between the Congress and the Presidency, I directed that members of the White House Staff should appear and testify voluntarily under oath before the Senate committee which was investigating Watergate.

I was determined that we should get to the bottom of the matter, and that the truth should be fully brought out—no matter who was involved.

At the same time, I was determined not to take precipitate action and to avoid, if at all possible, any action that would appear to reflect on innocent people. I wanted to be fair. But I knew that in the final analysis, the integrity of this office—public faith in the integrity of this office—would have to take priority over all personal considerations.

Today, in one of the most difficult decisions of my Presidency, I accepted the resignations of two of my closest associates in the White House—Bob Haldeman, John Ehrlichman—two of the finest public servants it has been my privilege to know.

I want to stress that in accepting these resignations, I mean to leave no implication whatever of personal wrongdoing on their part, and I leave no implication tonight of implication on the part of others who have been charged in this matter. But in matters as sensitive as guarding the integrity of our democratic process, it is essential not only that rigorous legal and ethical standards be observed but also that the public, you, have total confidence that they are both being observed and enforced by those in authority and particularly by the President of the United States. They agreed with me that this move was necessary in order to restore that confidence.

Because Attorney General Kleindienst—though a distinguished public servant, my personal friend for 20 years, with no personal involvement whatever in this matter—has been a close personal and professional associate of some of those who are involved in this case, he and I both felt that it was also necessary to name a new Attorney General.

The Counsel to the President, John Dean, has also resigned.

As the new Attorney General, I have today named Elliot Richardson, a man of unimpeachable integrity and rigorously high principle. I have directed him to do everything necessary to ensure that the Department of Justice has the confidence and the trust of every law-abiding person in this country.

I have given him absolute authority to make all decisions bearing upon the prosecution of the Watergate case and related matters. I have instructed him that if he should consider it appropriate, he has the authority to name a special supervising prosecutor for matters arising out of the case.

Whatever may appear to have been the case before, whatever improper activities may yet be discovered in connection with this whole sordid affair, I want the American people, I want you to know beyond the shadow of a doubt that during my term as President, justice will be pursued fairly, fully, and impartially, no matter who is involved. This office is a sacred trust and I am determined to be worthy of that trust.

Looking back at the history of this case, two questions arise:

How could it have happened?
Who is to blame?

Political commentators have correctly observed that during my 27 years in politics I have always previously insisted on running my own campaigns for office.

But 1972 presented a very different situation. In both domestic and foreign policy, 1972 was a year of crucially important decisions, of intense negotiations, of vital new directions, particularly in working toward the goal which has been my overriding concern throughout my political career—the goal of bringing peace to America, peace to the world.

That is why I decided, as the 1972 campaign approached, that the Presidency should come first and politics second. To the maximum extent possible, therefore, I sought to delegate campaign operations, to remove the day-to-day campaign decisions from the President's office and from the White House. I also, as you recall, severely limited the number of my own campaign appearances.

Who, then, is to blame for what happened in this case?

For specific criminal actions by specific individuals, those who committed those actions must, of course, bear the liability and pay the penalty.

For the fact that alleged improper actions took place within the White House or within my campaign organization, the easiest course would be for me to blame those to whom I delegated the responsibility to run the campaign. But that would be a cowardly thing to do.

I will not place the blame on subordinates—on people whose zeal exceeded their judgment and who may have done wrong in a cause they deeply believed to be right.

In any organization, the man at the top must bear the responsibility. That responsibility, therefore, belongs here, in this office. I accept it. And I pledge to you tonight, from this office, that I will do everything in my power to ensure that the guilty are brought to justice and that such abuses are purged from our political processes in the years to come, long after I have left this office.

Some people, quite properly appalled at the abuses that occurred, will say that Watergate demonstrates the bankruptcy of the American political system. I believe precisely the opposite is true. Watergate represented a series of illegal acts and bad judgments by a number of individuals. It was the system that has brought the facts to light and that will bring those guilty to justice—a system that in this case has included a determined grand jury, honest prosecutors, a courageous judge, John Sirica, and a vigorous free press.

It is essential now that we place our faith in that system—and especially in the judicial system. It is essential that we let the judicial process go forward, respecting those safeguards that are established to protect the innocent as well as to convict the guilty. It is essential that in reacting to the excesses of others, we not fall into excesses ourselves.

It is also essential that we not be so distracted by events such as this that we neglect the vital work before us, before this Nation, before America, at a time of critical importance to America and the world.

Since March, when I first learned that the Watergate affair might in fact be far more serious than I had been led to believe, it has claimed far too much of my time and my attention. Whatever may now transpire in the case, whatever the actions of the grand jury, whatever the outcome of any eventual trials, I must now turn my full attention—and I shall do so—once again to the larger duties of this office. I owe it to this great office that I hold, and I owe it to you—to my country.

I know that as Attorney General, Elliot Richardson will be both fair and he will be fearless in pursuing this case wherever it leads. I am confident that with him in charge, justice will be done.

There is vital work to be done toward our goal of a lasting structure of peace in the world—work that cannot wait, work that I must do.

Tomorrow, for example, Chancellor Brandt of West Germany will visit the White House for talks that are a vital element of "The

Year of Europe," as 1973 has been called. We are already preparing for the next Soviet-American summit meeting later this year.

This is also a year in which we are seeking to negotiate a mutual and balanced reduction of armed forces in Europe, which will reduce our defense budget and allow us to have funds for other purposes at home so desperately needed. It is the year when the United States and Soviet negotiators will seek to work out the second and even more important round of our talks on limiting nuclear arms and of reducing the danger of a nuclear war that would destroy civilization as we know it. It is a year in which we confront the difficult tasks of maintaining peace in Southeast Asia and in the potentially explosive Middle East.

There is also vital work to be done right here in America: to ensure prosperity, and that means a good job for everyone who wants to work; to control inflation, that I know worries every housewife, everyone who tries to balance a family budget in America; to set in motion new and better ways of ensuring progress toward a better life for all Americans.

When I think of this office—of what it means—I think of all the things that I want to accomplish for this Nation, of all the things I want to accomplish for you.

On Christmas Eve, during my terrible personal ordeal of the renewed bombing of North Vietnam, which after 12 years of war finally helped to bring America peace with honor, I sat down just before midnight. I wrote out some of my goals for my second term as President.

Let me read them to you:

"To make it possible for our children, and for our children's children, to live in a world of peace.

"To make this country be more than ever a land of opportunity—of equal opportunity, full opportunity for every American.

"To provide jobs for all who can work, and generous help for those who cannot work.

"To establish a climate of decency and civility, in which each person respects the feelings and the dignity and the God-given rights of his neighbor.

"To make this a land in which each person can dare to dream, can live his dreams—not in fear, but in hope—proud of his community, proud of his country, proud of what America has meant to himself and to the world."

These are great goals. I believe we can, we must work for them. We can achieve them. But we cannot achieve these goals unless we dedicate ourselves to another goal.

We must maintain the integrity of the White House, and that integrity must be real, not transparent. There can be no whitewash at the White House.

We must reform our political process—ridding it not only of the violations of the law but also of the ugly mob violence and other inexcusable campaign tactics that have been too often practiced and too readily accepted in the past, including those that may have been a response by one side to the excesses or expected excesses of the other side. Two wrongs do not make a right.

I have been in public life for more than a quarter of a century. Like any other calling, politics has good people and bad people. And let me tell you, the great majority in politics—in the Congress, in the Federal Government, in the State government—are good people. I know that it can be very easy, under the intensive pressures of a campaign, for even well-intentioned people to fall into shady tactics—to rationalize this on the grounds that what is at stake is of such importance to the Nation that the end justifies the means. And both of our great parties have been guilty of such tactics in the past.

In recent years, however, the campaign excesses that have occurred on all sides have provided a sobering demonstration of how far this false doctrine can take us. The lesson is clear: America, in its political campaigns, must not again fall into the trap of letting the end, however great that end is, justify the means.

I urge the leaders of both political parties, I urge citizens, all of you, everywhere, to join in working toward a new set of standards, new rules and procedures to ensure that future elections will be as nearly free of such abuses as they possibly can be made. This is my goal. I ask you to join in making it America's goal.

When I was inaugurated for a second time this past January 20, I gave each member of my Cabinet and each member of my senior White House Staff a special four-year calendar, with each day marked to show the number of days remaining to the Administration. In the inscription on each calendar, I wrote these words: "The Presidential term which begins today consists of 1,461 days—no more, no less. Each can be a day of strengthening and renewal for America; each can add depth and dimension to the American experience. If we strive together, if we make the most of the challenge and the opportunity that these days offer us, they can stand out as great days for America, and great moments in the history of the world."

I looked at my own calendar this morning up at Camp David as I was working on this speech. It showed exactly 1,361 days remaining in my term. I want these to be the best days in America's history, because I love America. I deeply believe that America is the hope of the world. And I know that in the quality and wisdom of the leadership America gives lies the only hope for millions of people all over the world that they can live their lives in peace and freedom. We must be worthy of that hope, in every sense of the word. Tonight, I ask for your prayers to help me in everything that I do throughout the days of my Presidency to be worthy of their hopes and of yours.

God bless America and God bless each and every one of you.

[IS]

Russell Means, Speech, the American Indian Movement

1973

Means (1939-2012) was a founder of the American Indian Movement (AIM), which, in 1973, in their seventy-one day occupation of Wounded Knee, galvanized support from many tribes but at the same time encountered armed assault from a tribal government and the U.S. Government. During that occupation, Means, an Oglala Sioux, spoke about the revival of the Ghost Dance.

THE WHITE MAN says that the 1890 massacre was the end of the wars with the Indian, that it was the end of the Indian, the end of the Ghost Dance. Yet here we are at war, we're still Indians, and we're Ghost Dancing again. And the spirits of Big Foot and his people are all around us. They suffered through here once before, in the snow and the cold, and they were hungry, they were surrounded at that time with the finest weapons the United States had available to them, brand new machine guns and cannons.

What came to me was that Big Foot and his band were like a grandfather. It was time for them to go to sleep, but they had a child that was just born. And this child had to grow and learn all kinds of new things before it once again could return here to Wounded Knee. World War I came along, and the United States asked the American Indian if they would fight their war for them. So we went out and saw around the world what was happening, and we came back. Then another war happened. This time they not only took Indians into the army, but into the defense plants all across America, and into the big cities. And we learned the ways of the white man, right here in this country, found out about the white man to bring that knowledge back for the use of our people. But we still had patience, and all this time we had been watching the white men.

When armed white men were fighting in the labor movement, riots and armed clashes with the pigs, we watched that. And in the '50s when the Communist scare was going throughout the country. And white man was fighting white man, arresting him and putting him in jail. And in the '60s, we watched the black man, that black cloud that Black Elk prophesied would cover this country. Then the 1970s came. And as a people we are beginning to see ...

[GSNA]

Harvey Milk,
"The Hope Speech"

March 10, 1978

*Harvey Milk (1930–1978), a Korean War veteran born on Long Island,
New York, moved in the early 1970s to San Francisco, where he owned a
small business. He began taking an interest in politics, and in 1977 became
the first openly gay person in the United States to be elected to civil office,
as city and county supervisor in San Francisco. He and the mayor of San
Francisco, George Moscone, were assassinated in 1978.*

MY NAME IS Harvey Milk and I'm here to recruit you.

I've been saving this one for years. It's a political joke. I can't
help it—I've got to tell it. I've never been able to talk to this many
political people before, so if I tell you nothing else you may be able
to go home laughing a bit.

This ocean liner was going across the ocean and it sank. And
there was one little piece of wood floating and three people swam
to it and they realized only one person could hold on to it. So they
had a little debate about which was the person. It so happened the
three people were the Pope, the President, and Mayor Daley. The
Pope said he was titular head of one of the great religions of the
world and he was spiritual adviser to many, many millions and he
went on and pontificated and they thought it was a good argument.
Then the President said he was leader of the largest and most powerful nation of the world. What takes place in this country affects
the whole world and they thought that was a good argument. And
Mayor Daley said he was mayor of the backbone of the United
States and what took place in Chicago affected the world, and what

took place in the archdiocese of Chicago affected Catholicism. And they thought that was a good argument. So they did it the democratic way and voted. And Daley won, seven to two.

About six months ago, Anita Bryant in her speaking to God said that the drought in California was because of the gay people. On November 9, the day after I got elected, it started to rain. On the day I got sworn in, we walked to City Hall and it was kind of nice, and as soon as I said the word "I do," it started to rain again. It's been raining since then and the people of San Francisco figure the only way to stop it is to do a recall petition. That's a local joke.

So much for that. Why are we here? Why are gay people here? And what's happening? What's happening to me is the antithesis of what you read about in the papers and what you hear about on the radio. You hear about and read about this movement to the right. That we must band together and fight back this movement to the right. And I'm here to go ahead and say that what you hear and read is what they want you to think because it's not happening. The major media in this country has talked about the movement to the right so much that they've got even us thinking that way. Because they want the legislators to think that there is indeed a movement to the right and that the Congress and the legislators and the city councils will start to move to the right the way the major media want them. So they keep on talking about this move to the right.

So let's look at 1977 and see if there was indeed a move to the right. In 1977, gay people had their rights taken away from them in Miami. But you must remember that in the week before Miami and the week after that, the word homosexual or gay appeared in every single newspaper in this nation in articles both pro and con. In every radio station, in every TV station and every household. For the first time in the history of the world, everybody was talking about it, good or bad. Unless you have dialogue, unless you open the walls of dialogue, you can never reach to change people's opinion. In those two weeks, more good and bad, but *more* about the word homosexual and gay was written than probably in the history of mankind. Once you have dialogue starting, you know you can break down the prejudice. In 1977 we saw a dialogue start. In 1977, we saw a gay person elected in San Francisco. In 1977 we saw the state of Mississippi decriminalize marijuana. In 1977, we saw the convention of conventions in Houston. And I want to know where the movement to the right is happening.

What that is is a record of what happened last year. What we must do is make sure that 1978 continues the movement that is really happening that the media don't want you to know about, that is the movement to the left. It's up to CDC to put the pressures on Sacramento—not to just bring flowers to Sacramento—but to break down the walls and the barriers so the movement to the left continues and progress continues in the nation. We have before us coming up several issues we must speak out on. Probably the most important issue outside the Briggs—which we will come to—but we do know what will take place this June. We know there's an issue on the ballot called Jarvis-Gann. We hear the taxpayers talk about it on both sides. But what you don't hear is that it's probably the most racist issue on the ballot in a long time. In the city and county of San Francisco, if it passes and we indeed have to lay off people, who will they be? The last in, not the first in, and who are the last in but the minorities? Jarvis-Gann is a racist issue. We must address that issue. We must not talk away from it. We must not allow them to talk about the money it's going to save, because look at who's going to save the money and who's going to get hurt.

We also have another issue that we've started in some of the north counties and I hope in some of the south counties it continues. In San Francisco elections we're asking—at least we hope to ask—that the U.S. government put pressure on the closing of the South African consulate. That must happen. There is a major difference between an embassy in Washington which is a diplomatic bureau, and a consulate in major cities. A consulate is there for one reason only—to promote business, economic gains, tourism, and investment. And every time you have business going to South Africa, you're promoting a regime that's offensive.

In the city of San Francisco, if everyone of 51 percent of that city were to go to South Africa, they would be treated as second-class citizens. That is an offense to the people of San Francisco and I hope all my colleagues up there will take every step we can to close down that consulate and hope that people in other parts of the state follow us in that lead. The battles must be started some place and CDC is the greatest place to start the battles.

I know we are pressed for time so I'm going to cover just one more little point. That is to understand why it is important that gay people run for office and that gay people get elected. I know there are many people in this room who are running for central committee who are gay. I encourage you. There's a major reason why.

If my non-gay friends and supporters in this room understand it, they'll probably understand why I've run so often before I finally made it. Y'see right now, there's a controversy going on in this convention about the governor. Is he speaking out enough? Is he strong enough for gay rights? And there is a controversy and for us to say it is not would be foolish. Some people are satisfied and some people are not.

You see there is a major difference—and it remains a vital difference—between a friend and a gay person, a friend in office and a gay person in office. Gay people have been slandered nationwide. We've been tarred and we've been brushed with the picture of pornography. In Dade County, we were accused of child molestation. It's not enough anymore just to have friends represent us. No matter how good that friend may be.

The black community made up its mind to that a long time ago. That the myths against blacks can only be dispelled by electing black leaders, so the black community could be judged by the leaders and not by the myths or black criminals. The Spanish community must not be judged by Latin criminals or myths. The Asian community must not be judged by Asian criminals or myths. The Italian community should not be judged by the mafia, myths. And the time has come when the gay community must not be judged by our criminals and myths.

Like every other group, we must be judged by our leaders and by those who are themselves gay, those who are visible. For invisible, we remain in limbo—a myth, a person with no parents, no brothers, no sisters, no friends who are straight, no important positions in employment. A tenth of a nation supposedly composed of stereotypes and would-be seducers of children—and no offense meant to the stereotypes. But today, the black community is not judged by its friends, but by its black legislators and leaders. And we must give people the chance to judge us by our leaders and legislators. A gay person in office can set a tone, can command respect not only from the larger community, but from the young people in our own community who need both examples and hope.

The first gay people we elect must be strong. They must not be content to sit in the back of the bus. They must not be content to accept pablum. They must be above wheeling and dealing. They must be—for the good of all of us—independent, unbought. The anger and the frustrations that some of us feel is because we are misunderstood, and friends can't feel that anger and frustration. They can sense it in us, but they can't feel it. Because a friend has never gone through what is known as coming out. I will never forget what it was like coming out and having nobody to look up toward. I remember the lack of hope—and our friends can't fulfill that.

I can't forget the looks on faces of people who've lost hope. Be they gay, be they seniors, be they blacks looking for an almost-impossible job, and be they Latins trying to explain their problems and aspirations in a tongue that's foreign to them. I personally will never forget that people are more important than buildings. I use the word "I" because I'm proud. I stand here tonight in front of my gay sisters, brothers and friends because I'm proud of you. I think it's time that we have many legislators who are gay and proud of that fact and do not have to remain in the closet. I think that a gay person, up-front, will not walk away from a responsibility and be afraid of being tossed out of office. After Dade County, I walked among the angry and the frustrated night after night and I looked at their faces. And in San Francisco, three days before Gay Pride Day, a person was killed just because he was gay. And that night, I walked among the sad and the frustrated at City Hall in San Francisco and later that night as they lit candles on Castro Street and stood in silence, reaching out for some symbolic thing that would give them hope. These were strong people, people whose faces I knew from the shop, the streets, meetings and people who I never saw before but I knew. They were strong, but even they needed hope.

And the young gay people in the Altoona, Pennsylvanias and the Richmond, Minnesotas who are coming out and hear Anita Bryant on television and her story. The only thing they have to look forward to is hope. And you have to give them hope. Hope for a better world, hope for a better tomorrow, hope for a better place to come to if the pressures at home are too great. Hope that all will be all right. Without hope, not only gays, but the blacks, the seniors, the handicapped, the us'es, the us'es will give up. And if you help elect to the central committee and other offices, more gay people, that gives a green light to all who feel disenfranchised, a green light to move forward. It means hope to a nation that has given up, because if a gay person makes it, the doors are open to everyone.

So if there is a message I have to give, it is that if I've found one overriding thing abut my personal election, it's the fact that if a gay person can be elected, it's a green light. And you and you and you, you have to give people hope. Thank you very much.

[GSTC]

President Ronald Reagan, Address to the National Association of Evangelicals (the "Evil Empire" speech)

March 8, 1983

Ronald Reagan (1911–2004), one of the nation's most popular presidents during his two terms in office, had been, before being elected governor of California in 1966, a well-known movie actor. His charisma carried him through various crises and also enabled him to make controversial positions palatable. In this speech in Orlando, Florida, he decried what he saw as disintegrating American moral values while also lauding American religious conservatism. Most famously, he called out the leaders of Communist regimes, namely those of the Soviet Union, as leading a godless "evil empire."

THERE IS SIN and evil in the world, and we're enjoined by Scripture and the Lord Jesus to oppose it with all our might. Our nation, too, has a legacy of evil with which it must deal. The glory of this land has been its capacity for transcending the moral evils of our past. For example, the long struggle of minority citizens for equal rights, once a source of disunity and civil war, is now a point of pride for all Americans. We must never go back. There is no room for racism, anti-Semitism, or other forms of ethnic and racial hatred in this country. [*Long Applause*]

I know that you've been horrified, as have I, by the resurgence of some hate groups preaching bigotry and prejudice. Use the mighty voice of your pulpits and the powerful standing of your churches to denounce and isolate these hate groups in our midst. The commandment given us is clear and simple: "Thou shalt love thy neighbor as thyself." [*Applause*]

But whatever sad episodes exist in our past, any objective observer must hold a positive view of American history, a history that has been the story of hopes fulfilled and dreams made into reality. Especially in this century, America has kept alight the torch of freedom, but not just for ourselves, but for millions of others around the world.

And this brings me to my final point today. During my first press conference as president, in answer to a direct question, I pointed out that, as good Marxist-Leninists, the Soviet leaders have openly and publicly declared that the only morality they recognize is that which will further their cause, which is world revolution. I think I should point out I was only quoting Lenin, their guiding spirit, who said in 1920 that they repudiate all morality that proceeds from supernatural ideas—that's their name for religion—or ideas that are outside class conceptions. Morality is entirely subordinate to the interests of class war. And everything is moral that is necessary for the annihilation of the old exploiting social order and for uniting the proletariat.

Well, I think the refusal of many influential people to accept this elementary fact of Soviet doctrine illustrates an historical reluctance to see totalitarian powers for what they are. We saw this phenomenon in the 1930s. We see it too often today.

This doesn't mean we should isolate ourselves and refuse to seek an understanding with them. I intend to do everything I can to persuade them of our peaceful intent, to remind them that it was the West that refused to use its nuclear monopoly in the forties and fifties for territorial gain and which now proposes 50 percent cut in strategic ballistic missiles and the elimination of an entire class of land-based, intermediate-range nuclear missiles. [*Applause*]

At the same time, however, they must be made to understand: we will never compromise our principles and standards. We will never give away our freedom. We will never abandon our belief in God. [Long Applause] And we will never stop searching for a genuine peace, but we can assure none of these things America stands for through the so-called nuclear freeze solutions proposed by some.

The truth is that a freeze now would be a very dangerous fraud, for that is merely the illusion of peace. The reality is that we must find peace through strength. [*Applause*]

I would a—[*Applause continuing*]... I would agree to a freeze if only we could freeze the Soviets' global desires. [*Laughter, Applause*] A freeze at current levels of weapons would remove any incentive for the Soviets to negotiate seriously in Geneva and virtually end our chances to achieve the major arms reduction s which we have proposed. Instead, they would achieve their objectives through the freeze.

A freeze would reward the Soviet Union for its enormous and unparalleled military buildup. It would prevent the essential and long overdue modernization of United States and allied defenses and would leave our aging forces increasingly vulnerable. And an honest freeze would require extensive prior negotiations on the systems and numbers to be limited and on the measures to ensure effective verification and compliance. And the kind of a freeze that has been suggested would be virtually impossible to verify. Such a major effort would divert us completely from our current negotiations on achieving substantial reductions. [*Applause*]

I, a number of years ago, I heard a young father, a very prominent young man in the entertainment world, addressing a tremendous gathering in California. It was during the time of the cold war, and communism and our own way of life were very much on people's minds. And he was speaking to that subject. And suddenly, though, I heard him saying, "I love my little girls more than anything—" And I said to myself, "Oh, no, don't. You can't—don't say that." But I had underestimated him. He went on: "I would rather see my little girls die now; still believing in God, than have them grow up under communism and one day die no longer believing in God." [*Applause*]

There were thousands of young people in that audience. They came to their feet with shouts of joy. They had instantly recognized the profound truth in what he had said, with regard to the physical and the soul and what was truly important.

Yes, let us pray for the salvation of all of those who live in that totalitarian darkness—pray they will discover the joy of knowing God. But until they do, let us be aware that while they preach the supremacy of the State, declare its omnipotence over individual man, and predict its eventual domination of all peoples on the earth, they are the focus of evil in the modern world.

It was C.S. Lewis who, in his unforgettable "Screwtape Letters," wrote: "The greatest evil is not done now...in those sordid 'dens of crime' that Dickens loved to paint. It is...not even done in concentration camps and labor camps. In those we see its final result, but it is conceived and ordered; moved, seconded, carried and minuted in clear, carpeted, warmed, and well-lighted offices, by quiet men with white collars and cut fingernails and smooth-shaven cheeks who do not need to raise their voice."

Well, because these "quiet men" do not "raise their voices," because they sometimes speak in soothing tones of brotherhood and peace, because, like other dictators before them, they're always making "their final territorial demand," some would have us accept them at their word and accommodate ourselves to their aggressive impulses. But if history teaches anything, it teaches that simple-minded appeasement or wishful thinking about our adversaries is folly. It means the betrayal of our past, the squandering of our freedom.

So, I urge you to speak out against those who would place the United States in a position of military and moral inferiority. You know, I've always believed that old Screwtape reserved his best efforts for those of you in the Church. So, in your discussions of the nuclear freeze proposals, I urge you to beware the temptation of pride—the temptation of blithely declaring yourselves above it all and label both sides equally at fault, to ignore the facts of history and the aggressive impulses of an evil empire, to simply call the arms race a giant misunderstanding and thereby remove yourself from the struggle between right and wrong and good and evil.

I ask you to resist the attempts of those who would have you withhold your support for our efforts, this administration's efforts, to keep America strong and free, while we negotiate—real and verifiable reductions in the world's nuclear arsenals and one day, with God's help, their total elimination. [*Applause*]

While America's military strength is important, let me add here that I've always maintained that the struggle now going on for the world will never be decided by bombs or rockets, by armies or military might. The real crisis we face today is a spiritual one; at root, it is a test of moral will and faith. [...]

I believe we shall rise to the challenge. I believe that communism is another sad, bizarre chapter in human history whose last—last pages even now are being written. I believe this because the source of our strength in the quest for human freedom is not material, but spiritual. And because it knows no limitation, it must terrify and ultimately triumph over those who would enslave their fellow man. For in the words of Isaiah: "He giveth power to the faint; and to them that have no...might He increased strength. But they that wait upon the Lord shall renew their strength; they shall mount up with wings as eagles; they shall run, and not be weary." [*Applause*]

Yes, change your world. One of our founding fathers, Thomas Paine, said, "We have it within our power to begin the world over again." We can do it, doing together what no one church could do by itself.

God bless you and thank you very much. [*Long Applause*]

[VOD]

President Ronald Reagan, Addresses to the Nation on the Iran Arms and Contra Aid Controversy

November 13, 1986, and March 4, 1987

Elected President in 1980 and 1984, Ronald Reagan was famous for presenting his message. Through thick and thin, he delivered his lines convincingly. In the second speech, broadcast nationally, now having been caught in a lie about his administration's covert operations, he maintained the truth of the lie, while apologizing for its factual falseness. His apology, however, reads very well: "Now, what should happen when you make a mistake is this: You take your knocks, you learn your lessons, and then you move on."

PART I: NOVEMBER 13, 1986

GOOD EVENING. I know you've been reading, seeing, and hearing a lot of stories the past several days attributed to Danish sailors, unnamed observers at Italian ports and Spanish harbors, and especially unnamed government officials of my administration. Well, now you're going to hear the facts from a White House source, and you know my name.

I wanted this time to talk with you about an extremely sensitive and profoundly important matter of foreign policy. For 18 months now we have had underway a secret diplomatic initiative to Iran. That initiative was undertaken for the simplest and best of reasons: to renew a relationship with the nation of Iran, to bring an honorable end to the bloody 6-year war between Iran and Iraq, to eliminate state-sponsored terrorism and subversion, and to effect the safe return of all hostages. Without Iran's cooperation, we cannot bring an end to the Persian Gulf War; without Iran's concurrence, there can be no enduring peace in the Middle East. For 10 days now, the American and world press have been full of reports and rumors about this initiative and these objectives. Now, my fellow Americans, there's an old saying that nothing spreads so quickly as a rumor. So, I thought it was time to speak with you directly, to tell you firsthand about our dealings with Iran. As Will Rogers once said, "Rumor travels faster, but it don't stay put as long as truth." So, let's get to the facts.

The charge has been made that the United States has shipped weapons to Iran as ransom payment for the release of American hostages in Lebanon, that the United States undercut its allies and secretly violated American policy against trafficking with terrorists. Those charges are utterly false. The United States has not made concessions to those who hold our people captive in Lebanon. And we will not. The United States has not swapped boatloads or planeloads of American weapons for the return of American hostages. And we will not. Other reports have surfaced alleging U.S. involvement: reports of a sealift to Iran using Danish ships to carry American arms; of vessels in Spanish ports being employed in secret U.S. arms shipments; of Italian ports being used; of the U.S. sending spare parts and weapons for combat aircraft. All these reports are quite exciting, but as far as we're concerned, not one of them is true.

During the course of our secret discussions, I authorized the transfer of small amounts of defensive weapons and spare parts for defensive systems to Iran. My purpose was to convince Tehran that our negotiators were acting with my authority, to send a signal that the United States was prepared to replace the animosity between us with a new relationship. These modest deliveries, taken together, could easily fit into a single cargo plane. They could not, taken together, affect the outcome of the 6-year war between Iran and Iraq nor could they affect in any way the military balance between the two countries. Those with whom we were in contact took considerable risks and needed a signal of our serious intent if they were to carry on and broaden the dialog. At the same time we undertook this initiative, we made clear that Iran must oppose all forms of international terrorism as a condition of progress in our relationship. The most significant step which Iran could take, we indicated, would be to use its influence in Lebanon to secure the release of all hostages held there.

Some progress has already been made. Since U.S. Government contact began with Iran, there's been no evidence of Iranian Government complicity in acts of terrorism against the United States. Hostages have come home, and we welcome the efforts that the Government of Iran has taken in the past and is currently undertaking.

But why, you might ask, is any relationship with Iran important to the United States? Iran encompasses some of the most critical geography in the world. It lies between the Soviet Union and access to the warm waters of the Indian Ocean. Geography explains why the Soviet Union has sent an army into Afghanistan to dominate that country and, if they could, Iran and Pakistan. Iran's geography gives it a critical position from which adversaries could interfere with oil flows from the Arab States that border the Persian Gulf. Apart from geography, Iran's oil deposits are important to the long-term health of the world economy.

For these reasons, it is in our national interest to watch for changes within Iran that might offer hope for an improved relationship. Until last year there was little to justify that hope. Indeed, we have bitter and enduring disagreements that persist today. At the heart of our quarrel has been Iran's past sponsorship of international terrorism. Iranian policy has been devoted to expelling all Western influence from the Middle East. We cannot abide that because our interests in the Middle East are vital. At the same time, we seek no territory or special position in Iran. The Iranian revolution is a fact of history, but between American and Iranian basic national interests there need be no permanent conflict.

Since 1983 various countries have made overtures to stimulate direct contact between the United States and Iran; European, Near East, and Far East countries have attempted to serve as intermediaries. Despite a U.S. willingness to proceed, none of these overtures bore fruit. With this history in mind, we were receptive last year when we were alerted to the possibility of establishing a direct dialog with Iranian officials. Now, let me repeat: America's longstanding goals in the region have been to help preserve Iran's independence from Soviet domination; to bring an honorable end to the bloody Iran–Iraq war; to halt the export of subversion and terrorism in the region. A major impediment to those goals has been an absence of dialog, a cutoff in communication between us. It's because of Iran's strategic importance and its influence in the Islamic world that we chose to probe for a better relationship between our countries.

Our discussions continued into the spring of this year. Based upon the progress we felt we had made, we sought to raise the diplomatic level of contacts. A meeting was arranged in Tehran. I then asked my former national security adviser, Robert McFarlane, to undertake a secret mission and gave him explicit instructions. I asked him to go to Iran to open a dialog, making stark and clear our basic objectives and disagreements. The 4 days of talks were conducted in a civil fashion, and American personnel were not mistreated. Since then, the dialog has continued and step-by-step progress continues to be made. Let me repeat: Our interests are clearly served by opening a dialog with Iran and thereby helping to end the Iran-Iraq war. That war has dragged on for more than 6 years, with no prospect of a negotiated settlement. The slaughter on both sides has been enormous, and the adverse economic and political consequences for that vital region of the world have been growing. We sought to establish communication with both sides in that senseless struggle, so that we could assist in bringing about a cease-fire and, eventually, a settlement. We have sought to be evenhanded by working with both sides and with other interested nations to prevent a widening of the war.

This sensitive undertaking has entailed great risk for those involved. There is no question but that we could never have begun or continued this dialog had the initiative been disclosed earlier. Due to the publicity of the past week, the entire initiative is very much at risk today. There is ample precedent in our history for this kind of secret diplomacy. In 1971 then-President Nixon sent his national security adviser on a secret mission to China. In that case, as today, there was a basic requirement for discretion and for sensitivity to the situation in the nation we were attempting to engage.

Since the welcome return of former hostage David Jacobsen, there has been unprecedented speculation and countless reports that have not only been wrong but have been potentially dangerous to the hostages and destructive of the opportunity before us. The efforts of courageous people like Terry Waite have been jeopardized. So extensive have been the false rumors and erroneous reports that the risks of remaining silent now exceed the risks of speaking out.

And that's why I decided to address you tonight. It's been widely reported, for example, that the Congress, as well as top executive branch officials, were circumvented. Although the efforts we undertook were highly sensitive and involvement of government officials was limited to those with a strict need to know, all appropriate Cabinet officers were fully consulted. The actions I authorized were, and continue to be, in full compliance with Federal law. And the relevant committees of Congress are being, and will be, fully informed.

Another charge is that we have tilted toward Iran in the Gulf war. This, too, is unfounded. We have consistently condemned the violence on both sides. We have consistently sought a negotiated settlement that preserves the territorial integrity of both nations. The overtures we've made to the Government of Iran have not been a shift to supporting one side over the other, rather, it has been a diplomatic initiative to gain some degree of access and influence within Iran—as well as Iraq—and to bring about an honorable end to that bloody conflict. It is in the interests of all parties in the Gulf region to end that war as soon as possible.

To summarize: Our government has a firm policy not to capitulate to terrorist demands. That no concessions policy remains in force, in spite of the wildly speculative and false stories about arms for hostages and alleged ransom payments. We did not—repeat—did not trade weapons or anything else for hostages, nor will we. Those who think that we have gone soft on terrorism should take up the question with Colonel Qadhafi. We have not, nor will we, capitulate to terrorists. We will, however, get on with advancing the vital interests of our great nation—in spite of terrorists and radicals who seek to sabotage our efforts and immobilize the United States. Our goals have been, and remain, to restore a relationship with Iran; to bring an honorable end to the war in the Gulf; to bring a halt to state-supported terror in the Middle East; and finally, to effect the safe return of all hostages from Lebanon.

As President, I've always operated on the belief that, given the facts, the American people will make the right decision. I believe that to be true now. I cannot guarantee the outcome. But as in the past, I ask for your support because I believe you share the hope for peace in the Middle East, for freedom for all hostages, and for a world free of terrorism. Certainly there are risks in this pursuit, but there are greater risks if we do not persevere. It will take patience and understanding; it will take continued resistance to those who commit terrorist acts; and it will take cooperation with all who seek to rid the world of this scourge.

Thank you, and God bless you.

PART II: MARCH 4, 1987

My fellow Americans:

I've spoken to you from this historic office on many occasions and about many things. The power of the Presidency is often thought to reside within this Oval Office. Yet it doesn't rest here; it rests in you, the American people, and in your trust. Your trust is what gives a President his powers of leadership and his personal strength, and it's what I want to talk to you about this evening.

For the past 3 months, I've been silent on the revelations about Iran. And you must have been thinking: "Well, why doesn't he tell us what's happening? Why doesn't he just speak to us as he has in the past when we've faced troubles or tragedies?" Others of you, I guess, were thinking: "What's he doing hiding out in the White House?" Well, the reason I haven't spoken to you before now is this: You deserve the truth. And as frustrating as the waiting has been, I felt it was improper to come to you with sketchy reports, or possibly even erroneous statements, which would then have to be corrected, creating even more doubt and confusion. There's been enough of that. I've paid a price for my silence in terms of your trust and confidence. But I've had to wait, as you have, for the complete story. That's why I appointed Ambassador David Abshire as my Special Counsellor to help get out the thousands of documents to the various investigations. And I appointed a Special Review Board, the Tower board, which took on the chore of pulling the truth together for me and getting to the bottom of things. It has now issued its findings.

I'm often accused of being an optimist, and it's true I had to hunt pretty hard to find any good news in the Board's report. As you know, it's well-stocked with criticisms, which I'll discuss in a moment; but I was very relieved to read this sentence: "... the Board is convinced that the President does indeed want the full story to be told." And that will continue to be my pledge to you as the other investigations go forward. I want to thank the members of the panel: former Senator John Tower, former Secretary of State Edmund Muskie, and former national security adviser Brent

Scowcroft. They have done the Nation, as well as me personally, a great service by submitting a report of such integrity and depth. They have my genuine and enduring gratitude.

I've studied the Board's report. Its findings are honest, convincing, and highly critical; and I accept them. And tonight I want to share with you my thoughts on these findings and report to you on the actions I'm taking to implement the Board's recommendations. First, let me say I take full responsibility for my own actions and for those of my administration. As angry as I may be about activities undertaken without my knowledge, I am still accountable for those activities. As disappointed as I may be in some who served me, I'm still the one who must answer to the American people for this behavior. And as personally distasteful as I find secret bank accounts and diverted funds—well, as the Navy would say, this happened on my watch.

Let's start with the part that is the most controversial. A few months ago I told the American people I did not trade arms for hostages. My heart and my best intentions still tell me that's true, but the facts and the evidence tell me it is not. As the Tower board reported, what began as a strategic opening to Iran deteriorated, in its implementation, into trading arms for hostages. This runs counter to my own beliefs, to administration policy, and to the original strategy we had in mind. There are reasons why it happened, but no excuses. It was a mistake. I undertook the original Iran initiative in order to develop relations with those who might assume leadership in a post-Khomeini government.

It's clear from the Board's report, however, that I let my personal concern for the hostages spill over into the geopolitical strategy of reaching out to Iran. I asked so many questions about the hostages welfare that I didn't ask enough about the specifics of the total Iran plan. Let me say to the hostage families: We have not given up. We never will. And I promise you we'll use every legitimate means to free your loved ones from captivity. But I must also caution that those Americans who freely remain in such dangerous areas must know that they're responsible for their own safety.

Now, another major aspect of the Board's findings regards the transfer of funds to the Nicaraguan contras. The Tower board wasn't able to find out what happened to this money, so the facts here will be left to the continuing investigations of the court-appointed Independent Counsel and the two congressional investigating committees. I'm confident the truth will come out about this matter, as well. As I told the Tower board, I didn't know about any diversion of funds to the contras. But as President, I cannot escape responsibility.

Much has been said about my management style, a style that's worked successfully for me during 8 years as Governor of California and for most of my Presidency. The way I work is to identify the problem, find the right individuals to do the job, and then let them go to it. I've found this invariably brings out the best in people. They seem to rise to their full capability, and in the long run you get more done. When it came to managing the NSC staff, let's face it, my style didn't match its previous track record. I've already begun correcting this. As a start, yesterday I met with the entire professional staff of the National Security Council. I defined for them the values I want to guide the national security policies of this country. I told them that I wanted a policy that was as justifiable and understandable in public as it was in secret. I wanted a policy that reflected the will of the Congress as well as of the White House. And I told them that there'll be no more freelancing by individuals when it comes to our national security.

You've heard a lot about the staff of the National Security Council in recent months. Well, I can tell you, they are good and dedicated government employees, who put in long hours for the Nation's benefit. They are eager and anxious to serve their country. One thing still upsetting me, however, is that no one kept proper records of meetings or decisions. This led to my failure to recollect whether I approved an arms shipment before or after the fact. I did approve it; I just can't say specifically when. Well, rest assured, there's plenty of recordkeeping now going on at 1600 Pennsylvania Avenue.

For nearly a week now, I've been studying the Board's report. I want the American people to know that this wrenching ordeal of recent months has not been in vain. I endorse every one of the Tower board's recommendations. In fact, I'm going beyond its recommendations so as to put the house in even better order. I'm taking action in three basic areas: personnel, national security policy, and the process for making sure that the system works.

First, personnel—I've brought in an accomplished and highly respected new team here at the White House. They bring new blood, new energy, and new credibility and experience. Former

Senator Howard Baker, my new Chief of Staff, possesses a breadth of legislative and foreign affairs skills that's impossible to match. I'm hopeful that his experience as minority and majority leader of the Senate can help us forge a new partnership with the Congress, especially on foreign and national security policies. I'm genuinely honored that he's given up his own Presidential aspirations to serve the country as my Chief of Staff. Frank Carlucci, my new national security adviser, is respected for his experience in government and trusted for his judgment and counsel. Under him, the NSC staff is being rebuilt with proper management discipline. Already, almost half the NSC professional staff is comprised of new people.

Yesterday I nominated William Webster, a man of sterling reputation, to be Director of the Central Intelligence Agency. Mr. Webster has served as Director of the FBI and as a U.S. District Court judge. He understands the meaning of "rule of law." So that his knowledge of national security matters can be available to me on a continuing basis, I will also appoint John Tower to serve as a member of my Foreign Intelligence Advisory Board. I am considering other changes in personnel, and I'll move more furniture, as I see fit, in the weeks and months ahead.

Second, in the area of national security policy, I have ordered the NSC to begin a comprehensive review of all covert operations. I have also directed that any covert activity be in support of clear policy objectives and in compliance with American values. I expect a covert policy that, if Americans saw it on the front page of their newspaper, they'd say, "That makes sense." I have had issued a directive prohibiting the NSC staff itself from undertaking covert operations—no ifs, ands, or buts. I have asked Vice President Bush to reconvene his task force on terrorism to review our terrorist policy in light of the events that have occurred.

Third, in terms of the process of reaching national security decisions, I am adopting in total the Tower report's model of how the NSC process and staff should work. I am directing Mr. Carlucci to take the necessary steps to make that happen. He will report back to me on further reforms that might be needed. I've created the post of NSC legal adviser to assure a greater sensitivity to matters of law. I am also determined to make the congressional oversight process work. Proper procedures for consultation with the Congress will be followed, not only in letter but in spirit. Before the end of March, I will report to the Congress on all the steps I've taken in line with the Tower board's conclusions.

Now, what should happen when you make a mistake is this: You take your knocks, you learn your lessons, and then you move on. That's the healthiest way to deal with a problem. This in no way diminishes the importance of the other continuing investigations, but the business of our country and our people must proceed. I've gotten this message from Republicans and Democrats in Congress, from allies around the world, and—if we're reading the signals right—even from the Soviets. And of course, I've heard the message from you, the American people. You know, by the time you reach my age, you've made plenty of mistakes. And if you've lived your life properly—so, you learn. You put things in perspective. You pull your energies together. You change. You go forward.

My fellow Americans, I have a great deal that I want to accomplish with you and for you over the next 2 years. And the Lord willing, that's exactly what I intend to do.

Good night and God bless you.

[PPP]

Urvashi Vaid Gay Rights Speech at the March on Washington

April 25, 1993

Urvashi Vaid [born 1958] is an American attorney, writer, and political activist of Indian descent, known for her decades of work promoting gay rights and social justice. She currently serves as the executive director of the Arcus Foundation, an organization dedicated to the promotion of human rights and conservation throughout the world. The following speech was delivered at the second March on Washington in support of gay and lesbian rights.

— Note by James Daley

HELLO, LESBIAN AND gay Americans. I am proud to stand before you as a lesbian today.

With hearts full of love and an abiding faith in justice, we have come to Washington to speak to America. We have come to speak the truth of our lives and silence the liars. We have come to challenge the cowardly Congress to end its paralysis and exercise moral leadership. We have come to defend our honor and win our equality.

But most of all we have come in peace and with courage to say, "America, this day marks the end from exile of the gay and lesbian people. We are banished no more. We wander the wilderness of despair no more. We are afraid no more. For on this day, with love in our hearts, we have come out. We have come out across America to build a bridge of understanding, a bridge of progress, a bridge as solid as steel. A bridge to a land where no one suffers prejudice because of their sexual orientation, their race, their gender, their religion, or their human difference."

I have been asked by the March organizers to speak in five minutes about the Far Right. The Far Right, which threatens the
construction of that bridge. The extreme Right which has targeted
every one of you, and me, for extinction. The Supremacist Right
which seeks to redefine the very meaning of democracy.

Language itself fails in this task, my friends, for to call our opponents "the Right," states a profound untruth. They are wrong. They
are wrong morally, they are wrong spiritually, and they are wrong
politically.

The Christian supremacists are wrong spiritually when they de-
monize us. They are wrong when they reduce the complexity and
beauty of our spirit into a freak show.

They are wrong spiritually, because, if we are the untouchables
of America—if we are the untouchables—then we are, as Mahatma
Gandhi said, children of God. And as God's children we know that
the Gods of our understanding, the Gods of goodness and love and
righteousness, march right here with us today.

The supremacists who lead the anti-gay crusade are wrong morally. They are wrong because justice is moral, and prejudice is evil;
because truth is moral and the lie of the closet is the real sin; because the claim of morality is a subtle sort of subterfuge, a stratagem
which hides the real aim which is much more secular.

Christian supremacist leaders like Bill Bennett and Pat Robertson, Lou Sheldon and Pat Buchanan, supremacists like Phyllis
Schlafly, Ralph Reed, Bill Kristol, R. J. Rushdoony—these supremacists don't care about morality, they care about power. They
care about social control. And their goal, my friends, is the reconstruction of American Democracy into American Theocracy.

We who are gathered here today must prove the religious Right
wrong politically. And we can do it. That is our challenge.

You know they have made us into the communists of the nine-
ties. They say they have declared cultural war against us. It's war all
right. It's a war about values.

On one side are the values that everyone here stands for. Do you
know what those values are? Traditional American values of democracy
and pluralism. On the other side are those who want to turn the Christian church into government, those whose value is monotheism.

We believe in democracy, in many voices co-existing in peace,
and people of all faiths living together in harmony under a common
civil framework known as the United States Constitution.

Our opponents believe in monotheism. One way—theirs. One God—theirs. One law—the Old Testament. One nation supreme—the Christian Right one. Let's name it. Democracy battles theism in Oregon, in Colorado, in Florida, in Maine, in Arizona, in Michigan, in Ohio, in Idaho, in Washington, in Montana, in every state where my brothers and sisters are leading the fight to oppose the Right and to defend the United States Constitution.

We won the anti-gay measure in Oregon, but today 33 counties—33 counties and municipalities face local versions of that ordinance today.

The fight has just begun. We lost the big fight in Colorado, but, thanks to the hard work of all the people of Colorado, the Boycott Colorado movement is working and we are strong. And we are going to win our freedom there eventually.

To defeat the Right politically, my friends, is our challenge when we leave this march.

How can we do it? We've got to march from Washington into action at home.

I challenge every one of you, straight or gay, who can hear my voice, to join the national gay and lesbian movement. I challenge you to join the National Gay and Lesbian Task Force to fight the Right. We have got to match the power of the Christian supremacists, member for member, vote for vote, dollar for dollar.

I challenge each of you, not just buy a T-shirt, but [also] get involved in your movement. Get involved! Volunteer! Volunteer!

Every local organization in this country needs you. Every clinic, every hotline, every youth program needs you, needs your time and your love.

And I also challenge our straight liberal allies, liberals and libertarians, independent and conservative, republican or radical. I challenge and invite you to open your eyes and embrace us without fear.

The gay rights movement is not a party. It is not [a] lifestyle. It is not a hairstyle. It is not a fad or a fringe or a sickness. It is not about sin or salvation.

The gay rights movement is an integral part of the American promise of freedom.

We, you and I, each of us, we are the descendants of a proud tradition of people asserting our dignity.

It is fitting that the Holocaust Museum was dedicated the same weekend as this march, for not only were gay people persecuted by the Nazi state, but [also] gay people are indebted to the struggle of the Jewish people against bigotry and intolerance.

It is fitting that the NAACP marches with us, that feminist leaders march with us, because we are indebted to those movements.

When all of us who believe in freedom and diversity see this gathering, we see beauty and power.

When our enemies see this gathering, they see the millennium, the end of the world.

Perhaps the Right is right about something. We stand for the end of the world as we know it. We call for the end of racism and sexism and bigotry as we know it. We call for the end of violence and discrimination and homophobia as we know it. We call for the end of sexism as we know it.

We stand for freedom as we have yet to know it. And we will not be denied.

[GSGR]

Into the Twenty-first Century

Elizabeth Birch, First Convention Speech by a Gay Organization's Leader, the Democratic National Convention

August 15, 2000

Elizabeth Birch [born 1956] is an American attorney and gay rights activist best known for her work as the Executive Director of the Human Rights Campaign, an organization dedicated to working for Lesbian, Gay, Bisexual, and Transgender equal rights. This speech was the first ever given at a national political convention by the leader of a gay organization.

— Note by James Daley

I AM HONORED to speak here as a gay American. Tonight, we celebrate the American family. But we know that America's family is not yet whole.

For the color of his skin, James Byrd Jr. was dragged behind a truck in Jasper, Texas, until his body was shattered on a drainage ditch. Because of her faith, 14-year-old Kristi Beckel was gunned down as she worshipped in a Texas Baptist church.

Because Matthew Shepard was gay, he was driven into the countryside on a freezing Wyoming night, beaten and hung on a fence to die. His gentle voice still asks why, as do the families who have paid for our national lesson with their children's lives.

Tonight, we dedicate ourselves to healing the fractures—soothing the wounds—to making our American family truly whole. It is now well settled that Democrats are capable of strong and disciplined standards of governance for our economy, domestic and foreign affairs. But true leadership also requires a muscled heart for equality.

Wise leadership never takes refuge in silence.

I speak here tonight with the parents and political leaders whose action or apathy will determine the fullness of the American family. To parents—some of whom have left their gay children at the margins of family life and out of a vision for America, I say this: I want you to know that your gay children are gifted and strong. All are heroic in the way they have conquered barriers to their own self-respect. Many have suffered cruelty or violence. Some serve their communities with leadership and grace. Many are rich in faith, and have a deep love for this nation and democracy. Tens of thousands have served with distinction in the armed forces. Many have lost their lives.

Until this administration, many battled AIDS virtually alone in the face of a stony, silent government. Many have lost their jobs. All were created by God. And you have a right to be proud of each and every one of them.

I am proud to know the good heart of Al Gore. He has led this nation with wisdom and courage. His vision embraces every child and every family, including my family. I cannot imagine a better leader for our small twins than the next President of the United States, Al Gore.

The other party's vision for America excludes as many as it includes. To be blunt, the Republican platform remains shameful. Healing America's family requires resolve, not simply a refrain.

I do not believe that the Republican ticket is comprised of hateful men. But they are not wise men. They practice silent apathy in the face of hatred, and call it leadership. They forego invective but embrace indifference, and call it compassion.

Deep within their hearts, they know this to be true: that not a single gay American seeks special rights or favored treatment. We seek simple equality—the equal right to work, raise a family, serve our country in every way and be free from the shackles of brutality and hate.

Equality is a special right—a right so special that for two-and-a-quarter centuries it has motivated men and women to dream and to die and to animate the heart of America itself.

Al Gore and Joe Lieberman have taken strong, courageous, positions on behalf of equality. The Democratic platform they support is a work of art in democracy—unambiguously supporting inclusion for every American. They have never run for cover of silence.

Like most Americans, they understand that:

As long as a young man can be left on a fence to die, our American family is fractured;

As long as gay parents live in fear that their children might be taken from them, our family is torn;

As long as hardworking Americans can be fired in 30 states simply for being gay, our family is not whole;

As long as gay people are barred from serving openly and with dignity in the armed forces of the United States, our family is not just;

As long as gay, lesbian, bisexual and transgender youth are at risk for suicide;

Until there is a cure for AIDS for men, women and children here and around the world . . . then the American family we celebrate tonight is not yet healed. It is not enough to love your own child. Leaders must love all children and safeguard the family called America. This is what Al Gore knows. It is what George Bush has yet to learn. We don't have a single child to spare—and we don't have time for George Bush to learn on the job.

I do not know how our young twins will one day judge my partner Hilary and me as parents, or as people. Our hope and prayer is that we will measure up in the way Dr. Martin Luther King asked people to judge themselves. He said: "In the end, we will remember not the words of our enemies, but the silence of our friends."

Let us not follow the silence of George Bush. Let us follow a voice of courage and wisdom, and let us elect Al Gore President of the United States.

[GSGR]

9/11 Commission Report ("Heroism and Horror")

September 11, 2001

On September 11, 2001, there was a coordinated attack on the World Trade Center in New York City and the Pentagon in Washington, D.C., in which thousands of people died. In 2002, President George W. Bush formed the National Commission on Terrorist Attacks Upon the United States (informally known as the 9/11 Commission), "an independent, bipartisan commission ... to prepare a full and complete account of the circumstances surrounding the September 11, 2001, terrorist attacks, including preparedness for and the immediate response to the attacks." The excerpts below come from the ninth chapter, "Heroism and Horror," and describe the morning's minute by minute series of tragedies in New York. The commission's chair, Thomas H. Kean, and vice chair, Lee H. Hamilton, published the commission's report on July 22, 2004.

9.1 PREPAREDNESS AS OF SEPTEMBER 11

EMERGENCY RESPONSE IS a product of preparedness. On the morning of September 11, 2001, the last best hope for the community of people working in or visiting the World Trade Center rested not with national policymakers but with private firms and local public servants, especially the first responders: fire, police, emergency medical service, and building safety professionals.

Building Preparedness

The World Trade Center. The World Trade Center (WTC) complex was built for the Port Authority of New York and New Jersey. Construction began in 1966, and tenants began to occupy its space in 1970. The Twin Towers came to occupy a unique and symbolic place in the culture of New York City and America.

The WTC actually consisted of seven buildings, including one hotel, spread across 16 acres of land. The buildings were connected by an underground mall (the concourse). The Twin Towers (1 WTC, or the North Tower, and 2 WTC, or the South Tower) were the signature structures, containing 10.4 million square feet of office space. Both towers had 110 stories, were about 1,350 feet high, and were square; each wall measured 208 feet in length. On any given workday, up to 50,000 office workers occupied the towers, and 40,000 people passed through the complex.

Each tower contained three central stairwells, which ran essentially from top to bottom, and 99 elevators. Generally, elevators originating in the lobby ran to "sky lobbies" on higher floors, where additional elevators carried passengers to the tops of the buildings.

Stairwells A and C ran from the 110th floor to the raised mezzanine level of the lobby. Stairwell B ran from the 107th floor to level B6, six floors below ground, and was accessible from the West Street lobby level, which was one floor below the mezzanine. All three stairwells ran essentially straight up and down, except for two deviations in stairwells A and C where the staircase jutted out toward the perimeter of the building. On the upper and lower boundaries of these deviations were transfer hallways contained within the stairwell proper. Each hallway contained smoke doors to prevent smoke from rising from lower to upper portions of the building; they were kept closed but not locked. Doors leading from tenant space into the stairwells were never kept locked; reentry from the stairwells was generally possible on at least every fourth floor. Doors leading to the roof were locked. There was no rooftop evacuation plan. The roofs of both the North Tower and the South Tower were sloped and cluttered surfaces with radiation hazards, making them impractical for helicopter landings and as staging areas for civilians. Although the South Tower roof had a helipad, it did not meet 1994 Federal Aviation Administration guidelines. […]

9.2 SEPTEMBER 11, 2001

As we turn to the events of September 11, we are mindful of the unfair perspective afforded by hindsight. Nevertheless, we will try to describe what happened in the following 102 minutes:

- the 17 minutes from the crash of the hijacked American Airlines Flight 11 into 1 World Trade Center (the North Tower) at 8:46 until the South Tower was hit

- the 56 minutes from the crash of the hijacked United Airlines Flight 175 into 2 World Trade Center (the South Tower) at 9:03 until the collapse of the South Tower
- the 29 minutes from the collapse of the South Tower at 9:59 until the collapse of the North Tower at 10:28

From 8:46 until 9:03 A.M.

At 8:46:40, the hijacked American Airlines Flight 11 flew into the upper portion of the North Tower, cutting through floors 93 to 99. Evidence suggests that all three of the building's stairwells became impassable from the 92nd floor up. Hundreds of civilians were killed instantly by the impact. Hundreds more remained alive but trapped.

Civilians, Fire Safety Personnel, and 911 Calls

North Tower. A jet fuel fireball erupted upon impact and shot down at least one bank of elevators. The fireball exploded onto numerous lower floors, including the 77th and 22nd; the West Street lobby level; and the B4 level, four stories below ground. The burning jet fuel immediately created thick, black smoke that enveloped the upper floors and roof of the North Tower. The roof of the South Tower was also engulfed in smoke because of prevailing light winds from the northwest.

Within minutes, New York City's 911 system was flooded with eyewitness accounts of the event. Most callers correctly identified the target of the attack. Some identified the plane as a commercial airliner.

The first response came from private firms and individuals—the people and companies in the building. Everything that would happen to them during the next few minutes would turn on their circumstances and their preparedness, assisted by building personnel on-site.

Hundreds of civilians trapped on or above the 92nd floor gathered in large and small groups, primarily between the 103rd and 106th floors. A large group was reported on the 92nd floor, technically below the impact but unable to descend. Civilians were also trapped in elevators. Other civilians below the impact zone—mostly on floors in the 70s and 80s, but also on at least the 47th and 22nd floors—were either trapped or waiting for assistance.

It is unclear when the first full building evacuation order was attempted over the public-address system. The deputy fire safety

director in the lobby, while immediately aware that a major incident had occurred, did not know for approximately ten minutes
that a commercial jet had directly hit the building. Following protocol, he initially gave announcements to those floors that had
generated computerized alarms, advising those tenants to descend
to points of safety—at least two floors below the smoke or fire—and
to wait there for further instructions. The deputy fire safety director
has told us that he began instructing a full evacuation within about
ten minutes of the explosion. But the first FDNY chiefs to arrive
in the lobby were advised by the Port Authority fire safety
director—who had reported to the lobby although he was no longer the designated fire safety director—that the full building evacuation announcement had been made within one minute of the
building being hit.

Because of damage to building systems caused by the impact of
the plane, public-address announcements were not heard in many
locations. For the same reason, many civilians may have been unable to use the emergency intercom phones, as they had been advised to do in fire drills. Many called 911.

The 911 system was not equipped to handle the enormous volume of calls it received. Some callers were unable to connect with
911 operators, receiving an "all circuits busy" message. Standard
operating procedure was for calls relating to fire emergencies to be
transferred from 911 operators to FDNY dispatch operators in the
appropriate borough (in this case, Manhattan). Transfers were often
plagued by delays and were in some cases unsuccessful. Many calls
were also prematurely disconnected.

The 911 operators and FDNY dispatchers had no information
about either the location or the magnitude of the impact zone and
were therefore unable to provide information as fundamental as
whether callers were above or below the fire. Because the operators
were not informed of NYPD Aviation's determination of the impossibility of rooftop rescues from the Twin Towers on that day,
they could not knowledgeably answer when callers asked whether
to go up or down. In most instances, therefore, the operators and
the FDNY dispatchers relied on standard operating procedures for
high-rise fires—that civilians should stay low, remain where they
are, and wait for emergency personnel to reach them. This advice
was given to callers from the North Tower for locations both above
and below the impact zone. Fire chiefs told us that the evacuation

of tens of thousands of people from skyscrapers can create many new problems, especially for individuals who are disabled or in poor health. Many of the injuries after the 1993 bombing occurred during the evacuation.

Although the guidance to stay in place may seem understandable in cases of conventional high-rise fires, FDNY chiefs in the North Tower lobby determined at once that all building occupants should attempt to evacuate immediately. By 8:57, FDNY chiefs had instructed the PAPD and building personnel to evacuate the South Tower as well, because of the magnitude of the damage caused by the first plane's impact.

These critical decisions were not conveyed to 911 operators or to FDNY dispatchers. Departing from protocol, a number of operators told callers that they could break windows, and several operators advised callers to evacuate if they could. Civilians who called the Port Authority police desk located at 5 WTC were advised to leave if they could.

Most civilians who were not obstructed from proceeding began evacuating without waiting for instructions over the intercom system. Some remained to wait for help, as advised by 911 operators. Others simply continued to work or delayed to collect personal items, but in many cases were urged to leave by others. Some Port Authority civilian employees remained on various upper floors to help civilians who were trapped and to assist in the evacuation.

While evacuating, some civilians had trouble reaching the exits because of damage caused by the impact. Some were confused by deviations in the increasingly crowded stairwells, and impeded by doors that appeared to be locked but actually were jammed by debris or shifting that resulted from the impact of the plane. Despite these obstacles, the evacuation was relatively calm and orderly.

Within ten minutes of impact, smoke was beginning to rise to the upper floors in debilitating volumes and isolated fires were reported, although there were some pockets of refuge. Faced with insufferable heat, smoke, and fire, and with no prospect for relief, some jumped or fell from the building.

South Tower. Many civilians in the South Tower were initially unaware of what had happened in the other tower. Some believed an incident had occurred in their building; others were aware that a major explosion had occurred on the upper floors of the North

Tower. Many people decided to leave, and some were advised to do so by fire wardens. In addition, Morgan Stanley, which occupied more than 20 floors of the South Tower, evacuated its employees by the decision of company security officials.

Consistent with protocol, at 8:49 the deputy fire safety director in the South Tower told his counterpart in the North Tower that he would wait to hear from "the boss from the Fire Department or somebody" before ordering an evacuation. At about this time, an announcement over the public-address system in the South Tower stated that the incident had occurred in the building and advised tenants, generally that their building was safe and that they should remain on or return to their offices or floors. A statement from the deputy fire safety director informing tenants that the incident had occurred in the other building was consistent with protocol; the expanded advice did not correspond to any existing written protocol, and did not reflect any instruction known to have been given to the deputy fire safety director that day. We do not know the reason for the announcement, as both the deputy fire safety director believed to have made it and the director of fire safety for the WTC complex perished in the South Tower's collapse. Clearly, however, the prospect of another plane hitting the second building was beyond the contemplation of anyone giving advice. According to one of the first fire chiefs to arrive, such a scenario was unimaginable, "beyond our consciousness." As a result of the announcement, many civilians remained on their floors. Others reversed their evacuation and went back up.

Similar advice was given in person by security officials in both the ground-floor lobby—where a group of 20 that had descended by the elevators was personally instructed to go back upstairs—and in the upper sky lobby, where many waited for express elevators to take them down. Security officials who gave this advice were not part of the fire safety staff.

Several South Tower occupants called the Port Authority police desk in 5 WTC. Some were advised to stand by for further instructions; others were strongly advised to leave.

It is not known whether the order by the FDNY to evacuate the South Tower was received by the deputy fire safety director making announcements there. However, at approximately 9:02—less than a minute before the building was hit—an instruction over the South Towers public-address system advised civilians, generally, that they could begin an orderly evacuation if conditions warranted. Like the earlier advice to remain in place, it did not correspond to any prewritten emergency instruction.

FDNY Initial Response

Mobilization. The FDNY response began within five seconds of the crash. By 9:00, many senior FDNY leaders, including 7 of the 11 most highly ranked chiefs in the department, as well as the Commissioner and many of his deputies and assistants, had begun responding from headquarters in Brooklyn. While en route over the Brooklyn Bridge, the Chief of Department and the Chief of Operations had a clear view of the situation on the upper floors of the North Tower. They determined that because of the fire's magnitude and location near the top of the building, their mission would be primarily one of rescue. They called for a fifth alarm, which would bring additional engine and ladder companies, as well as for two more elite rescue units. The Chief of Department arrived at about 9:00; general FDNY Incident Command was transferred to his location on the West Side Highway. In all, 22 of the 32 senior chiefs and commissioners arrived at the WTC before 10:00.

As of 9:00, the units that were dispatched (including senior chiefs responding to headquarters) included approximately 235 firefighters. These units consisted of 21 engine companies, nine ladder companies, four of the departments elite rescue teams, the department's single Hazmat team, two of the city's elite squad companies, and support staff. In addition, at 8:53 nine Brooklyn units were staged on the Brooklyn side of the Brooklyn-Battery Tunnel to await possible dispatch orders.

Operations. A battalion chief and two ladder and two engine companies arrived at the North Tower at approximately 8:52. As they entered the lobby, they encountered badly burned civilians who had been caught in the path of the fireball. Floor-to-ceiling windows in the northwest corner of the West Street level of the lobby had been blown out; some large marble tiles had been dislodged from the walls; one entire elevator bank was destroyed by the fireball. Lights were functioning, however, and the air was clear of smoke.

As the highest-ranking officer on the scene, the battalion chief initially was the FDNY incident commander. Minutes later, the on-duty division chief for Lower Manhattan arrived and took over. Both chiefs immediately began speaking with the former fire safety director and other building personnel to learn whether building systems were working. They were advised that all 99 elevators in the North Tower appeared to be out, and there were no assurances that sprinklers or standpipes were working on upper floors. Chiefs also spoke with Port Authority police personnel and an OEM representative.

After conferring with the chiefs in the lobby, one engine and one Ladder Company began climbing stairwell C at about 8:57, with the goal of approaching the impact zone as scouting units and reporting back to the chiefs in the lobby. The radio channel they used was tactical 1. Following FDNY high-rise fire protocols, other units did not begin climbing immediately, as the chiefs worked to formulate a plan before sending them up. Units began mobilizing in the lobby, lining up and awaiting their marching orders.

Also by approximately 8:57, FDNY chiefs had asked both building personnel and a Port Authority police officer to evacuate the South Tower, because in their judgment the impact of the plane into the North Tower made the entire complex unsafe—not because of concerns about a possible second plane.

The FDNY chiefs in the increasingly crowded North Tower lobby were confronting critical choices with little to no information. They had ordered units up the stairs to report back on conditions, but did not know what the impact floors were; they did not know if any stairwells into the impact zone were clear; and they did not know whether water for firefighting would be available on the upper floors. They also did not know what the fire and impact zone looked like from the outside.

They did know that the explosion had been large enough to send down a fireball that blew out elevators and windows in the lobby and that conditions were so dire that some civilians on upper floors were jumping or falling from the building. They also knew from building personnel that some civilians were trapped in elevators and on specific floors. According to Division Chief for Lower Manhattan Peter Hayden, "We had a very strong sense we would lose firefighters and that we were in deep trouble, but we had estimates of 25,000 to 50,000 civilians, and we had to try to rescue them."

The chiefs concluded that this would be a rescue operation, not a firefighting operation. One of the chiefs present explained:

> We realized that, because of the impact of the plane, that there
> was some structural damage to the building, and most likely

that the fire suppression systems within the building were probably damaged and possibly inoperable....We knew that at the height of the day there were as many as 50,000 people in this building. We had a large volume of fire on the upper floors. Each floor was approximately an acre in size. Several floors of fire would have been beyond the fire-extinguishing capability of the forces that we had on hand. So we determined, very early on, that this was going to be strictly a rescue mission. We were going to vacate the building, get everybody out, and then we were going to get out.

The specifics of the mission were harder to determine, as they had almost no information about the situation 80 or more stories above them. They also received advice from senior FDNY chiefs that while the building might eventually suffer a partial collapse on upper floors, such structural failure was not imminent. No one anticipated the possibility of a total collapse.

Emergency medical services (EMS) personnel were directed to one of four triage areas being set up around the perimeter of the WTC. Some entered the lobby to respond to specific casualty reports. In addition, many ambulance paramedics from private hospitals were rushing to the WTC complex.

NYPD Initial Response

Numerous NYPD officers saw the plane strike the North Tower and immediately reported it to NYPD communications dispatchers.

At 8:58, while en route, the NYPD Chief of Department raised the NYPD's mobilization to level 4, thereby sending to the WTC approximately 22 lieutenants, 100 sergeants, and 800 police officers from all over the city. The Chief of Department arrived at Church and Vesey at 9:00.

At 9:01, the NYPD patrol mobilization point was moved to West and Vesey in order to handle the greater number of patrol officers dispatched in the higher-level mobilization. These officers would be stationed around the perimeter of the complex to direct the evacuation of civilians. Many were diverted on the way to the scene by intervening emergencies related to the attack.

At 8:50, the Aviation Unit of the NYPD dispatched two helicopters to the WTC to report on conditions and assess the feasibility of a rooftop landing or of special rescue operations. En route, the two helicopters communicated with air traffic controllers at the area's three major airports and informed them of the commercial airplane crash at the World Trade Center. The air traffic controllers had been unaware of the incident.

At 8:56, an NYPD ESU team asked to be picked up at the Wall Street heliport to initiate rooftop rescues. At 8:58, however, after assessing the North Tower roof, a helicopter pilot advised the ESU team that they could not land on the roof, because "it is too engulfed in flames and heavy smoke condition."

By 9:00, a third NYPD helicopter was responding to the WTC complex. NYPD helicopters and ESU officers remained on the scene throughout the morning, prepared to commence rescue operations on the roof if conditions improved. Both FDNY and NYPD protocols called for FDNY personnel to be placed in NYPD helicopters in the event of an attempted rooftop rescue at a high-rise fire. No FDNY personnel were placed in NYPD helicopters on September 11.

The 911 operators and FDNY dispatchers were not advised that rooftop rescues were not being undertaken. They thus were not able to communicate this fact to callers, some of whom spoke of attempting to climb to the roof.

Two on-duty NYPD officers were on the 20th floor of the North Tower at 8:46. They climbed to the 29th floor, urging civilians to evacuate, but did not locate a group of civilians trapped on the 22nd floor.

Just before 9:00, an ESU team began to walk from Church and Vesey to the North Tower lobby, with the goal of climbing toward and setting up a triage center on the upper floors for the severely injured. A second ESU team would follow them to assist in removing those individuals.

Numerous officers responded in order to help injured civilians and to urge those who could walk to vacate the area immediately. Putting themselves in danger of falling debris, several officers entered the plaza and successfully rescued at least one injured, nonambulatory civilian, and attempted to rescue others.

Also by about 9:00, transit officers began shutting down subway stations in the vicinity of the World Trade Center and evacuating civilians from those stations.

Around the city, the NYPD cleared major thoroughfares for emergency vehicles to access the WTC. The NYPD and PAPD coordinated the closing of bridges and tunnels into Manhattan. […]

Summary

In the 17-minute period between 8:46 and 9:03 A.M. on September 11, New York City and the Port Authority of New York and New Jersey had mobilized the largest rescue operation in the city's history. Well over a thousand first responders had been deployed, an evacuation had begun, and the critical decision that the fire could not be fought had been made.

Then the second plane hit.

From 9:03 until 9:59 A.M.

At 9:03:11, the hijacked United Airlines Flight 175 hit 2 WTC (the South Tower) from the south, crashing through the 77th to 85th floors. What had been the largest and most complicated rescue operation in city history instantly doubled in magnitude. The plane banked as it hit the building, leaving portions of the building undamaged on impact floors. As a consequence—and in contrast to the situation in the North Tower—one of the stairwells (A) initially remained passable from at least the 91st floor down, and likely from top to bottom.

Civilians, Fire Safety Personnel, and 911 Calls

South Tower. At the lower end of the impact, the 78th-floor sky lobby, hundreds had been waiting to evacuate when the plane hit. Many had attempted but failed to squeeze into packed express elevators. Upon impact, many were killed or severely injured; others were relatively unharmed. We know of at least one civilian who seized the initiative and shouted that anyone who could walk should walk to the stairs, and anyone who could help should help others in need of assistance. As a result, at least two small groups of civilians descended from that floor. Others remained on the floor to help the injured and move victims who were unable to walk to the stairwell to aid their rescue.

Still others remained alive in the impact zone above the 78th floor. Damage was extensive, and conditions were highly precarious. The only survivor known to have escaped from the heart of the impact zone described the 81st floor—where the wing of the plane had sliced through his office—as a "demolition" site in which everything was "broken up" and the smell of jet fuel was so strong that it was almost impossible to breathe. This person escaped by means of an unlikely rescue, aided by a civilian fire warden descending from a higher floor, who, critically, had been provided with a flashlight.

At least four people were able to descend stairwell A from the 81st floor or above. One left the 84th floor immediately after the building was hit. Even at that point, the stairway was dark, smoky, and difficult to navigate; glow strips on the stairs and handrails were a significant help. Several flights down, however, the evacuee became confused when he reached a smoke door that caused him to believe the stairway had ended. He was able to exit that stairwell and switch to another.

Many civilians in and above the impact zone ascended the stairs. One small group reversed its descent down stairwell A after being advised by another civilian that they were approaching a floor "in flames." The only known survivor has told us that their intention was to exit the stairwell in search of clearer air. At the 91st floor, joined by others from intervening floors, they perceived themselves to be trapped in the stairwell and began descending again. By this time, the stairwell was "pretty black," intensifying smoke caused many to pass out, and fire had ignited in the 82nd-floor transfer hallway.

Others ascended to attempt to reach the roof but were thwarted by locked doors. At approximately 9:30 a "lock release" order—which would unlock all areas in the complex controlled by the buildings' computerized security system, including doors leading to the roofs—was transmitted to the Security Command Center located on the 22nd floor of the North Tower. Damage to the software controlling the system, resulting from the impact of the plane, prevented this order from being executed.

Others, attempting to descend, were frustrated by jammed or locked doors in stairwells or confused by the structure of the stairwell deviations. By the lower 70s, however, stairwells A and B were well-lit, and conditions were generally normal.

Some civilians remained on affected floors, and at least one ascended from a lower point into the impact zone, to help evacuate colleagues or assist the injured.

Within 15 minutes after the impact, debilitating smoke had reached at least one location on the 100th floor, and severe smoke conditions were reported throughout floors in the 90s and 100s over the course of the following half hour. By 9:30, a number of civilians who had failed to reach the roof remained on the 105th floor, likely unable to descend because of intensifying smoke in the stairwell. There were reports of tremendous smoke on that floor, but at least one area remained less affected until shortly before the building collapsed. There were several areas between the impact zone and the uppermost floors where conditions were better. At least a hundred people remained alive on the 88th and 89th floors, in some cases calling 911 for direction. [...]

By 9:35, the West Street lobby level of the South Tower was becoming overwhelmed by injured people who had descended to the lobby but were having difficulty going on. Those who could continue were directed to exit north or east through the concourse and then out of the WTC complex.

By 9:59, at least one person had descended from as high as the 91st floor of that tower, and stairwell A was reported to have been almost empty. Stairwell B was also reported to have contained only a handful of descending civilians at an earlier point in the morning. But just before the tower collapsed, a team of NYPD ESU officers encountered a stream of civilians descending an unidentified stairwell in the 20s. These civilians may have been descending from at or above the impact zone.

North Tower. In the North Tower, civilians continued their evacuation. On the 91st floor, the highest floor with stairway access, all civilians but one was uninjured and able to descend. While some complained of smoke, heat, fumes, and crowding in the stairwells, conditions were otherwise fairly normal on floors below the impact. At least one stairwell was reported to have been "clear and bright" from the upper 80s down.

Those who called 911 from floors below the impact were generally advised to remain in place. One group trapped on the 83rd floor pleaded repeatedly to know whether the fire was above or below them, specifically asking if 911 operators had any information from the outside or from the news. The callers were transferred back and forth several times and advised to stay put. Evidence suggests that these callers died.

At 8:59, the Port Authority police desk at Newark Airport told a third party that a group of Port Authority civilian employees on the 64th floor should evacuate. (The third party was not at the WTC, but had been in phone contact with the group on the 64th floor.) At 9:10, in response to an inquiry from the employees themselves, the Port Authority police desk in Jersey City confirmed that employees on the 64th floor should "be careful, stay near the stairwells, and wait for the police to come up." When the third party inquired again at 9:31, the police desk at Newark Airport advised that they "absolutely" evacuate. The third party informed the police desk that the employees had previously received contrary advice from the FDNY, which could only have come via 911. These workers were not trapped, yet unlike most occupants on the upper floors, they had chosen not to descend immediately after impact. They eventually began to descend the stairs, but most of them died in the collapse of the North Tower.

All civilians who reached the lobby were directed by NYPD and PAPD officers into the concourse, where other police officers guided them to exit the concourse and complex to the north and east so that they might avoid falling debris and victims.

By 9:55, only a few civilians were descending above the 25th floor in stairwell B; these primarily were injured, handicapped, elderly, or severely overweight civilians, in some cases being assisted by other civilians.

By 9:59, tenants from the 91st floor had already descended the stairs and exited the concourse. However, a number of civilians remained in at least stairwell C, approaching lower floors. Other evacuees were killed earlier by debris falling on the street. [...]

FDNY North Tower Operations. Command and control decisions were affected by the lack of knowledge of what was happening 30, 60, 90, and 100 floors above. According to one of the chiefs in the lobby, "One of the most critical things in a major operation like this is to have information. We didn't have a lot of information coming in. We didn't receive any reports of what was seen from the [NYPD] helicopters. It was impossible to know how much damage was done on the upper floors, whether the stairwells were intact or not." According to another chief present, "People watching on TV certainly had more knowledge of what was happening a hundred floors above us than we did in the lobby.... [W]ithout critical information coming in... It's very difficult to make informed, critical decisions [.]"

As a result, chiefs in the lobby disagreed over whether anyone at or above the impact zone possibly could be rescued, or whether there should be even limited firefighting for the purpose of cutting exit routes through fire zones.

Many units were simply instructed to ascend toward the impact zone and report back to the lobby via radio. Some units were directed to assist specific groups of individuals trapped in elevators or in offices well below the impact zone. One FDNY company successfully rescued some civilians who were trapped on the 22nd floor as a result of damage caused by the initial fireball.

An attempt was made to track responding units' assignments on a magnetic board, but the number of units and individual firefighters arriving in the lobby made this an overwhelming task. As the fire companies were not advised to the contrary, they followed protocol and kept their radios on tactical channel 1, which would be monitored by the chiefs in the lobby. Those battalion chiefs who would climb would operate on a separate command channel, which also would be monitored by the chiefs in the lobby.

Fire companies began to ascend stairwell B at approximately 9:07, laden with about 100 pounds of heavy protective clothing, self-contained breathing apparatuses, and other equipment (including hoses for engine companies and heavy tools for ladder companies).

Firefighters found the stairways they entered intact, lit, and clear of smoke. Unbeknownst to the lobby command post, one battalion chief in the North Tower found a working elevator, which he took to the 16th floor before beginning to climb.

In ascending stairwell B, firefighters were passing a steady and heavy stream of descending civilians. Firemen were impressed with the composure and total lack of panic shown by almost all civilians. Many civilians were in awe of the firefighters and found their mere presence to be calming.

Firefighters periodically stopped on particular floors and searched to ensure that no civilians were still on it. In a few instances healthy civilians were found on floors, either because they still were collecting personal items or for no apparent reason; they were told to evacuate immediately. Firefighters deputized healthy civilians to be in charge of others who were struggling or injured.

Climbing up the stairs with heavy protective clothing and equipment was hard work even for physically fit firefighters. As firefighters began to suffer varying levels of fatigue, some became separated from others in their unit.

At 9:32, a senior chief radioed all units in the North Tower to return to the lobby, either because of a false report of a third plane approaching or because of his judgment about the deteriorating condition of the building. Once the rumor of the third plane was debunked, other chiefs continued operations, and there is no evidence that any units actually returned to the lobby. At the same time, a chief in the lobby was asked to consider the possibility of a rooftop rescue but was unable to reach FDNY dispatch by radio or phone. Out on West Street, however, the FDNY Chief of Department had already dismissed any rooftop rescue as impossible.

As units climbed higher, their ability to communicate with chiefs on tactical 1 became more limited and sporadic, both because of the limited effectiveness of FDNY radios in high-rises and because so many units on tactical 1 were trying to communicate at once. When attempting to reach a particular unit, chiefs in the lobby often heard nothing in response.

Just prior to 10:00, in the North Tower one engine company had climbed to the 54th floor, at least two other companies of firefighters had reached the sky lobby on the 44th floor, and numerous units were located between the 5th and 37th floors.

FDNY South Tower and Marriott Hotel Operations. [.....]

The first FDNY fatality of the day occurred at approximately 9:30, when a civilian landed on and killed a fireman near the intersection of West and Liberty streets. [...]

Between 9:45 and 9:58, the ascending battalion chief continued to lead FDNY operations on the upper floors of the South Tower. At 9:50, an FDNY ladder company encountered numerous seriously injured civilians on the 70th floor. With the assistance of a security guard, at 9:53 a group of civilians trapped in an elevator on the 78th-floor sky lobby were found by an FDNY company. They were freed from the elevator at 9:58. By that time the battalion chief had reached the 78th floor on stairwell A; he reported that it looked open to the 79th floor, well into the impact zone. He also reported numerous civilian fatalities in the area. [...]

NYPD Response

Immediately after the second plane hit, the Chief of Department of the NYPD ordered a second Level 4 mobilization, bringing the total number of NYPD officers responding to close to 2,000. [']

The first NYPD ESU team entered the West Street–level lobby of the North Tower and prepared to begin climbing at about 9:15 A.M. They attempted to check in with the FDNY chiefs present, but were rebuffed. OEM personnel did not intervene. The ESU team began to climb the stairs. Shortly thereafter, a second NYPD ESU team entered the South Tower. The OEM field responder present ensured that they check in with the FDNY chief in charge of the lobby, and it was agreed that the ESU team would ascend and support FDNY personnel.

A third ESU team subsequently entered the North Tower at its elevated mezzanine lobby level and made no effort to check in with the FDNY command post. A fourth ESU team entered the South Tower. By 9:59, a fifth ESU team was next to 6 WTC and preparing to enter the North Tower.

By approximately 9:50, the lead ESU team had reached the 31st floor, observing that there appeared to be no more civilians still descending. This ESU team encountered a large group of firefighters and administered oxygen to some of them who were exhausted.

At about 9:56, the officer running the ESU command post on Church and Vesey streets had a final radio communication with one of the ESU teams in the South Tower. The team then stated that it was ascending via stairs, was somewhere in the 20s, and was making slow progress because of the numerous descending civilians crowding the stairwell.

Three plainclothes NYPD officers without radios or protective gear had begun ascending either stairwell A or C of the North Tower. They began checking every other floor above the 12th for civilians. Only occasionally did they find any, and in those few cases they ordered the civilians to evacuate immediately. While checking floors, they used office phones to call their superiors. In one phone call an NYPD chief instructed them to leave the North Tower, but they refused to do so. As they climbed higher, they encountered increasing smoke and heat. Shortly before 10:00 they arrived on the 54th floor.

Throughout this period (9:03 to 9:59), a group of NYPD and Port Authority police officers, as well as two Secret Service agents, continued to assist civilians leaving the North Tower. They were positioned around the mezzanine lobby level of the North Tower, directing civilians leaving stairwells A and C to evacuate down an escalator to the concourse. The officers instructed those civilians who seemed composed to evacuate the complex calmly but rapidly. Other civilians exiting the stairs who were either injured or exhausted collapsed at the foot of these stairs; officers then assisted them out of the building.

When civilians reached the concourse, another NYPD officer stationed at the bottom of the escalator directed them to exit through the concourse to the north and east and then out of the WTC complex. This exit route ensured that civilians would not be endangered by falling debris and people on West Street, on the plaza between the towers, and on Liberty Street.

Some officers positioned themselves at the top of a flight of stairs by 5 WTC that led down into the concourse, going into the concourse when necessary to evacuate injured or disoriented civilians. Numerous other NYPD officers were stationed throughout the concourse, assisting burned, injured, and disoriented civilians, as well as directing all civilians to exit to the north and east. NYPD officers were also in the South Tower lobby to assist in civilian evacuation. NYPD officers stationed on Vesey Street between West Street and Church Street urged civilians not to remain in the area and instead to keep walking north.

At 9:06, the NYPD Chief of Department instructed that no units were to land on the roof of either tower. At about 9:30, one of the helicopters present advised that a rooftop evacuation still would not be possible. One NYPD helicopter pilot believed one portion of the North Tower roof to be free enough of smoke that a hoist could be lowered in order to rescue people, but there was no one on the roof. This pilot's helicopter never attempted to hover directly over the tower. Another helicopter did attempt to do so, and its pilot stated that the severity of the heat from the jet fuel—laden fire in the North Tower would have made it impossible to hover low enough for a rescue, because the high temperature would have destabilized the helicopter.

At 9:51, an aviation unit warned units of large pieces of debris hanging from the building. Prior to 9:59, no NYPD helicopter pilot predicted that either tower would collapse. [...]

Summary

The emergency response effort escalated with the crash of United 175 into the South Tower. With that escalation, communications as well as command and control became increasingly critical and increasingly difficult. First responders assisted thousands of civilians in evacuating the towers, even as incident commanders from responding agencies lacked knowledge of what other agencies and, in some cases, their own responders were doing.

From 9:59 until 10:28 A.M.

At 9:58:59, the South Tower collapsed in ten seconds, killing all civilians and emergency personnel inside, as well a number of individuals—both first responders and civilians—in the concourse, in the Marriott, and on neighboring streets. The building collapsed into itself, causing a ferocious windstorm and creating a massive debris cloud. The Marriott hotel suffered significant damage as a result of the collapse of the South Tower.

Civilian Response in the North Tower

The 911 calls placed from most locations in the North Tower grew increasingly desperate as time went on. As late as 10:28, people remained alive in some locations, including on the 92nd and 79th floors. Below the impact zone, it is likely that most civilians who were physically and emotionally capable of descending had exited the tower. The civilians who were nearing the bottom of stairwell C were assisted out of the building by NYPD, FDNY, and PAPD personnel. Others, who experienced difficulty evacuating, were being helped by first responders on lower floors.

FDNY Response

Immediate Impact of the Collapse of the South Tower. The FDNY overall command post and posts in the North Tower lobby, the Marriott lobby, and the staging area on West Street south of Liberty all ceased to operate upon the collapse of the South Tower, as did EMS staging areas, because of their proximity to the building.

Those who had been in the North Tower lobby had no way of knowing that the South Tower had suffered a complete collapse. Chiefs who had fled from the overall command post on the west side of West Street took shelter in the underground parking garage at 2 World Financial Center and were not available to influence FDNY operations for the next ten minutes or so.

When the South Tower collapsed, firefighters on upper floors of the North Tower heard a violent roar, and many were knocked off their feet; they saw debris coming up the stairs and observed that the power was lost and emergency lights activated. Nevertheless, those firefighters not standing near windows facing south had no way of knowing that the South Tower had collapsed; many surmised that a bomb had exploded, or that the North Tower had suffered a partial collapse on its upper floors.

We do not know whether the repeater channel continued to function after 9:59. [...]

FDNY Personnel above the Ground Floors of the North Tower. Within minutes, some firefighters began to hear evacuation orders over tactical 1. At least one chief also gave the evacuation instruction on the command channel used only by chiefs in the North Tower, which was much less crowded.

At least two battalion chiefs on upper floors of the North Tower—one on the 23rd floor and one on the 35th floor—heard the evacuation instruction on the command channel and repeated it to everyone they came across. The chief on the 23rd floor apparently aggressively took charge to ensure that all firefighters on the floors in the immediate area were evacuating. The chief on the 35th floor also heard a separate radio communication stating that the South Tower had collapsed (which the chief on the 23rd floor may have heard as well). He subsequently acted with a sense of urgency, and some firefighters heard the evacuation order for the first time when he repeated it on tactical 1. This chief also had a bullhorn and traveled to each of the stairwells and shouted the evacuation order: "All FDNY, get the fuck out!" As a result of his efforts, many firefighters who had not been in the process of evacuating began to do so.

Other firefighters did not receive the evacuation transmissions, for one of four reasons: First, some FDNY radios did not pick up the transmission because of the difficulties of radio communications in high-rises. Second, the numbers trying to use tactical 1 after the South Tower collapsed may have drowned out some evacuation instructions. According to one FDNY lieutenant who was on the 31st floor of the North Tower at the time, "[Tactical] channel 1 just might have been so bogged down that it may have been impossible to get that order through." Third, some firefighters in the North Tower were off-duty and did not have radios. Fourth, some firefighters in the North Tower had been dispatched to the South Tower and likely were on the different tactical channel assigned to that tower.

FDNY personnel in the North Tower who received the evacuation orders did not respond uniformly. Some units—including one whose officer knew that the South Tower had collapsed—either delayed or stopped their evacuation in order to assist nonambulatory civilians. Some units whose members had become separated during the climb attempted to regroup so they could descend together. Some units began to evacuate but, according to eyewitnesses, did not hurry. At least several firefighters who survived believed that they and others would have evacuated more urgently had they known of the South Tower's complete collapse. Other firefighters continued to sit and rest on floors while other companies descended past them and reminded them that they were supposed to evacuate. Some firefighters were determined not to leave the building while other FDNY personnel remained inside and, in one case, convinced others to remain with them. In another case, firefighters had successfully descended to the lobby, where another firefighter then persuaded them to rescind in order to look for specific FDNY personnel.

Other FDNY personnel did not hear the evacuation order on their radio but were advised orally to leave the building by other firefighters and police who were themselves evacuating.

By 10:24, approximately five FDNY companies reached the bottom of stairwell B and entered the North Tower lobby. They stood in the lobby for more than a minute, not certain what to do, as no chiefs were present. Finally, one firefighter—who had earlier seen from a window that the South Tower had collapsed—urged that they all leave, as this tower could fall as well. The units then proceeded to exit onto West Street. While they were doing so, the North Tower began its pancake collapse, killing some of these men.

Other FDNY Personnel. [...]

After the South Tower collapsed, some firefighters on the streets neighboring the North Tower remained where they were or came closer to the North Tower. Some of these firefighters did not know that the South Tower had collapsed, but many chose despite that knowledge to remain in an attempt to save additional lives. According to one such firefighter, a chief who was preparing to mount a search–and–rescue mission in the Marriott, "I would never think of myself as a leader of men if I had headed north on West Street after [the] South Tower collapsed." Just outside the North Tower on West Street one firefighter was directing others exiting the building, telling them when no jumpers were coming down and it was safe to run out. A senior chief had grabbed an NYPD bullhorn and was urging firefighters exiting onto West Street to continue running north, well away from the WTC. Three of the most senior and respected members of the FDNY were involved in attempting to rescue civilians and firefighters from the Marriott.

NYPD Response

A member of the NYPD Aviation Unit radioed that the South Tower had collapsed immediately after it happened, and further advised that all people in the WTC complex and nearby areas should be evacuated. At 10:04, NYPD aviation reported that the top 15 stories of the North Tower "were glowing red" and that they might collapse. At 10:08, a helicopter pilot warned that he did not believe the North Tower would last much longer. [...]

The ESU team on the 31st floor conferred with the FDNY personnel there to ensure that they, too, knew that they had to evacuate, then proceeded down stairwell B. During the descent, they reported seeing many firefighters who were resting and did not seem to be in the process of evacuating. They further reported advising these firefighters to evacuate, but said that at times they were not acknowledged. In the opinion of one of the ESU officers, some of these firefighters essentially refused to take orders from cops. At least one firefighter who was in the North Tower has supported that assessment, stating that he was not going to take an evacuation instruction from a cop that morning. However, another firefighter reports that ESU officers ran past him without advising him to evacuate.

The ESU team on the 11th floor began descending stairwell C after receiving the evacuation order. Once near the mezzanine level—where stairwell C ended—this team spread out in chain formation, stretching from several floors down to the mezzanine itself. They used their flashlights to provide a path of beacons through the darkness and debris for civilians climbing down the stairs. Eventually, when no one else appeared to be descending, the ESU team exited the North Tower and ran one at a time to 6 WTC, dodging those who still were jumping from the upper floors of the North Tower by acting as spotters for each other. They remained in the area, conducting additional searches for civilians; all but two of them died.

After surviving the South Tower's collapse, the ESU team that had been preparing to enter the North Tower spread into chain formation and created a path for civilians (who had exited from the

North Tower mezzanine) to evacuate the WTC complex by descending the stairs on the north side of 5 and 6 WTC, which led down to Vesey Street. They remained at this post until the North Tower collapsed, yet all survived.

The three plainclothes NYPD officers who had made it up to the 54th floor of the North Tower felt the building shake violently at 9:59 as the South Tower collapsed (though they did not know the cause). Immediately thereafter, they were joined by three firefighters from an FDNY engine company. One of the firefighters apparently heard an evacuation order on his radio, but responded in a return radio communication, "We're not fucking coming out!" However, the firefighters urged the police officers to descend because they lacked the protective gear and equipment needed to handle the increasing smoke and heat. The police officers reluctantly began descending, checking that the lower floors were clear of civilians. They proceeded down stairwell B, poking their heads into every floor and briefly looking for civilians.

Other NYPD officers helping evacuees on the mezzanine level of the North Tower were enveloped in the debris cloud that resulted from the South Tower's collapse. They struggled to regroup in the darkness and to evacuate both themselves and civilians they encountered. At least one of them died in the collapse of the North Tower. At least one NYPD officer from this area managed to evacuate out toward 5 WTC, where he teamed up with a Port Authority police officer and acted as a spotter in advising the civilians who were still exiting when they could safely run from 1 WTC to 5 WTC and avoid being struck by people and debris falling from the upper floors.

At the time of the collapse of the South Tower, there were numerous NYPD officers in the concourse, some of whom are believed to have died there. Those who survived struggled to evacuate themselves in darkness, assisting civilians as they exited the concourse in all directions. [...]

After 10:28 A.M.

The North Tower collapsed at 10:28:25 A.M., killing all civilians alive on upper floors, an undetermined number below, and scores of first responders. The FDNY Chief of Department, the Port Authority Police Department Superintendent, and many of their senior staff were killed. Incredibly, twelve firefighters, one PAPD officer, and three civilians who were descending stairwell B of the North Tower survived its collapse.

On September 11, the nation suffered the largest loss of life—2,973—on its soil as a result of hostile attack in its history. The FDNY suffered 343 fatalities—the largest loss of life of any emergency response agency in history. The PAPD suffered 37 fatalities—the largest loss of life of any police force in history. The NYPD suffered 23 fatalities—the second largest loss of life of any police force in history, exceeded only by the number of PAPD officers lost the same day.

Mayor Giuliani, along with the Police and Fire commissioners and the OEM director, moved quickly north and established an emergency operations command post at the Police Academy. Over the coming hours, weeks, and months, thousands of civilians and city, state, and federal employees devoted themselves around the clock to putting New York City back on its feet.

[TCR]

President George W. Bush, Speech, "Weapons of Mass Destruction"

March 17, 2003

In this speech from the White House, George W. Bush (born 1946), the 43rd President of the United States, justified his intention to attack Iraq by claiming evidence of "weapons of mass destruction." There was no evidence, but a national propaganda campaign suggesting links between Saddam Hussein, Iraq's leader, and Al-Qaeda, Osama bin Laden's terrorist group, helped the president receive overwhelming support in Congress and from the American public to launch the Iraq War, which began in the spring of 2003 and ended in 2011.

MY FELLOW CITIZENS, events in Iraq have now reached the final days of decision. For more than a decade, the United States and other nations have pursued patient and honorable efforts to disarm the Iraqi regime without war. That regime pledged to reveal and destroy all its weapons of mass destruction as a condition for ending the Persian Gulf War in 1991.

Since then, the world has engaged in twelve years of diplomacy. We have passed more than a dozen resolutions in the United Nations Security Council. We have sent hundreds of weapons inspectors to oversee the disarmament of Iraq. Our good faith has not been returned.

The Iraqi regime has used diplomacy as a ploy to gain time and advantage. It has uniformly defied Security Council resolutions demanding full disarmament. Over the years, U.N. weapon inspectors have been threatened by Iraqi officials, electronically bugged, and systematically deceived. Peaceful efforts to disarm the Iraqi regime have failed again and again—because we are not dealing with peaceful men.

Intelligence gathered by this and other governments leaves no doubt that the Iraq regime continues to possess and conceal some of the most lethal weapons ever devised. This regime has already used weapons of mass destruction against Iraq's neighbors and against Iraq's people.

The regime has a history of reckless aggression in the Middle East. It has a deep hatred of America and our friends. And it has aided, trained and harbored terrorists, including operatives of al Qaeda.

The danger is clear: using chemical, biological or, one day, nuclear weapons, obtained with the help of Iraq, the terrorists could fulfill their stated ambitions and kill thousands or hundreds of thousands of innocent people in our country, or any other.

The United States and other nations did nothing to deserve or invite this threat. But we will do everything to defeat it. Instead of drifting along toward tragedy, we will set a course toward safety. Before the day of horror can come, before it is too late to act, this danger will be removed.

The United States of America has the sovereign authority to use force in assuring its own national security. That duty falls to me, as Commander-in-Chief, by the oath I have sworn, by the oath I will keep.

Recognizing the threat to our country, the United States Congress voted overwhelmingly last year to support the use of force against Iraq. America tried to work with the United Nations to address this threat because we wanted to resolve the issue peacefully. We believe in the mission of the United Nations. One reason the UN was founded after the second world war was to confront aggressive dictators, actively and early, before they can attack the innocent and destroy the peace.

In the case of Iraq, the Security Council did act, in the early 1990s. Under Resolutions 678 and 687—both still in effect—the United States and our allies are authorized to use force in ridding Iraq of weapons of mass destruction. This is not a question of authority, it is a question of will.

Last September, I went to the U.N. General Assembly and urged the nations of the world to unite and bring an end to this danger.

On November 8, the Security Council unanimously passed Resolution 1441, finding Iraq in material breach of its obligations, and vowing serious consequences if Iraq did not fully and immediately disarm.

Today, no nation can possibly claim that Iraq has disarmed. And it will not disarm so long as Saddam Hussein holds power. For the last four-and-a-half months, the United States and our allies have worked within the Security Council to enforce that Council's long-standing demands. Yet, some permanent members of the Security Council have publicly announced they will veto any resolution that compels the disarmament of Iraq. These governments share our assessment of the danger, but not our resolve to meet it. Many nations, however, do have the resolve and fortitude to act against this threat to peace, and a broad coalition is now gathering to enforce the just demands of the world. The United Nations Security Council has not lived up to its responsibilities, so we will rise to ours.

In recent days, some governments in the Middle East have been doing their part. They have delivered public and private messages urging the dictator to leave Iraq, so that disarmament can proceed peacefully. He has thus far refused. All the decades of deceit and cruelty have now reached an end. Saddam Hussein and his sons must leave Iraq within 48 hours. Their refusal to do so will result in military conflict, commenced at a time of our choosing. For their own safety, all foreign nationals—including journalists and inspectors—should leave Iraq immediately.

Many Iraqis can hear me tonight in a translated radio broadcast, and I have a message for them. If we must begin a military campaign, it will be directed against the lawless men who rule your country and not against you. As our coalition takes away their power, we will deliver the food and medicine you need. We will tear down the apparatus of terror and we will help you to build a new Iraq that is prosperous and free. In a free Iraq, there will be no more wars of aggression against your neighbors, no more poison factories, no more executions of dissidents, no more torture chambers and rape rooms. The tyrant will soon be gone. The day of your liberation is near.

It is too late for Saddam Hussein to remain in power. It is not too late for the Iraqi military to act with honor and protect your country by permitting the peaceful entry of coalition forces to eliminate weapons of mass destruction. Our forces will give Iraqi military units clear instructions on actions they can take to avoid being attacked and destroyed. I urge every member of the Iraqi military and intelligence services, if war comes, do not fight for a dying regime that is not worth your own life.

And all Iraqi military and civilian personnel should listen carefully to this warning. In any conflict, your fate will depend on your action. Do not destroy oil wells, a source of wealth that belongs to the Iraqi people. Do not obey any command to use weapons of mass destruction against anyone, including the Iraqi people. War crimes will be prosecuted. War criminals will be punished. And it will be no defense to say, "I was just following orders."

Should Saddam Hussein choose confrontation, the American people can know that every measure has been taken to avoid war, and every measure will be taken to win it. Americans understand the costs of conflict because we have paid them in the past. War has no certainty, except the certainty of sacrifice.

Yet, the only way to reduce the harm and duration of war is to apply the full force and might of our military, and we are prepared to do so. If Saddam Hussein attempts to cling to power, he will remain a deadly foe until the end. In desperation, he and terrorists groups might try to conduct terrorist operations against the American people and our friends. These attacks are not inevitable. They are, however, possible. And this very fact underscores the reason we cannot live under the threat of blackmail. The terrorist threat to America and the world will be diminished the moment that Saddam Hussein is disarmed.

Our government is on heightened watch against these dangers. Just as we are preparing to ensure victory in Iraq, we are taking further actions to protect our homeland. In recent days, American authorities have expelled from the country certain individuals with ties to Iraqi intelligence services. Among other measures, I have directed additional security of our airports, and increased Coast Guard patrols of major seaports. The Department of Homeland Security is working closely with the nation's governors to increase armed security at critical facilities across America.

Should enemies strike our country, they would be attempting to shift our attention with panic and weaken our morale with fear. In this, they would fail. No act of theirs can alter the course or shake the resolve of this country. We are a peaceful people—yet we're not a fragile people, and we will not be intimidated by thugs and killers. If our enemies dare to strike us, they and all who have aided them, will face fearful consequences.

We are now acting because the risks of inaction would be far greater. In one year, or five years, the power of Iraq to inflict harm on all free nations would be multiplied many times over. With these capabilities, Saddam Hussein and his terrorist allies could choose the moment of deadly conflict when they are strongest. We choose to meet that threat now, where it arises, before it can appear suddenly in our skies and cities.

The cause of peace requires all free nations to recognize new and undeniable realities. In the 20th century, some chose to appease murderous dictators, whose threats were allowed to grow into genocide and global war. In this century, when evil men plot chemical, biological and nuclear terror, a policy of appeasement could bring destruction of a kind never before seen on this earth.

Terrorists and terror states do not reveal these threats with fair notice, in formal declarations—and responding to such enemies only after they have struck first is not self-defense, it is suicide. The security of the world requires disarming Saddam Hussein now.

As we enforce the just demands of the world, we will also honor the deepest commitments of our country. Unlike Saddam Hussein, we believe the Iraqi people are deserving and capable of human liberty. And when the dictator has departed, they can set an example to all the Middle East of a vital and peaceful and self-governing nation.

The United States, with other countries, will work to advance liberty and peace in that region. Our goal will not be achieved overnight, but it can come over time. The power and appeal of human liberty is felt in every life and every land. And the greatest power of freedom is to overcome hatred and violence, and turn the creative gifts of men and women to the pursuits of peace.

That is the future we choose. Free nations have a duty to defend our people by uniting against the violent. And tonight, as we have done before, America and our allies accept that responsibility.

Good night, and may God continue to bless America.

[TG]

State Senator Barack Obama, Keynote Address, Democratic National Convention

July 27, 2004

At the time of this speech, which brought him to national prominence, Barack Hussein Obama (born 1961) was a state senator from Chicago. Here in Boston he told his own story in his testimonial for the Democratic Party nominee for President, John Kerry. Four years later, Obama himself would be elected President.

[...] ON BEHALF OF the great state of Illinois, crossroads of a nation, land of Lincoln, let me express my deepest gratitude for the privilege of addressing this convention. Tonight is a particular honor for me because, let's face it, my presence on this stage is pretty unlikely. My father was a foreign student, born and raised in a small village in Kenya. He grew up herding goats, went to school in a tin-roof shack. His father, my grandfather, was a cook, a domestic servant to the British.

But my grandfather had larger dreams for his son. Through hard work and perseverance my father got a scholarship to study in a magical place; America, that shone as a beacon of freedom and opportunity to so many who had come before. While studying here, my father met my mother. She was born in a town on the other side of the world, in Kansas. Her father worked on oil rigs and farms through most of the Depression. The day after Pearl Harbor my grandfather signed up for duty, joined Patton's army, marched across Europe. Back home, my grandmother raised a baby and went to work on a bomber assembly line. After the war, they studied on the GI Bill, bought a house through FHA, and later moved west—all the way to Hawaii—in search of opportunity.

And they, too, had big dreams for their daughter, a common dream, born of two continents. My parents shared not only an improbable love; they shared an abiding faith in the possibilities of this nation. They would give me an African name, Barack, or "blessed," believing that in a tolerant America your name is no barrier to success. They imagined me going to the best schools in the land, even though they weren't rich, because in a generous America you don't have to be rich to achieve your potential. They are both passed away now. And yet, I know that on this night, they look down on me with great pride.

They stand here and I stand here today, grateful for the diversity of my heritage, aware that my parents' dreams live on in my two precious daughters. I stand here knowing that my story is part of the larger American story, that I owe a debt to all of those who came before me, and that in no other country on earth is my story even possible. Tonight, we gather to affirm the greatness of our nation, not because of the height of our skyscrapers, or the power of our military, or the size of our economy. Our pride is based on a very simple premise, summed up in a declaration made over two hundred years ago, "We hold these truths to be self-evident, that all men are created equal. That they are endowed by their Creator with certain inalienable rights. That among these are life, liberty and the pursuit of happiness."

That is the true genius of America, a faith in the simple dreams, an insistence on small miracles. That we can tuck in our children at night and know that they are fed and clothed and safe from harm. That we can say what we think, write what we think, without hearing a sudden knock on the door. That we can have an idea and start our own business without paying a bribe. That we can participate in the political process without fear of retribution, and that our votes will be counted—at least most of the time.

This year, in this election, we are called to reaffirm our values and our commitments, to hold them against a hard reality and see how we are measuring up, to the legacy of our forbearers, and the promise of future generations. And fellow Americans—Democrats, Republicans, and Independents—I say to you tonight: we have more work to do. More work to do for the workers I met in

Galesburg, Illinois, who are losing their union jobs at the Maytag plant that's moving to Mexico, and now are having to compete with their own children for jobs that pay seven bucks an hour. More to do for the father that I met who was losing his job and choking back the tears, wondering how he would pay $4,500 a month for the drugs his son needs without the health benefits that he counted on. More to do for the young woman in East St. Louis, and thousands more like her, who has the grades, has the drive, has the will, but doesn't have the money to go to college.

Now don't get me wrong. The people I meet in small towns and big cities, in diners and office parks, they don't expect government to solve all their problems. They know they have to work hard to get ahead and they want to. Go into the collar counties around Chicago, and people will tell you they don't want their tax money wasted by a welfare agency or by the Pentagon. Go into any inner city neighborhood, and folks will tell you that government alone can't teach our kids to learn. They know that parents have to teach, that children can't achieve unless we raise their expectations and turn off the television sets and eradicate the slander that says a black youth with a book is acting white. They know those things. People don't expect government to solve all their problems. But they sense, deep in their bones, that with just a slight change in priorities, we can make sure that every child in America has a decent shot at life, and that the doors of opportunity remain open to all. They know we can do better. And they want that choice.

In this election, we offer that choice. Our party has chosen a man to lead us who embodies the best this country has to offer, and that man is John Kerry. John Kerry understands the ideals of community, faith, and service, because they've defined his life. From his heroic service to [in] Vietnam to his years as prosecutor and lieutenant governor, through two decades in the United States Senate, he has devoted himself to this country. Again and again, we've seen him make tough choices when easier ones were available. His values and his record affirm what is best in us.

John Kerry believes in an America where hard work is rewarded. So instead of offering tax breaks to companies shipping jobs overseas, he offers them to companies creating jobs here at home. John Kerry believes in an America where all Americans can afford the same health coverage our politicians in Washington have for themselves. John Kerry believes in energy independence, so we aren't held hostage to the profits of oil companies or the sabotage of foreign oil fields. John Kerry believes in the constitutional freedoms that have made our country the envy of the world, and he will never sacrifice our basic liberties nor use faith as a wedge to divide us. And John Kerry believes that in a dangerous world, war must be an option sometimes, but it should never be the first option.

You know a while back I met a young man named Shamus in a VFW Hall in East Moline, Illinois. He was a good-looking kid, six-two, six-three, clear eyed, with an easy smile. He told me he'd joined the Marines and was heading to Iraq the following week. And as I listened to him explain why he'd enlisted, the absolute faith he had in our country and its leaders, his devotion to duty and service, I thought this young man was all any of us might ever hope for in a child. But then I asked myself: Are we serving Shamus as well as he's serving us? I thought of the 900 men and women, sons and daughters, husbands and wives, friends and neighbors, who won't be returning to their own hometowns. I thought of families I had met who were struggling to get by without a loved one's full income, or whose loved ones had returned with a limb missing or nerves shattered, but still lacked long-term health benefits because they were reservists. When we send our young men and women into harm's way, we have a solemn obligation not to fudge the numbers or shade the truth about why they're going, to care for their families while they're gone, to tend to the soldiers upon their return, and to never ever go to war without enough troops to win the war, secure the peace, and earn the respect of the world.

Now let me be clear. We have real enemies in the world. These enemies must be found. They must be pursued and they must be defeated. John Kerry knows this. And just as Lieutenant Kerry did not hesitate to risk his life to protect the men who served with him in Vietnam, President Kerry will not hesitate one moment to use our military might to keep America safe and secure. John Kerry believes in America. And he knows that it's not enough for just some of us to prosper. For alongside our famous individualism, there's another ingredient in the American saga.

A belief that we're all connected as one people. If there's a child on the south side of Chicago who can't read, that matters to me, even if it's not my child. If there's a senior citizen somewhere who can't pay for their prescription drugs and having to choose between medicine and the rent, that makes my life poorer, even if it's not my grandparent. If there's an Arab American family being rounded up without benefit of an attorney or due process, that threatens my civil liberties. It is that fundamental belief—I am my brother's keeper, I am my sister's keeper—that makes this country work. It's what allows us to pursue our individual dreams, and yet still come together as one American family. "E pluribus unum." Out of many, one.

Now even as we speak, there are those who are preparing to divide us, the spin masters, the negative ad peddlers who embrace the politics of anything goes. Well, I say to them tonight, there is not a liberal America and a conservative America—there is the United States of America. There is not a black America and white America and Latino America and Asian America; there is the United States of America. The pundits like to slice-and-dice our country into Red States and Blue States; Red States for Republicans, Blue States for Democrats. But I've got news for them, too. We worship an awesome God in the Blue States, and we don't like federal agents poking around our libraries in the Red States. We coach Little League in the Blue States, and yes we've got some gay friends in the Red States. There are patriots who opposed the war in Iraq and there are patriots who supported the war in Iraq. We are one people, all of us pledging allegiance to the stars and stripes, all of us defending the United States of America.

In the end, that's what this election is about. Do we participate in a politics of cynicism or do we participate in a politics of hope? John Kerry calls on us to hope. John Edwards calls on us to hope. I'm not talking about blind optimism here—the almost willful ignorance that thinks unemployment will go away if we just don't think about it, or the health care crisis will solve itself if we just ignore it. That's not what I'm talking about. I'm talking about something more substantial. It's the hope of slaves sitting around a fire singing freedom songs; the hope of immigrants setting out for distant shores; the hope of a young naval lieutenant bravely patrolling the Mekong Delta; the hope of a millworker's son who dares to defy the odds; the hope of a skinny kid with a funny name who believes that America has a place for him, too. Hope in the face of difficulty. Hope in the face of uncertainty. The audacity of hope!

In the end, that is God's greatest gift to us, the bedrock of this nation; a belief in things not seen; a belief that there are better days ahead. I believe that we can give our middle class relief and provide working families with a road to opportunity. I believe we can provide jobs to the jobless, homes to the homeless, and reclaim young people in cities across America from violence and despair. I believe that we have a righteous wind at our backs and that as we stand on the crossroads of history, we can make the right choices, and meet the challenges that face us.

America, tonight, if you feel the same energy I do, if you feel the same urgency I do, if you feel the same passion I do, if you feel the same hopefulness I do—if we do what we must do, then I have no doubt that all across the country, from Florida to Oregon, from Washington to Maine, the people will rise up in November, and John Kerry will be sworn in as president, and John Edwards will be sworn in as vice president, and this country will reclaim its promise, and out of this long political darkness a brighter day will come. Thank you very much everybody. God bless you.

[DIA]

Senator Barack Obama, Presidential Election Night Speech

November 4, 2008

The 2008 presidential election ended on November 4, with the Democratic senator of Illinois, Barack Obama, defeating Republican John McCain, senator from Arizona. Obama's father, from Kenya, and mother, from Kansas were no longer alive to see their son become the first African-American president. Just after midnight, in Chicago, Obama made his acceptance speech to a jubilant crowd.

Hello, Chicago. [*Applause*]

IF THERE IS anyone out there who still doubts that America is a place where all things are possible, who still wonders if the dream of our founders is alive in our time, who still questions the power of our democracy, tonight is your answer. [*Applause*]

It's the answer told by lines that stretched around schools and churches in numbers this nation has never seen, by people who waited three hours and four hours, many for the first time in their lives, because they believed that this time must be different, that their voices could be that difference.

It's the answer spoken by young and old, rich and poor, Democrat and Republican, black, white, Hispanic, Asian, Native American, gay, straight, disabled and not disabled. Americans who sent a message to the world that we have never been just a collection of individuals or a collection of red states and blue states.

We are, and always will be, the United States of America. [*Applause*]

It's the answer that led those who've been told for so long by so many to be cynical and fearful and doubtful about what we can achieve to put their hands on the arc of history and bend it once more toward the hope of a better day.

It's been a long time coming, but tonight, because of what we did on this date in this election at this defining moment change has come to America. [*Applause*]

It's the answer that led those who've been told for so long by so many to be cynical and fearful and doubtful about what we can achieve to put their hands on the arc of history and bend it once more toward the hope of a better day.

It's been a long time coming, but tonight, because of what we did on this date in this election at this defining moment change has come to America. [*Applause*]

A little bit earlier this evening, I received an extraordinarily gracious call from Senator McCain. [*Applause*]

Senator McCain fought long and hard in this campaign. And he's fought even longer and harder for the country that he loves. He has endured sacrifices for America that most of us cannot begin to imagine. We are better off for the service rendered by this brave and selfless leader.

I congratulate him; I congratulate Governor Palin for all that they've achieved. And I look forward to working with them to renew this nation's promise in the months ahead. [*Applause*]

I want to thank my partner in this journey, a man who campaigned from his heart, and spoke for the men and women he grew up with on the streets of Scranton . . . [*Applause*] . . . and rode with on the train home to Delaware, the vice president–elect of the United States, Joe Biden. [*Applause*]

And I would not be standing here tonight without the unyielding support of my best friend for the last sixteen years . . . [*Applause*] . . . the rock of our family; the love of my life, the nation's next first lady . . . [*Applause*] . . . Michelle Obama. [*Applause*] Sasha and Malia . . . [*Applause*] . . . I love you both more than you can imagine. And you have earned the new puppy that's coming with us . . . (Laughter) . . . to the new White House. [*Applause*];

And while she's no longer with us, I know my grandmother's watching, along with the family that made me who I am. I miss them tonight. I know that my debt to them is beyond measure.

To my sister Maya, my sister Alma, all my other brothers and sisters, thank you so much for all the support that you've given me. I am grateful to them. [*Applause*] And to my campaign manager, David Plouffe . . . [*Applause*] the unsung hero of this campaign, who built the best—the best political campaign, I think, in the history of the United States of America. [*Applause*]

To my chief strategist David Axelrod . . . [*Applause*] . . . who's been a partner with me every step of the way. To the best campaign team ever assembled in the history of politics . . . [*Applause*] . . . you made this happen, and I am forever grateful for what you've sacrificed to get it done.

But above all, I will never forget who this victory truly belongs to. It belongs to you. It belongs to you.

I was never the likeliest candidate for this office. We didn't start with much money or many endorsements. Our campaign was not hatched in the halls of Washington. It began in the backyards of Des Moines and the living rooms of Concord and the front porches of Charleston. It was built by working men and women who dug into what little savings they had to give $5 and $10 and $20 to the cause.

It grew strength from the young people who rejected the myth of their generation's apathy . . . [*Applause*] . . . who left their homes and their families for jobs that offered little pay and less sleep.

It drew strength from the not-so-young people who braved the bitter cold and scorching heat to knock on doors of perfect strangers, and from the millions of Americans who volunteered and organized and proved that more than two centuries later a government of the people, by the people, and for the people has not perished from the Earth.

This is your victory. [*Applause*]

And I know you didn't do this just to win an election. And I know you didn't do it for me.

You did it because you understand the enormity of the task that lies ahead. For even as we celebrate tonight, we know the challenges that tomorrow will bring are the greatest of our lifetime—two wars, a planet in peril, the worst financial crisis in a century.

Even as we stand here tonight, we know there are brave Americans waking up in the deserts of Iraq and the mountains of Afghanistan to risk their lives for us.

There are mothers and fathers who will lie awake after the children fall asleep and wonder how they'll make the mortgage or pay their doctors' bills or save enough for their child's college education.

There's new energy to harness, new jobs to be created, new schools to build, and threats to meet, alliances to repair.

The road ahead will be long. Our climb will be steep. We may not get there in one year or even in one term. But, America, I have never been more hopeful than I am tonight that we will get there.

I promise you, we as a people will get there. [*Applause*]

AUDIENCE: Yes we can! Yes we can! Yes we can!

OBAMA: There will be setbacks and false starts. There are many who won't agree with every decision or policy I make as president. And we know the government can't solve every problem.

But I will always be honest with you about the challenges we face. I will listen to you, especially when we disagree. And, above all, I will ask you to join in the work of remaking this nation, the only way it's been done in America for 221 years—block by block, brick by brick, calloused hand by calloused hand.

What began 21 months ago in the depths of winter cannot end on this autumn night.

This victory alone is not the change we seek. It is only the chance for us to make that change. And that cannot happen if we go back to the way things were.

It can't happen without you, without a new spirit of service, a new spirit of sacrifice.

So let us summon a new spirit of patriotism, of responsibility, where each of us resolves to pitch in and work harder and look after not only ourselves but each other.

Let us remember that, if this financial crisis taught us anything, it's that we cannot have a thriving Wall Street while Main Street suffers.

In this country, we rise or fall as one nation, as one people. Let's resist the temptation to fall back on the same partisanship and pettiness and immaturity that has poisoned our politics for so long.

Let's remember that it was a man from this state who first carried the banner of the Republican Party to the White House, a party founded on the values of self-reliance and individual liberty and national unity.

Those are values that we all share. And while the Democratic Party has won a great victory tonight, we do so with a measure of humility and determination to heal the divides that have held back our progress. [*Applause*]

As Lincoln said to a nation far more divided than ours, we are not enemies but friends. Though passion may have strained, it must not break our bonds of affection.

And to those Americans whose support I have yet to earn, I may not have won your vote tonight, but I hear your voices. I need your help. And I will be your president, too. [*Applause*]

And to all those watching tonight from beyond our shores, from parliaments and palaces, to those who are huddled around radios in the forgotten corners of the world, our stories are singular, but our destiny is shared, and a new dawn of American leadership is at hand. [*Applause*]

To those—to those who would tear the world down: We will defeat you. To those who seek peace and security: We support you. And to all those who have wondered if America's beacon still burns as bright: Tonight we proved once more that the true strength of our nation comes not from the might of our arms or the scale of our wealth, but from the enduring power of our ideals: democracy, liberty, opportunity and unyielding hope. [*Applause*]

That's the true genius of America: that America can change. Our union can be perfected. What we've already achieved gives us hope for what we can and must achieve tomorrow.

This election had many firsts and many stories that will be told for generations. But one that's on my mind tonight's about a woman who cast her ballot in Atlanta. She's a lot like the millions of others who stood in line to make their voice heard in this election except for one thing: Ann Nixon Cooper is 106 years old. [*Applause*]

She was born just a generation past slavery; a time when there were no cars on the road or planes in the sky; when someone like her couldn't vote for two reasons—because she was a woman and because of the color of her skin. And tonight, I think about all that she's seen throughout her century in America—the heartache and the hope; the struggle and the progress; the times we were told that we can't, and the people who pressed on with that American creed: Yes we can. At a time when women's voices were silenced and their hopes dismissed, she lived to see them stand up and speak out and reach for the ballot. Yes we can. When there was despair in the dust bowl and depression across the land, she saw a nation conquer fear itself with a New Deal, new jobs, a new sense of common purpose. Yes we can.

AUDIENCE: Yes we can.

OBAMA: When the bombs fell on our harbor and tyranny threatened the world, she was there to witness a generation rise to greatness and a democracy was saved. Yes we can.

AUDIENCE: Yes we can.

OBAMA: She was there for the buses in Montgomery, the hoses in Birmingham, a bridge in Selma, and a preacher from Atlanta who told a people that "We Shall Overcome." Yes we can.

AUDIENCE: Yes we can.

OBAMA: A man touched down on the moon, a wall came down in Berlin, a world was connected by our own science and imagination.

And this year, in this election, she touched her finger to a screen, and cast her vote, because after 106 years in America, through the best of times and the darkest of hours, she knows how America can change.

Yes we can.

AUDIENCE: Yes we can.

OBAMA: America, we have come so far. We have seen so much. But there is so much more to do. So tonight, let us ask ourselves—if our children should live to see the next century; if my daughters should be so lucky to live as long as Ann Nixon Cooper, what change will they see? What progress will we have made?

This is our chance to answer that call. This is our moment.

This is our time, to put our people back to work and open doors of opportunity for our kids; to restore prosperity and promote the cause of peace; to reclaim the American dream and reaffirm that fundamental truth, that, out of many, we are one; that while we breathe, we hope. And where we are met with cynicism and doubts and those who tell us that we can't, we will respond with that timeless creed that sums up the spirit of a people: Yes, we can. [*Applause*]

Thank you. God bless you. And may God bless the United States of America. [*Applause*]

[GSTC]

Source and Author Guide

[AAA]   *The Annals of the American Academy of Political and Social Science.* Philadelphia. November 1908.

[ACF]   Atlantic Charter Foundation. http://www.atlanticcharter.ca/

[ACH]   *Source Book and Bibliographical Guide for American Church History.* Edited by Peter G. Mode. Menasha, Wisconsin: George Banta Publishing Company. 1921.

[AE]   American Experience. http://www.pbs.org/wgbh/amex/macarthur/sfeature/officialdocs03.html

[AEM]   Apollo: Expeditions to the Moon. Edgar M. Cortright. Washington, D.C.: NASA. 1975

[AHD]   *American Historical Documents 1000–1904.* The Harvard Classics. Edited by Charles W. Eliot. Volume 43. New York: P. F. Collier and Son Company. 1910.

[AIH]   *Great Documents in American Indian History.* Wayne Moquin and Charles Van Doren. New York: Da Capo. 1995.

[APP]   *The American Presidency Project* by Gerhard Peters and John T. Woolley. http://www.presidency.ucsb.edu/index.php

[ARCH]   Archives.gov/exhibits

[AVA]   Yale University ... Avalon.org

[CD]   Helen Hunt Jackson. *A Century of Dishonor.* New York: Harper and Brothers. 1881.

[CGI]   *Annual Report of the Commissioner General of Immigration to the Secretary of Labor.* Washington: Government Printing Office. 1923.

[CM]   *The Communist Manifesto and Other Revolutionary Documents.* Bob Blaisdell. Mineola, New York: Dover. 2003.

[DAAL]   *The Dover Anthology of American Literature,* Volume 1. Bob Blaisdell. Mineola, New York: Dover. 2014.

[DAH]   *Documents of American History.* Volume I: to 1898; 10th ed. Henry Steele Commager and Milton Cantor. Englewood Cliffs, New Jersey: Prentice Hall. 1988. Volume 2: Since 1898; 7th ed. Henry Steele Commager. New York: Appleton-Century-Crofts. 1963.

[DB]   *W. E. B. Du Bois: Selections from His Writings.* Bob Blaisdell. Mineola, New York: Dover. 2014.

[DH]   Digital History. University of Houston, digitalhistory. uh.edu

[DIA]   Democracy in Action. George washington University. http://www.gwu.edu/~action/2004/demconv04/ obama072704spt.html

[FDR]   Franklin Delano Roosevelt. *Great Speeches.* John Grafton. Mineola, New York: Dover. 1999.

[FP]   Free Republic, http://www.freerepublic.com/focus/f-news/1556858/posts

[GCM]   The George C. Marshall Foundation, http://marshall-foundation.org/marshall/the-marshall-plan/marshall-plan-speech/

[GIA]   *Great Inaugural Addresses.* James Daley. Mineola, New York: Dover. 2010.

[GSAA]   *Great Speeches by African Americans.* James Daley. Dover. 2006.

[GSAW]   *Great Speeches by American Women.* James Daley. Dover. 2008.

[GSNA]   *Great Speeches by Native Americans.* Bob Blaisdell. Mineola, New York: Dover. 2000.

[GSTC]   *Great Speeches of the Twentieth Century.* Bob Blaisdell. Mineola, New York: Dover. 2011.

[GSGR]   *Great Speeches on Gay Rights.* James Daley. Mineola, New York: Dover. 2010.

[HM]   History Matters. http://historymatters.gmu.edu/d/5361/

[IS]   *Infamous Speeches: From Robespierre to Osama bin Laden.* Bob Blaisdell. Mineola, New York: Dover. 2011.

[LD]   *Landmark Decisions of the U. S. Supreme Court.* James Daley. Dover. 2006.

[MC]   Miller Center.

[NARA] National Archives & Records Adminstration. archives. gov (also ourdocuments.gov)

[PPP] The Public Papers of President: Ronald W. Reagan, 1981–1989. Ronald Reagan Presidential Library. University of Texas. http://www.reagan.utexas.edu/ archives/speeches/1987/030487h.htm

[SAJ] *Supplement to the American Journal of International Law.* Volume 9. New York: Baker, Voorhis and Company. July 1915.

[SI] Spartacus International. http://spartacus-educational. com/USAvanzetti.htm

[TCR] The 9/11 Commission Report: Final Report of the National Commission on Terrorist Attacks upon the United States. 2004

[TG] *The Guardian,* http://www.guardian.co.uk/world/ 2003/mar/18/usa.iraq

[TR] *Addresses and Papers of Theodore Roosevelt.* Edited by Willis Fletcher Johnson. New York: The Unit Book Publishing Company. 1909.

[TY] John Muir. *The Yosemite.* New York: The Century Company. 1912.

[USC] *The United States Constitution: The Full Text with Supplementary Materials.* Bob Blaisdell. Mineola, New York: Dover. 2009.

[VOD] *Voices of Democracy, voicesofdemocracy.umd.edu*

[WJB] Speeches of William Jennings Bryan, Revised and Arranged by Himself. Biographical Introduction by Mary Baird Bryan. Volume I. New York: Funk and Wagnalls. 1913.

[WGS] *The World's Great Speeches.* Fourth edition. Lewis Copeland, Lawrence W. Lamm and Stephen J. McKenna. Mineola, New York: Dover. 1999.

Bibliography

Richard D. Heffner. *A Documentary History of the United States.* Expanded edition. New American Library, Mentor: New York. 1965.

Robert V. Hine and Edwin R. Bingham. *The American Frontier: Readings and Documents.* Boston: Little, Brown. 1972.

Edwin Clarence Stedman and Ellen Mackay Hutchinson. *A Library of American Literature from the Earliest Settlement to the Present Time.* New York. 1888–1890.

David R. Wrone and Russell S. Nelson, Jr. *Who's the Savage?: A Documentary History of the Mistreatment of the Native North Americans.* Greenwich, Connecticut. New York: Fawcett. 1973.

A CATALOG OF SELECTED
DOVER BOOKS
IN ALL FIELDS OF INTEREST

A CATALOG OF SELECTED DOVER
BOOKS IN ALL FIELDS OF INTEREST

100 BEST-LOVED POEMS, Edited by Philip Smith. "The Passionate Shepherd to His Love," "Shall I compare thee to a summer's day?" "Death, be not proud," "The Raven," "The Road Not Taken," plus works by Blake, Wordsworth, Byron, Shelley, Keats, many others. 96pp. 5³⁄₁₆ x 8¼.					0-486-28553-7

100 SMALL HOUSES OF THE THIRTIES, Brown-Blodgett Company. Exterior photographs and floor plans for 100 charming structures. Illustrations of models accompanied by descriptions of interiors, color schemes, closet space, and other amenities. 200 illustrations. 112pp. 8⅜ x 11.					0-486-44131-8

1000 TURN-OF-THE-CENTURY HOUSES: With Illustrations and Floor Plans, Herbert C. Chivers. Reproduced from a rare edition, this showcase of homes ranges from cottages and bungalows to sprawling mansions. Each house is meticulously illustrated and accompanied by complete floor plans. 256pp. 9⅜ x 12¼.

0-486-45596-3

101 GREAT AMERICAN POEMS, Edited by The American Poetry & Literacy Project. Rich treasury of verse from the 19th and 20th centuries includes works by Edgar Allan Poe, Robert Frost, Walt Whitman, Langston Hughes, Emily Dickinson, T. S. Eliot, other notables. 96pp. 5³⁄₁₆ x 8¼.					0-486-40158-8

101 GREAT SAMURAI PRINTS, Utagawa Kuniyoshi. Kuniyoshi was a master of the warrior woodblock print — and these 18th-century illustrations represent the pinnacle of his craft. Full-color portraits of renowned Japanese samurais pulse with movement, passion, and remarkably fine detail. 112pp. 8⅜ x 11.		0-486-46523-3

ABC OF BALLET, Janet Grosser. Clearly worded, abundantly illustrated little guide defines basic ballet-related terms: arabesque, battement, pas de chat, relevé, sissonne, many others. Pronunciation guide included. Excellent primer. 48pp. 4³⁄₁₆ x 5¾.

0-486-40871-X

ACCESSORIES OF DRESS: An Illustrated Encyclopedia, Katherine Lester and Bess Viola Oerke. Illustrations of hats, veils, wigs, cravats, shawls, shoes, gloves, and other accessories enhance an engaging commentary that reveals the humor and charm of the many-sided story of accessorized apparel. 644 figures and 59 plates. 608pp. 6⅛ x 9¼.

0-486-43378-1

ADVENTURES OF HUCKLEBERRY FINN, Mark Twain. Join Huck and Jim as their boyhood adventures along the Mississippi River lead them into a world of excitement, danger, and self-discovery. Humorous narrative, lyrical descriptions of the Mississippi valley, and memorable characters. 224pp. 5³⁄₁₆ x 8¼.		0-486-28061-6

ALICE STARMORE'S BOOK OF FAIR ISLE KNITTING, Alice Starmore. A noted designer from the region of Scotland's Fair Isle explores the history and techniques of this distinctive, stranded-color knitting style and provides copious illustrated instructions for 14 original knitwear designs. 208pp. 8⅜ x 10⅞.		0-486-47218-3

Browse over 9,000 books at www.doverpublications.com

ALICE'S ADVENTURES IN WONDERLAND, Lewis Carroll. Beloved classic about a little girl lost in a topsy-turvy land and her encounters with the White Rabbit, March Hare, Mad Hatter, Cheshire Cat, and other delightfully improbable characters. 42 illustrations by Sir John Tenniel. 96pp. 5³⁄₁₆ x 8¼. 0-486-27543-4

AMERICA'S LIGHTHOUSES: An Illustrated History, Francis Ross Holland. Profusely illustrated fact-filled survey of American lighthouses since 1716. Over 200 stations — East, Gulf, and West coasts, Great Lakes, Hawaii, Alaska, Puerto Rico, the Virgin Islands, and the Mississippi and St. Lawrence Rivers. 240pp. 8 x 10¾.
0-486-25576-X

AN ENCYCLOPEDIA OF THE VIOLIN, Alberto Bachmann. Translated by Frederick H. Martens. Introduction by Eugene Ysaÿe. First published in 1925, this renowned reference remains unsurpassed as a source of essential information, from construction and evolution to repertoire and technique. Includes a glossary and 73 illustrations. 496pp. 6⅛ x 9¼. 0-486-46618-3

ANIMALS: 1,419 Copyright-Free Illustrations of Mammals, Birds, Fish, Insects, etc., Selected by Jim Harter. Selected for its visual impact and ease of use, this outstanding collection of wood engravings presents over 1,000 species of animals in extremely lifelike poses. Includes mammals, birds, reptiles, amphibians, fish, insects, and other invertebrates. 284pp. 9 x 12. 0-486-23766-4

THE ANNALS, Tacitus. Translated by Alfred John Church and William Jackson Brodribb. This vital chronicle of Imperial Rome, written by the era's great historian, spans A.D. 14-68 and paints incisive psychological portraits of major figures, from Tiberius to Nero. 416pp. 5³⁄₁₆ x 8¼. 0-486-45236-0

ANTIGONE, Sophocles. Filled with passionate speeches and sensitive probing of moral and philosophical issues, this powerful and often-performed Greek drama reveals the grim fate that befalls the children of Oedipus. Footnotes. 64pp. 5³⁄₁₆ x 8 ¼. 0-486-27804-2

ART DECO DECORATIVE PATTERNS IN FULL COLOR, Christian Stoll. Reprinted from a rare 1910 portfolio, 160 sensuous and exotic images depict a breathtaking array of florals, geometrics, and abstracts — all elegant in their stark simplicity. 64pp. 8⅜ x 11. 0-486-44862-2

THE ARTHUR RACKHAM TREASURY: 86 Full-Color Illustrations, Arthur Rackham. Selected and Edited by Jeff A. Menges. A stunning treasury of 86 full-page plates span the famed English artist's career, from *Rip Van Winkle* (1905) to masterworks such as *Undine, A Midsummer Night's Dream,* and *Wind in the Willows* (1939). 96pp. 8⅜ x 11.
0-486-44685-9

THE AUTHENTIC GILBERT & SULLIVAN SONGBOOK, W. S. Gilbert and A. S. Sullivan. The most comprehensive collection available, this songbook includes selections from every one of Gilbert and Sullivan's light operas. Ninety-two numbers are presented uncut and unedited, and in their original keys. 410pp. 9 x 12.
0-486-23482-7

THE AWAKENING, Kate Chopin. First published in 1899, this controversial novel of a New Orleans wife's search for love outside a stifling marriage shocked readers. Today, it remains a first-rate narrative with superb characterization. New introductory Note. 128pp. 5³⁄₁₆ x 8¼. 0-486-27786-0

BASIC DRAWING, Louis Priscilla. Beginning with perspective, this commonsense manual progresses to the figure in movement, light and shade, anatomy, drapery, composition, trees and landscape, and outdoor sketching. Black-and-white illustrations throughout. 128pp. 8⅜ x 11. 0-486-45815-6

THE BATTLES THAT CHANGED HISTORY, Fletcher Pratt. Historian profiles 16 crucial conflicts, ancient to modern, that changed the course of Western civilization. Gripping accounts of battles led by Alexander the Great, Joan of Arc, Ulysses S. Grant, other commanders. 27 maps. 352pp. 5⅜ x 8½. 0-486-41129-X

BEETHOVEN'S LETTERS, Ludwig van Beethoven. Edited by Dr. A. C. Kalischer. Features 457 letters to fellow musicians, friends, greats, patrons, and literary men. Reveals musical thoughts, quirks of personality, insights, and daily events. Includes 15 plates. 410pp. 5⅜ x 8½. 0-486-22769-3

BERNICE BOBS HER HAIR AND OTHER STORIES, F. Scott Fitzgerald. This brilliant anthology includes 6 of Fitzgerald's most popular stories: "The Diamond as Big as the Ritz," the title tale, "The Offshore Pirate," "The Ice Palace," "The Jelly Bean," and "May Day." 176pp. 5⅜ x 8½. 0-486-47049-0

BESLER'S BOOK OF FLOWERS AND PLANTS: 73 Full-Color Plates from Hortus Eystettensis, 1613, Basilius Besler. Here is a selection of magnificent plates from the *Hortus Eystettensis,* which vividly illustrated and identified the plants, flowers, and trees that thrived in the legendary German garden at Eichstätt. 80pp. 8⅜ x 11.
0-486-46005-3

THE BOOK OF KELLS, Edited by Blanche Cirker. Painstakingly reproduced from a rare facsimile edition, this volume contains full-page decorations, portraits, illustrations, plus a sampling of textual leaves with exquisite calligraphy and ornamentation. 32 full-color illustrations. 32pp. 9⅜ x 12¼. 0-486-24345-1

THE BOOK OF THE CROSSBOW: With an Additional Section on Catapults and Other Siege Engines, Ralph Payne-Gallwey. Fascinating study traces history and use of crossbow as military and sporting weapon, from Middle Ages to modern times. Also covers related weapons: balistas, catapults, Turkish bows, more. Over 240 illustrations. 400pp. 7¼ x 10⅛. 0-486-28720-3

THE BUNGALOW BOOK: Floor Plans and Photos of 112 Houses, 1910, Henry L. Wilson. Here are 112 of the most popular and economic blueprints of the early 20th century — plus an illustration or photograph of each completed house. A wonderful time capsule that still offers a wealth of valuable insights. 160pp. 8⅜ x 11.
0-486-45104-6

THE CALL OF THE WILD, Jack London. A classic novel of adventure, drawn from London's own experiences as a Klondike adventurer, relating the story of a heroic dog caught in the brutal life of the Alaska Gold Rush. Note. 64pp. 5³⁄₁₆ x 8¼.
0-486-26472-6

CANDIDE, Voltaire. Edited by Francois-Marie Arouet. One of the world's great satires since its first publication in 1759. Witty, caustic skewering of romance, science, philosophy, religion, government — nearly all human ideals and institutions. 112pp. 5³⁄₁₆ x 8¼. 0-486-26689-3

CELEBRATED IN THEIR TIME: Photographic Portraits from the George Grantham Bain Collection, Edited by Amy Pastan. With an Introduction by Michael Carlebach. Remarkable portrait gallery features 112 rare images of Albert Einstein, Charlie Chaplin, the Wright Brothers, Henry Ford, and other luminaries from the worlds of politics, art, entertainment, and industry. 128pp. 8⅜ x 11. 0-486-46754-6

CHARIOTS FOR APOLLO: The NASA History of Manned Lunar Spacecraft to 1969, Courtney G. Brooks, James M. Grimwood, and Loyd S. Swenson, Jr. This illustrated history by a trio of experts is the definitive reference on the Apollo spacecraft and lunar modules. It traces the vehicles' design, development, and operation in space. More than 100 photographs and illustrations. 576pp. 6¾ x 9¼. 0-486-46756-2

A CHRISTMAS CAROL, Charles Dickens. This engrossing tale relates Ebenezer Scrooge's ghostly journeys through Christmases past, present, and future and his ultimate transformation from a harsh and grasping old miser to a charitable and compassionate human being. 80pp. 5³⁄₁₆ x 8¼.   0-486-26865-9

COMMON SENSE, Thomas Paine. First published in January of 1776, this highly influential landmark document clearly and persuasively argued for American separation from Great Britain and paved the way for the Declaration of Independence. 64pp. 5³⁄₁₆ x 8¼.   0-486-29602-4

THE COMPLETE SHORT STORIES OF OSCAR WILDE, Oscar Wilde. Complete texts of "The Happy Prince and Other Tales," "A House of Pomegranates," "Lord Arthur Savile's Crime and Other Stories," "Poems in Prose," and "The Portrait of Mr. W. H." 208pp. 5³⁄₁₆ x 8¼.   0-486-45216-6

COMPLETE SONNETS, William Shakespeare. Over 150 exquisite poems deal with love, friendship, the tyranny of time, beauty's evanescence, death, and other themes in language of remarkable power, precision, and beauty. Glossary of archaic terms. 80pp. 5³⁄₁₆ x 8¼.   0-486-26686-9

THE COUNT OF MONTE CRISTO: Abridged Edition, Alexandre Dumas. Falsely accused of treason, Edmond Dantès is imprisoned in the bleak Chateau d'If. After a hair-raising escape, he launches an elaborate plot to extract a bitter revenge against those who betrayed him. 448pp. 5³⁄₁₆ x 8¼.   0-486-45643-9

CRAFTSMAN BUNGALOWS: Designs from the Pacific Northwest, Yoho & Merritt. This reprint of a rare catalog, showcasing the charming simplicity and cozy style of Craftsman bungalows, is filled with photos of completed homes, plus floor plans and estimated costs. An indispensable resource for architects, historians, and illustrators. 112pp. 10 x 7.   0-486-46875-5

CRAFTSMAN BUNGALOWS: 59 Homes from "The Craftsman," Edited by Gustav Stickley. Best and most attractive designs from Arts and Crafts Movement publication — 1903–1916 — includes sketches, photographs of homes, floor plans, descriptive text. 128pp. 8¼ x 11.   0-486-25829-7

CRIME AND PUNISHMENT, Fyodor Dostoyevsky. Translated by Constance Garnett. Supreme masterpiece tells the story of Raskolnikov, a student tormented by his own thoughts after he murders an old woman. Overwhelmed by guilt and terror, he confesses and goes to prison. 480pp. 5³⁄₁₆ x 8¼.   0-486-41587-2

THE DECLARATION OF INDEPENDENCE AND OTHER GREAT DOCUMENTS OF AMERICAN HISTORY: 1775-1865, Edited by John Grafton. Thirteen compelling and influential documents: Henry's "Give Me Liberty or Give Me Death," Declaration of Independence, The Constitution, Washington's First Inaugural Address, The Monroe Doctrine, The Emancipation Proclamation, Gettysburg Address, more. 64pp. 5³⁄₁₆ x 8¼.   0-486-41124-9

THE DESERT AND THE SOWN: Travels in Palestine and Syria, Gertrude Bell. "The female Lawrence of Arabia," Gertrude Bell wrote captivating, perceptive accounts of her travels in the Middle East. This intriguing narrative, accompanied by 160 photos, traces her 1905 sojourn in Lebanon, Syria, and Palestine. 368pp. 5⅜ x 8½.
0-486-46876-3

A DOLL'S HOUSE, Henrik Ibsen. Ibsen's best-known play displays his genius for realistic prose drama. An expression of women's rights, the play climaxes when the central character, Nora, rejects a smothering marriage and life in "a doll's house." 80pp. 5³⁄₁₆ x 8¼.   0-486-27062-9

DOOMED SHIPS: Great Ocean Liner Disasters, William H. Miller, Jr. Nearly 200 photographs, many from private collections, highlight tales of some of the vessels whose pleasure cruises ended in catastrophe: the *Morro Castle, Normandie, Andrea Doria, Europa,* and many others. 128pp. 8⅞ x 11¼. 0-486-45366-9

THE DORÉ BIBLE ILLUSTRATIONS, Gustave Doré. Detailed plates from the Bible: the Creation scenes, Adam and Eve, horrifying visions of the Flood, the battle sequences with their monumental crowds, depictions of the life of Jesus, 241 plates in all. 241pp. 9 x 12. 0-486-23004-X

DRAWING DRAPERY FROM HEAD TO TOE, Cliff Young. Expert guidance on how to draw shirts, pants, skirts, gloves, hats, and coats on the human figure, including folds in relation to the body, pull and crush, action folds, creases, more. Over 200 drawings. 48pp. 8¼ x 11. 0-486-45591-2

DUBLINERS, James Joyce. A fine and accessible introduction to the work of one of the 20th century's most influential writers, this collection features 15 tales, including a masterpiece of the short-story genre, "The Dead." 160pp. 5³⁄₁₆ x 8¼.
0-486-26870-5

EASY-TO-MAKE POP-UPS, Joan Irvine. Illustrated by Barbara Reid. Dozens of wonderful ideas for three-dimensional paper fun — from holiday greeting cards with moving parts to a pop-up menagerie. Easy-to-follow, illustrated instructions for more than 30 projects. 299 black-and-white illustrations. 96pp. 8⅜ x 11.
0-486-44622-0

EASY-TO-MAKE STORYBOOK DOLLS: A "Novel" Approach to Cloth Dollmaking, Sherralyn St. Clair. Favorite fictional characters come alive in this unique beginner's dollmaking guide. Includes patterns for Pollyanna, Dorothy from *The Wonderful Wizard of Oz,* Mary of *The Secret Garden,* plus easy-to-follow instructions, 263 black-and-white illustrations, and an 8-page color insert. 112pp. 8¼ x 11. 0-486-47360-0

EINSTEIN'S ESSAYS IN SCIENCE, Albert Einstein. Speeches and essays in accessible, everyday language profile influential physicists such as Niels Bohr and Isaac Newton. They also explore areas of physics to which the author made major contributions. 128pp. 5 x 8. 0-486-47011-3

EL DORADO: Further Adventures of the Scarlet Pimpernel, Baroness Orczy. A popular sequel to *The Scarlet Pimpernel,* this suspenseful story recounts the Pimpernel's attempts to rescue the Dauphin from imprisonment during the French Revolution. An irresistible blend of intrigue, period detail, and vibrant characterizations. 352pp. 5³⁄₁₆ x 8¼. 0-486-44026-5

ELEGANT SMALL HOMES OF THE TWENTIES: 99 Designs from a Competition, Chicago Tribune. Nearly 100 designs for five- and six-room houses feature New England and Southern colonials, Normandy cottages, stately Italianate dwellings, and other fascinating snapshots of American domestic architecture of the 1920s. 112pp. 9 x 12. 0-486-46910-7

THE ELEMENTS OF STYLE: The Original Edition, William Strunk, Jr. This is the book that generations of writers have relied upon for timeless advice on grammar, diction, syntax, and other essentials. In concise terms, it identifies the principal requirements of proper style and common errors. 64pp. 5⅜ x 8½. 0-486-44798-7

THE ELUSIVE PIMPERNEL, Baroness Orczy. Robespierre's revolutionaries find their wicked schemes thwarted by the heroic Pimpernel — Sir Percival Blakeney. In this thrilling sequel, Chauvelin devises a plot to eliminate the Pimpernel and his wife. 272pp. 5³⁄₁₆ x 8¼. 0-486-45464-9

AN ENCYCLOPEDIA OF BATTLES: Accounts of Over 1,560 Battles from 1479 B.C. to the Present, David Eggenberger. Essential details of every major battle in recorded history from the first battle of Megiddo in 1479 B.C. to Grenada in 1984. List of battle maps. 99 illustrations. 544pp. 6½ x 9¼. 0-486-24913-1

ENCYCLOPEDIA OF EMBROIDERY STITCHES, INCLUDING CREWEL, Marion Nichols. Precise explanations and instructions, clearly illustrated, on how to work chain, back, cross, knotted, woven stitches, and many more — 178 in all, including Cable Outline, Whipped Satin, and Eyelet Buttonhole. Over 1400 illustrations. 219pp. 8⅜ x 11¼. 0-486-22929-7

ENTER JEEVES: 15 Early Stories, P. G. Wodehouse. Splendid collection contains first 8 stories featuring Bertie Wooster, the deliciously dim aristocrat and Jeeves, his brainy, imperturbable manservant. Also, the complete Reggie Pepper (Bertie's prototype) series. 288pp. 5⅜ x 8½. 0-486-29717-9

ERIC SLOANE'S AMERICA: Paintings in Oil, Michael Wigley. With a Foreword by Mimi Sloane. Eric Sloane's evocative oils of America's landscape and material culture shimmer with immense historical and nostalgic appeal. This original hardcover collection gathers nearly a hundred of his finest paintings, with subjects ranging from New England to the American Southwest. 128pp. 10⅝ x 9. 0-486-46525-X

ETHAN FROME, Edith Wharton. Classic story of wasted lives, set against a bleak New England background. Superbly delineated characters in a hauntingly grim tale of thwarted love. Considered by many to be Wharton's masterpiece. 96pp. 5³⁄₁₆ x 8 ¼. 0-486-26690-7

THE EVERLASTING MAN, G. K. Chesterton. Chesterton's view of Christianity — as a blend of philosophy and mythology, satisfying intellect and spirit — applies to his brilliant book, which appeals to readers' heads as well as their hearts. 288pp. 5⅜ x 8½. 0-486-46036-3

THE FIELD AND FOREST HANDY BOOK, Daniel Beard. Written by a co-founder of the Boy Scouts, this appealing guide offers illustrated instructions for building kites, birdhouses, boats, igloos, and other fun projects, plus numerous helpful tips for campers. 448pp. 5³⁄₁₆ x 8¼. 0-486-46191-2

FINDING YOUR WAY WITHOUT MAP OR COMPASS, Harold Gatty. Useful, instructive manual shows would-be explorers, hikers, bikers, scouts, sailors, and survivalists how to find their way outdoors by observing animals, weather patterns, shifting sands, and other elements of nature. 288pp. 5⅜ x 8½. 0-486-40613-X

FIRST FRENCH READER: A Beginner's Dual-Language Book, Edited and Translated by Stanley Appelbaum. This anthology introduces 50 legendary writers — Voltaire, Balzac, Baudelaire, Proust, more — through passages from *The Red and the Black, Les Misérables, Madame Bovary,* and other classics. Original French text plus English translation on facing pages. 240pp. 5⅜ x 8½. 0-486-46178-5

FIRST GERMAN READER: A Beginner's Dual-Language Book, Edited by Harry Steinhauer. Specially chosen for their power to evoke German life and culture, these short, simple readings include poems, stories, essays, and anecdotes by Goethe, Hesse, Heine, Schiller, and others. 224pp. 5⅜ x 8½. 0-486-46179-3

FIRST SPANISH READER: A Beginner's Dual-Language Book, Angel Flores. Delightful stories, other material based on works of Don Juan Manuel, Luis Taboada, Ricardo Palma, other noted writers. Complete faithful English translations on facing pages. Exercises. 176pp. 5⅜ x 8½. 0-486-25810-6

Browse over 9,000 books at www.doverpublications.com

FIVE ACRES AND INDEPENDENCE, Maurice G. Kains. Great back-to-the-land classic explains basics of self-sufficient farming. The one book to get. 95 illustrations. 397pp. 5⅜ x 8½.   0-486-20974-1

FLAGG'S SMALL HOUSES: Their Economic Design and Construction, 1922, Ernest Flagg. Although most famous for his skyscrapers, Flagg was also a proponent of the well-designed single-family dwelling. His classic treatise features innovations that save space, materials, and cost. 526 illustrations. 160pp. 9⅜ x 12¼.

0-486-45197-6

FLATLAND: A Romance of Many Dimensions, Edwin A. Abbott. Classic of science (and mathematical) fiction — charmingly illustrated by the author — describes the adventures of A. Square, a resident of Flatland, in Spaceland (three dimensions), Lineland (one dimension), and Pointland (no dimensions). 96pp. 5³⁄₁₆ x 8¼.

0-486-27263-X

FRANKENSTEIN, Mary Shelley. The story of Victor Frankenstein's monstrous creation and the havoc it caused has enthralled generations of readers and inspired countless writers of horror and suspense. With the author's own 1831 introduction. 176pp. 5³⁄₁₆ x 8¼.   0-486-28211-2

THE GARGOYLE BOOK: 572 Examples from Gothic Architecture, Lester Burbank Bridaham. Dispelling the conventional wisdom that French Gothic architectural flourishes were born of despair or gloom, Bridaham reveals the whimsical nature of these creations and the ingenious artisans who made them. 572 illustrations. 224pp. 8⅜ x 11.   0-486-44754-5

THE GIFT OF THE MAGI AND OTHER SHORT STORIES, O. Henry. Sixteen captivating stories by one of America's most popular storytellers. Included are such classics as "The Gift of the Magi," "The Last Leaf," and "The Ransom of Red Chief." Publisher's Note. 96pp. 5³⁄₁₆ x 8¼.   0-486-27061-0

THE GOETHE TREASURY: Selected Prose and Poetry, Johann Wolfgang von Goethe. Edited, Selected, and with an Introduction by Thomas Mann. In addition to his lyric poetry, Goethe wrote travel sketches, autobiographical studies, essays, letters, and proverbs in rhyme and prose. This collection presents outstanding examples from each genre. 368pp. 5⅜ x 8½.   0-486-44780-4

GREAT EXPECTATIONS, Charles Dickens. Orphaned Pip is apprenticed to the dirty work of the forge but dreams of becoming a gentleman — and one day finds himself in possession of "great expectations." Dickens' finest novel. 400pp. 5³⁄₁₆ x 8¼.

0-486-41586-4

GREAT WRITERS ON THE ART OF FICTION: From Mark Twain to Joyce Carol Oates, Edited by James Daley. An indispensable source of advice and inspiration, this anthology features essays by Henry James, Kate Chopin, Willa Cather, Sinclair Lewis, Jack London, Raymond Chandler, Raymond Carver, Eudora Welty, and Kurt Vonnegut, Jr. 192pp. 5⅜ x 8½.   0-486-45128-3

HAMLET, William Shakespeare. The quintessential Shakespearean tragedy, whose highly charged confrontations and anguished soliloquies probe depths of human feeling rarely sounded in any art. Reprinted from an authoritative British edition complete with illuminating footnotes. 128pp. 5³⁄₁₆ x 8¼.   0-486-27278-8

THE HAUNTED HOUSE, Charles Dickens. A Yuletide gathering in an eerie country retreat provides the backdrop for Dickens and his friends — including Elizabeth Gaskell and Wilkie Collins — who take turns spinning supernatural yarns. 144pp. 5⅜ x 8½.   0-486-46309-5

HEART OF DARKNESS, Joseph Conrad. Dark allegory of a journey up the Congo River and the narrator's encounter with the mysterious Mr. Kurtz. Masterly blend of adventure, character study, psychological penetration. For many, Conrad's finest, most enigmatic story. 80pp. 5³⁄₁₆ x 8¼. 0-486-26464-5

HENSON AT THE NORTH POLE, Matthew A. Henson. This thrilling memoir by the heroic African-American who was Peary's companion through two decades of Arctic exploration recounts a tale of danger, courage, and determination. "Fascinating and exciting." — *Commonweal.* 128pp. 5⅜ x 8½. 0-486-45472-X

HISTORIC COSTUMES AND HOW TO MAKE THEM, Mary Fernald and E. Shenton. Practical, informative guidebook shows how to create everything from short tunics worn by Saxon men in the fifth century to a lady's bustle dress of the late 1800s. 81 illustrations. 176pp. 5⅜ x 8½. 0-486-44906-8

THE HOUND OF THE BASKERVILLES, Arthur Conan Doyle. A deadly curse in the form of a legendary ferocious beast continues to claim its victims from the Baskerville family until Holmes and Watson intervene. Often called the best detective story ever written. 128pp. 5³⁄₁₆ x 8¼. 0-486-28214-7

THE HOUSE BEHIND THE CEDARS, Charles W. Chesnutt. Originally published in 1900, this groundbreaking novel by a distinguished African-American author recounts the drama of a brother and sister who "pass for white" during the dangerous days of Reconstruction. 208pp. 5⅜ x 8½. 0-486-46144-0

THE HUMAN FIGURE IN MOTION, Eadweard Muybridge. The 4,789 photographs in this definitive selection show the human figure — models almost all undraped — engaged in over 160 different types of action: running, climbing stairs, etc. 390pp. 7⅞ x 10⅝. 0-486-20204-6

THE IMPORTANCE OF BEING EARNEST, Oscar Wilde. Wilde's witty and buoyant comedy of manners, filled with some of literature's most famous epigrams, reprinted from an authoritative British edition. Considered Wilde's most perfect work. 64pp. 5³⁄₁₆ x 8¼. 0-486-26478-5

THE INFERNO, Dante Alighieri. Translated and with notes by Henry Wadsworth Longfellow. The first stop on Dante's famous journey from Hell to Purgatory to Paradise, this 14th-century allegorical poem blends vivid and shocking imagery with graceful lyricism. Translated by the beloved 19th-century poet, Henry Wadsworth Longfellow. 256pp. 5³⁄₁₆ x 8¼. 0-486-44288-8

JANE EYRE, Charlotte Brontë. Written in 1847, *Jane Eyre* tells the tale of an orphan girl's progress from the custody of cruel relatives to an oppressive boarding school and its culmination in a troubled career as a governess. 448pp. 5³⁄₁₆ x 8¼.
0-486-42449-9

JAPANESE WOODBLOCK FLOWER PRINTS, Tanigami Kônan. Extraordinary collection of Japanese woodblock prints by a well-known artist features 120 plates in brilliant color. Realistic images from a rare edition include daffodils, tulips, and other familiar and unusual flowers. 128pp. 11 x 8¼. 0-486-46442-3

JEWELRY MAKING AND DESIGN, Augustus F. Rose and Antonio Cirino. Professional secrets of jewelry making are revealed in a thorough, practical guide. Over 200 illustrations. 306pp. 5⅜ x 8½. 0-486-21750-7

JULIUS CAESAR, William Shakespeare. Great tragedy based on Plutarch's account of the lives of Brutus, Julius Caesar and Mark Antony. Evil plotting, ringing oratory, high tragedy with Shakespeare's incomparable insight, dramatic power. Explanatory footnotes. 96pp. 5³⁄₁₆ x 8¼. 0-486-26876-4

Browse over 9,000 books at www.doverpublications.com